STANDARDS AND COLORS OF THE AMERICAN REVOLUTION

STANDARDS AND COLORS OF THE AMERICAN REVOLUTION

Edward W. Richardson

The University of Pennsylvania Press and the
Pennsylvania Society of Sons of the Revolution
and Its Color Guard
1982

Standards and Colors of the American Revolution
is a joint publication of the University of Pennsylvania Press
and the Pennsylvania Society of Sons of the Revolution
and Its Color Guard.

Copyright © 1982 by the
University of Pennsylvania Press
All rights reserved.

Library of Congress Catalog Card Number 82–050447
ISBN 0–8122–7839–9

Printed in the United States of America

This book is dedicated to the memory of
HERBERT C. RORER,
who was a president of the Pennsylvania Society of Sons of the Revolution
and a captain of its Color Guard
and whose bequest made publication possible.

Contents

Preface

This book is an encyclopedic reference on the design, emblems, and unit designations of flags of the American Revolution. Primary source material—surviving originals; contemporary paintings, drawings, and prints; and the orders, journals, and letters of participants—have been used, in the main, to avoid the interpretation errors of earlier historians.

Emphasis is placed on describing and picturing the flags and giving accurate official designations for the units that carried them. Digressions into campaigns, battles, and personalities have been held to a minimum and, if included, are meant to provide some clue to the flag's design, date, or unit.

The author is indebted to the pioneer work of earlier historians, and he acknowledges that ten times the amount of material is accessible today than was forty years ago. What is generally not realized is that there are large and scattered collections of Revolutionary War records not yet properly catalogued. Indeed, most of the cataloguing that has been done was done after 1945, except for that of the most important documents, events, and people. Thus, flag historians are faced with a very difficult task in finding and correlating Revolutionary War documents. Projects which are currently underway—such as the compilation and publishing of the naval documents of the Revolution and the papers of members of the Continental Congress—will broaden the scope of future research.

The book provides as accurate a description of the flags as is possible to develop within the time that could be spent in research over a number of years. It is definitely not the last and final word. The author has studied the Revolution for over twenty years and has concentrated on flags for a number of those years. Although several thousand hours were spent in research, this time allowed only a small part of the available records and source material to be studied, possibly only twenty percent of the pertinent material. Of course, research by earlier historians had already pinpointed some important source data and provided a starting base for the author's work. It is hoped that this book will, in turn, encourage and support further work. There are still large amounts of data that time and effort, hopefully, will bring to light. The author has tried to indicate where questions still remain.

The book is divided into chapters on design and symbols; on early Liberty flags; on Union flags; on flags of the Continental Army and Navy; on units of the thirteen states; on French, British, and Loyalist flags, and on German and early post-war flags. There are appendices on flag-related orders and letters and on flag makers, including Betsy Ross. Reference notes and a glossary of flag terminology, which includes a summary of American Revolutionary Army and Navy organizations, have also been included. Each flag description stands alone except for the general grouping by chapter and function of the flag's unit.

There is fairly extensive coverage on the stars and stripes, but it is kept in proportion to the discussion of the far more numerous individualized state and unit flags. The author has concentrated on those renderings of the stars and stripes that can be dated confidently to the Revolutionary War era. There are quite a number of early thirteen-stars-and-stripes extant. This is not surprising, since the thirteen-star canton continued to be used throughout the nineteenth century—particularly by ships and for commemorations. Some of these flags have quite a bit of age and look ancient enough. Whether they really date to the Revolution can only be settled, if ever, by textile historians, and there has been much disagreement. Therefore, except for these early flags, the primary reference sources used for stars and stripes are paintings and drawings of which there are a satisfactory number.

The flags found in paintings, drawings, and maps are frequently of small scale or are shown in a swirl. Close-up photography cannot always bring out details, proportions, and shadings visible to the eye in the original. Therefore, drawings are employed to interpret the flag as it would actually appear in the flat. Often a drawing is shown together with a photograph of the original, if it seemed helpful. The same approach has been taken with originals that are faded or have missing parts.

One of the main messages of the book is that Revolutionary War standards and colors were carefully made and decorated with all the meticulous craftsmanship of the age. Surviving flags, such as the Philadelphia Light Horse standard and that of

Webb's regiment, are significant examples of early American patriotic art and deserve to be recognized as such. They were of far finer workmanship than later copies indicate.

Three sponsors have joined together to finance the preparation and publication of this book. The Pennsylvania Society of Sons of the Revolution and the University of Pennsylvania Press are responsible for the final editing, design, typesetting, printing, and publication. The Color Guard of the Society initiated the project, requested the author to write the book, and funded preparation of the manuscript, artwork, photography, and initial typesetting and design. All are nonprofit organizations. All of the author's time and efforts have been donated.

The Pennsylvania Society of Sons of the Revolution has taken a strong interest in flags since the early years of its founding some ninety years ago. This book is the fifth publication on Revolutionary War flags sponsored by the Society, and each publication has been more comprehensive than its predecessor. In addition, the Society sponsors a standing committee on flags, the Color Guard, of some eighty members who are responsible for the care and display of the Society's collection of about fifty copies of Revolutionary and current-day standards and colors. The publication of this latest "flag book" has been made possible by a bequest from Herbert C. Rorer, who served as a president of the Society and a captain of its Color Guard and to whose memory the book is dedicated.

The author appreciates the strong, continuing support of members of the Guard and the Society. There are many names that should be acknowledged if space permitted. The author particularly appreciates the interest and support of Theodore Clattenburg; F. M. H. Currie; D. W. Darby, Jr.; G. W. Evans; J. D. Evans; R. N. Ferrer; W. B. Gold, Jr.; C. E. Hires; G. J. Lincoln, III; R. L. McNeil, Jr.; R. F. Morris; Dr.

C. W. Muckle; J. P. Richards, Jr.; Dr. S. B. Sturgis; R. W. Thorington; T. E. Wynne; Captain Harris C. Aller, USN Ret.; the late W. S. Emmons and B. L. Lessig; all members of the Society; and the members and officers of the Color Guard and officers and managers of the Society.

The author also appreciates the interest and professionalism of the staff of the University of Pennsylvania Press, in particular, Mr. Maurice English, Mr. Malcolm Call, Mrs. Ingalill Hjelm, and Mr. E. Johnson-Muller, who were faced with some unique challenges in bringing the book out.

The majority of the excellent flag paintings are by J. Carlton Jones of Hatboro and Penndel, Pennsylvania, a businessman, artist, and student of heraldry. The photographs of Mr. Jones' paintings and of the majority of illustrations are by the author.

The author gratefully acknowledges the assistance of the many institutions and individuals in the list of credits who furnished data, photographs, and encouragement. Particular thanks are given to Dr. Whitney Smith of the Flag Research Center, who reviewed the galleys and offered encouragement and a number of helpful suggestions, many of which were incorporated. Also to be acknowledged are the data, photographs, and interest provided by Captain Fitzhugh McMaster, USN Ret.; Dr. Howard C. Rice, Jr.; Donald W. Holst; Dr. F. W. Headman; Dr. H. D. Langley; Donald Kloster; Kenneth Newman; Dittmar Finke; Craig Nannos; William Guthman; James V. Murfin and the late Harold L. Peterson of the National Park Service; R. L. McNeil; J. F. Reed; E. N. Smith; Comte de Rochambeau; Hughes Cauffman; and Dr. James Mooney. The author also wishes to thank the staffs of the many institutions and organizations noted in the credits, with particular thanks to the Library Company of Philadelphia, Historical Society of Pennsylvania, First Troop-Philadelphia City Cavalry, Pennsylvania Academy of Fine Arts, Philadelphia Maritime Museum, Independence National Historical Park, Valley Forge Historical Society, the Library of Congress, National Archives, Society of the Cincinnati, West Point Museum, National Museum of History and Technology, Alexandria-Washington Lodge No. 22, Maryland Historical Property Commission, Delaware Historical Society, New York Historical Society, New York Public Library, St. Paul's Chapel (Trinity Parish)-New York City, Metropolitan Museum of Art, Connecticut Historical Society, Yale University Art Gallery, Rhode Island Historical Society, Massachusetts Historical Society, New Hampshire Historical Society, Boston Museum of Grand Lodge of Masons, John Carter Brown Library, Museum of the King's Royal Rifle Corps, New Brunswick Museum, and many others listed under credits.

EDWARD W. RICHARDSON

List of Illustrations

xvii

Flag Design and Symbols

ARMY AND NAVY FLAGS

The flags carried by the American revolutionary armies were primarily individualistically-designed silk "colors" on which were painted or embroidered symbolic emblems. The emblems were based on old world heraldic as well as new world symbolism. Included were an unbelievable variety of objects. These included such things as beehive, rattlesnake, eagle, lion, bear, crane, beaver, horse, sword, armored hand and arm, rifle, cannon, trees, plants, vines, Indians, arrows, women, children, soldiers, anchor, victory wreath, liberty pole and cap, rising sun, new moon, stars, angels, beheaded king, harp, altar, Masonic symbols and many other devices. The "union" was frequently represented by thirteen swords, arrows, hands, chain links, ribbons, stripes or stars. On many of the colors were Latin or English mottos as well as the unit's designation.

Some of the colors were elaborate, others very plain. Almost all colors carried by units of the land forces were of lightweight solid-color silk. These were readily visible and would readily stream in a light breeze, or when on parade. The devices were usually painted in oils, although some were embroidered. Colors of mounted units were usually fringed; but those of foot or infantry units were generally not fringed.

The color was fixed to a wooden staff headed with a decorative brass or wooden spear-pointed finial. A pair of tasseled cords or ribbons formed part of the decoration.

Flag staffs of foot units were "pikes" while those of mounted troops were "lances." Colors were furled and cased most of the time and displayed in battle and on parade.

Simpler, smaller, more rugged "camp colors," about 18 inches square, served for identification at encampments. Strong bunting was used for marine and garrison flags.

The colors carried by land forces were of squarish proportions to allow for maximum streaming and ease of carrying. Naval and garrison ensigns were rectangular. Sizes varied from eighteen inches square (Pulaski's Legion) up to the five-by-seven foot standard of the Rhode Island Regiment of 1781 and the seven foot square standard of the Third New York Regiment. Generally, the regimental standards were the largest.

The Revolutionary soldier fought, rallied, and paraded under his regimental, battalion, divisional or independent company or troop colors. The stars and stripes, of which there were a number of evolutionary designs, was flown by ships, forts, garrison towns and at the headquarters of an army or corps.

A national standard for the Army was apparently not defined until late in the war. The thirteen-stars-and-stripes flag resolution of June 14, 1777 originated with the Marine Committee of the Continental Congress and was probably intended primarily for ships. As late as September 3, 1779, the War Office wrote to Washington inquiring about the proper design for a standard for the Army that would be "variant" from the marine flag. Washington replied that he preferred "the Union and Emblems in the Center . . . with . . . the Number of the Regiment and the State . . . within the curve of the Serpent. . . ."

Individual American land force units were not officially authorized to carry a stars and stripes along with their regimental or battalion colors until 1834. At that time the artillery received such authorization followed by the infantry in 1841. Some Revolutionary army units, however, did carry a stars and stripes, as evidenced by Major John Ross' sketch of the Order of Battle for General Sullivan's army, dated July 30, 1779. Also, at Yorktown, in 1781, the American forces hoisted a large blue-and-red stripe flag with a blue canton with stars, according to an on-the-spot sketch by British Lt. Col. John Graves Simcoe.

Naval ensigns and other outdoor flags were made of bunting, a strongly woven cloth of linen and wool. They were rectangular with thread whipped grommets and a reinforcing strip of heavy cloth along the hoist. There was no fringe. Marine flags depended on bold simple designs and bright colors for visibility. This is the reason the Continental Navy readily adopted the thirteen stripes. Contemporary paintings show the Continental Navy favored red, white and blue stripes but also used red and white stripes, and there are accounts of other color combinations. Such tri-colored marine ensigns continued in use throughout the war and for many years after. They were also flown on land. A red-white-blue striped flag was flown over Mud Island Fort (Mifflin) at Philadelphia in October 1777 and in August 1777 over Fort Stanwyx in western New York. As to the stars, John Paul Jones speaks of hoisting the "American stars" on the *Ranger* on April 24, 1778, while off the Irish Coast. He had sailed from New Hampshire in November 1777. In October 1779, at anchor in the Texel, a port of Holland, Jones flew a red and white striped ensign with a union of stars over the *Alliance* and a red-white-blue striped ensign with a union of stars over the *Serapis*.

While the design of naval flags was, for the most part, simple, there were some of fairly complex design. For instance, a pine tree symbol on a white flag with the motto, "An Appeal to Heaven," was flown by the Massachusetts Navy in the early years. Then there was the yellow standard with rattlesnake emblem designed in late 1775-early 1776 as the standard of the Commander-in-Chief of the Continental Navy. South Carolina authorized a blue flag with crescent emblem, and a white flag bearing thirteen stars and a sheaf of rice, and thirteen stripes with a rattlesnake as ensigns for its Navy.

The size of marine flags varied. A Philadelphia ship chandler's journal for December 1775-January 1776 lists Continental Navy flags 7½ by 13½ feet and 5 by 7½ feet, pendants 10 inches by 55 feet, and an ensign 18 by 30 feet. There would also have been garrison and fort flags of 5 by 8 feet and larger. The few union flags carried by land forces probably were of silk and square in proportions.

Commanders, such as Washington, Gates and Sullivan, had national standards which were carried next to them in battle. Washington's and Gates' standards have been variously depicted in paintings as consisting of an all blue field with a rectilinear or circular pattern of thirteen stars.

From the beginning of the Revolution, there was a strong demand for flags. Flags served to establish the Americans as a sovereign force. They also helped in recruiting, built morale, and helped to nullify any psychological advantage of flags carried by the British or Hessian forces. The Americans tended to adopt the general designs and sizes of the British colors for their own, but with appropriate changes to the unions and emblems.

Many early American Revolutionary colors displayed the crosses of the British Union in the canton to show basic loyalty to the King and mother country. Within the first year or so, however, the spirit of independence had stiffened and the cantons were gradually changed to a union of thirteen stripes and then to stars. An eagle with stars was introduced about 1783.

It should be noted that the *stripes* came first and then the stars. The "stripes" are also called out first in the flag resolutions of 1777, 1795 and 1818 and in the national anthem.

ORIGINAL COLORS

There were apparently many hundreds of American Revolutionary Army and Marine colors. By 1777, the American Continental Army alone had over one hundred authorized regiments, totaling about 38,000 men. In addition, there were many "State" or local militia units—probably as many again as the Continental Army. As to naval or marine flags, there were not only the Continental and State Navies but a total of 3,500 privateers commissioned.

Each regiment carried a "stand" of two, three or more colors. In the National Archives there is an inventory dated July-August 1778, which describes thirteen sets (or stands) of regimental colors ready for issue. Each "set" consisted of a main regimental standard and two "division colors" of simpler design, each of a different color. One of the regimental standards of that inventory still exists and is on display at the Smithsonian.

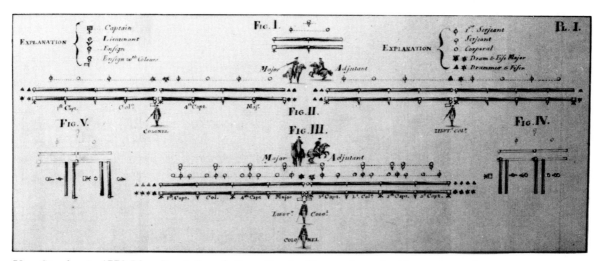

Von Steuben's 1779 Blue Book Regulations for the Formation of a Company and a Regiment. Posts for various officers, including the "Ensign with Colors," are shown in this engraving by L'enfant.

Von Steuben's Regulations of 1779, the "Blue Book," specified that, "a regiment is to consist of two battalions, if of over 160 files, and one color shall be posted in the center of each battalion. If the regiment is of less than 160 files it shall consist of one battalion and both colors shall be in the center," and further, "As there are two colors to a regiment, the ensigns must carry them in turn."

While some regiments may have had only one color, the records indicate that many had two or three. Therefore, it is likely that something on the order of one hundred or more regimental standards—one to two hundred division colors and several hundred or more state regimental, battalion, company·and troop colors and standards—originally existed at various times for a total of at least five hundred or more. Twenty-five original colors survive to this date. There are descriptions of about another one hundred. Those that have not survived were lost, through normal wear and tear, souvenir hunters, natural deterioration and neglect.

In 1814, Congress called for an inventory and preservation of captured flags and other trophies. Of the forty or more British and Hessian regimental colors captured during the Revolution only six could be found; and, unfortunately, two of these have disappeared since the 1920's. Such disappearances have also marked the American colors—even more so because of the lack, with very few exceptions, of any serious preservation efforts during the first one hundred and eighty years following the Revolution. Of the known originals that survive, all are now in collections and receiving proper care.

FLAG CLOTH

There are a number of records regarding purchases of silk. E. C. Knight in "New York in the Revolution," Supplement 1901, quotes an invoice for material for "Colours," as follows:

"1776"

"June 17 to 24	7 pieces Brown Hessian linen	£14.14
	8 yards yellow taffeta	5.12
	4½ yards white taffeta	3.3
	19 yards blue Italian silk	12.16.6
	1⅔ yards green silk	1. 3.7
	7½ yards pink lute string	3.15
	2⅔ yards green lute string	1. 6.8
		£42.16.1

The above was for "Colours for the Regiments in the New York Line. deld, Richd Kip." Assuming a selvage width of 28½ inches, as for the Webb Regimental Standard, there would be sufficient taffeta and silk in the above invoice to make eight or nine regimental colors.

According to the records of the Williamsburg Public Store in late 1775, the captain of a company bought a stand of colors and, on the same day, eight yards of white shalloon were received for camp colors for the army in Williamsburg. Earlier, the same company had been issued 1¾ yards of "best [Swanskin] for Ensign."

Preble wrote that Governor Daniel Rodney of Delaware received a bill in 1783 for "materials for a continental flag" which included "a piece of Green silk."

For the Continental Congress, the Board of War and Ordnance submitted an estimate dated June 11, 1779 for silk, cord, and fringe to be imported from France for regimental colors for the army.

The estimate included:
"Plain strong silk for regimental colours of

crimson	300	
deep blue	1100	1760 yds
Wite [sic]	280	
Buff	80	

"Tassils [sic] & cords
of deep blue silk and
gold mixed for the
colours   400"

Samuel Hodgdon, Commissary General of Military Stores, submitted to the Hon'ble Secretary at [sic] War an estimate dated Philadelphia, 2 July 1782 for one hundred standards for the Army of the United States, as follows:

"100 Standards at £12 each = £1200

"To be made of the best materials the silk estimated at 25 [shillings] per yard, each colour to be 4¼ yards. The name of the state and the number of the Regiment to be done in a garter of blue with pure gold leaf. Two silk tassels to each Standard and the ends of the staff mounted with brass"

At the bottom margin of the estimate is a note; "NB. 50 Only was admitted at this time."

SYMBOLS

Copying of the seals used on Continental and State currency for flag emblems appears to have been accepted practice. For instance, the device of three grapevines on a shield and the motto of a still surviving standard of the II Battalion, II Connecticut Regiment, appear on Connecticut paper currency as the state seal. An early union symbol—a circle of thirteen stars with the all-seeing eye of Providence—was designed by Francis Hopkinson of the Continental Congress. It appears on the standard of Pulaski's Legion and also on the Continental 40 dollar bill first issued on April 11, 1778. Benjamin Franklin's design of a circle of thirteen chain links (each with a state's name), the sun, and the motto "WE ARE ONE" placed on one of the standards of the Second New Hampshire Regiment of 1777 appears on the Continental two-thirds of a dollar bill, issue of February 17, 1776.

According to the "Record of Connecticut Men . . . during the War of the Revolution" under date of September 10, 1780, a regulation for regimental colors in the Connecticut Line required that ". . . each to bear the number of the Regt. in large characters: The devise on one side, the Conn. Arms on the other, the devise and motto of the 30 Dollar Bills . . ."

Seven of the thirteen regimental standards

5

listed in the Major Jonathan Gostelowe Return (inventory) of July–August 1778 have devices described which are identical to those that appear on different denominations of Continental paper currency. The reverse was also the case; the Continental Grand Union flag appears on North Carolina paper currency issued April 1, 1776.

According to Eric P. Newman, the emblems and mottos for the Continental dollar bills, $1 through $6, and $30 were taken from the 1702 Mainz edition of "Symbolorum ac Emblematum Ethico–Politicorum" by Joachim Camerarius. This book was in Franklin's library. The emblem and motto of the $40 bill, as well as those of six other denominations, were designed by Francis Hopkinson. He is also credited with the design of the national seal. In addition, Hopkinson claimed to be the designer of the stars and stripes.

The use of currency emblems and mottos for Revolutionary flags probably extended beyond the above known examples. For example, the Virginia state seal of Victory triumphing over Tyranny with the motto "Sic Semper Tyrannis," which appeared on Virginia currency as early as 1776, was the emblem for Virginia regimental standards of the War of 1812. It may also have been used on flags during the Revolution.

Vermont issued a Two-Shilling-Six Pence bill in February 1781. This featured the emblem of a circle of fourteen chain links (one loose) similar to the thirteen links-emblem on one of the colors of the 2nd New Hampshire Regiment of 1777.

South Carolina currency emblems, appropriate for flag design, included a rattlesnake attacking the British lion, thirteen hearts, an arm with sword (ET DEUS OMNIPOTENS), and a splay of 12 arrows.

Rhode Island's currency symbols included the rope entwined anchor. This symbol had been used in the Colonial era. It was also used on a Rhode Island regimental standard.

North Carolina currency symbols included the Continental Grand Union (issue of April 2, 1776); the rattlesnake and famous "Don't Tread on Me" motto; and a hand grasping a splay of thirteen arrows.

New York currency emblems included the state seal (see New York III Regiment), a sword, a candelabra of thirteen lights, an elephant, eagle, a hand planting a tree, and others.

New Jersey currency used the symbol of Liberty and Ceres with a shield picturing plows topped by a horse head. It also showed the "VI CONCITATAE" symbol of a strong wind blowing—the same as on the Continental $20 and the back of the 1775–1777 $30 bills.

New Hampshire currency used the thorn bush and hand (and in a Colonial-era issue, the pine tree).

Massachusetts currency emblems included the pine tree, the "VI CONCITATAE" strong wind emblem of the Continental $20 (a storm is followed by a peaceful calm), a soldier brandishing a sword and the Magna Carta (Paul Revere engraving). Some colonial-era currency also featured an Indian.

Maryland currency symbols included the eagle and crane (Continental $3 and Gostelowe Standard No. 8), an arm and hand extending a branch "SUB. CLY.PEO." The $4 bill of 1776 used an elaborate woodcut depicting Britannia, America, Liberty Cap, and An Appeal to Heaven.

Georgia currency emblems included a wild boar, dove and sword, rattlesnake, thirteen links, liberty cap, frontiersman, sea anemone, justice, an Indian and many others.

Delaware currency symbols included a soldier and sailor on either side of a shield topped with a ship.

Connecticut currency used the state's three grapevines and "Qui Trans Sust" motto.

Virginia ten-dollar bill—
October 7, 1776
Liberty Slaying Tyranny
The Seal of the Commonwealth of
Virginia

Delaware five shilling bill—
May 1, 1777
Arms of the State of Delaware

Page from a 1702 book on
symbols. A copy was in Franklin's
library

Massachusetts thirty-six shilling
bill by Paul Revere,
December 7, 1775

National and State Arms. Early Census of the United States. The circle of links was a popular design symbolizing the union

NATIONAL AND STATE COATS OF ARMS AS SYMBOLS ON REVOLUTIONARY STANDARDS

The seal of the United States and the seals of some of the individual States were employed as symbols on Revolutionary standards. The Smithsonian's Headman Color, which was ready for issue to a Continental regiment in 1778, bears the seal placed on the title page of the Journal of the Continental Congress of 1774. The spread eagle arms of the United States, which was adopted in June 1782, appears as the canton of the United States standard in L'enfant's 1783 diploma for the Society of the Cincinnati. The eagle seal might have been placed on the "National Standards of the Army" in 1782.

Versions of the arms of the states of Connecticut, Rhode Island, New York and South Carolina are found on surviving Revolutionary regimental standards. Shortly after the war, in the 1780's and 90's, legislation called for the arms of Massachusetts, Pennsylvania and New Hampshire to be placed on state regimental standards. Virginia regiments were definitely carrying standards bearing the arms of their state by 1812; and by the time of the Civil War, the use of state arms on colors was widespread.

It is possible that some form of state arms was placed on the standard of one or more regiments by all eleven original states that possessed arms during the War. Since the regiments raised by a state for the Continental service were to have facings on their uniforms of a specified color, and since they were to carry standards whose fields matched these facings, the principal elements of a number of standards could be constructed. For instance, New Jersey adopted a state seal in 1776. Its troops had red facings in 1777 which were changed to buff in 1779. Possibly, one of the New Jersey regiments carried a standard with a red or buff field bearing the state seal as the emblem.

Contemporary illustrations of the state arms are to be found on paper currency issued by the various states during the Revolutionary era. Detailed information on the Revolutionary arms and seals is provided by Admiral Preble's 1880 edition. Many of Preble's illustrations, however, show the state seal as evolved up to the 1870's. Therefore, the illustrations should be studied with their Revolutionary descriptions as given by Preble and then compared to the seals as they appeared on various issues of state Revolutionary currency. These should provide relatively crude, but probably more accurate depictions. It is likely that the original drawings of some of the Revolutionary-era state seals have been preserved in state archives. They should be included in any future research on this subject.

There has been considerable puzzlement as to why Washington and the Board of War in 1779 felt the need to define a design for a "national standard" for the army in view of the stars and stripes resolution of June 1777. The author suggests that they planned to use the "Arms of the United States" as the symbol on the "national standard." This was eventually realized in the army's national standards—a blue field bearing the great eagle seal. The Marine Committee, however, after waiting for almost a year after July 4, 1776, for the Seal Committee to develop an acceptable design, decided to specify the stripes and stars because of their urgent need to standardize on a flag. Washington, the Board of War, and apparently many others, did not consider the marine committee's flag to be the official "national standard" and referred to it as the "marine flag." It's interesting to note that Washington's proposal to use the union of stars alone, as the national standard for the army, paralleled the British practice of using a union of crosses as the national flag for their regiments.

The development of a "national standard" for the army was delayed until the adoption of an official U.S. seal which did not come about until June 1782.

Original die of the Great Seal of the United States

Reverse of the Great Seal of the United States of America

THE GREAT SEAL OF THE UNITED STATES OF AMERICA

The development of the seal and arms of the United States is well documented and gives a clear picture of the importance attached to such heraldic devices by the leaders and artists of the Revolution. The following description of the development of the Seal is based primarily on Patterson and Dougall's work.

The Continental Congress appointed Franklin, John Adams, and Jefferson as a committee, on July 4, 1776, to prepare a device for the great seal of the United States of America. The Committee turned to a Philadelphia silhouette and miniature artist, Pierre Eugene du Simitiere, from the French West Indies, who was familiar with heraldry.

Du Simitiere proposed a typical elaborate design, similar in format to a number of Colonial state seals then in use. Basically, the design consisted of a shield bearing the traditional symbols (rose, thistle, harp, fleur de lys, eagle and lion) representing the six

principal European nations which had settled North America. The shield was flanked by "Supporters," which were the Goddess of Liberty and an American rifleman. The seal also bore the eye of Providence and the motto "Bello Vel Pace."

Franklin, reflecting the widespread tendency to identify America with Old Testament stories and wandering tribes, proposed Moses with his wand, the Red Sea engulfing Pharaoh's army and, as a motto, the typical metaphor, "Rebellion to Tyrants is Obedience to God." Adams, reflecting the classical education and knowledge of mythology then expected of all learned men, proposed Hercules with his club being urged by Virtue to climb her rugged mountain, while at the same time he is being tempted by the sensuous Goddess of Sloth to accompany her down the flowery paths of pleasure. Jefferson proposed the Israelites being led by the cloud and pillar of fire and, on the reverse, the Saxon chiefs, Hengist and Horsa, early freedom fighters.

Eventually, Jefferson combined the various proposals. He eliminated Hengist and Horsa and "Bello Vel Pace," kept the circle

10

of thirteen linked shields, each bearing the designation of a state and also du Simitiere's motto ''E Pluribus Unum,'' the date MDCCLXXVI, and Providence's eye within a Masonic triangle. The design was submitted on August 20, 1776, but events forced the subject to be tabled for the next several years.

Franklin's words appeared on a standard of a Continental Army regiment in 1778 and was engraved on Jefferson's ''life-motto'' ring. A simplified version of the circle of thirteen chain-linked states was placed on one of the colors of the 2nd New Hampshire Regiment of 1777 and also on various issues of Continental and State paper currency.

The proposed design of the first Committee contributed the Eye of Providence, the date, and ''E Pluribus Unum'' to the final version of the Seal, and, also, the shield.

On March 25, 1780, the war having shifted to the South, Congress again called for a seal and appointed James Lovell, John M. Scott, and William C. Houston to continue its development. Their design, submitted on May 10, called for a shield with thirteen diagonal red and white stripes flanked by a Roman soldier and by the Goddess of Peace with an olive branch, the motto ''Bello Vel Pace,'' crested by a constellation of thirteen stars, all encircled by the words ''The Great Seal of the United States of America.''

On the reverse, the seated figure of Liberty, in an eighteenth century hooped gown, held a Liberty staff and cap and with the motto ''Semper'' and date MDCCLXXVI. On 17 May, minor changes were made and there the matter again rested. This proposed version contributed the 13 red and white stripes, the constellation of 13 stars, and the olive branch. Hooped-skirted Goddesses of Liberty and Justice also appeared on the standard of the 3rd New York Regiment.

In 1780, the Roman soldier was substituted for an Indian warrior, and the date and mottos changed. A lone Indian warrior as a symbol of America was adopted in the arms of the seal of Massachusetts on December 13, 1780.

The 1776 proposed designs are indicative of the artistic talent of du Simitiere. It is logical to assume that he also painted devices on some of the colors and standards of Revolutionary Army units. Only a skilled heraldic artist could have painted the Headman Color which is now at the Smithsonian. This was one of thirteen such elaborate standards described by Philadelphia Major Jonathan Gostelowe in his ''Return'' of July–August 1778 as a ''Comissary of Military Stores.'' Six of the thirteen standards bore devices taken directly from early heraldry reference books and the devices described for the other seven are heraldic in principle. Undoubtedly, it was artists such as du Simitiere who provided sketches for the seals found on paper currency.

The third and final committee for the Seal was appointed in May, 1782, and included Middleton, Boudinot and Rutledge. Charles Thomson, Secretary of Congress, also became involved as did William Barton, a young Philadelphia lawyer with a knowledge of heraldry. Barton's proposed design was basically similar to du Simitiere's and included a central shield with 13 stripes and stars flanked by the maiden America and a knight in armor, plus other devices and mottos. For the reverse, he proposed an unfinished 13 tier pyramid topped by the eye of God. The knight was subsequently changed to a Continental officer. Other changes were also made and an eagle added.

Thomson made a major contribution by greatly simplifying and thereby strengthening the design. Thus refined, it was submitted to Congress and adopted on June 20, 1782.

The final version of the Seal appears on the present-day $1.00 bill. The central device is the American spread eagle (independence and strength) bearing a shield of thirteen red and white stripes (the states) supporting a blue horizontal bar (congress). The right talon clutches an olive branch; the

Barton's proposed seal, Third Committee, 1782
Note the stars and stripes with the stars in a circle

other, thirteen arrows. Above the eagle is placed a constellation of thirteen five-point stars breaking through the clouds (a new nation). The motto "E Pluribus Unum" is on a scroll held in the eagle's beak. The reverse of the seal features Barton's thirteen step pyramid capped by the watchful eye of Providence together with MDCCLXXVI, and the mottos "Annuit Coeptis" (He Has Favored Our Undertaking) and "Novus Ordo Seclorum" (A New Order of the Ages).

Thomson's report stated that, "The colors of the pales are those used in the flag of the United States of America; white, signifies purity and innocence; red, hardiness

and valor; and blue, the color of the chief, signifies vigilance, perseverance, and justice." Barton had earlier given the same significance to the three colors.

The earliest published representation of the great seal of the United States of America appears on the title page of a French publication of the state constitutions which was sponsored by Franklin and printed in 1783 by Chez Ph.-D. Pierres (&) Pissot, Paris. A copy is at the American Philosophical Society, Philadelphia. It is also illustrated in the catalog of the Bicentennial Exhibit "A Rising People" published by the Historical Society of Pennsylvania.

——2——

Liberty Flags

SONS OF LIBERTY

Liberty Poles, Liberty Trees, and Liberty Flags were mentioned with increased frequency as protests began to grow within the colonies prior to the Revolution.

Men banded together into "Sons of Liberty" societies and would meet under some large oak or other distinctive tree on the green. They erected Liberty Poles which local authorities and Loyalists would, of course, try to chop down. In one instance, after their Pole had been destroyed for the second time, the local Liberty Boys raised a massive replacement sheathed in iron.

Liberty Flag

Flags also began to appear. These were usually red ensigns bearing such mottos as "LIBERTY" or "CONGRESS." General Charles Lee, in 1775, urged that Army flags bear the motto "Liberty."

"LIBERTY AND UNION" FLAG, TAUNTON, MASSACHUSETTS—1774

The Boston Evening Post of Monday, October 24, 1774, reported "We have just received the following intelligence from Taunton—that on Friday last a liberty pole 112 feet long was raised there on which a vane, and a Union flag flying with the words Liberty and Union thereon."

VERTICAL STRIPED LIBERTY FLAG *(Plate 2)*

According to Mastai, in "The Stars and the Stripes," early Revolutionary accounts speak of a Sons of Liberty flag which had nine vertical red and white stripes. Such a design could have been inspired by Paul Revere's engraving of a snake cut into nine parts, labeled NE, NY, NJ, PA, MD, VA, NC, SC, GA, which appeared in The Massachusetts Spy in 1774. The motto was "JOIN OR DIE". Franklin, in 1754, had originated the drawing with a snake cut into eight parts (Georgia was not included).

Sons of Liberty Flag. Artist's Imaginative Sketch Showing the Possible Relation to Franklin's and Revere's Disjointed Snake

Franklin's Pennsylvania Gazette, May 9, 1754

"The taking of Miss Mud Island." Satiric English cartoon on the capture of Fort Mifflin, Philadelphia, October 1777. Engraved by W. Faden, Charing Cross, 1778. Note vertical striped flag with snake

Nine colonies participated in the Stamp Act Convention's Declaration of Rights in 1765. The present-day Coast Guard and Customs ensign, which stems from the Revenue Cutter ensign of 1799, has sixteen vertical red and white stripes.

A satiric English cartoon of the siege of Mud Island Fort (Mifflin) on the Delaware at Philadelphia, includes a vertically striped American standard bearing a running rattlesnake. There is also a British union flag depicted. Copies of the cartoon were sold by W. Humphrey, 227 Strand, London, and date from about December 1777. It should not be assumed that such a flag actually flew over Mud Island, but only that vertical striped flags were among the various ver-

14

sions of American Union flags known to English printmakers. The Mud Island Fort standard was actually of red, white, and blue horizontal stripes according to an eyewitness drawing made by a military mapmaker.

LIBERTY FLAG AND POLE CONCORD—1775

British Lieutenant Barker recorded that when the British column marched into Concord on April 19, 1775, they took possession of a nearby hill "with a liberty pole on it and a flag flying which was cut down."

"LIBERTY COLOURS" GEORGIA COAST—1776

Following the repulse of the British invasion fleet at Charleston on 28 June 1776, the Continental and State Forces of the Southern Department, under General Charles Lee, launched an abortive expedition against British East Florida. Some armed vessels accompanied the American forces and, as a result, Lt. William Grant, Royal Navy, of H. M. Schooner "St. John" recorded in his ship's journal and also reported to Royal Governor Patrick Tonyn that while off "St. Marie's Barr [sic] 7th August 1776, . . . saw a large flat resembling a Vessel cut down and made into a Floating Battery with one Mast and Liberty Colours flying near Cumberland Point. . . ."

"LIBERTY" FLAGS—BATTLE OF LONG ISLAND AUGUST 1776

Adjutant General Major Baurmeister of the Hessian forces reported that " . . . We came into possession of eleven enemy flags with the motto 'Liberty' . . ." at the battle of Long Island fought August 26, 1776. Subsequently, upon the occupation of New York, he noted: ". . . All the captured guns, ammunition, provisions and flags in the army were carefully listed, and the list turned over to the Commandant of New York, General Robertson . . ."

Liberty Flag.
Schenectady, N.Y.

"LIBERTY" FLAG SCHENECTADY/SCOTIA, N.Y.

A fragment, measuring 42 by 37 inches, of an original flag with the motto "LIBERTY" is in the collection of the Schenectady Historical Society. The fabric appears to be silk, originally blue-green but now indistinguishable. The motto is formed of three-inch high white silk letters and placed in what was the approximate center of the field. There is a three and one-half inch sleeve formed by a hem along one side for a staff.

The flag came into the collection of the Schenectady County Historical Society between 1905 and 1910 through the Glen-Sanders family of Scotia, New York. After years of typical quiet obscurity it was discovered in a closet in the "family mansion." Nothing else of the flag's origin is known. It is the author's opinion that the flag probably dates to the opening years of the Revolution.

LIBERTY FLAG, BOSTON, 1767

A flag of five red and four white stripes, measuring six feet ten inches by thirteen feet was given to the Bostonian Society in 1893. Traditionally, it had been flown on Boston Common in August 1767.

PHILADELPHIA; taken by *GEORGE HEAP* from the

To the Honourable Thomas Penn and Richard Penn true and Counties of NEWCASTLE, KENT *and* SUSSEX *on* DELAWARE.

Detail of a view of Philadelphia on the Delaware by George Heap, 1754.
Note Striped Ensign with Grand Union Canton

—3—

Continental and Union Colors

CONTINENTAL UNION

There are numerous references to "Continental" and "Union" colors throughout Revolutionary records. During the early period from late 1775 to mid-1777, such references generally meant a flag with a field of thirteen red and white stripes, with a blue canton bearing the crosses of St. George and St. Andrew. While no original survives, there are a number of contemporary paintings and sketches. Also, the "Continental Union" flag appears on the seal of the North Carolina $7.50 Bill of April 2, 1776. And we know that the Continental Navy sometimes flew a Continental Union with red, white and blue stripes.

Nineteenth century flag historians identify the above colors by calling it the "Continental Grand Union." However, Revolutionary records do not support the use of that name; instead, it would seem that "Continental" or "Union" would be closer to Revolutionary usage. For ease of identification, we will use the term "Continental Union" or "Continental Colors."

THE STRIPES WITH BRITISH GRAND UNION *(Plate 2)*

The Continental Union was simply the British red ensign with a striped field. The British ensign or, more accurately, the British Union flag, displayed the symbol of the Grand Union of England and Scotland; this was the superimposed crosses of the two patron saints. For some British colors, the Union was placed in the center, so as to cover the full field, while for others it was borne as a canton (see chapter on British and Loyalist Colors). When the Grand (or Great) Union occupied the canton, the field of the British national ensign was usually red. Some ensigns, however, had fields of blue or white or

"Union Flag" —red, white stripes
Ship Alfred —December 3, 1775
Cambridge —January 1, 1776

of distinctive colors. The British Grand Union ensign with a red field was the sovereign flag of colonial America. The Americans, simply by adding six white stripes, divided the field into thirteen stripes to symbolize their union.

Brig Sukey. Captured by the Privateer Washington, January 15, 1776.
Entering Newburyport under a prize crew. Note Continental Colors

The ensign of the "nation of East India" had red and white stripes. Also, the British national ensign was flown with a red and white striped field by ships of the British East Indies Company for many years before the Revolution. Some historians suggest that such stripes provided greater visibility at sea. There is a remarkable panoramic print of Philadelphia, as viewed from across the Delaware, by Scull, 1754. It shows, among the many vessels on the river, an armed ship flying a nine-striped field, Grand Union-cantoned ensign. The ship is heavily armed for its size and must have belonged to the Royal Navy or, possibly, some provincial navy. In either case, the ensign is what we now call a Continental Grand Union and the date was some twenty years before the Revolution. A copy of the print is at the Historical Society of Pennsylvania.

When the fighting began in 1775, and militia units from the various colonies joined together in besieging the British garrison at Boston, the Continental Congress voted to take all such troops into the services of the United Provinces of North America and appointed Washington as their Commander-in-chief. There was no United Colonies flag at the time.

Washington states in a letter that on January 1, 1776, he raised "the Union flag" for the first time in observance of the newly reorganized Continental army. He did not use the term "Grand Union" or "Continental Grand Union." Even so it seems almost certain that the flag had thirteen red and white stripes with a Grand Union canton.

Some historians suggest that the Continental Grand Union design was probably decided upon by the three-man Continental Congress committee that conferred with Washington at Cambridge in October 1775, but no original record appears to support this.

The Continental Union was apparently raised at Philadelphia by John Paul Jones

18

over the Continental ship ''Alfred'' on December 3, 1775, as discussed under the Continental Navy.

The Continental Union closely resembled the British ensign and, as noted above, was almost identical to the British East Indies Company ensign; therefore, when Washington first raised the flag, the British in Boston assumed the American Army was surrendering! Washington subsequently gave orders that this ensign should be hoisted only on special occasions.

Some time after the flag resolution of June 14, 1777, Washington adopted as his headquarters standard a flag with an all blue field bearing thirteen white six-point stars. In 1779, he urged that a version of this design be designated as the national standard for the Continental Army as discussed under that section. He spoke of this design as having the ''union in the center.''

An etching of Fort Schuyler on John McGraw's powder horn shows a continental union over the fort dated ''Decr 25, 1777.'' His Union bears only St. Andrews cross.

The Continental Union was a natural selection for the Americans in 1775. It did not signify rebellion but rather continued loyalty to the mother country. It was only after the Declaration of Independence and

the bitter fighting of 1776 that the British Grand Union canton lost favor. It was first replaced by the union of thirteen stripes, as with the Philadelphia Light Horse standard, and then by a union of thirteen stars.

THE STRIPES WITH PINE TREE CANTON *(Plate 23)*

One of the four flags depicted in a coat of arms, which John Paul Jones had painted for himself in late 1776 or early 1777 has red, blue, and white stripes and a white canton bearing a pine tree. The coat of arms, in the Masonic Library of Boston, is accepted as authentic by historians. A colored photograph and information on the arms were furnished by the Library.

Fort Schuyler, N.Y.—December 25, 1777 John McGraw's powder horn—
N.Y. State Militia
Note stripes with Scottish Cross Union

19

STRIPES WITH RATTLESNAKE CANTON—RHODE ISLAND MILITIA, SULLIVAN'S LIFE GUARDS *(Plate 20)*

The original silk standard is stored at the Rhode Island Historical Society. Traditionally, the standard was that of General Sullivan's Life Guards Company and was carried in Sullivan's Expedition against the Indians in 1779. There are, however, no early records concerning the flag, and its recorded history apparently starts with H. M. Chapin's article "Early Rhode Island Flags," in the October 1925 issue of the R. I. Historical Society's Collections.

The remaining fragment measures 45 (hoist) by 46 (fly) inches with the original estimated to have been 49 by 60 or 66 inches. It is badly deteriorated. The field consists of twelve stripes, probably thirteen originally. The stripes were red, white and blue, but the exact sequence cannot be determined accurately due to fading and some heavy-handed retouching. The sequence appears to be, starting with the missing bottom stripe, as follows: red, white, blue, r, w, b, r, w, b, r, w, b, and red. The canton, of which most is missing, bears a coiled rattlesnake with the motto "DON'T TREAD ON ME" on a scroll. The field of the canton appears to have been of white silk, with the snake painted in brown and gold and the motto in black letters on a blue scroll.

The flag has been pictured as having four narrow greenish-blue stripes on a white field forming nine stripes in total. However, close examination reveals there are actually twelve stripes of equal width remaining and that they were originally red, white and blue. The blue stripes were apparently tinted in this century.

This flag was reportedly carried by "Sullivan's Life Guards during the 1778 battle of Rhode Island." General John Sullivan commanded the 1778-79 expedition against the Iroquois and Loyalist forces that had

been raiding the Western Pennsylvania and New York settlements. It has been suggested that the flag was probably General Sullivan's personal command standard. There is no primary source information on the flag known to the author or to the Rhode Island Historical Society staff members contacted.

South Carolina State Navy
(Present day Ceremonial Banner)

STRIPES WITH RATTLESNAKE *(Plate 45)*

Franklin and Adams, as commissioners to France, stated in a letter, dated Oct. 9, 1778, to the Ambassador of the King of the Two Sicilies that the ships of the South Carolina Navy carried a flag with a rattlesnake in the middle of the 13 stripes. They do not state the colors of the stripes or whether the snake is coiled or stretched out (running) but the letter had simply described the flag of the United States as having red, white and blue stripes with a small union of stars.

An English print, dated in 1776, of Commodore Ezek Hopkins of the Continental Navy, shows two ships in the background. One ship flies an ensign with stripes with a rattlesnake stretched diagonally across the field. The second ship has an ensign with the Pine Tree or Liberty Tree symbol and the motto "An Appeal to God." It could be assumed the artist was indicating the two flags represented the northern and southern colonies united under Hopkins as Commander-in-Chief of the Continental Navy.

Union Flag "The Rebel Stripes"

THE STRIPES AND THE STARS AND STRIPES *(Plates 2-9)*

The Continental Congress on June 14, 1777 passed a resolution which was apparently proposed by the Marine Committee, as follows: "Resolved that the flag of the United States be 13 stripes alternate red and white, that the Union be 13 stars white in a blue field representing a new constellation." There was nothing stated as to the design or arrangement of the stars, or which stripe the union should rest on, or whether there was to be six or seven white or red stripes. These details were left for later Congressional representatives to resolve. This was just as well, because in the following years flag makers demonstrated their artistic independence and imagination by interpreting the 1777 "Resolve" into a wonderful variety of "stars and stripes" designs.

It should be noted in the above resolution that the stripes—the "rebellious stripes" as the British termed them—are defined first, and then the stars. This was also the case in the 1795 and 1818 Flag Resolutions and in the National Anthem. As late as the Civil War, the stripes were addressed first and then the stars.

The basic design of the stars and stripes evolved from the British red ensign which was modified with six white stripes to form the Continental Union, the first (but unofficial) American national standard. Once independence had been declared the crosses of the British union had to be replaced. On American regimental and other military unit colors, the canton became thirteen stripes and, later, stars. However, since the field of the Continental flag was composed of red-and-white stripes, changing the canton to a union of stripes would have been redundant. Therefore, the canton was dropped altogether and a standard of thirteen red and white or red, white and blue stripes was flown by some ships. The "stripes" design persisted as one of the accepted versions into the 1790's . At the same time, a new

Reading the Declaration of Independence at Philadelphia. Note Stripes

21

canton was desired. Various symbols for the union abounded, such as thirteen links or hands or swords or a rattlesnake. Stars, however, proved the final choice as representing a "new constellation."

Francis Hopkinson was a member of the Continental Congress and chairman of the Marine Committee. He was charged with the task of developing a seal for the United States. Of all candidates, he is the most likely designer of the stripes and stars. He is properly credited with the design of thirteen stars in a circle, a symbol which was used on the Continental $40 bill of September 26, 1778. He was also co-designer of the eagle seal of the United States introduced in 1782.

Once the Congress had passed the June 1777 flag resolution, artists, statesmen, military commanders, naval captains and flag-makers gave individual interpretations to the design. There are records of red-and-white stripes, red-and-blue stripes, blue-and-white stripes, red-and-green stripes and red-white-and-blue stripes; all in various sequences and varying widths. The stars were of eight points, six points and five points and varied in proportion from slender-rayed starfish types to fat discs with stubby rays. Star pattern arrangements included (from the top) 3-2-3-2-3, 4-5-4, 1-3-3-3-3, 1-3-5-3-1, 3-3-3-3-1, and the circle, oval and square. The canton varied as to size and proportions and as to which stripe it rested on.

At Yorktown, in 1781, a British officer, Lieutenant Colonel Simcoe, sketched the American ensign as having red and blue stripes, a large, light blue canton and dark blue stars.

Franklin and Adams in a letter dated October 9, 1778 from Paris to the Ambassador of the King of the Two Sicilies wrote that "it is with pleasure that we acquaint Your Excellency that the flag of the United States of America consists of 13 stripes, alternately red, white, and blue; a small square in the

Franklin & Adams —October 9, 1778

upper angle, next to the flag staff, is a blue field, with 13 white stars, denoting a new Constellation. Some of the States have vessels of war distinct from those of the United States. For example, the vessels of war of the State of Massachusetts Bay have sometimes a pine tree; and those of South Carolina a rattlesnake, in the middle of the 13 stripes; but the Flag of the United States, ordained by Congress, is the 13 stripes and 13 stars above described."

"B. Franklin"
"John Adams"

Note, again, that the stripes are called out first.

Arthur Lee, the third of the commissioners to France, wrote on September 20, 1778 to Henry Laurens, then President of Congress, that a "... ship's colours should be white, red and blue alternately to thirteen, and in the upper angle next to the staff a blue field with thirteen stars."

Arthur Lee —September 20, 1778

22

RED, WHITE AND
BLUE STRIPES *(Plate 2)*

Fort Stanwyx Garrison Flag, New York
August 1777

Lt. Colonel Marinus Willett, who was in Fort Stanwyx when under the command of Colonel Peter Gansevoort (Third New York Regiment of 1777), described a flag improvised out of various articles of clothing to provide "white stripes," "blue stripes," and "red stripes." Nothing as to the canton, either stars or British Union, is mentioned, and it appears that this flag consisted only of white, blue and red stripes. During Burgoyne's invasion, the flag was hoisted on August 3, 1777, the morning after the fort was surrounded by British General Barry St. Leger with 2,000 Regulars, Tories and Indians. The Americans withstood the siege and forced Leger's force to retreat.

A powder horn of a John McGraw is inscribed with a view of Fort Schuyler. It shows a Continental Grand Union flag flying over the fort and is dated December 25, 1777. It could therefore be assumed that the improvised flag of August 1777 as described by Lt. Colonel Willett was the Continental Grand Union—although this is not in line with his description. The red-white-blue striped flag, without canton, was a well known version of the national standard; one that was still recognized as an American ensign in the 1790's.

F. J. Hudleston in "Gentleman Johnny Burgoyne" writes that the Fort Stanwyx garrison standard was made out of "a woman's petticoat, the soldiers' shirt and Colonel Gansevoort's military coat." He gives no reference and assumes that the standard was a stars and stripes, although this was not stated by any original source consulted.

Lt. Col. Marinus Willett referred to the flag as a "Continental" flag in papers edited by his son in 1831. Willett said the blue cloak was owned by Captain Swarthout (Gansevoort-Lansing papers). The bill submitted by Captain Swarthout to replace his coat makes no mention of stars, only that the cloth was cut into stripes.

Some claim that the "first" stars and stripes was flown over Fort Stanwyx. There is little to support this, however. Possibly, the flag could have been a Continental Grand Union—but the British/Scottish union of crosses was being deleted from American flags. It is therefore not likely, considering the time and circumstances, that a British symbol would have been used.

A soldier of Colonel Gansevoort's Regiment at Fort Stanwyx recorded in his journal on August 3, 1777, that early in the morning a Continental flag, made by the officers of Colonel Gansevoort's Regiment, was hoisted and a cannon fired at the enemy's camp. On August 6, he described the rally against the enemy's camp and mentions that among the articles captured there were four colors which were immediately hoisted "on our flagstaff under the Continental Flag, as trophies of victory." Lt. Col. Marinus Willet, who led the rally, reported that five colors were captured.

Fort Mifflin and Fort Mercer
Union Flags—November 1777 (Plate 5)

Very small sketches of two American flags are depicted flying over Fort Mifflin and Fort Mercer during the October-November, 1777 siege in a panoramic inset to "A Survey of the City of Philadelphia and its Environs . . . likewise the attacks against Fort Mifflin on Mud Island and its Reduction 16 November 1777," John Montresor, Chief Engineer (surveyed and drawn by Pierre Nicole). The map is in the Peter Force Collection, Liberty of Congress.

The larger flag (in the drawing it measures ¼ x ½ inches) is seen flying over Fort Mifflin; it is of red, white and blue stripes without a canton. The smaller flag (3/32 x 5/32 inches) is over Red Bank (Fort Mercer). It shows blue and white stripes and a red canton with white dots (stars). The British shore batteries and ships which had been shelling Fort Mifflin for two months are shown at positions reached by November 15, 1777. This sketch is the first depiction of the stars and stripes known to the author.

The Fort was evacuated on the night of the 15th. On the 16th, British sailors entered the Fort "and took down the rebel colours." On the 15th, with the Fort battered to ruins, Major Simeon Thayer of Rhode Island, commander of Fort Mifflin in the final days of the siege "... ordered the blue flag to be hoisted as a signal of distress to the Commodore." Possibly there is a connection between the "blue flag" and the one depicted on the map.

In Scharf & Wescott's *History of Philadelphia* there is a black and white print of "Mud Island in 1777 before the British attack (from an old drawing made by Colonel Downman of the British Army)." No source is given.

The print is a panoramic view of the fort with ships in the background on the other side of the island indicating that Colonel Downman's viewpoint was from the western shore. It shows a tall flagpole towering over the fort's buildings from which streams a large stars and stripes. The scale of the print in Scharf & Westcott is small with the flag measuring about ⅛ x ¼ inch. There are seven dark and six white stripes and a dark canton resting on the ninth stripe. Within the canton is a circle of nine white dots (stars) plus one in the middle. The engraver probably tried for thirteen dots but the scale precluded precise details.

The print conflicts with the above original water-color drawing of the fort by British Major Montresor's staff draughtsman, Pierre Nicole. His drawing showed a principal flag of all stripes, red-white-and-blue, with no canton. The original should, of course, be accepted over the illustration re-produced in Scharf & Westcott. It would be of great interest to see Colonel Downman's original drawing.

RED, WHITE, BLUE STRIPES MERCHANT SHIPS, 1778

There is a painting signed "F. Holman, 1778" depicting four captured American merchantships guarded by a British Brig. Each merchantman flies an ensign of red, white and blue stripes (no canton) below a British ensign. The painting is in the National Maritime Museum, Greenwich, England.

STRIPED-UNION FLAGS

Revolutionary flags frequently used thirteen stripes, instead of stars, to represent the union in the canton or in the central device. The striped union is found in the troop colors of the Philadelphia Light Horse—1775 (original British Union canton beneath the stripes), the squadron colors of the Second Regiment, Continental Light Dragoons—1777, the "Delaware Militia Colour"—1777, and the Division Color carried by Captain Robert Wilson's Company, Seventh Pennsylvania Regiment—1777. In addition, the following striped union flags have been noted in Revolutionary War documents:

Blue Field with Striped-Union—1777

On July 24, 1777, Grenadier Lt. William Digby, of the 53rd Regiment of Foot (Shropshires) recorded in his journal that the 9th Regiment had captured "... a flag of the United States, 13 stripes alternate red and white in a blue field representing a new constellation." The 53rd was with Burgoyne's army (see 2nd New Hampshire Regiment).

Blue Field, Red Field and White Field Striped-Union Regiment Flags at Lancaster, Pa.—1780

British Captain Thomas Hughs, 53rd Re-

24

giment of Foot, while a prisoner on parole in Lancaster, Pa., noted that he saw on January 19, 1780, an American regiment of "400 men with three standards... The colours were blue, red and white with thirteen stripes in the corner of each." Captain Hughs was undoubtedly saying that one colour had a blue field, another a red field, the third a white field.

Blue Field with Striped-Union—(1814?)

This flag was reportedly made in Easton, Pa., for Captain Abraham Horn's Company of Northampton County in 1814. It has a blue field with thirteen stars (twelve circling one) and a canton union of thirteen red and white stripes. In spite of the above date, there is a possibility that this is actually a Revolutionary flag.

Buff Field with Striped-Union (possible XIth Virginia Regiment—1778-1780)

The Reynolds portrait of Lt. Col. Banastre Tarleton, Commander of The British Legion, shows three captured colors one of which has a buff field with a union of red and buff stripes.

STARS AND STRIPES IN TRUMBULL AND PEALE PAINTINGS *(Plates 6, 7)*

John Trumbull and Charles Wilson Peale, the artist-historians of the Revolution, served as officers during the War. Throughout the conflict and afterwards, both artists sketched and painted. Peale is best known for his paintings of prominent personages. Trumbull also painted portraits but, primarily, he painted his great National History series of a half dozen events and battles. While some artistic license is taken to allow grouping of principals and events, it is believed that both artists were meticulous as to the accuracy of uniforms and accoutrements. Therefore, the flags depicted in their paintings should be considered as accurate versions at the time of the painting.

CHARLES WILLSON PEALE'S 13-STARS AND STRIPES

(Partial List)

Painting (Date of Battle or Event)	Location (1950)	Date Painted	Stars Pattern Points	Stripes (From Top)
G. W. at Princeton (Jan. '77)	Pa. Acad	1779	Circle/6	None
G. W. at Princeton (Jan '77)	Mt. Vernon		Circle/6	None
G. W. at Princeton (Jan '77)	Yale		Circle/6	None
G. W. at Trenton (Dec '76)	Met	1779-82 (Study)	Circle/5	White Field
G. W. at Trenton (Dec '76)	Met	ca. 1780	Circle/6	None
G. W. at Trenton (Dec '76)	Nassau Hall	1783-84	Eagle & Stars	Red, White
G. W. at Yorktown (Oct '81)	Annapolis	1784	Eagle & Stars	Red, White
Samuel Smith —	Indep Hall	—	Eagle & Stars	Red, White

JOHN TRUMBULL'S 13-STARS AND STRIPES
(Partial List)

Painting (Date of Battle or Event)	Location (1950)	Date Painted	Stars Pattern/ Points	Stripes (From Top)
J. Wadsworth & Son	Private	1784	No Canton	Red, White
G. W. at West Point	Met	1780	No Canton	White, Red
G. W. at Trenton (Dec '76)	Met	—	Circle/?	White, Red
G. W. at Trenton (Dec '76)	Yale	1792	Circle/?	White, Red
G. W. at Trenton (Dec '76)	Yale	1786-before 1797	3 Rows	White, Red
Battle of Princeton (Jan '77)	Yale	1786-87 (Sketch)	No Canton	White, Red, Blue
Battle of Princeton (Jan '77)	Yale	1787-before 1797	Square/?	Red, White
Surrender at Saratoga (Oct '77)	Yale	ca. 1816	Square/?	Red, White
Surrender at Yorktown (Oct '81)	Yale	before 1797	Square/?	Red, White (14)
Surrender at Yorktown (Oct '81)	Detroit	1787 (Study)	Circle/6	Red, White, Blue
Surrender at Yorktown (Oct '81)	Capitol	1824	Square/8	Red, White

Note: Trumbull's squares and circles have one star in center. John Trumbull served as an officer in the Continental Army from 1775 to 1777 when he resigned to study art. In 1780, he went to London to study under Benjamin West and, thereafter, alternately lived in the States and in London until 1816 when he settled in New York. Much of his painting was done in London based on memory and sketches.

Peale depicted a wide circle of small six-pointed stars in a square blue field in his paintings of Washington at Trenton. In the majority of the replicas of this portrait the edges of the field are hidden by other objects. In the Pennsylvania Academy copy the edges of the blue field are visible—there are no stripes. The Metropolitan copy has the stars on a blue canton with an all-white field without stripes.

Trumbull depicted the stars as six-pointed, and only once as five pointed. His favorite star pattern was a square of twelve with one in the middle (Yale's Yorktown, and Burgoyne, and Princeton). He also used the circle (Detroit Institute's Yorktown) and rectilinear (Yale's Washington at Trenton) patterns. Cantons were blue. Stripes were red and white or white and red with, once, a red-white-blue sequence (Detroit's Yorktown). Trumbull also pictured the standard as thirteen red and white stripes without a canton.

"UNION FLAGS" PHILADELPHIA, 1777

The Pennsylvania Packet, dated August 24, 1777, carried the following item: "... Yesterday being the anniversary of his most Christian Majesty, LEWIS [sic] the XVIth, the vessels in the harbor of Philadelphia were decorated with union flags, ..."
It is possible that these "union flags" were stars and stripes.

Division Colors, 7th Pa Regt
September 1777

STARS AND STRIPES AT BRANDYWINE SEPTEMBER 1777 *(Plate 34)*

7th Pennsylvania Regiment Colors

An early interpretation of the "stars and stripes" is found in the canton of the still existing red silk division color carried by Captain Robert Wilson's Company, Seventh Pennsylvania Regiment of 1777. According to family tradition, this flag was carried at Brandywine on September 11, 1777—about three months after the Continental Congress resolution had defined the flag of the United States. The color, which is discussed under the section on Pennsylvania flags, has a plain red silk field with a canton formed of stars and stripes; thirteen eight-pointed red stars against a white canton with seven white and six red stripes. The original standard is at Independence National Historical Park. Whether the canton was on the flag at Brandywine or added later is not known. Possibly, the color had a canton union of thirteen stripes, originally—as with the Delaware Militia Color and Philadelphia Light Horse standard—and the stars were a subsequent addition.

"The flag of our country droops from yonder staff"—Brandywine Eve, September 10, 1777

Reverend Joab Trout preached a sermon to a large portion of the American Army on the eve of Brandywine, September 10th, 1777. In part, he said:

"Soldiers and Countrymen"—

"... It is a solemn moment. Brethren, does not the voice of nature seem to echo the sympathies of the hour? The flag of our country droops heavily from yonder staff; the breeze has died away along the green plains of Chadd's Ford—the heights of the Brandywine arise gloomily beyond yonder stream—all nature pauses in solemn silence, on the eve of tomorrow...."

Reverend Trout, in his rather gloomy sermon, does not describe the flag. It could have been the thirteen stripes or the stars and stripes.

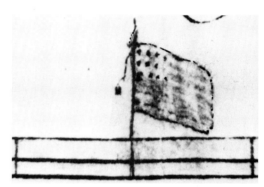

Brig Gen Clinton's Brigade
Major Gen Sullivan's expedition

SULLIVAN'S "ORDER OF BATTLE" STARS AND STRIPES JULY 30, 1779 *(Plate 8)*

The "Journal of Sullivan's Campaign" kept by Lt. Col. Henry Dearborn, commanding the 3rd New Hampshire (Scammell's) Regiment of Poor's Brigade, was published in 1887. It contains sketches of the Order of March and the Order of Battle of Sullivan's Army. As reproduced in 1887, Dearborn's sketches are essentially the same as those of Major John Ross whose original sketches are in the du Simitiere papers at the Historical Society of Pennsylvania, but Dearborn's have less detail and notation. No flags are shown by Dearborn or Ross in the Order of March. Three are shown in the Order of Battle, one at the center of each of the three brigades: Clinton's, Poor's and Maxwell's. In Dearborn's sketch, all three flags are stars and stripes with a rectilinear arrangement of the stars. Ross' original sketch shows two regimental colors with unions of stars (rectilinear pattern) and one stars and stripes (Clinton's Brigade).

Whether Dearborn's original sketch in his journal agrees with the 1887 print is not known to the author.

JOHN PAUL JONES' STARS AND STRIPES, HARBOR OF THE TEXEL, HOLLAND OCTOBER 4-5, 1779 *(Plates 6, 21)*

Original watercolor drawings of the stars and stripes flown in October 1779 by the Continental Frigate "Alliance" and the captured H.M.S. Serapis are in the Gunther collection at the Chicago Historical Society.

The ensign of the Alliance has seven white and six red stripes with a small blue canton

Serapis—The Texel—October 5, 1779

and thirteen eight-point stars in a 3-2-3-2-3 pattern. The drawing is dated October 4, 1779 and the location given as the harbor of The Texel Holland. The caption is in longhand Dutch, possibly by Jones.

The ensign of Serapis has thirteen red, white and blue stripes in an irregular sequence and a blue canton with thirteen eight-point stars in a 4-5-4 arrangement. The

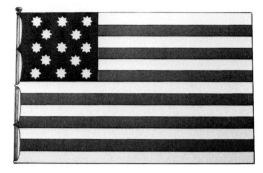

Alliance—The Texel—October 4, 1779

drawing is dated October 5, 1779.

Jones had taken refuge in The Texel following the engagement between the Richard and Serapis.

ST. PATRICK'S DAY AMERICAN FLAG—MORRISTOWN ENCAMPMENT, 1780

A loyalist New York City newspaper, "Gaine's Weekly Mercury," in its April 29, 1780 edition, published an account obtained from "rebel . . . deserters" of the "hoisting" of a special St. Patrick's Day flag on March 17, 1780. This took place at the American army's encampment at Morristown. The flag, together with music, a proclamation, and a holiday, were ordered by Washington to appease some disgruntled Irish-American troops who were being detained beyond their enlistment and who planned to leave the camp as a body on St. Patrick's Day. The flag was described as "exhibiting the thirteen stripes, the favorite harp, and an inscription declaring in capitals, THE INDEPENDENCE OF IRELAND." The flag, some music, a proclamation, and a keg of spirits persuaded the men to stay.

"OUR FLAG"—YORKTOWN, OCTOBER 19, 1781

Colonel Richard Butler of Pennsylvania wrote to General Irvine from "Camp at York, October 22nd, 1781," and briefly described the siege and surrender. He reported "... Their Flag was struck, and Major Hamilton, with 100 men (Americans) took possession of one work and planted our flag, and a French major, with 100 men (French) another. . . .''

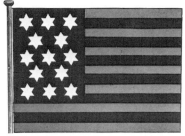

British Lt. Col. Simcoe, Yorktown— October 1781

YORKTOWN, LT. COLONEL SIMCOE, OCTOBER 1781
(Plates 3, 9)

A stars and stripes with red and blue stripes and a large blue canton with dark stars was flown on the right flank of the American lines at Yorktown, October 1781, according to a watercolor panoramic terrain sketch by Loyalist Lt. Colonel John Graves Simcoe, Commander of the Queen's Rangers, who was stationed at Gloucester, across the river.

YORKTOWN, MAJOR SEBASTIAN BAUMAN, OCTOBER 1781 *(Plates 3, 46, 47)*

A stars and stripes with red on white stripes and a small blue canton with six-point stars in a 3-2-3-2-3 pattern is shown in the title vignette of a 1782 map of the siege of Yorktown; "Plan of the Investment of York and Gloucester—by Sebastian Bauman 1781—Major of the New York or 2nd Regiment of Artillery—Dedicated to General Washington—taken between 22-28 October 1781," R. Scott, Sculp, Phila. 1782. Bauman commanded the Continental Artillery in 1783.

STARS AND STRIPES WITH FLEUR de LYS *(Plate 9)*

The American-French alliance brought about flag designs which coupled the fleur-de-lys within the union of stars, as shown in the Mondhare Flag Sheet of 1781 and the Lotter Flag Sheet of 1782.

MONDHARE FLAG SHEET, (FRANCE) 1781, NAVAL ENSIGNS *(Plate 9)*

A stars and stripes with white on red stripes and a large blue canton with twelve five-point stars and a fleur-de-lys is shown in the Mondhare Flag Sheet, Paris, 1781.

Major Bauman's Map of Yorktown Philadelphia 1782

Mondhare Flag Sheet—1781

Lotter Flag Sheet—1782

LOTTER SEUTTER FLAG SHEET, AUGSPURG [sic] 1782
(Plate 9)

A stars and stripes with white on red stripes and a blue canton with thirteen six-point stars and a fleur-de-lys is shown in the Lotter Flag sheet (Matthews Seutter, Augsberg) 1782.

WEATHERWISE ALMANACK, 1782

The "Town and Country Almanack" published by Abraham Weatherwise in 1782 shows a flag with thirteen five-pointed stars in a 3-5-5 arrangement (top to bottom rows).   (no illustration)

JOHN WALLIS MAP, LONDON
(Plate 9)

A stars and stripes with a 3-2-3-2-3 arrangement of stars (number of points not distinguishable) is shown on the John Wallis map of the "United States of America," London, April 3, 1783.

John Wallis Map, London—1783

Pennants, Mondhare Flag Sheet–1781

Title block of map, John Wallis, London —1783

30

BOWLES FLAG SHEET, LONDON 1783

A stars and stripes with thirteen five-pointed stars in a 3-2-3-2-3 arrangement is shown on "Bowles Universal Display of Naval Flags," London, 1783. (not illustrated)

L'ENFANT—CINCINNATI DIPLOMA, JUNE 10, 1783

A stars and stripes with seven white and six red stripes and a blue canton with an oval of thirteen five-point stars is shown in an original drawing by Major Pierre Charles L'Enfant. This was made for the diploma adopted on June 10, 1783 by the Society of the Cincinnati. The canton of the flag of the diploma was changed shortly thereafter to the eagle, stars and stripes.

Original design for the Diploma of the Society of the Cincinnati—June 10, 1783

ALMANAC, 1784 *(Plates 9, 20)*

A stars and stripes with red, white and blue stripes and a canton with stars in a 3-2-3-2-3 pattern is pictured in an article by Matthias Sprengel in a Berlin Almanac of 1784.

THIRTEEN REBEL STRIPES ON THE THAMES, FEBRUARY 3, 1783

A London periodical, The *Political Magazine*, in 1783 reported that "The ship Bedford, Captain Mooers, belonging to Massachusetts arrived in the Downs on 3rd of February . . . wears the rebel colors . . . This is the first vessel which has displayed the thirteen rebellious stripes of America in any British port . . ."

The same magazine summarized parliamentary debate under the date February 7—"Mr. Hammet begged leave to inform the House . . . [that there was] an American ship in the Thames, with the thirteen stripes flying on board . . ."

Peter Van Shaack wrote from London, February 19, 1783, ". . . One or two vessels with the thirteen stripes flying are now in the river Thames . . .

(Note that the above reports speak *only of stripes* not of the *stars* and stripes.)

BUELL MAP, 1783 *(Plate 4)*

A stars and stripes with white on red stripes and a blue canton with five-point stars in a 3-2-3-2-3 pattern is shown on "A New and Correct Map of the United States of North America" by Abel Buell, New Haven, 1783.

Abel Buell—1783

Stars and Stripes on Flag of Society of Pewterers, Constitution Parade, New York, July 23, 1788

CIRCLE OF STARS—TWELVE ENCIRCLING ONE: PEWTERERS' PARADE BANNER, NEW YORK—1788

The New York Historical Society has in its collection a painted silk banner which was carried on July 23, 1788 by the Society of Pewterers. The banner appeared in the "Federal Procession" in New York, celebrating the ratification of the Constitution. The standard includes a painting of a pewterer's work shop, the Pewterers' Society coat of arms, and in the canton a painted rendition of the stars and stripes. There are seven red and six white stripes. The canton bears twelve stars encircling one. The number of star points varies from five to eight. The banner is in excellent condition.

THE EASTON STARS AND STRIPES *(Plate 63)*

An early silk flag of stars and stripes is in the collection of the Easton Public Library, Easton, Pa. The standard is unique in having a circle of thirteen stars in the center of the blue field and a canton of thirteen red and white stripes. Its recorded history apparently dates to September 6, 1814, when the flag was presented to a local militia company, called up for the War of 1812.

There are some authorities in Easton who believe the flag dates back to the Revolution on the basis of its design; and also because a standard, "the device for which is the Thirteen United Colonies," was displayed at Easton on July 8, 1776, as reported in the *Pennsylvania Evening Post,* July 11, 1776.

32

Washington at Princeton —James Peale Polk, ca 1800. Note Easton Type Stripes and Stars

Those who support the Revolutionary origin of the flag point out that the use of thirteen stars and the reversed location of the stars and the stripes are at variance with the authorized and accepted design of the 1814 period, indicating that the flag predates the 1777 (and 1795) flag resolutions.

The standard measures 55 (hoist) by 97 (fly) inches. The eight point stars are seven inches in diameter. The striped canton, judging by photograph proportions, measures approximately 25 by 31 inches, hoist to fly. Twelve stars are encircling one. There appears (in the photographs) to be a sleeve along the hoist side. The blue field is of India silk and the stripes are of grosgrain (a silk with crosswise cotton ribs). The material of the stars is not stated in the available information.

The standard was offered to the Library in 1818 and delivered in 1821.

There is a portrait of Washington by

Easton Stripes and Stars carried by Capt. Abraham Horn's Company, September 6, 1814, possibly of Revolutionary Origin

James Peale Polk at the Historical Society of Pennsylvania, portraying Washington as he appeared during the Revolution. The painting is undated but Polk's career extended from the 1790's into the 19th century. In the background of the painting is a military encampment with a standard identical in design to the Easton flag. Why Polk selected this particular design is not known to the author. Perhaps he believed it to be of Revolutionary origin. There might be some connection with Washington's stated preference for a design which placed the stars in the center.

For the details and history of the Easton flag the author is indebted to Mr. John P. Cassidy of Easton and the staff of the Easton Public Library.

MILITIA STANDARD AT EASTON—JULY 9-10, 1776

The Pennsylvania Evening Post, July 11, 1776, reported:

"The Declaration was received at Easton, in Pennsylvania, and proclaimed in the following order:—The Colonel and all the other field officers of the first battalion repaired to the court-house, the light infantry company marching there with their drums beating, fifes playing, and the standard (the device for which is the Thirteen United Colonies,) which was ordered to be displayed.

After that the Declaration was read aloud to a great number of spectators, who gave their hearty assent with their loud huzzas, and cried out 'May God long preserve and unite the FREE and INDEPENDENT States of America.'"

The above description implies a flag with the motto "THIRTEEN UNITED COLONIES." In the opinion of the author the field would have been of a solid color.

THE EAGLE AND STARS—THE ARMS OF THE UNITED STATES

Possibly, the eagle seal or arms of the United States was placed on the first "National Standard of the U.S. Army." Copies of this standard were reported to have reached Washington in March 1783, long after he had requested them.

The original design of the 1783 standards has not been found, unfortunately. The pattern could have been the stars and stripes; the eagle canton and stripes; or, an all-blue field with the eagle seal centered on it. Such all-blue, eagle-symbol Army National Standards were definitely in use by the early 1790's and, probably, the latter 1780's.

For fifty or more years following the Revolution, the flag with the eagle and stars in the canton was a popular alternate to the stars and stripes.

EAGLE, STARS AND STRIPES NATIONAL STANDARD GENERAL PHILIP SCHUYLER
(Plate 11)

An original national standard with a canton bearing an eagle and thirteen white stars can be seen at Independence National Park, Philadelphia. Its recorded history begins in 1922 when it was presented by Miss Elizabeth Schuyler and Mrs. Anna Schuyler Killie, great-great-great-grandaughters of General Philip John Schuyler of the Revolution.

Early 13 Stars and Stripes,
Curtis—Clinton Family,
Stratford, Connecticut

13 Stars and Stripes—Flag carried by
Maryland and District of Columbia
Battalion of Volunteers—Mexican
War—1846–48

"America" Beauvais Tapestry,
ca. 1790. Commissioned 1783
by Louis XVI for Washington.
Note stars and stripes with fleur-de-lis

Elizabeth Schuyler Hamilton Stars and
Stripes. Blue canton originally bore
British union crosses. Cotton stars and
stripes added later

Porter Stars and Stripes. Hand woven
cotton; handsewn, 26 x 34 inches.
From the Old Porter house,
Nelsonville, Putnam Co., N.Y.

The flag is of silk with a red silk fringe. It has seven white and six red stripes and a blue canton which bears the eagle seal of the United States. The flag measures forty-two inches on the hoist by sixty-two inches on the fly and is in remarkably good condition. The canton rests on the seventh white stripe from the top. There is a sleeve for the staff.

The eagle, stars, olive branch and arrows symbol was adopted as the seal of the United States in 1782. It was used thereafter as a canton device for many national standards well into the nineteenth century. General Schuyler, although a competent leader and credited with a large share of the preparations which led to Burgoyne's defeat, was replaced by Congress with General Horatio Gates in August 1777 as commander of the northern army. He held no command thereafter.

The flag was examined in recent years by a textile historian who is on the staff of the Smithsonian. She concluded that the flag could be of eighteenth century origin but, based on the use of the eagle seal, not earlier than about 1784.

Schuyler's flag is probably associated with the Society of the Cincinnati of which General Schuyler was an active member.

L'ENFANT'S CINCINNATI DIPLOMA EAGLE-CANTONED STARS AND STRIPES

The L'enfant designed membership diploma of the Society of the Cincinnati shows an eagle-cantoned stars and stripes. L'enfant's initial design for the diploma, believed to have been drawn in 1783, displays the stars in an oval. The final diploma, probably drawn shortly after the first, introduced the great eagle seal symbol in the canton.

PEALE'S EAGLE AND STRIPES
(Plate 10)

The Charles Wilson Peale painting of Washington at Yorktown which hangs at the House of Delegates, Annapolis, pictures an American and a French standard in the background. The American standard has red and white stripes and a blue canton with the great eagle seal of the United States.

The scene depicted is the surrender which took place on October 17, 1781, some eight months before the eagle seal was adopted by Congress. This incongruity is probably explained by Peale having rendered the painting after the war and that the he used a later version of the national standard. This does help to establish that the eagle and stripes was recognized as a version of the national standard at the close of the Revolution and for some years after. Of course, if the painting is interpreted literally, it would indicate that the eagle and stripes came into use in the latter part of 1781.

Original Eagle and Stripes.
General Philip Schuyler, circa 1780's

Stripes with eagle and stars.
Society of Cincinnati Diploma, circa 1783

—4—

Continental Army

CONTINENTAL ARMY REGIMENTAL STANDARDS AND COLORS

Development of the standards and colors of the Continental Army can be followed through the orders and correspondence of Washington and associated Army and Congress inventories and records. A chronology and quotations from some of those orders and records are in Appendix I.

The first record of a military color being hoisted by the Army was the red flag of Putnam's Third Connecticut State Regiment of 1775. The flag was displayed on July 18, 1775 at an assembly of the troops besieging the British garrison in Boston.

As the concept of a union took hold, the colonies sought a suitable "union flag." At some time during the Fall or Winter of 1775, it was decided that such a flag would be the British red ensign with a red and white striped field. Some historians believe this continental union was selected by a Continental Congress Committee which conferred with Washington outside of Boston in October 1775 on future organization and supplies for the Army. This is logical but the author has not been able to find a primary source reference to support this claim.

After hoisting "the Union flag" for the first time on January 1, 1776, Washington wrote to his former aide, Joseph Reed, that the Loyalists and British in Boston had mistaken the flag as a signal that the American army was surrendering.

On February 20, 1776, orders were issued at Cambridge calling on the colonels to fix on a "standard (or Regimental Colours) and Colours for each Grand Division" with some kind of "similitude" to their uniform. Lt. Col. Hand, commander of the 1st Pennsylvania Continental Regiment, writes of this order and describes the standard for his regiment as being green with a centered red field bearing a hunter and lion. The standard is extant.

In May 1776, Washington again urged his colonels to obtain colors and, apparently, there were quite a number of flags carried during the following New York Campaign of 1776. Hessian Adjutant General Baurmeister reported that eleven

"LIBERTY" flags were captured at the battle of Long Island. Also a number of flags were taken at the fall of Fort Washington on Manhattan Island, including Pennsylvania Colonel Magaw's purple standard.

As the war continued, it became increasingly apparent there was a need for greater standardization on the design, color and number of colors for a regiment and for some overall system of color coding to identify the regiment's home state and function. This was eventually defined but the shortage of silk hampered its implementation.

The extent of the continuing shortage of colors was evidenced on September 2, 1778, when Adjutant General Scammell of the main army encamped at White Plains called for a report from each brigade on the number and condition of their colors. The fifteen brigades, totaling about fifty regiments, reported a total of 26 regimental standards, 1 regimental color, and 47 grand division colors on hand—about half the number needed, and 29 of these were in bad condition.

Perhaps Scammell's survey had some connection with the standards described in the Gostelowe "Return" of August 1778. Thirteen sets of new colors, each set consisting of one regimental standard and two division colors, were listed in the stores of Major Jonathan Gostelowe of Philadelphia, a Commissary of Military Stores. Each flag was of a basic color—red, yellow, blue or green. These sets of colors might possibly have been made for the thirteen Pennsylvania Continental regiments authorized at the time.

CONTINENTAL ARMY "SYSTEMS" AND "PLANS" FOR COLORS

In 1779, Von Steuben, the Army's Inspector General, published his "Regulations for the Order and Discipline of the Troops of the United States," the famous "Blue Book." As regards the system for flags, he said, there were to be "two colours to a regiment" and that "the ensigns must carry them in turn." The diagrams by L'enfant in Steuben's Regulations show where the two colors and the ensigns who served as color bearers were to be posted. Steuben's system of two colors—a national and a regimental standard—followed the British practice and is still in use today.

In addition to Von Steuben's, there were several other "systems" for regimental colors used during the Revolution. One was for each regiment to have a pair of regimental colors with different colored grounds, such as the blue and red colors of the 2nd S. C. Regiment of 1775, presented in 1776.

There were also variations on a basic plan that called for a main regimental standard plus smaller, plainer "colours" for each double-size company or grand subdivision. A retired British officer, Charles Lee, later a Major General in the Revolutionary Army, proposed this arrangement in early 1775; he also suggested that the word "LIBERTY" be placed on each color. That Lee's plan gained considerable acceptance is evidenced by the colors of Webb's Additional Continental Regiment of 1777, which had a regimental standard and at least four smaller subdivision colors. Webb's regimental standard and three of the subdivision colors are extant. A copy of Lee's plan was found among Webb's papers.

Lee's plan appears again in an arrangement that provided a regimental standard and two "division colors" as reflected by the Gostelowe Return of July-August 1778.

Matching the ground color of a regiment's "colours" to the color of the regiment's uniform or uniform facings was an accepted practice in "systems for colours" at the time. Webb's Regiment, above, wore captured scarlet uniforms faced with yellow. They carried a yellow regimental standard.

Of course, matching of uniforms and colors required that the color of uniforms be specified. There was little standardization of uniforms during the early years of the War, although brown was specified as the official color by the Continental Congress on November 4, 1776, with facings to be of different colors. Lefferts notes that blue was the favorite color for officers and, by the end of 1778, for the men also. On October 2, 1779, Washington issued General Orders which specified blue for the uniforms of the army with facings as follows:

Branch or State	Facings	Linings
Artillery	Scarlet	Scarlet
Light Dragoons	White	White
Infantry		
New Hampshire	White	White
Massachusetts	"	"
Rhode Island	"	"
Connecticut	"	"
New York	Buff	"
New Jersey	"	"
Pennsylvania	Red	"
Delaware	"	"
Maryland	"	"
Virginia	"	"
North Carolina	Blue	"
South Carolina	"	"
Georgia	"	"

As had been agreed earlier between the Board of War, Washington and Von Steuben, the regimental colors were to be of the same color as the regiment's facings. It follows that blue would be the preferred color of the "national standard for the army" carried by all regiments.

A direct comparison can be drawn between the number of regiments in 1779, the above regulations on uniforms, and the quantities of silk estimated for army standards by the Board of War on June 11, 1779 (see chapter 1). The estimate called for 1100 yards of deep blue silk, 300 of crimson (red), 280 of white and 80 of buff. Those quantities would have provided almost exactly for one regimental and one national standard, plus two spares of each, for each active regiment. The color of the regimental would match the facings and the national would match the basic uniform with an all blue field.

There were about eighty continental state foot regiments and about eight "Additional" and "Congress" regiments in 1779, plus eight artillery and dragoon regiments—a total of ninety-six. By the above regulations, thirty-one foot regiments were to have red facings, thirteen blue, twenty-eight white, and eight buff. On May 10, 1779, the Board of War wrote to Washington that, as recommended by Von Steuben, each regiment was to have a regimental color matching its facings and a "Standard of the United States" the same throughout the Army. The Board asked for Washington's opinion on the design of the standards and uniforms so that material could be ordered.

Typical foot regiment standards were about five feet square consisting of two horizontally seamed lengths of twenty-eight inch wide silk. This required ten feet or three and one-third linear yards of material per standard or ten yards with two spares. The estimate provided enough silk for thirty regiments assigned red regimentals, enough white for twenty-eight, and buff for eight. The blue silk would provide for the thirteen regiments with blue facings plus ninety-seven army regiments with blue field United States standards.

A NATIONAL STANDARD FOR THE ARMY

Steuben's two colors, above, were to be "The Standard of the United States" and "the Regimental Colour which should vary according to the facings of the Regiments" according to a May 10, 1779 letter from Secretary Richard Peters of the Board of War to Washington. Peters also said that as soon as a "Standard of the United States" was established by Congress and the color of the uniform decided, that colours for every Regiment would be ordered.

Peters' words were "But it is not yet settled what is the standard of the U. States." Viewed from today, Peters' statement is seemingly completely at odds with the June

14, 1777 resolution that established "the flag of the United States" as the stars and stripes.

In the author's opinion, the explanation is that the Board of War and Washington and apparently many others considered the stars and stripes to be primarily a marine flag and *not* the national standard. Probably, they were waiting for the official seal of the United States to be established so that the national standard could bear the arms of the new nation. In any case, Washington and his legislative superiors, the Board of War and Ordnance of the Continental Congress, corresponded at length on the design for a national standard for the Army, which employed "the Union and Emblems in the Middle."

The "union" of a stars and stripes, in the terminology of that day, was the canton of thirteen stars. This indicates that Washington and the Board wanted to place the stars in the center of the field. The "emblem" was apparently the rattlesnake, since the "curve of the serpent" is spoken of.

With the above guidelines, a standard can be pictured with a solid blue field bearing thirteen stars in rows across the field or in a cluster or circle, and with a looped rattlesnake among the stars, possibly as a canton. The regimental number and state were to be placed within the loop formed by the serpent.

Seal of the Board of War and Ordnance of the Continental Congress. Adopted 1778. This impression is on Benjamin Tall-madge's Commission as a Lieutenant Colonel, dated 10 December 1783

However, a contradiction to the above (and part of the puzzle), is that the Board of War had adopted a seal in 1778 bearing two flags with crossed staffs together with a rattlesnake and the motto "This We Will Defend." One flag is a stars and stripes with the stars in rows; the other flag is plain. This seal is still in use by the Department of the Army.

A strong indication that the Army's national standard was to be blue is provided by an estimate, dated June 11, 1779, for a large quantity of French silk, mainly deep blue, that was submitted by the Board of War to Congress for regimental colors for the Army (see Chapter 2). However, the silk did not arrive as expected, and Washington and the Board of War continued to correspond on the need for colors. Whether any standards for regimental use to the above design were ever made is doubtful. However, Washington's Headquarters Standard has the union of stars centered across its blue field.

The great eagle seal of the United States was adopted on June 20, 1782. This, finally, could have triggered the making of some national standards for the army.

Another estimate, this time for one hundred standards for "the Army of the United States," dated 2 July 1782, was submitted by Samuel Hodgdon, Commissary General of Military Stores, to the "Hon'ble Secretary at War." The color of the silk required is not stated. A total of only fifty standards was approved, probably because the regiments were being demobilized and consolidated.

On August 2, 1782, Washington again wrote to the Secretary of the Board of War requesting that the colors be forwarded, saying that he had heard they were ready. After several more exchanges of letters, the standards arrived in late February or early March, 1783. On March 14, 1783, orders were issued that those regiments without colors could obtain them from the Commissary of Military Stores. News of the peace treaty arrived March 27, 1783.

Nothing has been uncovered to tell us the design of these standards or whether they were national standards or regimental colors or both. However, in 1783, Major Pierre L'enfant of the Continental Army created a membership diploma for the Cincinnati which depicts a flag with thirteen stripes and a canton bearing the eagle arms. An earlier proposed design by L'enfant for this diploma depicts a stars and stripes. The diploma was adopted on June 10, 1783.

Another slim clue to the design is that Secretary Lincoln in replying to Washington's letter of February 17, 1783, says that the colours "will be sent on" and adds, "I wish they were better than they are." Since a stars and stripes is a straightforward design and easily made by any skilled seamstress, there might have been some feature about the standards that caused them to be more difficult to make, such as, possibly, a painted eagle on blue silk.

Whether the standards bore the eagle seal is not known. However, when St. Clair's and Wayne's Federal Armies were campaigning against the Indians in the early 1790's an eagle-seal national standard was carried. The use of this standard continued well into the nineteenth century. It is still carried today as a regimental color.

A gold medal was awarded by Congress to General Daniel Morgan for the victory at Cowpens, South Carolina, on January 17, 1781. The medal was made in Paris in the late-1780's and its scene depicts a striped flag with an eagle canton as does also the medal for John Paul Jones by the same artist, Augustin Dupré.

13th Continental Regiment of 1776

STANDARD OF THE THIRTEENTH CONTINENTAL REGIMENT OF 1776 *(Plate 26)*

No original has survived. The illustration is based on a contemporary description.

A Nineteenth Century historian wrote that in the *American Archives* there is a description of the standard of the Thirteenth Regiment, dated September 8, 1776. The ground is described as light buff. The device was a pine tree and field of Indian corn (emblematic of New England) with two officers in the uniform of the regiment. One officer is bleeding from a chest wound. Several children stand under the pine, and one officer points to them. The motto is "FOR POSTERITY WE BLEED."

Such a standard would have been made of silk, with overall dimensions of about five feet square. The symbolic scene is the same type of elaborate tableaux as the standard of Webb's Additional Continental Regiment of 1777, and of certain standards of the Gostelowe Return of 1778.

The 13th Continental Regiment of 1776 was raised in Massachusetts and was one of twenty-six Continental regiments authorized. It served from January 1 to December 31, 1776, with Colonel Joseph Reed commanding. For subsequent organizations, the regimental designations employed the State Line number, such as the "1st Massachusetts Continental Regiment." There was also a 13th Virginia Regiment formed in November 1776 under Colonel William Russel, and a 13th Massachusetts Regiment formed January 1, 1777 under Colonel Edmund Wigglesworth. However, the only Thirteenth Regiment listed by Berg as active on September 8, 1776, is that of Colonel Joseph Reed's 13th Continental Regiment. Also, the flag's device of a pine-tree and Indian corn strongly suggests a Massachusetts origin.

REGIMENTAL STANDARDS AND COLORS OF THE GOSTELOWE RETURN
(Plates 12-15)

Among the papers of the Continental Congress at the National Archives is an extensive inventory or "Return" of arms and other military stores on hand for the months of July and August 1778 at Philadelphia and outlying stores and repair locations. The Return was prepared by Philadelphia Major Jonathan Gostelowe, one of the Commissaries of Military Stores, for Lt. Col. Benjamin Flower, Commissary General of Military Stores for the Continental Army. A separate section of the report is titled "A Return of ye New Standards & Division Colours for ye Use of ye Army of ye United States of America In the Possession of Major Jonathan Gostelowe, Com'y Mil'y Stores." There are thirteen regimental "Standards," of which each of the first eleven have two "Division Colours" listed. The color of the fields of these first eleven sets is given. The "Device of the Standard" and "Their Motto" are described and quoted for all thirteen standards. A footnote states: "N.B. The Union agreeable to the Resolve of Congress, Thirteen Stars is Painted on each Standard." Apparently the Division colors were plain as no device is indicated.

The Gostelowe Return was analyzed by co-authors Donald W. Holst and Marko Zlatich in an article illustrated by Peter Copeland and published in the Journal of The Company of Military Historians for Winter 1967. It is one of the most important writings ever published on American Revolutionary War regimental standards and colors.

The above authors point out that the color of the field and the description of the device of Standard No. 1 match a surviving silk flag, known as the "Headman Color" which descended in the Pennsylvania family of that name. The color is now at the Smithsonian. The authors also matched the devices described on seven standards with the seals used on seven denominations of paper Continental currency. Some of the seals were designed by Francis Hopkinson and Benjamin Franklin and others were taken from early books on seals and emblems in Franklin's library.

Holst and Zlatich also point out that versions of the device of Standard No. 13, which featured thirteen arrows and a motto, "United We Stand" are on three powderhorns. Drawings of these are at the New York Historical Society. One of the powderhorns belonged to a soldier in the 1st New York Regiment of 1777.

Similarities between the devices of the Gostelowe Standards and other Revolutionary flags, seals and symbols are pointed out by the above authors. The most important aspect of their analysis, beyond bringing the inventory to light, is the relationship between the devices on the standards and the symbols on currency and state arms. Conclusions and comments hereafter are the responsibility of the author.

Major Jonathan Gostelowe was a Philadelphia resident and cabinetmaker. His name appears on various tax lists and rolls during the War, including one list where the letters "C.M.S." (Commissary of Military Stores) are entered after his name. He is listed as a member of a Philadelphia militia artillery unit during the post-war period and in 1789, presented a baptismal font to Christ Church. See Notes for further discussion.

Number of the Standards	Their Colour	No. of the Division Colours	Their Colour	The Device of the Standards	No. of Ye Standards	Their Motto
1st	Green	2	Blue & Yellow	A Pillow on the Top of which is the Cap of Liberty Supported by thirteen Hands.	1st	This we will defend or Die.
2nd	Redd	2	Green & Yellow	An Arm in Armour with a drawn Sword in its Hand, & Thirteen drawn Swords linked together.	2	Manus hec Inimica Tyranis. We are always ready.
3rd	Redd	2	Blue & Yellow	A Golden Harp.	3d	Majora. Minoribus. Consanant.
4th	Yellow	2	Blue & Redd	Brittania Setting on an Old Stump weeping a Tree behind her whithered, her Spear broken, an Olive Branch lying at her Feet, an Indian on the Opposite Side with his Bow Strung holding an Arrow in his hand, by his Side a Dog, (an Emblem of Fidelity). Under his Feet a Shield, behind him a Palm Tree in full bloom, before the Indian, the Sun Rising upon the New Empire, between the Two is Fame Flying Towards the Indian holding the Cap of Liberty and Proclaiming; Be Liberty Thine.	4th / 5th / 6th / 7th / 8th / 9th	Behold the Rising Empire / Sustine. vel. Abstine.— / Aut. Mors. Aut. Vita Decora. / Perseverando. / Exitus in dubio est. / Si. Recte. Facies.
5th	Blue	2	Yellow & Green	A Thorn Bush and Hand.	10th	Resistance to Tyrants is Obedience to God.
6th	Yellow	2	Redd & Blue	The Boar and Spear.	11th	This is mine & I'll defend it.
7th	Ditto	2	Blue & Redd	The Beaver & Tree.	12th	Depressa. Resurget.
8th	Redd	2	D° & D°	The Eagle & Craine.	13th	United we Stand.
9th	Blue	2	Redd & Yellow	A Laurel Reath on a Pedestall		
10th	Yellow	2	Blue & Redd	An Arm in Armour with a drawn Sword in its Hand.	NB.	The Union agreeable to the Resolve of Congress, Thirteen Stars is Painted on each Standard.—
11th	Blue	2	Redd & Green	An Indian Representing America, Laying his Hand on the Cap of Liberty, placed on a Pedestall, with his Bow Strung, and his Dog by his side.		
12th				The Plant Acanthus Sprouting out on all sides under a Weight		
13th				Thirteen Darts.		

A Return of ye New Standards & Division Colours for Ye Use of Ye Army of the United States of America. In the Possession of Major Jonathan Gostelowe, Com'l Mil'y Stores.

A Return of y[e] New Standards of Division Colours for y[e] Use of y[e] Army of y[e] United States of America In the Possession of Major Jonathan Gostelowe Com[y] Mil[y] Stores.

Whether deliv'd or Rec'd for the half Y[ea]r	No. of the Standard	Their Colour	No. of the Division	Their Colour	The Device of the Standards	No. of the Division	Their Motto
480	1.	Green	2.	Blue & Yellow	A Pillow on the Top of which is the Cap of Liberty supported by thirteen Hands.	1.	This we will defend or Die.
79	2.	Redd	2.	Green & Yellow	An Arm in Armour with a drawn Sword in its Hand, & thirteen drawn Swords linked together	2.	Manus hæc Inimica Tyrannis. We are always ready.
565	3.	Redd	2.	Blue & Yellow	A Golden Harp.	3.	Majora Minoribus Consonant.
468	4.	Yellow	2.	Blue & Redd	Brittania sitting on an Old Stump weeping a Tree behind her whithered, her Speer broken, an Olive Branch lying at her Feet, and an Indian on the Opposite Side with his Bow Strung, holding an Arrow in his hand, by his Side a Dog, (an Emblem of Fidelity) Under his Feet a Shield, behind him a Palm Tree in full bloom, before the Indian, the Sun Rising upon the New Empire between the two, is Fame Flying towards the Indian holding the Cap of Liberty and Proclaiming; Be Liberty thine.	4.	Behold the Rising Empire.
468						5.	Justine Vel Hostine.
79						6.	Aut Mors Aut Vita Decora.
468						7.	Perseverando.
						8.	Exitus in dubio est.
						9.	Si Recte Facies.
						10.	Resistance to Tyrants, is Obedience to God.
						11.	This is mine & I'll defend it.
						12.	Depressa Resurget.
						13.	United we Stand.
	5.	Blue	2	Yellow & Green	A Thorn Bush and Hand.		
	6.	Yellow	2	Redd & Blue	The Beaver & Tree.		N.B. The Union agreable to the Resolve of Congress, Thirteen Stars is Painted on each Standard.
	7.	Ditto	2.	Blue & Redd	The Beaver & Tree.		
	8.	Redd	2.	D[itt]o & D[itt]o	The Eagle & Crane.		
468	9.	Blue	2.	Redd & Yallow	A Laurel Wreath on a Pedestall.		
486	10.	Yallow	2	Blue & Redd	An Arm in Armour with a Drawn Sword in the Hand.		
79	11.	Blue	2	Redd & Grun	An Indian Representing America, laying his Hand on the Cap of Liberty, placed on a Pedestal, with his Bow Strung, and his Dog by his Side.		
565	12.				The Plant Acanthus Sprouting out on all Sides, under a Weight.		
	13.				Thirteen Darts.		

This is part of a detailed Return of the Artillery, Arms, Accoutrements, Etc., at various magazines under the command of Colonel Benjamin Flower, Com'y Gen'l Mil'y Stores, for the months of July and August 1778

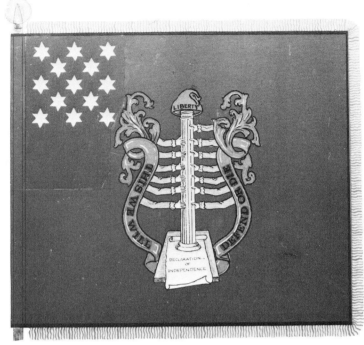

The Headman Color of 1778

STANDARD NO. 1
HEADMAN COLOR *(Plate 12)*

The Headman Color features a device with a fluted column supported by thirteen hands and topped by a Liberty Cap. This same symbol, but showing only twelve hands, appears on the title page of the proceedings of the Continental Congress of 1774. It was used as a masthead by Holt's newspaper in New York in 1775.

In the 1774 Congress seal, the pillar rests on a copy of the Magna Carta; but the bottom of the pillar in the Headman Color is missing. Therefore, the author has elected to place the Declaration of Independence at the base of the pillar on the assumption that the Headman Color device was based on the original 1774 design, and that the Declaration of Independence would have been substituted for the Magna Carta by 1778.

JOURNAL

OF THE

PROCEEDINGS

OF THE

CONGRESS,

Held at PHILADELPHIA,
September 5, 1774.

PHILADELPHIA:
Printed by WILLIAM and THOMAS BRADFORD,
at the *London Coffee-House.*
M,DC C,LXXI V.

45

Detail of the Painted Device on the Headman Color and the Seal on the cover of the Journal of 1774 Congress

The Color descended from Sergeant Francis William Headman. He had served in a Philadelphia militia company composed of potters and according to family tradition had carried the Color at Trenton and Germantown. The Color was donated to the Smithsonian in the 1940's by a descendant.

William Headman served with the associators and the militia of Philadelphia throughout the War. He appears repeatedly in the muster roll returns as published in the Pennsylvania Archives. For example, he was a member of Captain Christian Schaeffer's Company of Colonel John Bayard's 4th Battalion of the Philadelphia militia in July 1777. The Philadelphia militia was in the field at the time of Trenton, Brandywine, Germantown, etc.

Headman continued to serve in Philadelphia militia companies after the war. When and how he secured the Color is not known. Since Trenton and Germantown were fought before the Gostelowe Return was drawn up, and the standards were "new" at that time, the Color could not have been carried at these battles. Also, it is listed as being for the "Army of the United States." Whether such a scarce and highly desirable flag would have gone to a militia battalion has been questioned. However, Headman apparently saw active service at the time of Trenton and Germantown. It is quite possible that he acquired the Color later, even after the War.

Also, militia units were frequently better equipped than Continental units, as evidenced by the standards of the Philadelphia Light Horse, Proctor's Westmoreland Battalion and others.

The Color stayed in the Headman family until donated to the Smithsonian. It was exhibited on patriotic occasions during the nineteenth century. One descendant reportedly had the Color with him during a period of residence in Savannah.

The sketch is of the assumed original configuration of the Headman Color. The missing half of the motto and device appear on the reverse, according to Messrs. Holst, Zlatich and Copeland's article and allows accurate reconstruction. The field is of green silk, and measures 70 inches on the hoist. Originally, it was probably about 78 inches on the fly. Since the device is painted, it is assumed that the stars in the missing union were also painted. The arrangement of the stars is hypothesized by the author. It is believed that in later years—probably during the 1876 Centennial—the inscription, ". . . Old 76" was painted on the field. A water stain, incurred when the flag was rolled up, has left an odd waveform mark across the field.

Inclusion of the Declaration of Independence is, again, hypothesized by this author and is based on the 1774 Seal which had its pillar resting on the Magna Carta. This area of the flag is missing. After July 4, 1776, drawings which had included the Carta replaced it with the Declaration. See notes for further discussion.

STANDARD NO. 2 (Plate 12)
UNITED DEFENSE

An armor-clad arm with sword encircled by thirteen linked swords, and the words: "Manus hec Inimica Tyrannis" (This hand is inimicable to tyrants). The motto is taken from a famous quote by Algernon Sidney who took an active part in the rebellion of the 1640's. The second part of Sidney's saying is the motto of the state of Massachusetts.

Captain James Duncan, a Pennsylvanian and a member of "Congress' Own," or Hazen's Regiment, recorded in his journal that the "Manus haec inimica tyrannis" motto was on a color he planted on the ramparts of the trenches at Yorktown. Hazen's Regiment was assigned to Lafayette's Division at Yorktown.

Franklin created the circle of thirteen chain links which was used on the fractional continental bills.

Continental $2/3 bill

STANDARD NO. 3 (Plate 12)
HARMONIOUS UNION

A harp with 13 strings. "Major Minoribus Consonant" (The large colonies are in harmony with the small colonies). Used on the $8 bill. The symbol and motto are from a 1660 edition of Saavedra's *Symbolis,* possibly in Franklin's library.

Continental $8 bill

STANDARD NO. 4 (Plate 13)
AMERICA TRIUMPHANT

Britannia defeated; America (the Indian) triumphant; the sun rising on the New Empire, etc. "Behold the Rising Empire." Britannia is seated as in the colonial Louisburg expedition flag (New York Historical Society). New York adopted the rising sun into its state arms.

Louisburg Standard

Continental $5 bill

STANDARD NO. 5 *(Plate 13)*
SUSTAIN OR ABSTAIN

A thorn bush and bleeding hand. "Sustine Vel Abstine" (Either sustain yourself or abstain). Used on the $5 bill. The symbol is from the 1702 Mainz edition of Camerarius' *Symbolorum*.

Continental $6 bill

STANDARD NO. 7 *(Plate 13)*
PERSEVERANCE

A beaver and tree. "Perseveranda" (By perseverance). Used on the $6 bill. Possible New York association. The symbol is from Camerarius' *Symbolorum*, 1702 edition, in Franklin's library.

Continental $4 bill

STANDARD NO. 6 *(Plate 13)*
DEATH OR HONOR

A wild boar charging a spear. "Aut Mors Aut Vita Decora" (Either death or an honorable life). The symbol is from Camerarius' *Symbolorum*.

Continental $3 bill

STANDARD NO. 8 *(Plate 13)*
FIGHT BACK

An eagle and crane. "Exitus In Dubio Est" (The outcome is in doubt). The crane is spearing the hawk. Used on Continental $3 bill. The symbol is from Camerarius' *Symbolorum*.

Continental $30 bill

Motto and Arms of Massachusetts

STANDARD NO. 9 *(Plate 14)*
HONORABLE REMEMBRANCE

A wreath on a tomb. "Si Recte Facies" (If you have lived righteously). Used on $30 bill. Connecticut ordered all its regiments to use this device on its colors in 1780. The symbol is from Camerarius.

STANDARD NO. 11 *(Plate 14)*
AMERICAN DEFENSE

An Indian (America) with a Liberty Cap, strung bow (vigilance) and dog (loyalty). "This is mine & I'll defend it." The arms of Massachusetts has an Indian.

Bedford Minutemen Standard

Continental $1 bill

STANDARD NO. 10 *(Plate 14)*
ARMED RESISTANCE

An armored arm with sword. "Resistance to Tyrants Is Obedience to God." The saying is by Franklin. Jefferson had it engraved on his ring. An upraised arm with sword was used on the standard of the Bedford Troop of Minutemen and is in the Arms of Massachusetts.

STANDARD NO. 12 *(Plate 15)*
RESURGENT

A weighted basket (of toys) on an acanthus plant. "Depressa Resurget" (Though crushed it arises again). This seal was used on the Continental $1 bill. The symbol is from ancient Greek history and was taken from Camerarius.

49

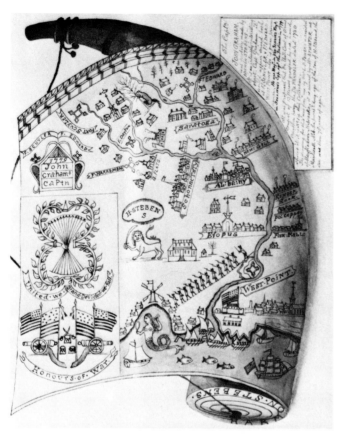

Same symbol of thirteen arrows as for Gostelowe's Standard No. 13. Harmon Stebens Powderhorn, Captain John Graham's Company, 1779. First New York Regiment of 1777

Same symbol of thirteen arrows as for Gostelowe's Standard No. 13. John DeWandeler's Powderhorn (Detail)

STANDARD NO. 13 *(Plate 15)*

Thirteen Darts (arrows). "United We Stand." A splay of arrows was a favored device symbolizing united might and is used in the seal of the United States. The device, a splay of thirteen arrows encircled by a vine, together with mottos similar to the above, are etched on three powderhorns, drawings of which are in the Rufus Grider collection at the New York Historical Society. One of the horns belonged to Harmon Stebens, Captain John Graham's Company, of the 1st New York Regiment. Another of the three horns was found in Rome, N.Y., and the third bears the name, John DeWandeler, which suggests an upstate New York Dutch origin. Possibly, Gostelowe Set No. 13 was assigned to the 1st New York Regiment.

SQUADRON COLORS OF THE SECOND REGIMENT, CONTINENTAL LIGHT DRAGOONS and later of THE SECOND LEGIONARY CORPS *(Plates 16, 17)*

Two colors of this regiment still exist: one with a blue field, now at the Connecticut State Library in Hartford; and one with a "light beige" or "pink" field (which may have been red, originally), now at the Smithsonian. There was a third color, almost identical in design to the surviving pink color, but it disappeared between the years 1907 and 1943. The recorded history of the colors apparently starts in 1904 with a book on the life of Benjamin Tallmadge. There is also mention of "red and blue" colors in 1776 in connection with this regiment.

The blue flag is of lightweight silk. It is intact and measures 25½ (hoist) by 38½ (fly) inches. It has no fringe. The painted device is a blue disc with a pair of gold wings, horizontally outstretched and heading downward, and with ten gold thunderbolts radiating to all points. Painted in dark letters on gold scrolls is the unit designation, "2^D REG^T L^T DRAGOONS," above the sun, and the motto "PAT^A. CONCITA. FLUM^{NT}. NATI." below. The canton measures 9¾ by 12 inches and its thirteen stripes are formed by seven gold-painted stripes against the blue silk. The canton is not inset, and is bordered on its fly edge by a thin gold stripe. There is a vertical seam at the midpoint of the standard. Thread-whipped eyelets are spaced about one and one-half inches apart. Morgan B. Brainard, of Hartford, owned this flag in 1943. Of the two colors, the one with the blue field is more likely to have been the regimental standard since it bears the regiment's designation.

The "pink" or red field squadron color at the Smithsonian was donated in 1968 by Emily Howell Wilkins, a descendant of Col-

onel Benjamin Tallmadge. Tallmadge was initially Captain of the First Troop, and later Major and Adjutant of the Regiment. The pink silk is now faded to a light buff. The flag is intact and measures about 29 (hoist) by 33 (fly) inches. It has no fringe, and appears to have threadwhipped eyelets for tying the flag to its staff.

The basic design of the painted device is the same as that of the blue standard. The disc is blue, the wings silver, and the thunderbolts are gold outlined in black or blue. The Latin motto, below the disc and rays, is painted in dark letters on a silver scroll, and reads the same as on the blue flag. There is no unit designation on the flag, and no scroll above the device. A canton of thirteen stripes is formed by seven silver stripes. The canton is not inset and is bordered by a narrow vertical silver stripe on its outer (fly) edge. A ribbonlike tie about thirty-six inches long is knotted through the lowermost eyelet.

The 2nd Regiment was one of four Light Dragoon Regiments authorized by the Continental Congress in December 1776. Each regiment consisted of the commandant, a colonel, his staff and six troops, each of forty-four officers and men, headed by a Troop Captain. A "squadron" of cavalry consists of two to four troops.

The 2nd saw action in many campaigns and battles, including Saratoga, Fort Stanwyx, Brandywine, Germantown, and the Long Island raids. It was also at Valley Forge. The Second was officially discharged in November 1783.

A standard of Sheldon's Regiment of Light Dragoons was captured by a detachment of Tarleton's cavalry in the neighborhood of Bedford/Pound-Ridge, near New York, July 1, 1779. Tarleton surprised and routed the Americans, inflicted a number of casualties, "... destroyed their whole baggage, and brought off a standard, about a hundred helmets, and seventeen prisoners ...".

51

REGIMENTAL STANDARD OF THE THIRD REGIMENT OF CONTINENTAL LIGHT DRAGOONS also known as THE EUTAW STANDARD of COLONEL WILLIAM WASHINGTON'S THIRD LEGIONARY CORPS (Plate 45)

The Eutaw Flag

The standard is of pink damask, originally crimson. Judging by Davis' photograph, the flag measures about eighteen inches square with fringe included. There is a sleeve for a staff or, more properly termed, a "lance." In Davis' photograph, there appears to be a reinforcement of heavy cross-stitching or netting.

According to family tradition, Miss Jane Elliott, daughter of Colonel Elliott of Sandy Hill Plantation near Charleston, cut the flag material from the back of a dining room chair when her fiancee, Colonel William Washington, told her his regiment was without a standard. That was in the Spring of 1780.

Lieutenant Colonel William Washington, who warned Miss Elliott that the British were coming, was a third cousin of George. He was initially a Captain with the 3rd Virginia Regiment of 1776 and was wounded at Brooklyn and Trenton. He joined the Dragoons in 1778 and assumed command of the 3rd Regiment of Continental Light Dragoons (of 1777) after Colonel George Baylor was

seriously wounded at Old Tappan, New Jersey, September 27, 1778.

The regiment lost heavily in the southern campaign of 1780–81. After the battle of Camden, August 1780, the remaining men of the 1st, 3rd and 4th Light Dragoon detachments were combined under Colonel Washington and served at Cowpens, Guilford Courthouse, Hobkirk Hill (the second battle of Camden) and Eutaw Springs. The combined unit was designated the 3rd Legionary Corps in 1781, according to Berg. This Corps fought in the final pitched battle of the war in September 1781 at Eutaw Springs, South Carolina, where Colonel Washington was wounded and taken prisoner. Lee wrote that "... Baylor's regiment of horse, with Kirkwood's infantry of Delaware, composed the reserve led by Lieutenant Colonel Washington."

The battle was marked by headlong charges by the North and South Carolina militia, state troops and Continentals. The British were driven back about a mile from their camp. The Americans stopped to force some Britishers out of a brick house and to plunder their camp. This gave the British a chance to re-form and drive the Americans back. After the battle, the British retired within their lines at Charleston.

At Eutaw Springs, some of the American troops were so poor in clothing, they went into battle naked, according to General Nathaniel Greene's report. Greene was awarded a gold medal for his victory at Eutaw Springs. Colonel Washington was voted a silver medal by Congress for his leadership of the dragoons at Cowpens. And his regimental standard is linked to romance: he married Miss Elliott in 1782 and settled in Charleston.

STANDARD OF PULASKI'S LEGION OF 1778 (Plate 15)

The original is at the Maryland Historical Society. Its recorded history starts in 1824. The standard is eighteen inches square with a deep green bullion fringe, originally silver,

Reverse   *Obverse*

Original Standard of Pulaski's Legion

and has a sleeve for its staff. The field is made of two layers of crimson silk, now faded, with emblems embroidered in yellow silk. The letters are yellow, shaded with green. The obverse side of the flag shows a brown "All-Seeing Eye" within a circle of thirteen eight-pointed yellow stars surrounded by the motto "NON ALIUS REGIT" (No Other Governs). This emblem was designed by Francis Hopkinson and was used for the Continental $40 bill, issue of September 26, 1778. The reverse side has the letters "U.S." encircled with the motto, "UNITAS VIRTUS FORCIOR" (Union Makes Valor Stronger). In the corners are exploding hand grenades depicted in yellow and white thread.

Tradition tells us the standard was made for Colonel Casimir Pulaski by the Moravian Sisters at Bethlehem, Pennsylvania in 1777–78. The Colonel was in Bethlehem to visit Lafayette who was recovering from a wound received at Brandywine.

Pulaski was, initially, commander of the Corps of Light Dragoons, but requested reassignment. He was then authorized to raise and organize an independent corps of sixty-eight horse and two hundred foot soldiers, principally at Baltimore, Maryland in 1778.

Pulaski's Legion was "cut to pieces" at Little Egg Harbor, New Jersey in Fall 1778. When Pulaski joined the Southern Continental Army in 1779, his Legion was down to 120 lancers and infantry.

Pulaski was mortally wounded at Savannah, Georgia, during the American and French assault on the British lines at Savannah on October 9, 1779. The flag was saved by his adjutant and aide, Captain Paul Bentalou. It reached Baltimore after the close of the war. Captain Bentalou allowed the flag to be carried in the procession that welcomed Lafayette to that city in 1824. It was then deposited in Peale's Museum. In 1844 the flag was removed to the Maryland Historical Society.

Presentation of the flag to Pulaski, and his heroic death, are the subject of a poem by Longfellow, "Hymn of the Moravian Nuns."

Battalion Colors of Lafayette's Continental Light Infantry Corps

CORPS OF LIGHT INFANTRY MAIN CONTINENTAL ARMY

No known original has survived, but there were a number of light infantry colors recorded. Lafayette briefly mentioned the devices on two of the flags when he presented a flag to each battalion of the Corps in 1780. One of the Lafayette flags may be pictured on Major Bauman's map of the Siege of Yorktown.

The Corps of Light Infantry was not a permanent standing organization. It was formed as the need arose by combining the light infantry companies detached from the various regiments into battalions. The men in these companies were specially chosen for their soldiering qualities, including endurance and the ability to travel light and fast. They were intended to form the initial line of defense, thus allowing the full strength of the regiments to come up behind them.

Wayne commanded the Main Army's Light Infantry when it captured by bayonet the British-held Fort at Stoney Point on July 16, 1779. Two British union standards and two colors of the 17th British Regiment were captured. Wayne was awarded a gold medal by Congress for this victory.

The Corps of Light Infantry which Lafayette twice commanded actually operated more as a small army during the Virginia campaign of 1780–81 against Arnold and Cornwallis.

Webb's Light Infantry Corps was organized by Washington on August 12, 1782, and consisted of five battalions formed by detachments of light infantry companies totaling 1200 men. The battalions, in turn, were formed into two regiments, Webb's and Jackson's, and "Major Forman's Battalion." Webb also continued to be listed as commander of the 3rd Connecticut. On September 5, 1782, orders were issued at Verplank's Point to turn in all the light infantry colors presented by Lafayette (see Chronology). The next day, Adjutant General Hand wrote to Colonel Webb, as follows:

"Camp Verplanks Point
6 September, 1782

Dear Sir:

By direction of the Commander-in-chief I send you two of the Lt. Infantry Standards, one for the use of your own and the other for Col. Jackson's Regt.
I am very sincerely yours,
Edw.₀ Hand
A. Gen.

Brand Whitlock relates that Lafayette, on his return from France in 1780, brought with him a large supply of leather helmets with red and black plumes (Charlemagne Tower says "black and white") as well as a supply of swords which he distributed to his Light Infantry Corps. He had also ordered uniforms, but they were delayed in shipment from France. They were to be brought over, first, by Ternay's fleet, but never arrived. Then they were to be carried here by the U.S. Frigate Alliance, but, again, they were left on the dock by the Alliance's Captain, Pierre Landais. Among other things that Lafayette brought with him were flags which he had purchased in France. These flags he distributed in 1780 to his Light Infantry Corps, one to each battalion just prior to the Virginia campaign. One flag, according to Whitlock, was "embroidered with a cannon and the device: "ULTIMA RATIO"—he (Lafayette) had left out the "REGUM," since kings had gone out of favor in America; the other was embroidered with a civic crown and a wreath of laurel, and carried the motto "NO OTHER."

Gold Medal awarded by the Continental Congress to Pennsylvania General Anthony Wayne for leading the Light Infantry Corps in capture of the British Fort at Stoney Point on the Hudson, July 15, 1779. The medal was engraved by Gatteaux, Paris, 1789

Continental Congress Silver Medal awarded to Maryland Major John Stewart for his role at Stoney Point—July 15, 1779

There is a 1782 map of the siege of Yorktown, published by New York Major Sebastian Bauman who was at Yorktown, which has a decorative display of various flags flanking the block of explanatory notes at the bottom. The flags on the lefthand side are apparently French and include, as the topmost, a white standard with a simplified cartouche of the royal arms of France. On the righthand side, just below the stars and stripes, is a large white standard with a single device—a gold wreath of closely intertwined leaves encircling what appears to be a gold monogram " S." The scale is too small for the artist to have incorporated much detail. As noted above, a wreath of oak leaves and acorns is a "civic crown." This flag could be one that Lafayette gave to his Corps of Light Infantry, and the letter "S" could stand for Lt. Col. Scammell or for Scot, engraver of the map.

A 1782 mezzotint by Noel Le Mire, published in France, of Lafayette at Yorktown pictures the Marquis in the uniform of an American major-general with his Negro orderly in the helmet and plume that Lafayette had designed for his Corps of Light Infantry. Centered in the legend to the engraving is a wreath of what appears to be laurel encircling the motto "LIBERTE" and a liberty pole and cap.

An 1831 French lithograph picturing Lafayette as "Le Heros Des Deux Mondes" features a wreath composed of branches of laurel and oak leaves on both sides of the wreath.

LAURENS' LIGHT INFANTRY STANDARD

In Hirsch's *"Huguenots of Colonial South Carolina"* there is a black-and-white photograph of "an original portrait in oil by Copley" of Lt. Col. John Laurens (1754–1782). In the background is a standard held by a junior officer. Both officers are in full regimentals with a dark (blue?) coat, white breeches, and black gaiters or boots. Laurens wears two epaulets, the junior officer one. The "high hat" type helmet worn by the junior officer is decorated with the crescent emblem of the South Carolina regiments. Laurens, bare-headed, holds his hat, but no emblem is visible. Judging by the height of the color bearer, the flag was about four feet square and sleeved to an eight-foot staff.

Laurens commanded a Light Infantry Battalion at Yorktown in 1781 and Light Infantry divisions of the Southern Continental Army during various campaigns starting in 1779.

There is in existence a Peale miniature of Lt. Col. Laurens. There may also be another miniature which would have been painted when Laurens visited France in 1781.

The photograph unfortunately does not allow any details of the standard to be distinguished, although it is a prominent feature of

56

the painting. Mr. and Mrs. John Laurens of Charleston, the present day owners of the painting, kindly informed the author that the color of the standard is now a faded grayish-blue but that no decipherable symbols or designations could be distinguished, visually.

Washington's Headquarters Standard

WASHINGTON'S HEADQUARTERS STANDARD
(Plates 18, 19)

The original is in the collection of the Valley Forge Historical Society. The field is a single width of faded blue silk about 27½ (hoist) by 35½ (fly) inches. the 27½ inch dimension is a reasonable selvage width for silk woven during the eighteenth century. Thirteen large six-pointed six-inch stars with elongated rays are arranged in a rectilinear 3-2-3-2-3 pattern covering the field. The stars are not clocked precisely the same; some are rotated from an exact vertical, as shown. Since the stars are appliqued to the obverse side, the blue silk is cut out to show the stars through to the reverse side with the result that they are smaller on the reverse. All stitching is by hand. A narrow strip of once-white heavy cloth is stitched along the hoist. The stars are white silk.

Recorded history of the flag starts in 1912 when it was donated by Miss Frances B. Lovell, a descendant of Betty Washington Lewis, the only sister of George Washington. Miss Lovell said that the flag was known in the family as "Washington's Headquarters Flag." This attribution has been questioned by some writers.

Based on the Analysis provided in the Notes Appendix, and after examining the original flag with the kind assistance of Mr. John Reed, this author is of the opinion that the Washington Headquarters Flag at Valley Forge is exactly what Miss Lovell claimed it to be—Washington's Revolutionary-era command standard. It was possibly succeeded in the 1780's or '90's by a version with a circle of stars.

Dr. Burk, a founder of both the Washington Memorial Chapel at Valley Forge and the Valley Forge Historical Society, states in his "Valley Forge Guide Book," that this flag has the original homespun linen heading. The heading material appears to be the same as that of Washington's marquee. This was pointed out to the author by the historian of the Valley Forge Historical Society, Mr. John F. Reed.

Two early postwar paintings, supervised by eyewitnesses, show a large blue standard with a linear arrangement of stars. One painting is that of the battle of Princeton by Wm. Mercer, son of the General and a student of Peale. The second painting is by Van Blarenberghe, a French military artist who depicted the siege and surrender of Yorktown. The surrender scene shows several regimental standards similar to Washington's standard. In addition, there are the paintings by Peale which show just a blue canton with a circle of stars. Also, there is an all blue standard with a circle of stars as the device on the standard of Washington's Life Guards. Washington and the Board of War corresponded in 1779 on the design of a national standard for the army. The blue flag with stars was probably Washington's choice.

Proposed design for the Seal of the Board of War and Ordnance. An undated and unsigned item found among the papers of General Anthony Wayne, probably from a friend. Note Washington's Standard

STANDARD OF GENERAL WASHINGTON'S LIFE GUARDS
(Plate 19)

An original standard of the Commander-in-Chief's Guard or "General Washington's Life Guard" is on display at the George Washington Masonic National Memorial, Alexandria, Virigina. The standard is of white silk (now light beige) and measures 28 inches on the hoist by 37½ inches on the fly, and originally was probably edged with gold-colored fringe. The standard bears an elaborate, delicately painted scene covering most of the flag's surface, which depicts a horse, an officer, a blue standard with a circle or oval of stars, a woman representing the Genius of Liberty supporting a shield of the United States, and a spread eagle. Liberty is presenting the blue standard to the officer. Above the figures is a yellow-gold scroll with the motto "CONQUER OR DIE." The standard dates after 1782 when the shield and eagle were adopted into the seal of the United States. The officer is uniformed in a blue coat with white facings, white waistcoat and breeches, black boots (or, perhaps, half gaiters), spurs, gold epaulets and a glossy black helmet with a bearskin crest and brim. He wears a gold-hilted saber on his right side. Liberty is dressed in a pink and blue gown and is crowned with a symbolic gold flame. The shield has red and blue stripes topped by a blue upper quarter. The eagle rests on the ground next to the shield.

The standard was presented to the Alexandria Masonic Lodge in the early 1800's by George Washington Parke Custis, Martha's grandson, together with other colors and Washington memorabilia. It was sketched by Lossing about 1850. When the Masonic Museum was destroyed by fire in 1871, this flag was thought to have been destroyed, but it was later, in 1926, found safely stored away.

The Commander-in-Chief's Guard (1777–1783), often called "Washington's Life Guard" and "Body Guard," was a company-size unit of selected men representing all thirteen states. It was, primarily, an infantry unit although it did include some mounted troops. Its primary function was to guard the person, headquarters, papers and effects of the Commander-in-Chief. The dragoons provided escorts, patrols and videttes and took part in battle when required.

One of the duties of the Guard was to carry the Commander-in-Chief's standard, and therefore, it is undoubtedly Washington's standard which "Liberty" is handing to the officer. Washington's standard is depicted as being an all-blue flag with an oval or circle of eight-pointed, slender-rayed, white stars occupying the full field. It has a gold-colored fringe, a spear-headed staff and two short tasseled cords. The standard is rectangular and judging by the size of the officer (who had to be between 5'9" and 5'10" to qualify for the Guard), was approximately 22 inches on the hoist by 36 inches on the fly.

In recent years, the opinion has been expressed that the Lifeguards' standard might actually date to the 1780's or 90's because of certain features of the officer's uniform. Perhaps the Guard was reactivated for Washington's inauguration.

PINE TREE ENSIGNS OF WASHINGTON'S ARMED VESSELS—1775 *(Plate 27)*

Washington commissioned two floating batteries and six armed vessels to operate against the beseiged British in Boston and their supply transports. The ensign flown bore a pine-tree symbol and the motto "AN APPEAL TO HEAVEN."

The first captain commissioned was Nicholas Broughton of Marblehead. His orders, dated September 2, 1775, called for him "to take the command of a detachment of said army, and proceed on board the Schooner Hannah, at Beverly."

Charles Blaskowitz, a mapmaker with Howe's army in Boston, drew a colored pen-sketch of one of the rebels' floating batteries. It flies an ensign that appears to bear a tree with a motto beneath.

On October 20, 1775, Washington's aide, Colonel Joseph Reed, wrote to Colonel Glover and Stephen Moylan: "Please fix upon some particular flag, and a signal by which our vessels may know one another. What do you think of a flag with a white ground, a tree in the middle, the motto, 'Appeal to Heaven.' This is a flag of our floating batteries. We are fitting out two vessels at Plymouth, and when I next hear from you on this subject I will let them know the flag and the signal, that we may distinguish our friends from our foes."

Mr. Moylan replies: "The schooner sailed this morning. As they had none but their old colors, we appointed them a signal that they may know each other by, and be known to their friends—as the ensign up the main topping lift."

Preble, without giving a reference, states: "The floating batteries of Pennsylvania, in the Delaware, carried the pine-tree flag in the autumn of 1775."

HAZEN'S REGIMENT, "CONGRESS' OWN" *(Plate 49)*

"The Colors were planted
on the Paparet,"
Captain James Duncan,
Hazen's Regiment,
Yorktown, October 7, 1781

Captain James Duncan was born in Philadelphia in 1756. He graduated at Princeton and prepared for the ministry. He was commissioned in Colonel Moses Hazen's Regiment ("Congress' Own"), originally the 2nd Canadian Regt of 1775, which included 153 Pennsylvanians in 1779. Duncan served to the end of the War and died in Mercer County on June 24, 1844.

Captain Duncan marched from White

Plains with his regiment as part of Washington's army and arrived at Williamsburg, Virginia on September 26, 1781. His Yorktown Journal starts with a summary of the march and deployment before Yorktown.

Duncan recorded the following operations for October 7:

"The regiments ordered for the extra duty were last night employed in drawing the line of circumvallation. This line extends itself to the river on each side the town, and at all places nearly equally distant and better than 200 yards in front of the former works. The enemy discovered us, although the night was pretty favorable, but the chief of their fire was directly against the French. They were, no doubt, much astonished in the morning to find themselves so completely hemmed in on all sides, and trenches so deep that we could sustain little or no harm from their fire. The trenches were this day to be enlivened with drums beating and colors flying, and this honor was conferred on our division of light infantry. And now I must confess, although I was fond of the honor, I had some fear as I had no notion of a covered way, and more especially as I was posted in the center with the colors. We however did not lose a man in relieving, although the enemy fired much. The covered way was of infinite service. Immediately upon our arrival the colors were planted on the parapet with this motto: Manus Haec inimica tyrannis. Our next maneuver was rather extraordinary. We were ordered to mount the bank, front the enemy, and there by word of command go through all the ceremony of soldiery, ordering and grounding our arms; and although the enemy had been firing a little before, they did not give us a single shot. I suppose their astonishment at our conduct must have prevented them, for I can assign no other reason. Colonel Hamilton gave the orders, and although I esteem him one of the first officers in the American army, must beg leave in this instance to think he wantonly exposed the lives of his men. Our orders were this night that if the enemy made a sortie and attempted to storm the trenches we were to give them one fire from the barquet, rush over the parapet and meet them with the bayonet."

The question remains as to the regimental identity of the above "colors." Either it was the standard of Hazen's "Congress' Own" Regiment, which was Duncan's regular unit, or it belonged to one of Lafayette's light infantry battalions to which Duncan might have been assigned during the siege. Lafayette had purchased some standards in France and given one to each battalion of his light infantry before the Virginia Campaign.

—5—

Continental Navy and Privateers

THE FIRST CRUISE

The Continental Congress in late 1775 appointed a committee to fit out armed vessels to form the Continental Navy, also called the "American Navy" and the "Fleet of the United Colonies." Washington, at Boston, had already commissioned a number of small cruisers in the service of the United Colonies. The Committee was variously referred to as a Committee of Congress, the Marine Committee, the Naval Committee, the Committee for Naval Affairs, Board of Admiralty (Samuel Adams' term), or simply as "the Committee."

Samuel Adams writing to John Adams from "Philadelphia Decr. 22, 1775" reports that ". . . Hopkins is appointed Commander in Chiefe . . . I dare promise that he will on all occasions distinguish his bravery, as he always has, and do honor to the American Flag."

A Loyalist identified only as "B. P." wrote to Lord Dartmouth from Maryland, December 20, 1775, that on ". . . the 3d instant, the Continental flag on board the *Black Prince* [Alfred], opposite Philadelphia was hoisted . . ."

Gilbert Barkley wrote Sir Gray Cooper in New York from Philadelphia, on January 10th, 1776, that the Continental ships and brigantines with large crews and companies of marines "fell down the river the 4th Currt" [sic] and ". . . they have hoisted what they call the Ammerican [sic] Flag viz the British Union, with thirteen stripes red and white, for its field, Representing the thirteen United Collonies [sic] . . ."

The fleet started downriver on January 4, 1776, but was held up by ice until January 17, as noted in his journal by Lieutenant James Josiah of the *Andrew Doria*, as follows:

"Thursday, January 4th. At 2 PM Cast off from the Warf in Company with the Commodore Ship *Alfred, Columbus & Cabot*, Light airs from the Westward & much Ice in the River. At 6 Do Came to at the Pierse at Liberty Island, & was there detain'd by the ice till the 17th."

As Hopkins' Continental fleet prepared to sail from the Capes of the Delaware, orders were issued on February 14, 1776, giving the day-signals that were to be hoisted by the Flagship when calling for certain maneuvers. Among the signals to be employed were listed the following flags which would have had to be in the *Alfred's* flag locker:

Commodore Ezek Hopkins,
Commander-In-Chief, Continental Navy.
The flags are the Standard of the
Commander-in-Chief of the Navy and The
Liberty Tree with "An Appeal to God"
(Massachusetts)

Flags Used in Signals Continental Frigate "Alfred"	Author's Notes
"a white pendant"	(see ship chandler's list)
"the ensign"	(Continental Grand Union) (see ship chandler's list)
"the broad pendant"	(see ship chandler's list)
"a Dutch flag"	(red, blue, white stripes) (see ship chandler's list)
"a St. George's ensign with stripes"	(Continental Union) (same as "the ensign" above)
"a red pendant"	(see ship chandler's list)
"For a General Attack . . . *The Standard* at the maintopmast head with *the Striped jack* and *ensign* at their proper places"	(rattlesnake on yellow field) (13 red and white stripes at bow) (Continental Union at stern)
"a white flag"	(see ship chandler's list)
"a weft in a jack" at the mizzen top mast head	(same as striped jack, above)

Vessels in the fleet wanting to speak with the Commodore were to display a "weft in the Ensign." Also the Continental Frigate "Columbus" of Hopkins' fleet was to answer a signal (to chase) by "a weft in the ensign...." This evidences that the other vessels also carried a Continental Grand Union. Copies of Hopkins' instructions on signals, using the above flags, are at the Rhode Island Historical Society.

Preble gives the following without reference:

"Among the signal flags to be used by the fleet under Abraham Whipple, commodore commanding, given under his hand on board the continental frigate, Providence, Nantasket Roads, Nov. 22, 1779, are mentioned:

A continental ensign.
A continental jack.

A Dutch jack and ensign.
A white ensign.

A striped flag, and
A white jack.

A red ensign.

"Among the signals prescribed to be observed by commanders in the continental navy, and issued by order of the Marine Committee, Jan. 14, 1778, are mentioned as to be used: A French jack and A continental jack."

Author's Note: Of course, none of the above ensigns or jacks would have carried the British Union Canton by 1778 or '79.

CONTINENTAL NAVY PENDANTS—1776

Preble quotes the Journal of Congress, Tuesday, October 29, 1776, vol. i, p. 531 that, "Resolved, that no private ship or vessel of war, merchant ship or other vessel, belonging to the subjects of these States, be permitted to wear pendants when in company with continental ships or vessels of war, without leave from the commanding officer thereof..."

CONTINENTAL COLOURS, NEW YORK AND MARYLAND, MARCH 1776

Colonel Alexander McDougall wrote to John Jay (New York Delegate to Continental Congress), as follows:

"Hq (New York) 7 March 1776 "The sloop we are fitting out is ready but wait to know ... the description of the Continental Colours ..."

Among the Purviance Papers, Maryland Historical Society, is a letter from Wm. Lux to the York County Committee which includes the following:

"Baltimore, 12 March 1776 [The Ship *Defense*, Capt Nicholson had the] ... honor of displaying the Continental Colors to a British Man of War, without a return ..."

CONTINENTAL NAVY COLORS THE ENSIGN, PENDANTS, STRIPED UNION JACKS, THE STANDARD

The Day Book of Philadelphia ship chandler, James Wharton, who supplied all types of naval stores and materials to several of the new Continental Navy ships during the winter of 1775–76, lists hundreds of items including pendants, ensigns, jacks and bunting. The book is in the collection of the Historical Society of Pennsylvania.

The entry for December 2, 1775, is as follows:

"Ship Alfred   Dr
     49 yds Broad Buntg @ 2/   4.18.-
     52½ yds Narrow   do   1/   2.12.6
     To makg an Ensign
        Canvas & Shd   1. 2.8
                                      _____
                                      £ 8.13.2
"Cr (credit) Margt Manny for
     makg an Ensign   £ 1. 2.8"

The above entry identifies Philadelphia seamstress, Margaret Manny, as the maker of the first United Colonies ensign for the Continental Navy. This ensign for the *Alfred*, as noted further on, was a "St. George's ensign with stripes." This was probably the "flag of America" hoisted by John Paul Jones on December 3, 1775, on the Delaware River.

Many of the flags furnished by Wharton were charged directly to a "Committee of Congress," whereas almost all other items were charged to a specific ship. Further, the listings are arranged and indented to indicate that the flags were also delivered to the Committee, or to a representative of the Committee; just as Marline, Needles, Rope, Nails, Tarr, etc. were delivered to a particular ship.

Some miscellaneous items, such as "3 Skains of housline, 6 Bed laces, 2 lb Twine, 1 Logline, 2 Quires Sheathg paper (del'd Thos Tr (ask))," were also charged and possibly delivered to the "Committee of Congress."

The following colors were furnished by Wharton:

Ship Alfred		*Cost*	
Dec 2	49 yds Broad Bunting	£	4.18.–
	55½ yds Narrow Do		2.12.6
	Ensign (credit Margt		
	Manny)		1.2 .8
Dec 13	145 yds Broad Bunting		14.10.0
	8½ yds Narrow Do		8.6
	Making an Ensign thread		
	& Oznabrigs		1.14.10
Dec 29	21 yds Red Cloth		—
Jan 1	20 yds Broad Red		
	Bunting		—
	20 yds Broad Blue		—
	20 yds Do White		—
Jan 2	1 Broad Pendant		—
Jan 3	2 Dutch flags Red White		
	& Blue 7½ x 13½		—
	1 Pendant—55 feet long		—
	1 Jack Red & White		
	—13 half breaths narrow		—
Jan 8	1 lb thread, red, blue		
	& white		—

Committee of Congress		*Cost*	
Dec 6	1 Flagg Blue & White		—
	(dd Cap; Allen Moore)		
	[Moore was with Pa.		
	Navy]		
Dec 12	1 Flag 5 Feet by 7½	£	1.10.11
Dec 19	1 Pendant 10 inches—		
	55 feet long		—
	1 Jack (Union) Red,		
	Blew & White		—
Dec 20	1 Union Flagg Green &		
	Red, 13 Stripes		—
	3 Pendants, 1 Green,		
	1 White & 1 Red		—
Dec 23	4 Union Pendants,		
	55 Feet long		—
Jan 1	2 Blue & White Flags		—
	1 Green, Blue, White		
	& Red Do		—
	1 Red—1 Green &		
	1 White Pendant		—
	1 Jack, & 1 Pendant		
	blue, White & Red		—

Ship Columbus		*Cost*
Dec 12	1 Union Flag	—
Dec 23	1 Ensign 18 feet by 30	—

Sloop Fly		*Cost*
Jan 17	1 Jack 35/. 1 Pendant 27/6	—

RED, WHITE, BLUE STRIPED CANTON—BATTLE OF LAKE CHAMPLAIN, 11-13 OCTOBER, 1776. *(Plate 21)*

In a series of battles on Lake Champlain, October 11-13, 1776, an American fleet of schooners, row galleys and gondolas, under Brigadier General Arnold, was defeated by a British fleet, under General Carleton. A hand-colored line engraving of the final action of the engagement was printed in London for *"Robert Sayer & Jno Bennett, No.*

5th, Fleet Street, as the Act directs, 22d Decr. 1776.''

The British vessels fly a blue field ensign with a Grand Union canton. The American vessels fly ensigns with cantons of stripes. The most prominently depicted American ensign has a canton of red, white and blue stripes on a field of nondescript gray. Of the two other American ensigns, partially visible, one has a canton of stripes with a solid field; the other, almost wholly obscured, shows a few stripes at the bottom of the field. Both of the latter two ensigns are gray and white in the print.

The print is illustrated in color in *"American Naval Broadsides"* by Edgar Newbold Smith, published by the Philadelphia Maritime Museum, 1974.

Following the battle, Carleton withdrew his forces to Canada, since it was too late in the season to continue campaigning. Though defeated in the engagement, the defense provided by Arnold's fleet delayed the British invasion from Canada for a year.

Among the Philip Scuyler papers at the New York Public Library is an undated watercolor by Marine Lieutenant James Calderwood of the schooner *Royal Savage* flying a continental union ensign. Calderwood, an ensign in Colonel William Irvine's 6th Pennsylvania Regiment, was appointed lieutenant of marines on board the *Royal Savage* on 1 August 1776 and the schooner was lost in battle on 11 October 1776. The painting was probably done within the above dates. Because of Calderwood's painting, it has been generally assumed that Arnold's fleet flew the continental union. However, with the increased harshness of the War in 1776 and the Declaration of Independence, the British union canton was being dropped in favor of thirteen stripes. Therefore, there is a strong possibility that the London mezzotint accurately depicts the American ensigns flown in the battle.

Calderwood survived the Lake Champlain battle but was mortally wounded at Brandywine in 1777.

Continental schooner "Royal Savage". Lake Champlain August-October 1776.
Drawn by Marine Lt. John Calderwood

Continental Brigantine Lexington.

CONTINENTAL BRIGANTINE LEXINGTON—RED-WHITE-BLUE STRIPED CONTINENTAL GRAND UNION SEPTEMBER 1777 *(Plate 3)*

The *Lexington* took part in a number of actions during 1776 and 1777. She sailed from Baltimore for Europe in March 1777 and was detained at the port of Morlaix by the French government. Upon being released in September 1777, she sailed and was captured by the British cutter *Ariel*; this after action of an hour and one-half and a chase of four hours. The *Lexington* was commanded by Captain Johnson and, when captured, was flying a Continental Grand Union with thirteen red, white and blue stripes and a British Union Canton.

"CONTINENTAL COLORS" U.S. FRIGATE TRUMBULL JUNE 2, 1780

Captain James Nicholson of the Continental Frigate Trumbull, in his account of the June 2, 1780 engagement with the British Letter of Marque "Watt," states that he attempted to decoy the "Watt" by hoisting British colours, then hoisted the "Continental Colours" as the engagement began. The Captain of the "Watt" recorded that his opponent hoisted "rebel colours."

STANDARD OF THE COMMANDER IN CHIEF, CONTINENTAL NAVY *(Plate 20)*

No original of this standard survives. It had a yellow field with a rattlesnake coiled to strike and the motto "DON'T TREAD ON ME," according to a description recorded in the Journal of the Provincial Congress of South Carolina. John Jay attributed the design to Christopher Gadsden, a South Carolina delegate to the Continental Congress, and, briefly, chairman of the marine committee in December 1775–January 1776. Jay speaks of the standard in a letter dated March 23, 1776. Drayton's Memoirs also includes a description.

There is strong evidence that Commodore Esek Hopkins flew this standard from the mainmast of his flagship, the "Alfred," during the Continental Navy's first expedition against Nassau, Bahamas, in Spring 1776. As Hopkins' fleet prepared to sail from Delaware Bay, he issued a list of flag signals that included "the ensign," "a striped jack," and "the standard at the maintopmast."

Preble provides a crude illustration of this standard, which has been much copied, but gives no source other than the above description. He might have located an English print which depicted the standard. If so, it would probably have been some artist's secondhand interpretation of a description. Preble's rattlesnake more closely resembles a spiral coiled spring than a self-respecting, all-American rattler. One would expect a more realistic rattler in any flag painted by an American artist.

Preble wrote: "John Jay, in a letter dated July, 1776 . . . expressly states Congress had made no order, at that date, concerning continental colors, and that captains of the armed vessels had followed their own fancies." He names as one device a rattlesnake rearing its crest and shaking its rattles, and having the motto, "Don't tread on me."

Preble also wrote; "DeBenvouloir, the

discreet emissary of Vergennes, who arrived in Philadelphia the latter part of 1775, just after Congress had ordered all thirteen ships of war, reports to the French minister: 'They have given up the English flag, and have taken for their devices a rattlesnake with thirteen rattles, and a mailed arm holding thirteen arrows.' ''

Lossing's 1849 version of the Standard of The Commander-In-Chief Continental Navy. The "Gadsden Flag"

On December 11 and 14, 1775, the Continental Congress officially appointed a marine or naval committee ''for carrying into execution the resolutions of Congress, for fitting out armed vessels.'' One delegate was chosen from each colony, including Christopher Gadsden of South Carolina. Gadsden served as chairman until January 14, 1776, at which time he received orders to return to South Carolina.

Upon his arrival in Charleston, Gadsden presented a rattlesnake standard to the Provincial Congress of South Carolina as recorded in their Journal for Friday, February 9, 1776, as follows:

''Col. Gadsden presented to the Congress an elegant standard, such as is to be used by the commander in chief of the American navy; being a yellow field, with a lively representation of a rattlesnake in the middle, in the attitude of going to strike, and these words underneath, 'DON'T TREAD ON ME!' 'Ordered, that the said standard be carefully preserved, and suspended in the Congress room.' From that time on it was placed in the south-west corner of that room, at the left hand, of the President's chair.''

Arthur Lee, September 20, 1778

Franklin and Adams, October 9, 1778

CONTINENTAL NAVY RED, WHITE AND BLUE STRIPED ENSIGN *(Plates 2, 6, 9)*

The use of red, white, and blue striped ensigns by ships of the Continental Navy was so commonly recorded, that the historians, Admiral Samuel Eliot Morison and Hugh E. Rankin, concluded it was the accepted ensign of the Continental Navy until the stars and stripes was adopted on June 14, 1777. Merchant ships continued to fly tricolored-striped ensigns into the 1790's.

Some tri-color-striped ensigns did not have a canton—the Union was symbolized by the thirteen stripes. Other examples had cantons, either bearing the British Union (see Jones' Coat of Arms and the Continental Brig *Lexington*), a Pine Tree (see Jones), or the Union of Stars (see Jones' Serapis and Alliance ensigns). Franklin and Adams in a diplomatic letter dated October 2, 1778 from Passy described "The flag of the United States of America" as consisting of thirteen red, white and blue stripes with a small union of stars. The two men also described the flags flown by "vessels of war" of Massachusetts and South Carolina. Arthur Lee wrote from Paris on September 20, 1779 to Henry Laurens, President of the Continental Congress, that a ship's colours should be thirteen white, red and blue stripes with a small blue union of "stars."

JOHN PAUL JONES
HIS COAT OF ARMS
(Plates 22, 23)

In the Masonic Library, Boston, there is an original watercolor of a coat of arms which John Paul Jones had painted for himself in late 1776 or early 1777. There are four flags depicted in this coat of arms: a British red ensign with a Grand Union canton; an American Union ensign with red, white, blue stripes and a Grand Union canton; an American Union ensign with red, blue, white stripes and a white canton bearing a pine tree; and a blue commodore's standard. The library kindly furnished a colored photograph and available information.

Jones' coat of arms is accepted as authentic by historians. Samuel Eliot Morison has described the arms and several of Jones' letters sealed with an impression of the arms. Morison wrote that the earliest known use of the seal by Jones is on a letter "to John Wendall of Portsmouth, New Hampshire, dated from Nantes, 11 December 1777." The absence of the stars and stripes indicates that Jones had the arms painted before the June 14, 1777 flag resolution.

"THE FLAG OF AMERICA"
JOHN PAUL JONES,
3 DECEMBER 1775

John Paul Jones wrote to Robert Morris of the Continental Congress on October 10, 1783, "... It was my fortune, as the senior first lieutenant, to hoist the 'flag of America' the first time it was displayed. Though this was but a light circumstance, yet I feel for its honor more than I think I should have done if it had not happened..."

Jones also wrote to Baron Van der Capellan: "... I had the honor to hoist with my

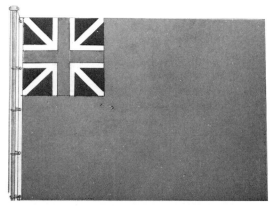

British Red Field Ensign With Grand Union Canton. John Paul Jones Coat of Arms, 1776-77

Tri-Colored Stripes and British Union John Paul Jones Coat of Arms, 1776-77

*Continental Congress Gold Medal awarded to Captain John Paul Jones for the
Bonhomme Richard's Victory over HMS Serapis September 23, 1779*

*Detail of John Paul Jones' Medal. The Richard's striped ensign bears an eagle
canton, a symbol that was not adopted until 1782. The medal was engraved in
France in 1789 and the artist used a design popular at that time*

Red, white, blue stripes with Pine Tree Union John Paul Jones Coat of Arms, 1776-77

Commodore's Blue Command Pendant John Paul Jones Coat of Arms, 1776-77

own hands the flag of freedom, the first time it was displayed on the Delaware; and I have attended it with veneration ever since on the ocean . . .''

A letter to the Earl of Dartmouth from a Loyalist, ''B.P.,'' dated from Maryland, December 20, 1775, states in part that ''Their harbors by spring will swarm with privateers; an admiral is appointed, a court established and on the 3rd inst. (December) the continental flag on board the Black Prince opposite Philadelphia was hoisted.''

The ''flag of America'' hoisted by Jones would have been one of the colors supplied by Philadelphia ship chandler, James Wharton. It is his Day Book that lists an ''En-

sign,'' as well as ''Union'' flags, pendants, and jacks delivered to the *Alfred* in December 1775, including a 13-stripe green and red ''Union'' flag and a ''union jack'' of red, blue and white (see Continental Navy). The ''ensign'' was made by ''Margaret Manny'' according to Wharton's entries and was delivered to the *Alfred* on December 2, 1775. In his signaling instructions to the captains of his fleet on February 14, 1776, Commodore Hopkins lists a ''St. George's ensign with stripes'' as one of the flags to be hoisted by the *Alfred* (see the Appendix on Philadelphia Flagpainters and Flagmakers).

THE STARS AND STRIPES JOHN PAUL JONES *(Plate 6)*

Continental Frigates Ranger, Bonhomme Richard and Alliance and Captured HMS Serapis

There are documents indicating John Paul Jones flew some version of the stars and stripes when in command of the Ranger in 1777–1778, and of the Bonhomme Richard in 1779. Jones was definitely aware of the June 14, 1777 Congressional flag resolution, since the resolution appointing him commander of the Ranger was adopted immediately following the flag resolution—a fact he enjoyed pointing out.

The records also show that Jones obtained the first salute to the new flag from a sovereign power. This was on February 14, 1778, when he exchanged cannon salutes with Admiral D'Orvilliers' fleet at Quiberon Bay.

In a letter dated ''Brest, May 27, 1778,'' from Jones to the American Commissioners in Paris, Jones describes the capture of ''the British ship-of-war Drake'' on 24 April by the Ranger. Jones writes: ''. . . The Drake hoisted English colors, and, at the same instant, the American stars were displayed on board the Ranger.''

The American and French ships of the squadron commanded by Jones during his famous cruise of 1779 were ordered to fly American colors. The ensign of the Bonhomme Richard was probably thirteen red, white and blue stripes, possibly with a blue canton bearing thirteen stars. Such tricolored striped ensigns were apparently favored by the Continental Navy at the time, particularly in European waters. The Richard's ensign was shot off during the battle.

In his report from the Texel in Holland, October 3, 1779, to Franklin, concerning the Bonhomme Richard's August–October 1779 cruise, Jones states that during the September 23, 1779 engagement with HMS Serapis, there was an attempt by the panic-stricken "gunner to run aft on the poop, without my knowledge, to strike the colors; fortunately for me, a cannon ball had done that before, by carrying away the ensign staff; ..." There is no mention in the accounts by Jones or by Midshipman Nathaniel Fanning of any attempt to find or recover the ensign. The battle was fought at night and all able hands were fully occupied after the battle in fighting fires, pumping, clearing wreckage, getting under way, and caring for the wounded. The Richard could not be kept afloat and sank about 10:00 A.M. September 25. Jones wrote he lost the "best part of my clothes, books and papers; and several of my officers lost all their clothes and effects." If the flag had been recovered, Jones would have stated so in his report.

There is strong documentary evidence accepted by historians that Jones hoisted over the captured HMS Serapis a stars-and-stripes with an irregularly sequenced arrangement of blue, red and white stripes and a blue canton with thirteen eight-pointed stars in a 4-5-4 pattern. At the same time, Jones' escort, the Continental Frigate Alliance, flew a stars-and-stripes with seven white and six red stripes and a blue canton with thirteen eight-pointed stars in a 3-2-3-2-3 pattern.

The two flags were carefully sketched either by Jones or possibly by a Dutch admiralty artist on October 4 and 5, 1779. This was shortly after Jones put in to the harbor of the Texel to repair battle damages, and to avoid British warships dispatched to intercept him. The flags flown by the two ships were of utmost importance to Jones, the Dutch, and to the English Ambassador who was demanding return of the Serapis and the arrest of Jones as a pirate. Under these circumstances, the sketches would have been rendered with meticulous accuracy to details.

The Alliance had arrived from America with Lafayette some months previous. It is, therefore, reasonable to assume that the Alliance's stars-and-stripes was an accurate interpretation of the intent of the Congressional Resolve of 1777. Having white stripes on the outer edges is correct from a heraldic standpoint and eight-point stars were frequently used during the period.

The fine watercolor sketches were brought to light in 1924 by Captain Byron McCandless, U.S.N. when he was examining the Gunther Collection acquired by the Chicago Historical Society in 1923. How the sketches came into the Gunther collection is not known. In 1961, Wilmer R. Leech of the New York Historical Society wrote to Roy E. Appleman, of The National Park Service, as to the probable origin of the sketches. Mr. Leech pointed out that the identifying notations on the sketches match Jones' handwriting. Mr. Leech also said that the sketches might have been among the papers of John de Neufville, the American agent at Amsterdam with whom Jones corresponded. DeNeufville later came to the United States; his papers are now in various collections in the U.S.

CONTINENTAL AND STATE MARINES

The Marines, as part of the Continental Navy, did not create a specific standard of their own until the nineteenth century. During the Revolution they fought under the Continental Colors, the stripes, the stars, the stripes and stars and the rattlesnake and pine-tree standards flown by the Navy.

The Marine Corps was established by Congress on November 10, 1775. Two battalions were authorized on the recommendation of the Committee on Nova Scotia with the personnel to be recruited by Washington from his army besieging Boston. Washington recommended against the plan, and Congress, on November 30, ordered the battalions to be raised outside the Army.

Five companies of Marines were recruited in the Philadelphia area in November–December 1775. Captain Samuel Nicholas was the first commissioned Marine officer. He was joined by fellow members of the Gloucester Fox Hunting Club a number of whose members had formed the Philadelphia Light Horse. Nicholas was also a member of The Schuylkill Fishing Company, a sportsmen's club, which is still active.

The first action seen by the Continental Marines was the 1776 expedition against New Providence in the Bahamas. Detachments of Marines were an integral part of all Continental combatant ships. The victory of Bonhomme Richard over Serapis was due almost entirely to the sharpshooting and grenading of the Richard's marines and naval personnel.

There were also marines in the small navies created by Washington at Boston and New York. Arnold's squadron on Lake Champlain in 1776 included marines. The state navies also had marines. Middlebrook's "*Maritime Connecticut during the American Revolution*" contains numerous references to Connecticut State Marines. Such State Marines should be identified with the ensigns of their state navies.

Philadelphia's Tun Tavern became the recruiting station for the Continental Marines in 1776.

A "Letter from Philadelphia" dated December 27, 1775, states: "I observed on one of the drums belonging to the Marines, now raising, there was painted a Rattlesnake, with this modest motto under it, "Don't Tread on me . . ."" The writer is not identified.

PRIVATEERS AND LETTERS OF MARQUE

Although there were approximately 3500 American privateers and "letters of marque," apparently no original ensigns carried by any of these vessels have survived. That they carried flags is well attested by contemporary accounts. And in almost all cases their flags were the Continental and state naval colors. There were probably some special ensigns flown by a few such ships, but not many. There was no recognized, unique "naval privateer ensign" which one hoisted when setting out to capture prizes. In fact, the exact opposite was the case, and logically so. Privateers were privately-owned and civilian-manned sea raiders. They operated under a commission (or for armed cargo carriers under a "letter of marque") issued by the Continental Congress or a state government. Sailing without a commission or under some unrecorded flag could lead to a charge of piracy—the penalty for which was death. So privateers took care to fly as official an ensign as possible. For Continental privateers the flag was usually the striped ensign, or union with thirteen stripes of various colors. State commissioned privateers flew the Continental stripes or the naval ensign of their state.

Privateering was one of the most successful and extensive operations of the Revolution. Privately financed and manned by expert merchant officers and seamen, Continental and state privateers inflicted significant damage on British military transport and merchant fleets. They also brought needed supplies to the combat forces. Privateers were fast. Most were lightly armed. They were not fitted for standup battles with combatant ships; although some, when necessary, successfully fought sizable armed merchantships and smaller combatants. The objective of the privateer was to make captures, with the crew and owners sharing in the proceeds.

——6——

Connecticut

CONNECTICUT STATE SEAL

The present-day Connecticut state seal is of Colonial origin. It was in use before 1656, and consists of a shield bearing grapevines with the motto "Qui Transtulit Sustinet" (Who Transporteth Sustaineth), which refers to the Biblical transplanting of the vines from Egypt. This was because the Puritans related their migrations to the wanderings of the Israelites.

Early colonial versions of the seal had as many as fifteen vines. Most issues of state paper currency starting with 1709 carried the grapevine and motto seal with three vines, each holding three clusters of grapes. Other detail changes have been made which are described by Preble. It is believed that the three vines symbolize the original settlements of Hartford, Windsor and Wethersfield, or possibly, the "three virtues," Knowledge, Liberty, and Religion.

The "Colony arms, with the motto 'qui transtulit sustinet' round it in gold" was placed on the standards and drums carried by Connecticut troops who marched to Boston in 1775. The surviving standard of the 2nd Battalion, 2nd Regiment has the state arms and motto on one side and the unit designation on the other.

On September 10, 1780, the Connecticut Assembly directed that the standards of the regiments bear the state seal on one side and the unit's designation, together with the device from the Continental $30.00 bill, on the other.

CONNECTICUT STATE NAVY ENSIGN *(Plate 27)*

No original survives, but there is a contemporary drawing of a Connecticut naval ensign and, also, records of purchases of cloth for colors.

Eleven of the thirteen states had their own navy. Connecticut was among the most active, having both state naval and marine personnel.

A voucher in the state records indicates that the flag of the Connecticut Colony Brig "Defence," fitted out at New Haven in 1776, was blue and white. Also, among

*Blue Ensign of the
Connecticut State Navy*

73

Maritime Court papers concerning the British schooner, "True Love," captured by the Connecticut privateer "Retaliation," there is an untitled and undated black and white drawing of a flag with a solid blue field and a white canton featuring a single grapevine the symbol of Connecticut. The flag's hoist-to-fly are proportioned 1.0 to 1.3. The solid blue field is indicated heraldically by horizontal lines.

Among original vouchers on file at the Connecticut State Library for fitting out the "Defence" in January 1776 there is this item: "11 yards blue tammie, 26 yards white tammie for the colors of ye brig Defence paid to Anthony Perit Feb. 23, 1776—L.2-2-9". There is also an item, dated April 3, 1776 for "cash paid for making the Colours L.1-5-0." "Tammie" was a kind of woolen or woolen and cotton used for marine flags.

CONNECTICUT REGIMENTAL STANDARDS—11 MAY, 1775

In his history of Connecticut, G. H. Hollister, in 1857, reports the following: "On the 11th of May [1775]... the Assembly again met... Guns, tents... and standards were ordered to be procured. For each regiment the new standard was to be of a particular color. That of Wooster's was to be yellow, Spencer's blue, Putnam's scarlet, Hinman's crimson, Waterbury's white and Parson's azure..."

In "Record of Service of Connecticut Men in the Revolution," compiled by the State Adj. General, Hartford, p 93, the colors of the "Regimental Standards" are given as follows: 1st Regt, yellow; 2d, blue; 3d, scarlet; 4th, crimson; 5th, white; 6th, azure; 7th, blue (?); 8th, orange.

CONNECTICUT REGIMENTAL COLORS, SEPTEMBER 10, 1780

Among the camp orders issued to the Connecticut Division, was the following, dated Sept 10, 1780:

Continental $30 bill—July 22, 1776
The symbol was taken from Camerarius' "Symbolorum", 1702. A copy of the book was in Franklin's Library

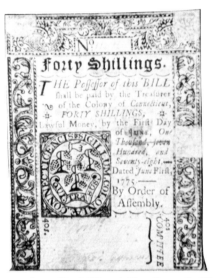

Connecticut 40 shilling bill—June 1, 1775
Grapevine Seal and Motto "Qui. Tra. Sust."

"Regulation for regimental colours in the Connecticut Line. The ground of each to be different—each to bear the number of the Regt. in large character:—The device on one side, the Conn- Arms—on the other, the device and motto of the 30 dollar Bills. If the ground of (any) two colours should be so alike as not to be distinguishable 3 or 400 yards, a small field of 13 stripes in the Lower

Quarter of one of them may serve as a distinction."

STANDARD OF THE THIRD CONNECTICUT REGIMENT OF 1775 *(Plate 24)*

Although no original has survived, records tell us that on Prospect Hill outside of Boston, on July 18, 1775, the scarlet standard of the Third Connecticut Regiment was unfurled. It had been recently sent to General Putnam and bore on the one side the Connecticut motto "Qui Transtulit Sustinet" and on the other the recognized motto of Massachusetts, "An Appeal to Heaven." Putnam had been the commander of the Third up until June 19, 1775. The Connecticut General Assembly in the Spring of 1775 directed that the standard of the Third Regiment (of 1775) be scarlet. Eyewitness and historian accounts differ somewhat as to the design of the standard.

Hollister wrote, "On July 20, 1775, the declaration of the Continental Congress, setting forth their reasons for taking up arms, was read to the American Troops before Boston. Putnam's division was paraded upon Prospect Hill to hear the declaration. The troops shouted "Amen" three times, a signal gun was fired from the fort, ... and suddenly the new standard that had just arrived from Connecticut, rose and unfurled itself ... exhibiting on one side, in large golden letters, the words An Appeal to Heaven! and, on the other, the armorial bearings of Connecticut, with its simple shield unsupported and without a crest, marked with the three vines ... and with the scroll, Qui Transtulit Sustinet."

The New England Chronicle for July 21, 1775, reported the event, as follows: "Cambridge, July 21. On Tuesday morning the standard lately sent to General Putnam was exhibited flourishing in the air, bearing on one side this motto, 'An Appeal to Heaven', and on the other, 'Qui Transtulit Sustinet'. The whole was conducted with the utmost

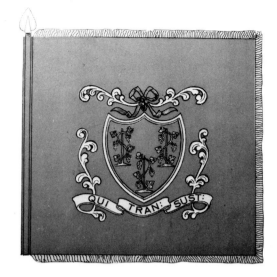

Standard of the Third Connecticut Regiment of 1775

decency, good order, and regularity, and to the universal acceptance of all present. All the Philistines on Bunker's Hill heard the shout of the Israelites, and, being very fearful, paraded themselves in battle array."

Newburyport Lieutenant Paul Lunt recorded in his diary the following: "May 10, 1775, marched from Newburyport with sixty men, Captain Ezra Lunt, commander, and May 12, at 11 o'clock, arrived at Cambridge. ... June 16, our men went to Charlestown and entrenched on a hill beyond Bunker's

Hill . . . June 17, the regulars landed a number of troops, and we engaged them. They drove us off the hill and burned Charlestown. July 2, General Washington came into the camp . . . July 18th. This morning a manifesto from the grand Continental Congress was read by the Rev. Mr. Leonard, chaplain of the Connecticut forces upon Prospect Hill in Charlestown. Our standard was presented in the midst of the regiments, with this inscription upon it, 'Appeal to Heaven,' after which Mr. Leonard made a short prayer, and then we were dismissed, by the discharge of a cannon, three cheers, and a war-whoop by the Indians.''

REGIMENTAL STANDARD AND DIVISION COLORS OF WEBB'S ADDITIONAL CONTINENTAL REGIMENT OF 1777, Later the NINTH OF 1780, and then the THIRD CONNECTICUT REG. OF 1781
(Plates 24, 25, 26)

Gherardi Davis in *"Regimental Colors of the War of the Revolution"* published in 1907, states that two Revolutionary flags were presented to the Pennsylvania Society of Sons of the Revolution in 1905 by Mr. Francis Parsons Webb of New York City, through Mr. Oliver Hough as "having belonged to Colonel Samuel B. Webb's Third Connecticut Regiment" of 1781. This Regiment had been initially raised as Webb's Additional Continental Regiment of 1777. Later it was redesignated the Ninth Connecticut Regiment of 1780, and finally consolidated into the Third of 1781.

The report in the Society's *"Annual Proceedings for 1905-06"* lists the gift from Mr. Hough of "two original flags carried . . . by regiments of the New York Continental Line." Apparently, the flags were identified with New York because Mr. Francis P. Webb was a native of New York. The flags should have been identified with Col. S. B.

Colors of the 1st Grand Subdivision Webb's Additional Continental Regiment of 1777. (Present-day painting)

Original colors of the 1st Grand Subdivision

Webb's Connecticut Regiment, as correctly stated by G. Davis in 1907, by Schermerhorn in 1948, and by Adm. G. H. Preble in 1880. Francis P. Webb was a great-grandson of Colonel S. B. Webb, who had moved from Connecticut to New York after the close of the Revolutionary War.

One of the flags is intact. It measures 29 x 35 inches and is in comparably good condition. Made of yellow silk, it has a painted sword, victory wreath and the numeral "I". The flag was pictured by Gherardi Davis in

Standard of Webb's Additional Continental Regiment of 1777. Later the 9th Connecticut Regiment of 1780, then the 3rd Connecticut Regiment of 1781. (Present-day painting)

1907; by E. N. Avery in "A History of the United States and Its People," 1909; and in the National Geographic Magazine, October 1917 and September 1934. The flag is believed to be the Colors of the "1st" Grand Sub-Division of the regiment. A regiment usually consisted of eight companies, as Webb's. During battles and parades, two companies were, at times, grouped together to form a "grand division", or "division."

The second flag is of large size; originally, about five feet square, of which 46 inches of the hoist and 45 inches of the fly remain. The flag's size and elaborate device indicate that it is a regimental standard. It was mentioned but not pictured or described by Schermerhorn. Gherardi Davis described and pictured both flags in 1907.

The regimental standard was exhibited at Independence Hall in 1876, according to Admiral G. H. Preble's *"History of the Flag of the United States of America"*, published in 1880. The flag is essentially in the same condition today as when photographed in 1905-1907. According to Preble, it was in "mutilated" condition when exhibited in 1876. The 1905-07 photograph indicates the standard had been unrolled from a furled condition. It shows what appears to be a staff sleeve with a portion of the staff, which is now missing. Evidence of a sleeve still remains. Preble described the emblem and stated that the flag was of yellow silk and "once belonged to Colonel O. B. Webb, [sic] aid to General Putnam and ... Washington." Both Webb flags were described in detail in The Philadelphia Inquirer in the mid-1930's.

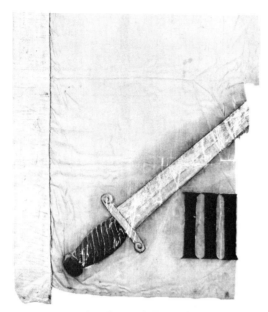

Original colors of the IIIrd and IIIIth Grand Subdivisions of Webb's Additional Continental Regiment of 1777

The larger of the above Webb flags represents an important American Revolutionary regimental standard and justifies close attention. Although portions of the field are missing, the principal elements of the standard's symbolic scene are intact. The motto can be read by combining the surviving letters on both sides. The colors of the paint and of the yellow silk are still bright—probably because the standard has been in storage most of the past two hundred years. Placement of the scene, motto scroll, and the width of the upper panel of silk (28½ inches selvage-to-selvage width) indicate the flag was originally about 57 x 65 inches. This size is in keeping with regimental standards of the Revolutionary period.

Two additional division colors of Webb's Regiment, both originals, are at the New York Historical Society. These were also donated by descendants of Samuel B. Webb. One, the III Division Colors, was presented by Francis Egerton Webb in 1942. Made of a single width of tan silk, it measures 28½ x 33½ inches. It has the same sword and wreath emblem as the I Division

Colors and bears the Roman numeral "III". The flag is intact and is sleeved for its staff.

The second flag was presented by Mrs. Jorge R. André, daughter of Col. G. Creighton Webb, in 1948. The outer half is missing. It is also made of silk and measures about 28½ inches on the hoist with about 15 inches of the fly remaining. The hoist is sleeved and the inner half of the same sword as found on the "I" and "III" Division Colors is present with the numeral "III" remaining. The tear is at the outer edge of the "III" and the missing portion probably had the last "I" digit to form a "IIII" for that Division as well as the outer portion of the sword blade and the Victory wreath.

The above flags form the only matched set of Revolutionary War regimental and grand subdivision colors that has survived to this date. The flags are of particular interest to historians for reasons of their relative sizes, designs, and use of the same sword and wreath emblem on each of the three extant division colors.

The use of a single large distinctive regimental standard and smaller colors for a regiment with four companies the size of grand subdivisions follows the system proposed by General Charles Lee in 1775, and recommended by Washington in 1776. A copy of Lee's system for regimental colors was found in Colonel Webb's papers. Webb's regiment actually had eight full size companies. Such companies were, at times, grouped into grand subdivisions for battles and parades.

The symbolic scene of the Webb regimental flag reveals the same type of graphic tableau as described for two of the regimental standards listed in the Mayor Jonathan Gostelowe's Return of 1778. The same symbol was adopted during the Revolution by the state of Virginia and symbolizes the Declaration of Independence.

The scene pictures a brown-haired, white skinned Indian maiden, ''America,'' robed in a light-red, classical-style gown with a blue belt. In classical style, one breast is exposed. She wears gold bracelets and armlets and a headdress of upright red, green, white and blue feathers. One hand supports a spiral-wrapped pole which is topped with a black Cavalier-style Liberty hat. From the pole streams a swallow-tailed pennant of seven red and six white stripes. In her other hand is a horizontally outstretched sword with a blue blade and gold hilt. A gold, studded, round shield is clasped to the arm which holds the flagpole. Standing below the sword, is an alert-looking brownish-tan lion with an upright swishing tail. Lying on the ground, in front of the lion, is the severed head of a bald-headed king pierced through the temple by an arrow. His red-and-gold crown lies nearby. Green grass and plants lightly cover the ground, which is now a nondescript dark gray with a red undercoat.

That portion of the scene which included some of the lower part of the gown of the maiden is missing, along with half of the ground on which she stands. It undoubtedly pictured the headless body of the king. The outline and colors of the missing half of the ground would have been the same as that half which is still present.

The motto reads ''*IN MERIDIEM PROGRED ETC*'' and has defied exact translation by the author, but appears to express the thought ''ADVANCE BEYOND HIGH NOON.'' The letters are gold, on a deep blue ribbon-like tassel-ended scroll which curves across the top of the flag. The scene, Cavalier hat, and the ''HIGH NOON'' of the motto refer to the Parliamentary Cromwellian Revolution of the 1640's which led to the beheading of Charles I. The existing

Detail of the Standard of Webb's Additional Continental Regiment of 1777. A symbolic representation of the Declaration of Independence. America, symbolized by an Indian princess, holding the Liberty Pole and ''cap''

Revolutionary-era flag of the II Battalion, II Regiment of Connecticut has the motto "Raised 1640". Connecticut was generally in sympathy with the Cromwellians and sheltered two of the regicides following the Restoration.

Colonel Samuel Blatchley Webb (brevetted Brig-General, September 30, 1783) of Wethersfield, Connecticut, was one of the country's foremost patriots. A stepson of Silas Deane, he was on General Putnam's staff in 1775 and was Washington's aide and secretary in 1776. He was wounded at Bunker Hill, at White Plains and at Trenton. Taken prisoner by a British frigate while leading an expedition against Setauket, Long Island, in December 1777, he was exchanged in December 1780. He raised Webb's Additional Continental Regiment in 1777, which was designated the Ninth Connecticut in 1780, then merged in 1781 with Colonel Charles Webb's Second Connecticut Regiment of 1777 to form the (new) Third Connecticut Regiment of 1781. For additional information on Webb's Third Regiment, see notes.

STANDARD OF THE II BATTALION II CONNECTICUT REGT.
(Plate 24)

The original is in the collection of the Connecticut Historical Society and on display in the State House, Hartford. Its recorded history started in 1812 or 1839.

The flag is of red silk and now measures 34 (hoist) by 44 (fly) inches. Originally, it appears to have measured at least 36 by 48 inches. On the obverse side, painted in 3½ inch high gold letters, is the following:

II. BAT:
II. REG:
CONNECTICUT
Raised 1640

On the reverse is a large painting of the seal of Connecticut, a shield with three grapevines, representing Hartford, Windsor, and Wethersfield, with the abbreviated motto "QUI TRAN: SUST" for "Qui Transtulit Sustinet." The vines, scroll and outer edge of the shield are gold. The

Colors of the II Battalion, II Connecticut Regiment

Present-day Artist's Rendition

Original Standard of the II Battalion, II Connecticut Regiment
(1907 Photograph, Gherardi Davis)

inner edge of the shield and the ribbon are blue. Lettering, outlines and shading are black.

Traditionally, the standard was deposited in the State Arsenal by Colonel John Mix of Farmington. The Arsenal was built in 1812. Mix was the Adjutant of the Second Connecticut Regiment of 1777 from June 1, 1778 to January 1, 1781. He was Connecticut's Quartermaster-General from 1796 to 1814. He died in 1834. The standard was moved to the Connecticut Secretary of State's office in 1839 and placed in the custody of the Connecticut Historical Society in 1846.

Davis expressed some concern that the flag is red, whereas in 1775 the Connecticut Assembly established "blue" as the color for the second regiment. Since the regiments of 1775 ceased to exist on 1 January 1776 (to be replaced by newly authorized regiments) it is possible that the 1775 color designations became obsolete at that time.

Use of the Connecticut state seal and the unit's designation is partially in accordance with the September 10, 1780 regulation defining the design for regimental colors. It has also been pointed out that the standard conforms to Connecticut militia regulations of 1792. The motto, "Raised 1640"; refers to the Cromwellian Rebellion.

Continental Congress Gold Medal awarded to Daniel Morgan for Cowpens—January 17, 1781. This medal was engraved in Paris in 1789 and depicts the American Standard as thirteen stripes with an eagle canton, a design which came into use after 1782 when the eagle seal was adopted

Morgan calls for the charge at Cowpens. Note Eagle Canton and stripes. Engraved by A. Dupré. Paris, 1789

———7———

Delaware

ARMS OF STATE OF DELAWARE

The arms of Delaware, adopted in 1793, are an azure shield, or escutcheon, divided into two equal parts by a white band or girdle. A cow proper is pictured in the lower division, and in the other a sheaf of wheat and a bundle of leaf tobacco. At the crest is a ship under full sail, displaying an American flag, and supported on a wreath. On a white field around the escutcheon were placed wreaths of flowers, and olive branches. There are two supporters, a mariner and a hunter. At the bottom of the seal, in numeral letters, is the date of its adoption, "MD.CCXCIII."; and around the border, in Roman capitals, are the words, "GREAT SEAL OF THE STATE OF DELAWARE." Underneath the shield is the motto, "Liberty and Independence."

An issue of Delaware state currency of 1777 bears a seal with a mariner and hunter.

DELAWARE MILITIA COLOR *(Plate 27)*

The original of this silk flag is now at the Delaware Historical Society. It is initially recorded in a letter written by a British officer on October 11, 1777.

The flag's olive green field is now a faded greenish brown. It has a painted canton union of seven red and six white stripes. The hoist is 47 inches, the fly 62 inches, and the inset canton 17½ x 17½ inches. There is a remnant of green fringe (made "from the material itself") along the flag's border. Two blue and white tassels on cords are attached to the head.

The flag was captured by Captain William

Delaware Militia Color—1777
(Present-day painting)

Dansey, British 33rd Regiment of Foot, who wrote home on October 11, 1777 from his camp at Germantown: "Philadelphia has been taken and the Rebels twice defeated" and that "a few days before the Battle of Brandywine on a flanking party I took the Horse Arms, Colours and Drums belonging to a Rebel Colonel of the Delaware Militia, made his Brother Prisoner and caused all his Baggage to be taken which the General (Cornwallis) very politely sent back again but the Horse, Arms, and Colours came to my share, the later I hope to bring home as a Trophy to Brinsop." The battle of Brandywine was fought September 11, 1777.

The next record of the flag was when it was purchased in England in 1927 (at auction) as the property or estate of Captain Dansey's greatgrandson, along with forty-four Revolutionary War letters, including the above.

This information was kindly provided by Juanelle Crump and Mary Brady of the Delaware Historical Society.

It is hoped that research will eventually identify the specific Delaware unit. Mr. Holst of the Smithsonian believes the flag is a grand-divisional color of one of the Delaware militia battalions.

DELAWARE BATTALION COLORS—BATTLE OF LONG ISLAND

At the August 27, 1776 battle of Long Island, Colonel John Haslet commanding the Delaware Battalion described how his command and Smallwood's Marylanders held their position for four hours. Haslett said his men took position on the side of a hill in close array, their colours flying.

GOVERNOR DANIEL RODNEY'S CONTINENTAL FLAG

Preble refers to a letter he received from Dr. Rodney King of Roxboro, Pa. in 1875, in which Dr. King described a letter found among the papers of his grandfather, the Hon. Daniel Rodney, a Revolutionary War governor of Delaware. The letter dated 1783 lists "materials for a Continental Flag," one of the items being "for a piece of green silk." Preble remarks on the need for green silk for a continental flag, but offers no explanation. The author points out that the Delaware Militia Color described in this chapter was of green silk.

Original of the Delaware Militia Color—1777

8

Georgia

GEORGIA STATE SEAL

In response to the Declaration of Independence, Georgia drew up a state constitution between October 1776 and February 5, 1777, which included the following design for a great seal of state: ''On one side a scroll whereon shall be engraved 'The Constitution of the State of Georgia', and the motto 'Pro Bono Publico'; on the other side an elegant house and other buildings, fields of corn, and meadows covered with sheep and cattle; a river running through the same, with a ship under full sail; and the motto 'Deus Nobis Haec Otia Fecit'.''

UNION FLAG, SAVANNAH, GEORGIA—JUNE 1775

Two Nineteenth Century historians wrote as follows:

''... The first liberty pole erected in Georgia was elevated in Savannah on the 5th of June, 1775... The 'Liberty Boys'... drank as their first regular toast 'The King'. The second was 'American Liberty' ... On the 21st of June was published a call... to meet at the liberty pole on the following day at ten o'clock in the forenoon for the purpose of bringing about a union of Georgia with the other colonies in the cause of freedom... At the appointed place and designated hour many were present... The union flag was hoisted upon the liberty pole, and two field-pieces were posted at its foot. Thirteen patriotic toasts were drunk, each being responded to by a salute from the cannon and by martial music...''

Preble also wrote as follows, without giving a reference:

''June 19, 1775, two days after the battle of Bunker Hill, and before the news had reached Georgia there was a meeting of a committee of the leading men of Savannah, to enforce the requirements of the American Association. After the meeting, a dinner was had at Tondee's tavern, where a 'union flag' was hoisted upon a liberty pole, and two pieces of artillery placed under it.''

FLOATING BATTERY WITH "LIBERTY COLOURS" GEORGIA COAST—1776

Following the repulse of the British invasion fleet at Charleston on 28 June 1776, the army of the Southern Department, under the command of General Charles Lee, attempted to launch an expedition against East Florida. Scouting vessels were sent ahead and, as a result, Lt. William Grant, Royal Navy, of H.M. Schooner "St. John" recorded in his ship's journal and also reported to Royal Governor Patrick Tonyn the following: That while off "St Marie's Barr 7th August 1776, . . . saw a large flat resembling a Vessel cut down and made into a Floating Battery with one Mast and Liberty Colours flying near Cumberland Point . . ."

COLORS OF THE FIRST GEORGIA REGIMENT

There is a portrait in the Georgia Historical Society, Savannah, of Captain (later Major) John Habersham, painted between 1777 and 1779. Habersham served in the 1st Georgia Battalion or Regiment throughout the war. His uniform coat is dark blue with yellow or buff facings and he wears a gorget engraved with a coiled rattlesnake and the motto "DON'T TREAD ON ME." The camp colors of the Battalion in January 1778 had a blue field with yellow inscriptions. The author assumes that the gorget engraving could have been used as the symbol on the battalion's standard and that the camp colors and Habersham's uniform matched the standard. Thereby, it is possible to visualize a silk standard of 5 by 5½ feet with a blue field bearing a yellow rattlesnake and motto in the center with the unit designation "1st BAT" in the upper inside canton. The British captured a standard when Savannah was taken in December, 1778.

Continental Congress Gold Medal awarded to General Nathaniel Greene for Eutaw Springs. Greene led the Georgia forces in the final campaign of the War. He was awarded a rice plantation near Savannah and died there in 1786

86

9

Maryland

STATE SEAL OF MARYLAND

The Maryland state seal is the provincial great seal of 1658 with the arms of the United States on the reverse. The provincial seal bears the arms of Lord Baltimore on a shield supported by a fisherman and a ploughman. At the crest is a helmet with a ducal crown surmounted by two bannerets. The motto is, "Fatti maschii parole femine," which is translated, "Manly deeds and womanly words." Around the margin of the seal is inscribed, "Scuto Bonae Voluntatis Tuac Coronasti Nos," which is translated, "With the shield of Thy good will Thou has covered us."

STANDARD OF PULASKI'S LEGION *(Plate 15)*

The standard of this unit is described in the section on the Continental Army. Pulaski's Legion was raised principally in the Baltimore area. It was a Continental unit and not part of Maryland's regular quota.

Standard of Pulaski's Legion of 1778. (Painting)

Continental Congress Silver Medal awarded to Maryland Lt. Col. Howard for his role at Cowpens, January 17, 1781

MARYLAND STATE NAVY

The extensive records on the Maryland State Navy Ship *Defence* include the following inventory item:

"3 Sutes [sic] of Colours. A sufficient quantity of Bunting for Signals."

The inventory, signed by John Thomas Boucher, first lieutenant, is undated but is believed to have been submitted on March 1, 1776.

THE BATCHELOR STARS AND STRIPES, THE BATTLE OF COWPENS, AND THE 3RD MARYLAND REGIMENT

This flag has a canton of twelve, five-pointed stars encircling one in the middle. It measures 30 by 61 inches and is of an open weave material. Historians and textile experts disagree on the flag's date of origin, and on whether it is of the size and type that would be carried by an infantry unit.

Members of the 3rd Maryland Regiment were at Cowpens not as a regiment but as part of the combined light infantry commanded by Colonel Howard. The Maryland Brigades had incurred heavy losses at Camden on August 16, 1780, and the survivors were pooled with Delaware and Virginia troops to form a consolidated unit.

Although American regiments were not authorized to carry a stars and stripes until the Nineteenth Century, some brigades did, as evidenced by Major John Ross' sketch of General Sullivan's order-of-battle during the 1779 expedition against the Western New York Indians. (Historical Society of Pennsylvania, du Simentiere papers).

The author trusts that in time to come, continued research will resolve the issue of the Batchelor Standard.

The battle of Cowpens was to the Southern Campaign what Bennington was to Saratoga. Two British standards were captured. There are excellent descriptions of the battle by participants, quoted in the Notes. Cowpens was a classic example of field operations of the time, and the fierce attention given to capturing standards is evident in the descriptions.

——10——

Massachusetts

MASSACHUSETTS STATE SEAL

Massachusetts adopted its present seal on December 13, 1780. The arms consist of an Indian (America), a strung bow and arrow (readiness), a single star (Massachusetts), and an arm brandishing a sword (Defense) at the crest. The motto "Ense Petit Placidam Sub Liberate Quietam," (Seeks with the sword placid repose under liberty), is the second line of a 1660 politically defiant maxim by Algernon Sidney, a heroic figure (to the Puritans) of the Cromwellian rebellion. Sidney was subsequently beheaded for his political views.

The first line of Sidney's maxim, *"Manus Haec Inimica Tyrannis,"* appeared on a standard which was planted on the ramparts of the trenches at Yorktown by James Duncan, a Pennsylvania Captain in Hazen's (Congress' Own) Continental Regiment.

In June 1787, the Governor ordered that the standard for Massachusetts state troops be of white silk, with the arms of the state on one side and the crest of the arms, i.e., the arm and sword, on the other. The early Bedford Minuteman flag bears as a device an arm and sword.

Algernon Sidney's "Ense Petit..." quotation, above, together with an officer holding a "Magna Charta" scroll and brandishing a sword appeared on Massachusetts currency engraved by Revere, December 7, 1775. An Indian with a bow appears in the devices on two of the Gostelowe Continental Army regimental standards of 1778. Another of the Gostelowe standards has the first line of Sidney's poem, as quoted above, and has a device of an arm and sword encircled by thirteen linked swords.

John Q. Adams supplied the following translation of Sidney's lines:

"This hand, to tyrants ever sworn the foe,
For freedom only deals the deadly blow:
Then sheathe in calm repose the vengeful
    blade,
For gentle peace in freedom's hallowed
    shade."

THE MOULTON FLAG, 1745

There is an extant flag associated with the Louisbourg expedition of 1745 which was carried by the Third Massachusetts Regiment commanded by Colonel Jeremiah Moulton. The flag is of linen, 26½ inches square, and has as a painted device an oak tree holding a dagger and a motto, BELLO PAX QUAERITUR (By war seek peace). Only one side is painted. Two horizontal blue stripes are painted along the top edge.

MASSACHUSETTS STANDARDS "AN APPEAL TO HEAVEN"

The motto borne by Massachusetts standards, "An Appeal to Heaven", was apparently taken from "the closing paragraph of the 'address of the Provincial Congress of Massachusetts, to their brethren in Great Britain,' which was written shortly after the battle of Lexington, and ended thus: 'Appealing to Heaven for the justice of our cause, we determine to die or be free'."

There are numerous reports and English prints of "Appeal to Heaven" flags, particularly in the early years of the War. One such print of 1775 of Major General Charles Lee shows a flag in the background with the above motto.

PINE TREE ENSIGNS OF THE MASSACHUSETTS STATE NAVY AND OF THE FLOATING BATTERIES AND WASHINGTON'S CRUISERS OF 1775 *(Plate 27)*

The illustration of this ensign is based on contemporary sketches and descriptions. No original has survived.

In September 1775, the Americans launched two strong floating batteries on the Charles River, Massachusetts, and in the following month they opened fire on the enemy in Boston. In October, Washington also commissioned two schooners, the Lynch and the Franklin, to cruise the Bay. When speaking of these schooners, Colonel Joseph Reed, Washington's secretary, in a letter from Cambridge, Massachusetts, to Colonels Glover and Moylan, dated October 20, 1775, said "Please fix upon some particular color for a flag, and a signal by which our vessels may know one another. What do you think of a flag with a white ground and a tree in the middle, the motto 'AN APPEAL TO HEAVEN'—this is the flag of our floating batteries."

By February 1, 1776 a total of six such "Armed Vessels" of the "United Colonies of North America" had been commissioned by Washington. One of the Captains, Samuel Tucker, recalled that "the first cruise I made was in January, 1776, in the schooner Franklin, of seventy tons, equipped by order of General Washington, . . . and my wife made the banner I fought under the field of which was white and the union green, made therein in the

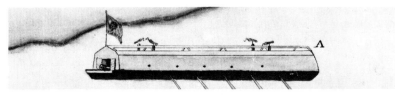

"Armaments of the American Rebels" —Boston, 1775. Pen sketch by Charles Blaskowitz, Mapmaker with Howe's army. Detail showing floating battery with flag bearing tree and motto

Ensign of the Massachusetts State Navy and Washington's armed vessels —1775 (Present-day ceremonial version with fringe)

figure of a pine-tree, made of cloth of her own purchasing, at her own expense.''

In April 1776, the Massachusetts council passed a series of resolutions for the regulation of the sea service, among which was the following:—''Resolved, that the uniform of the officers be green and white, and that the colors be a white flag, with a green pine-tree, and the inscription, 'An Appeal to Heaven'.''

The London Chronicle for January, 1776, states that an American provincial privateer had been captured, and in describing the flag, says ''the field is white bunting. On the middle is a green pine-tree and upon the opposite side is the motto 'An Appeal to Heaven.' ''

According to the English newspapers; ''Jan. 6, 1776, the Tartar, Captain Meadows, arrived at Portsmouth, England, from Boston, with over seventy men, the crew of an American privateer... her colors, which are a pale green palm-tree upon a white field, with this motto, 'We Appeal to Heaven.' She was taken on the Massachusetts coast... sent out by the council of that province.''

Probably, one or more of the first vessels commissioned soon afterwards by the Continental Congress sailed under the same device—a green pine tree in the center of a white field with the motto, ''Appeal to Heaven''. Also, Preble wrote that the floating batteries of the Pennsylvania Navy in the Delaware River carried this ensign in the Autumn of 1775 and during operations in the defence of Philadelphia in 1777 and 1778. However, Preble does not quote a reference nor has the author encountered a primary reference source.

Preble again quotes an unreferenced source concerning a pine tree ensign, as follows: ''Joseph Webb was paid by the Massachusetts Board of War, May 5, 1777, 'To mending an ensign and sewing in a pine tree, 6 s.'' ' He also quotes the following record, either a minute book or a voucher: ''State of Mass. Bay to Jos. Webb, Dr. Aug. 20, 1777. To making a suit colours, 44 s.; thread, 12 s; painting Pine Trees, etc. 24 s—£.4.00 'State Armed Brig Freedom   John Conston'' '

STANDARD OF THE BEDFORD MINUTEMEN OF 1775 *(Plate 27)*

The original flag is in the collection of the Bedford, Massachusetts Public Library. It is approximately 27¼ (hoist) by 29 (fly) inches, of red damask figured silk with painted emblem and motto, and, originally, silver fringe. The Library states: ''This flag was commissioned to Cornet Page in 1737, then a loyal subject of King George II. On April 19, 1775, it was carried at Concord to the fight at the bridge, by his son, Cornet Nathaniel. In 1875 it was carried at the Centennial Celebration at Concord and was presented by Captain Cyrus Page, grandson of Cornet Nathaniel Page, to the town of Bedford, October 19, 1885.'' The first hundred years of the history of the flag is based primarily on family tradition, as with most surviving flags.

There are records which indicate this flag was possibly associated with the standard of a colonial-era troop of mounted militia. When the New England Confederacy was formed in 1643 by the colonies of Massachusetts Bay, Plymouth, Connecticut and New Haven, three regiments were determined upon for Massachusetts to be formed from the three counties of Middlesex, Suffolk and Essex (joined with Norfolk). Out of this military formation grew a company of cavalry called the Three County Troop. The flag or "cavalry cornett" of this troop is shown by Preble. This was copied from a drawing in a manuscript book by a herald during the reign of Charles II (1660-85). It is now in the British Museum. The cornett is mounted on a knight's jousting lance and bears the inscription "Thre County Trom." Why the words "Thre" and "Trom" are used is unknown. Early records of Massachusetts refer at least nine times between 1659 and 1677, to the "Three County Troop." In his book the herald has included an itemized bill which speaks of "worke done for New England... painting in oyle on both sides... a Cornett one [on] rich crimson damask, with a hand and sword and invelloped with a scarfe [sic] about the arms of gold, black and silver." A staff, belt,

boote, "swible" and silver fringe are also mentioned. Total cost was £ 5.2.6.

There is an old copy of a seventeenth century manuscript which shows the banners and standards of the Parliamentarians of the Rebellion of the 1640's. One of these banners, that of Colonel Ridgly, shows a hand with a sword pointed at what appears to be a crown, and a motto on a scroll similar in design to the Bedford flag. The arm and sword symbol appears repeatedly as a device on the standards of both Parliamentary and Loyalist leaders.

Dr. Whitney Smith of The Flag Research Center, Winchester, Massachusetts, describes and analyzes the flag and its history in detail in his booklet, "The Bedford Flag." For instance, he tells us of a family tradition that the flag's missing silver fringe was used to trim a ball gown by Nathaniel Page's granddaughter, Mrs. Ruhamah Page Lane, when she was, by her own words, "a giddy girl."

The flag's painted device displays an armor-clad arm issuing from a cloud and brandishing an upraised sword. It also has a gilt ribbon scroll with the motto "VINCE AUT MORIRE" (Conquer or Die). The de-

Present-day copy of the Bedford Flag

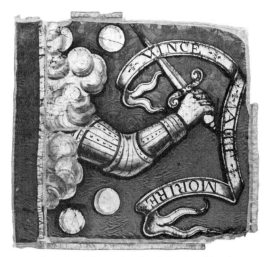

Original Standard of the Bedford Minutemen—1775

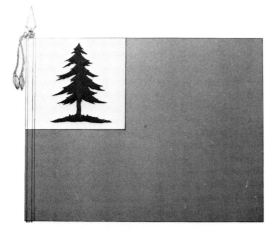

Bunker Hill Colors —1775
John Trumbull's version

vice and scroll are framed by a painted silver border which runs along the three outer edges, but is inset four inches from the hoist edge. The painted clouds appear to be white; the armor is silver with darker colored shading; the sword is silver with gold-colored hilt and pommel. There are stylized floral decorations between the words of the motto, while the scroll is edged and swallow-tailed. Whether there is a sleeve for a staff or lance is not discernible. The reverse side of the flag is essentially the same as the obverse, with the difference being that the sword is held by a left arm and the blade crosses in front of the scroll. Also, the motto reads from bottom to top. The silver fringe which once edged the flag is mentioned above.

BUNKER HILL *(Plates 27, 28)*

Red-Field New England Pine Tree Ensign
Blue-Field New England Pine Tree Ensign with St. George's Cross
Scarlet Standard of The Third Connecticut Regiment of 1775
White-Field "An Appeal to Heaven" Standard
"Nor did I see any colours to their regiments...," British Lieutenant Clarke

No original flag of the battle of Bunker's Hill has survived, although there are postwar descriptions of three flags reportedly flown there. Two of the three are versions of the New England pine tree ensign. The third was the scarlet standard of the Third Connecticut Regiment of 1775, which had the motto "Qui Transtulet Sustinet" on one side and "An Appeal to Heaven" on the other. Further, there is a possibility of a fourth flag which had a white field bearing only the motto "An Appeal to Heaven."

Offsetting the above reports is a recent in-depth study by a committee of flag historians who concluded that probably no flag was flown by the Americans on the hill. Supporting their conclusion is the eye witness account of a British lieutenant who wrote that there was none. And yet we find a red-field New England ensign with a white canton, bearing only a pine tree, prominently pictured in John Trumbull's post-war (1785-6) painting of the Battle of Bunker's Hill and Trumbull was also an eyewitness. The red ensign is the foremost of a pair of large (approximately five-by-seven feet) colors being held aloft in the midst of the Americans in the Breed's Hill redoubt. The second color of the pair has a yellow or gold field with no distinguishable device. There is the bare outline of a third color in the background.

Trumbull was the adjutant of a Connecticut regiment stationed at Roxbury about three miles across the bay from Bunker's Hill. He would have witnessed the battle and talked to participants. Trumbull served with the American forces from May 1775 to Spring 1777 including assignments as aide-to-camp to Washington and chief-of-staff to Gates. He was the son of Connecticut Governor Trumbull and his brother was Commissary-General of the Army at Boston. Trumbull was the leading documentary artist of the Revolution. He personally knew and sketched many of its leaders, was a member of the Cincinnati, visited the battlefields, and painted his great "National History" series of Revolutionary battles and events at the urging of Benjamin West and Thomas Jefferson.

Continental Congress Gold Medal awarded to George Washington for victory at Boston in 1776

Although Trumbull's paintings do not have the exact documentary quality of a photograph, and reflect some artistic license to allow for dramatic effect and the inclusion of the principal participants, his paintings do show meticulous attention to technical details, such as uniforms and accoutrements. Therefore, it seems that Trumbull must have been quite sure of the flag's presence at Bunker's Hill to have painted it so prominently and definitively with a red-field New England pine-tree ensign. Further, the ensign is of a color and type that might have been carried by the Massachusetts forces involved. Trumbull, however, may have added the flag for dramatic effect. It is known that he did place stars-and-stripes in some of his postwar paintings of battles fought before that flag was adopted.

Another version of the New England pine tree ensign reportedly flown at Bunker's Hill was described to Lossing, about 1848-50, by "an intelligent old lady (Mrs. Manning)" whom he saw "between the Brandywine and Kennet (sic) Square." Lossing is not specific as to exactly what was said by Mrs. Manning, but it would appear she said her father told her he was in the Breed's Hill redoubt and helped hoist a blue-field New England ensign with a white canton bearing a red cross with a pine tree in one corner of the cross. Lossing compares her description to a Colonial-era New England ensign in an "old Dutch work" at the New York Historical Society, which was the same design except for a quartered globe instead of a pine tree in the corner of the cross.

An important point is that both the Trum-

94

bull and the Lossing accounts agree that a New England pine-tree ensign was in the forward redoubt on Breed's Hill. This is reasonable because the majority of the troops in the redoubt and their commander, Colonel Samuel Prescott, were from Massachusetts and would have favored the pine-tree ensign. The red-field New England ensign, with a white canton bearing a red cross and quartered globe or pine tree, was used throughout the Colonial era. Blue field and green field versions are also recorded. The Puritans objected to the presence of the "idolatross" cross, and Governor Endicott, in 1636, created a furor by publicly cutting it out of the ensign. It would seem a likely thing for the Massachusetts revolutionary troops to delete the cross. In the opinion of the author, Trumbull's red-field pine-tree ensign has more basis for acceptance than Lossing's blue-field ensign.

A third flag, reportedly carried at Bunker's Hill was described by Botta in his "History of the American Revolution," and is referenced by both Lossing (1850) and Preble (1880). Botta wrote that in an attempt to rally the retreating troops, Dr. Joseph Warren, president of the Massachusetts Provincial Congress, reminded them of the mottos inscribed on "their ensigns," "An Appeal to Heaven," and, "Qui Transtulet Sustinet." Warren joined the troops in the Breed's Hill redoubt and was killed as the Americans retreated. Lossing discounts Botta's statement. Preble merely reports it without comment. However, both Lossing and Preble agree that a flag with the above mottos "recently sent" to General Putnam was displayed on July 18, 1775 at the American encampment at Prospect Hill, outside Boston. This would have been one month after the battle. But whether the flag arrived before or after the battle is not known. Preble states that the flag, which was "scarlet", was the standard of the Third Connecticut Regiment. He gives as references, Bancroft,

Frothingham and Greenwood. The Connecticut General Assembly, in May 1775, had specified colors for the standards of its six regiments with that of the Third to be scarlet.

Putnam was commander of the Third Connecticut Regiment from May 1, 1775 to June 19, 1775. He was in the thick of the battle of Bunker Hill where he urged troops forward from the Neck and with strong language tried to rally those retreating. Connecticut, New Hampshire and Massachusetts men manned the American left flank.

Preble also said "tradition states" a flag was hoisted at the Breed's Hill redoubt and that the British were puzzled "to read by their glasses its motto." Further, he mentions that a flag said to have been at Bunker Hill was at a patriotic celebration in 1825, but gives no reference.

Preble quotes from the diary of a Bunker Hill participant, Lieutenant Paul Lunt of Captain Ezra Lunt's company of sixty men. Lunt recorded that his company marched from Newburyport on May 10, 1775, arrived in Cambridge on May 12, entrenched on a hill (Breed's) beyond Bunker Hill on June 16, engaged the regulars who drove us off the hill on June 17, and that on July 18, upon Prospect Hill "our standard was presented in the midst of the regiments," with this inscription upon it, "An Appeal to Heaven."

A black-and-white engraving of Major-General Charles Lee, published by C. Shepherd, London, 31 October, 1775, pictures in the background a white flag bearing only the motto "An Appeal to Heaven." A copy of the engraving is in the Library of Congress. Lee arrived at Boston (Cambridge) with Washington on July 2, 1775, shortly after the Bunker Hill battle. Considering that Lee was appointed a Major General in June 1775, and that the above engraving probably reflected events at Boston, it is possible such a flag was at Bunker Hill.

In summary, the flags reportedly flown by the American forces at Bunker Hill included:

— A red-field New England pine-tree ensign (no cross)—Trumbull
— A blue-field New England pine-tree ensign (with cross)—Lossing
— The scarlet-field standard of the III Connecticut Regiment of 1775—Preble
— A white field standard with only the motto ''An Appeal to Heaven''—Preble

The question of whether the flag at Bunker Hill was blue or red, was examined quite thoroughly by a committee of flag historians in recent years. Their findings are set forth in an article by Dr. Emmet V. Mittlebeeler (with Dorothy Claybourne), ''What Flag Flew at Bunker Hill?'' published in ''The Flag Bulletin,'' XVII:2 (March—April 1978). The authors, after checking some twenty references, conclude that, probably, no flag was flown by the Americans but if one had been used it would most likely have been red. The most important of the references listed is an account published in London in 1775 by a British Marine Lieutenant, John Clarke, who took part in the battle. Clarke wrote that the Americans were not uniformly clothed ''nor did I see any colours to their regiments (on) the day of action . . .''

STANDARD OF A NEWBURYPORT COMPANY
(Plate 26)

According to Admiral Preble, one of the Revolutionary flags exhibited at Independence Hall in 1876 belonged to a ''Newburyport Company.'' The present whereabouts of the flag is unknown, although a search for it is now under way. Preble describes and illustrates the standard as a green silk flag with a white canton, on which is painted a green pine-tree centered in a blue field, surrounded by a chain circle of thirteen links—each link grasped by a

mailed hand coming out of a cloud. The size is not stated, but two and one-half feet square would seem reasonable.

The above flag is quite similar to one carried by a Colonial-era Newburyport militia company, commanded by Captain Thomas Noyes. A flag for the company was ordered from England on May 31, 1684 by Nathaniel Saltonstall of the Council of the Colonies. It had a green field with a white canton containing St. George's Red Cross. Replacing St. George's cross with a pine tree and union device would have been in keeping with similar flag modifications by the rebellious colonists. Possibly, the flag exhibited in 1876 originally belonged to the Colonial-era Newburyport Company and was modified and carried during the Revolution. For instance, the still surviving flag of the Colonial-era Three County Troop (two and one-half feet square) was carried at Concord by the Bedford Minute Men.

The chain link circle motif also appears on one of the Second New Hampshire regimental colors. The circle of thirteen chain links originated with Franklin and was used on Continental paper currency. The pine tree is a typical New England symbol. The device of a mailed hand (with a sword, in this case) coming out of a cloud is found on the above flag of the Bedford Minute Men. The Headman Color, one of the regimental standards listed in the military stores of American Major Jonathan Gostelowe in 1778, and now at the Smithsonian, has thirteen hands supporting a Liberty Pole or ''Pillow''. Another flag is described in the above Gostelowe Return as having ''an arm in armour with a drawn sword in its hand and Thirteen drawn swords Linked Together''. From the above, it can be seen that the Newburyport Company flag exhibited in 1876 is representative of American Revolutionary flags.

FORSTER COLORS MASSACHUSETTS

An intact red-field color with a striped canton and a fragment of a second color consisting of the striped-canton, only, were handed down in the family of Major Israel Forster of Manchester, Massachusetts.

The intact surviving flag appears to be the colors of a division (or "grand subdivision") of an American regiment. Family tradition says the flag was captured from the British during the Concord raid on May 19, 1775, and that the British union was replaced by the stripes. The color is now at the Flag Research Center, Massachusetts.

The field is scarlet with the only embellishment being six stubby white stripes in the first canton next to the staff which form thirteen red and white stripes. The scarlet field appears to be made up of two or, possibly, four widths of cloth, horizontally seamed

Preble's 1876 sketch of the Canton of the Standard of a Newburyport Massachusetts Company

A red color and the canton fragment of a white color that descended in the family of Major Israel Forster, Manchester, Massachusetts

(two of the "seams" might actually be folds). A pair of tassels are suspended by cords from the tip. There is no fringe. The hoist is sleeved rather than grommeted judging by a photograph. The dimensional ratio of the fly to the hoist is approximately 1.08. The type of material and actual dimensions are not known to the author. The white stripes appear to be pieces of cloth sewn directly on the field.

There is also extant the remnant of a white silk standard or division color with a striped

canton which was found in the house of Revolutionary War Major Israel Forster in Manchester. It is now at the Essex Institute, which kindly furnished a photograph and available information.

The remnant measures 11½ (hoist) by 14 (fly) inches and appears to be of white silk with seven stripes of blue cloth, approximately ⅞ inches wide, applied to form the thirteen stripes. The striped canton occupies almost the entire remnant. A narrow strip of the field remains on both sides of the canton.

Color of the Bucks of America

BUCKS OF AMERICA

There is a handsome painted silk color at The Massachusetts Historical Society, Boston, that is possibly of Revolutionary origin. Apparently, nothing of the flag's history or of the military unit to which it belonged has been found in contemporary records.

Davis described and illustrated the flag in 1907. He said the field is "a shade of buff, the union a faded blue, the stars were once gilded." The painted central device shows a brown-colored running deer and a pine tree of "blue-green shaded with brown." There are two scrolls, one above the tree with the initials, "J.H." and "G.W.," and one below with "BUCKS OF AMERICA." The scrolls, according to Davis, are dark robin's-egg blue shaded with dark green. The letters are gilded.

The flag measures about 41 (hoist) by 62 (fly) inches and is intact. The thirteen stars in the union are five-pointed; nine stars are encircling four. There appears to be a sleeve for the staff. The canton union is 18½ x 20½ inches.

The author has not been able to obtain any primary source information on the flag. Davis said the historian, Nell, in "*Colored Patriots of the Revolution*" claimed the flag was given to a unit of black men known as The Bucks of America at the close of the Revolution by Governor Hancock. However, Nell gives no reference. He has been repeatedly quoted but without a primary reference. It is odd that nothing of the history of such an important flag is recorded. There were many black men who served during the Revolution according to observations and records.

An April 1, 1976 letter from the Massachusetts Historical Society gives the color of the stars as silver and the device over the stag as blue.

—11—

New Hampshire

NEW HAMPSHIRE STATE SEAL

New Hampshire adopted its state seal on February 11, 1785, based on a design submitted in November 1784. The seal presents a shoreside scene, the principal elements of which are a rising sun, a ship on the stocks with "American banners" flying from the masts, and the inscription "Sigillum Republicae Neo Hantoniensis". On December 28, 1792, it was enacted that each regiment was to have one standard bearing the device of the arms of the United States and one suit of regimental colors bearing the arms of the State.

SECOND NEW HAMPSHIRE REGIMENT OF 1777
(Plates 30, 31)

Two of the finest surviving colors are those identified with the 2nd New Hampshire Continental Regiment of 1777. They are in the collection of the New Hampshire Historical Society and were purchased in 1912 by Mr. Edward Tuck from Colonel George W. Rogers of Wykeham, Sussex—a descendant of Lieutenant-Colonel John Hill, acting commander of the Ninth Regiment of Foot of Burgoyne's Army.

Traditionally, Colonel Hill's regiment captured the colors near Fort Anne, New York on July 8, 1777. Colonel Hill shipped the colors to England or carried them back in his personal baggage. He also secreted out the colors of his Ninth Regiment, rather than surrender them at Saratoga. The Ninth's regimental color is now at Sandhurst.

The recorded history of the colors begins in 1907 when they were pictured in Gherardi Davis' book. For Davis to have found the flags would seem to have required some earlier record of them. Perhaps Davis heard of Lt. Digby's journal which records the capture of a flag by the Ninth at Fort Anne.

The two colors are of silk and in well preserved condition. They are sleeved to staffs which have a style of spearhead illustrated by Davis as being of British design. Probably the staffs are not the originals. These may not have been carried back to England along with the silk colors in Colonel Hill's baggage, so that the colors would have been mounted on English staffs when they reached England.

Canton of the Blue Standard

Symbol of the Blue Standard

Each flag measures five (hoist) by five and one-half (fly) feet and has a relatively small inset canton (12 x 12 inches) with the crosses of the British Union.

The blue color is made up of two pieces of silk, seamed horizontally. The canton is formed of silk strips—a red, gold-edged St. George's cross, and a gold red-edged St. Andrew's cross. There is a lightweight one-inch gold fringe. The painted device measures in its extreme dimensions about 12 by 12 inches and is centered in the field. The device is a red shield edged with a gold vine shadowed in black. On the shield, in scroll-like gold letters, appears the following:

NH

$2^{d}_{..}$

REG^{t}.

Above the shield is a gold waviform scroll curving downward with the motto in black letters "THE GLORY NOT THE PREY."

The second color is light buff, with its field made up of two pieces of silk, seamed horizontally. The canton is made up of four red and four blue silk triangles, so as to form the outlines of the crosses of the British Union against the buff silk of the field. The central device is painted in gold with light brown shadowing and black lettering. There is an outer circle of thirteen circular chain links. Each link has the abbreviated name of one of the states. "N. HAMP   is at the top (or twelve o'clock) position; then, clockwise, "MASSACH-, CONNECT-, R. ISLAND, N. YORK, N. JERSEY, PENNSYLV-, DELAWARE, MARYLAND, VIRGINIA, N. CAROL-., S. CAROL-., GEORGIA." Inside the circle is a radiating sun with the motto: "WE ARE ONE." Rays from the sun touch each link.

Symbol of the Buff Color

Canton of the Buff Color

The design of thirteen joined chain links, credited to Benjamin Franklin, appears as the seal on the one-sixth of a dollar Continental bill, issue of February 17, 1776.

The Second New Hampshire Regiment of 1775 served from May to December 1775. It was succeeded by the 8th Continental Regiment of 1776 and by the 2nd New Hampshire Continental Regiment of 1777. Colonel Enoch Poor was commander of the 2nd, from May 1775 to February 1777, when he was promoted to Brigadier General. Poor was succeeded by Colonel Nathan Hale (no relation to Nathan Hale of Connecticut) who was commander until September 1780.

The Second New Hampshire Regiment of 1777 fought in the battles of Hubbardstown, Bemis Heights (Saratoga), the battles around Philadelphia, Monmouth, and in Sullivan's 1778-9 expedition against the Indian and Tory raiders of the Susquehanna Valley and Western New York. The Regiment was also at Valley Forge.

There is disagreement between the above traditional history of the capture of the 2nd's colors and eyewitness accounts by participants of the Burgoyne invasion. In brief, the 2nd New Hampshire Regiment was not at the battle of Fort Anne. The 2nd was at the battle of Hubbardstown, fought the prior day, but thirty-five miles away. At Hubbardstown, the rearguard of St. Clair's American army was defeated. Casualties were heavy and a large number captured, including Colonel Hale commander of the 2nd and about 140 of his men. Although Lt. Colonel Hill and a part of his regiment were at the Fort Anne battle, the light infantry flank companies of Hill's Ninth were at Hubbardstown and could have taken the colors of Hale's regiment.

There is a journal by a Lt. Digby of Burgoyne's army that tells of an American flag being captured at Fort Anne, but Digby's description of the flag does not fit either of the 2nd's colors.

A Sergeant Lamb of the 9th Regiment was in the thick of the Fort Anne battle and was left to tend the badly wounded. They stayed for two weeks in a woodcutter's cabin and could hear the Americans all around felling trees across streams and trails but were not attacked. Lamb wrote his memoirs in the early 1800's. He said nothing about any flags being captured.

The above points are discussed further in the notes.

JOHN STARK'S NEW HAMPSHIRE MILITIA BRIGADE (Plate 32)

"Flag of the Green Mountain Boys"

A fragment of the original standard is at the Bennington Historical Society, donated in the 1920's or 30's by the great-great-granddaughter of General John Stark. Its recorded history begins on August 15, 1877, when the Bennington Daily Banner announced it would be displayed.

The fragment consists of a 17 x 19 inch blue silk canton with remnants of green silk along its right hand edge. The canton has thirteen white, five-pointed stars, painted and arranged in a rough approximation of the crosses of the British Union. Apparently, the flag had a green silk field and measured, overall, at least 34 (hoist) by 38 (fly) inches, more likely, closer to 60 by 66 inches.

The donor of the flag wrote: "My mother . . . repeatedly told me that from time to time small pieces were cut from the float and given to different descendants of General Stark, and I have seen my aunt cut off such pieces." This was common practice with these early flags. The Fort McHenry flag lost quite a bit of its area to such requests. At the close of the Revolution, some standards were cut up to provide survivors with a souvenir piece. One of the pieces of Stark's flag was in the collection of the Pennsylvania Society of Sons of the Revolution until 1976 when it was donated to the Bennington Museum. Hopefully, other pieces will be returned by those still holding them.

Of the original flag, General Stark's granddaughter said in 1877: "the old man cherished this relic throughout his life." She said Stark told his children that the flag had been in the thick of the battle of Bennington, August 16, 1777. This indicates that the flag was either Stark's personal command standard or the standard of one of his units at Bennington, possibly of the New Hampshire Militia Brigade he commanded.

Stark was the first and only commander of the First New Hampshire Regiment of 1775; holding this command from April 23, 1775 to December 1775. In January, 1776 he was appointed commander of the Fifth Continental Regiment of 1776; then was commander of the First New Hampshire Regiment of 1777, from November 8, 1776 to March 23, 1777, before retiring in protest over promotion policies of the Continental Congress.

The New Hampshire Assembly called upon Stark to accept a commission as brigadier-general of the state militia and to take to the field again against Burgoyne. In the summer of 1777, Burgoyne's army had swept down Lake Champlain and into New York. Lossing wrote that the militia flocked to the "standard," for Stark was their favorite commander.

On August 11, 1777, Burgoyne dispatched a force of Hessians with some Tories and Indians under Colonel Baume to capture a supply dump and horses at Bennington. The Hessian force was wiped out and the relief column under Breymann driven back by Stark's brigade.

Colonel Seth Warner's Continental Regiment, made up of men from Northern New York and the Hampshire Grants (the Green Mountain Boys), was also in the thick of the battle, although not part of Stark's Brigade.

Congress appointed Stark a brigadier-general in the Continental Army after his Bennington victory and he and his men fought through the Saratoga campaign. Subsequently, he was promoted to Major-General, served at the Battle of Rhode Island in 1778 and in New Jersey in 1780. In 1781 he was in command of the entire Northern Army.

BENNINGTON STARS AND STRIPES

The original is at the Bennington Historical Museum. Its recorded history begins about 1928. The flag was donated to the Museum in the 1920s. Traditionally, it had been carried at the battle of Bennington on August 16, 1777, then handed down through the family of the flag bearer.

The flag was described in recent years by a textile historian and judged to date from the period of the Centennial of 1876. It measures five and one-half (hoist) by ten (fly) feet and has seven white and six red stripes. The blue canton is square and extends across nine stripes. The number "76" is placed at the bottom of the canton and is surmounted by a semicircle of eleven seven-pointed stars with two stars in the upper corners. It is a very handsome version of the stars and stripes.

Although family tradition claims the flag was "carried" at Bennington, the flag is too large, long, and heavy to have been carried on a staff and was probably flown from a flagpole.

As outlined on the preceding pages, Bennington was fought and won by a New Hampshire State Militia Brigade commanded by the New Hampshire State Militia General, John Stark. Stark refused to join his brigade to Schuyler's Northern Continental Army despite orders to do so. It is doubtful, in the author's opinion, that Stark would have carried the stars and stripes of the Continental Congress at Bennington.

—12—

New Jersey

NEW JERSEY STATE SEAL

New Jersey adopted its seal on October 3, 1776, and appointed Francis Hopkinson to employ "proper persons at Philadelphia" to prepare the seal itself. The arms are "three plows in an escutcheon" flanked by the Goddesses Liberty and Ceres with a horse's head at the crest. No record has been found of the use of these arms on any Revolutionary standard. The seal was placed on State currency issued in 1781 and 1786.

MONMOUTH COLOR *(Plate 34)*

There is an original gold silk color with a British union canton in the collection of the Monmouth County Historical Association. The color was presented to the Association many years ago by Mrs. Marguerite Potter Bixler a descendant of Captain William Wilson of the First Pennsylvania Regiment. Traditionally, the color was captured by Captain Wilson at Monmouth, Sunday, 28 June 1778. It was stained with the blood of Lt. Col. Monckton, 45th Regiment, Royal Grenadiers, who was killed leading his regiment. However, certain features of the flag indicate it may actually be American rather than British—possibly, a division color of the First Pennsylvania Regiment. The presence of the British union canton, frequently used on American colors in the early years of the war, could have led to the tradition that the color was British. If the color is American, it is of even greater historical interest.

The recorded history of the color starts with "an 1874 account in the *American Historical Review*" that the flag had been seen at the Bellefonte, Pennsylvania home of Captain William Wilson Potter, grandson of Captain Wilson, and that it was stained and torn along its staff edge.

The flag now measures 56 (hoist) by 61 (fly) inches. The donor said pieces had been lost to souvenir hunters. The field is made up of four horizontally-seamed widths of gold silk. The two still intact inner widths are fifteen inches wide (including selvage edges of ¼ inch) indicating that the hoist was sixty inches originally. There is a three inch sleeve for the staff.

Some authorities believe the flag to be American, rather than British, for the following reasons:

There is no emblem or unit designation on the field. American divisional colors were generally plain but a British color would have had both a symbol and unit designation.

The canton measures 21 by 20 inches and is inset. An officially made British color would not have an inset canton, although a number of surviving American colors do. The red and white crosses and blue field of the canton are formed of red silk (figured damask), blue silk (watered or moire effect), and white silk. The use of figured silk, the relative proportions of the crosses, and the very wide white edging to Saint George's cross are not correct for an official British flag.

STANDARD OF A NEW JERSEY REGIMENT OF MAXWELL'S BRIGADE—1779 *(Plate 8)*

Among the du Simitiere papers at the Historical Society of Pennsylvania is a water-color drawing by Major John Ross of New Jersey of the "Order of March" and the "Order of Battle" of General John Sullivan's army on July 30, 1779. It depicts the expedition against the Indian and Tory forces in Western Pennsylvania and New York by Sullivan's army. The watercolor drawing illustrates in block form the relative formation of the regiments, brigades, flankers, light troops, cannon, and packhorses.

The units are designated as General Hand's Light Corps (Pa.), and General Maxwell's, Poor's, and Clinton's Brigades.

General Maxwell's Brigade consisted of the 1st, 2nd, 3rd and 5th New Jersey Regiments of 1777. In Ross' Order of Battle drawing, Maxwell's Brigade is shown schematically as a block of four regiments in line abreast with a single regimental standard at the midpoint, as are also Poor's and Clinton's Brigades. This method of designating a brigade was also used by Brig. Gen. Weedon in his map of the Battle of Brandywine. Ross' tiny standard measures $8/32$ by $9/32$ inches. It has a solid light blue field and a white canton with three rows of dots depicting stars. In the center of the field is a horizontal S—shaped dark blue or black scroll. The illustration scales up the tiny flag and assumes that the dots in the canton are thirteen six-pointed stars. It appears that the standard is representative of those carried by one or more of the four regiments.

Poor's Brigade consisted of the 1st, 2nd, and 3rd New Hampshire Regiments of 1777 and the 6th Massachusetts Regiment. The standard posted at the center of Poor's Brigade is identical to Maxwell's, but the field is of light green. Clinton's Brigade, consisting of the 2nd, 3rd, 4th and 5th New York Regiments of 1777, is posted in the center and carries one standard, a stars and stripes with seven red and six white stripes and thirteen dots (stars) in three rows on a white canton.

On the basis of Ross' eyewitness drawing, it can be said that by 1779 a Continental Army was carrying a stars and stripes standard into battle. Whether the above brigades displayed only the one standard as shown, or that Ross was indicating that regimental colors were unfurled when in battle formation, is not definitely known, although the latter seems more likely.

—13—

New York

NEW YORK STATE SEAL

New York adopted a seal in 1777 or early 1778 designed by Morris, Jay, and Hobart which depicts on a shield a river (the Hudson), mountains (the Highlands), and a rising, radiant sun. Below the shield is a scroll and motto, "EXCELSIOR." At the crest is the upper part of the globe of the earth surmounted by an eagle. The Goddess of Liberty holding a Liberty pole with cap and spurning a crown at her feet is the righthand Supporter and the Goddess of Justice is the shield's lefthand Supporter. The reverse of the seal depicts a huge rock rising from the sea with the motto, "FRUSTRA, 1777."

The arms of New York appear on the standard of the 3rd New York Regiment; also on a military commission issued by Governor Geo. Clinton on June 12, 1778; and as a 1785 painting over Governor Clinton's pew in St. Paul's church in New York City.

LONG ISLAND FLAG—AUGUST 1776
WHITE PLAINS FLAG—OCTOBER 1776

No original has survived.

There is an account by a Hessian officer of the capture of a flag, apparently near Flatbush, upon the defeat of the American Army at the battle of Long Island, August 26, 1776. According to Colonel van Heeringen, "the captured flag, which is made of red damask, with the motto, 'LIBERTY' appeared with sixty men before Rall's regiment. They had all shouldered their guns upside down, and had their hats under their arms. They fell on their knees and begged piteously for their lives." Another Hessian account tells of the same incident but speaks of "fifty men" and tells of a quarrel over possession of the flag between Colonel Rall and General von Merbach. Adjutant General Baurmeister reported to his superior in Germany that

American Flag. "From an old English engraving of the Battle of White Plains, October 28, 1776"

eleven "LIBERTY" flags were captured at Long Island.

Preble writes of the above incident and states that he had an "undated engraving of what purports to be the battle of White Plains, but which seems to represent the scene above described, the Americans carrying a flag of which the annexed is a facsimile." Preble's drawing shows a flag with a sword crossed by a liberty pole with cap and topped with the motto: "Liberty or Death" (the "a" is reversed). It is titled "American Flag, from an Old Engraving of the Battle of White Plains, October 28, 1776."

Preble's flag appears in the National Geographic (September 1934) as a "White Plains" flag and that "American Troops surrendered this flag to Hessian troops at the battle of Long Island, August 26, 1776."

It appears to the author that the red damask flag with the motto "LIBERTY" captured at Long Island was an entirely different flag from the one with the sword, liberty pole and cap and its motto, which was captured at White Plains.

Probably the two flags should be described as follows:

— *Long Island—August 26, 1776*
Red Damask with "LIBERTY" motto (see chapter on "Liberty" flags)

— *White Plains—October 28, 1776*
Color—not specified. Emblem—sword crossed with Liberty pole topped with cap. Motto—"Liberty or Death"

The battle of White Plains was followed by the British and Hessian capture of Fort Washington on November 16, 1776, in which Colonel Rall took part. The capture of Fort Lee followed, on November 26. Washington then retreated down through New Jersey to the west bank of the Delaware. On December 25-26, Washington recrossed the Delaware and defeated the Hessians at Trenton. Colonel Rall was mortally wounded, his command wiped out, 900 Hessians captured, and his colors taken.

Liberty Flag captured at the Battle of Long Island, August 26, 1776

STANDARD of the FIRST NEW YORK REGIMENT OF 1777 (Possibly)

No original has survived. There is a regimental standard that might be associated with this regiment described in Major Jonathan Gostelowe's Return of August 1778, as standard number 13, which has a device of "thirteen darts" or arrows with the motto "United We Stand".

Three powder horns, drawings of which are in the New York Historical Society, are decorated with a splay of thirteen arrows bordered by a laurel vine with the respective motto "XIII U.S." (John DeWandeler's horn), "XIII Unit State" (Rome, N.Y.), and "UNITED . WE . STAND . DIVIDED .

WE . FALL'' (horn of Harmon Stebens of Captain John Graham's Company). John Graham is listed in Heitman as a captain in the First New York Regiment.

The First New York Regiment of 1777 was commanded by Colonel Goose Van Shaik, from its formation in November 1776 to its deactivation in November 1783. The regiment would have taken part in the battles of Burgoyne's invasion and was probably at Yorktown. The illustration of this standard is based on Gostelowe's description and on the above powder horns.

The suggested association of the above standard, powderhorns, and regiment is definitely theoretical, only, but is worth reporting and could inspire further research.

STANDARD OF THE THIRD NEW YORK REGT. OF 1777
(Plate 32)

The original 1778-9 standard of this regiment is at the Albany Institute of History and Art. It was donated about 1900 by Mrs. Catherine Gansevoort Lansing, a descendant of Colonel Peter Gansevoort, commander of the Third New York Regiment of 1777, from November 1776 to January 1781.

The recorded history of the standard starts with Preble in 1880 who stated: ''... In 1864 General Gansevoort wrote under his own hand a declaration that the flag was borne at the surrender of Yorktown in 1781...''. General Gansevoort was the grandson of Colonel Peter Gansevoort of the Revolution who died in 1812. Preble goes on to state that ''Mrs. Abraham Lansing of Albany'' was the owner of the flag when it was unfurled before 50,000 people at the centennial celebration at Oriskany in 1877. Near Oriskany, on 6 August, 1777, the Tryon County Militia under Herkimer, fought a drawn battle with a mixed British force in attempting to relieve Gansevoort besieged in Fort Stanwix.

The standard is of dark blue silk and is framed with its edges folded so as to reduce its size. The ''frame sight size'' is 53 by 65 inches. Preble wrote that the standard was about seven feet square overall and that the painted emblem of the arms or seal of New York covers a space four feet five inches wide by three feet five inches high, and that the two figures of women (''Justice'' blind folded with a sword and scales and ''Liberty'' with a liberty pole and cap) are each two feet two and one-half inches high. The women flank a central circular seal which pictures a rising sun with human face denoting America. An elaborate scroll encircles the seal; an eagle stands on a globe on top of the rising sun seal; and a vinelike scroll extends across the top of the emblem. There is a lower scroll upon which the figures stand with the motto ''EXCELSIOR''.

A photograph furnished by the Albany Institute shows the flag to be fringed the same shade as the field. The flag is made of three horizontally seamed widths of silk. Assuming a selvage width of 28½ inches, the hoist of this flag would be seven feet. Scaling of the photograph also verifies Preble's dimensions for the emblem and its figures. This is the largest regimental standard known to the author.

The painted central emblem of the Gansevoort Third Regiment standard was described in 1907 by Gherardi Davis, of the New York Society of Sons of the Revolution, as follows; ''The coloring of the arms is as in the present State Arms, except that the wreath is red and white, not blue and gold. The supporters, who are in costumes of the second half of the eighteenth century, have dresses of cloth of gold, red mantles and sandals, and blue sashes across their bodies. The scroll work is yellow-brown, shaded brown.'' (The flag is illustrated in color in Avery's History, 1909.) ''The flag was made in 1778 or 1779, is about six feet square, and is of dark blue silk. The fringe is also blue...'' The photograph in Davis' book shows the flag in the same frame and with edges folded as in the Albany Institute photograph furnished to the author.

Original Standard of the 3rd New York Regiment of 1777 (edges folded under)

Therefore, Davis' statement that the flag is "about six feet square" was probably an approximation; whereas, Preble's 1880 statement of "about seven feet square" was made before the flag was folded into its frame. Davis says the standard is the handsomest regimental color of the Revolution.

Mrs. Lansing believed the flag was made in 1778 or 1779, because the Regiment had to improvise a garrison flag at Fort Stanwix in 1777. Preble wrote that the colonels of the three New York regiments (there were actually four) petitioned the New York Committee of Safety as early as November 30, 1776 to be furnished with colors. When Gansevoort's Regiment was besieged within Fort Stanwix during August 1777, a flag of red, white and blue stripes was improvised and hoisted. Lt. Col. Marinus Willett's account as quoted by Spargo does not speak of a canton.

Knight quotes an invoice dated June 17, 1776 for material "for Colours for the Regi-

ments in the New York Line" which included "19 yards of blue Italian silk." This would be enough for three flags about the size of Gansevoort's Third Regimental standard.

There was a Third New York Regiment of 1775 (May 1775—March 1776, Colonel James Clinton), a Third of 1776 (March to November 1776, Colonel Rudolphus Ritzema), and the Third of 1777 (November 1776 to January 1781, Colonel Peter Gansevoort). In 1781, the remaining men of the Third were taken into the Second New York Regiment commanded by Colonel Philip Van Cortland, from November 1776 to November 1783. Gansevoort had been the commander of the Second of 1776 from August to November 1776. The men of the Third would have had to have taken their standard with them when they were incorporated into the Second in January 1781 to have carried the standard at Yorktown in October 1781.

North Carolina

NORTH CAROLINA STATE SEAL

Regarding this seal, Preble states the following: "In the original seal, on a white or silver field, are represented the Goddess Liberty on the right, and Ceres, the Goddess of Corn and of Harvests, on the left. In the right hand of the former is a scroll representing the Declaration of Independence, and the left supports a wand, surmounted by the cap of liberty. Ceres has in her right hand three heads or ears of wheat, and in her left the cornucopia or horn of plenty, filled with the products of the earth. In the background are mountains. Around the outer circle, starting from a star on the top, is the legend, 'GREAT SEAL OF THE STATE OF NORTH CAROLINA'."

EARLY NORTH CAROLINA FLAGS

The first flag of North Carolina appeared in June 1775. It was white and bore a hornet's nest and the date May 20, 1775. A little later, the people of Bladen and Brunswick Counties carried a flag which featured an emblem with a rattlesnake coiled at the root of a pine tree.

GUILFORD COURTHOUSE STARS AND STRIPES OR NORTH CAROLINA MILITIA FLAG *(Plate 33)*

A major fragment of the original standard is at the North Carolina Museum of History in Raleigh. Portions are missing and the edges are uneven. It measures thirty-one inches on the hoist (forty-two inches at the inner edge) by eight feet four inches on the fly. There are six blue cotton stripes and six red worsted stripes, alternating from the top, blue-red-blue-red, etc., with the remnant of two additional stripes (same original cloth and thread) at the bottom of the inner edge. The white

Beehive Flag of North Carolina

Flag of Bladen and Brunswick Counties, North Carolina

cotton canton is about twenty-five by seventy-three inches, with thirteen blue cotton, eight-pointed stars eight inches in diameter. These are arranged (from the top) 4-3-4, plus 2 paired and offset at the canton's outer edge. The inner edge has been cut off. The canton extends across the top eight stripes.

The *recorded* history of this flag begins in 1909 when it was presented to the Grand Masonic Lodge of North Carolina. It was transferred to the State in 1914. The standard is traced by family tradition to 1854 when it was delivered to the Mt. Energy Lodge, Granville County by Major Edward Bullock, who had received it from his father Micajah Bullock. Edward Bullock of Greenville County was 81 years old when he presented the flag. By family tradition, the flag had been brought back from "the battlefields of North and South Carolina about the close of the War of the Revolution". There is no evidence, written or otherwise, however, to link it to Guilford Courthouse; nor does the Bullock family tradition say anything about Guilford Courthouse.

There is disagreement as to the age of the flag. The use of cotton for the blue stripes, the canton and stars indicate to textile histo-

rians that it dates to the early Nineteenth Century. Also, at the bottom of the hoist edge are the stubs of two additional stripes of the same material and stitching as the full stripes; the placement of the stubs indicates that the flag had at least fourteen stripes, and probably fifteen originally. Further, there is the strong possibility that two additional stars had been originally present on the cutoff staff side of the canton for a balanced design of fifteen stars. The above factors, coupled with the flag's history, has led to the theory that the flag was originally a rare fifteen stars and stripes, or an even rarer sixteen stripe flag, dating possibly as early as 1795 and carried in the War of 1812. Other authorities disagree and point out that a Revolutionary-era drum at the Guilford Courthouse Museum has a painting of a flag with twenty-three stripes. If the 15-stripes, 15-stars theory is correct, the flag originally measured approximately three feet nine inches by twelve feet six inches.

With either the present (8′6″) or the above theoretical (12′6″) size, the standard would have been too long and heavy to have been carried by a flag bearer. It must have been suspended from a flag pole, or carried horizontally by two or more men as a processional or ceremonial display standard.

110

—15—

Pennsylvania

PENNSYLVANIA STATE SEAL

Pennsylvania appointed a committee to prepare seals on July 28, 1776. Members were Rittenhouse, Jacobs and Clymer. The resulting design, which was based primarily on the seal of the city of Philadelphia, consisted of an escutcheon bearing wheat sheafs, a ship and a plow with the motto "agriculture, commerce, husbandry." This seal was first placed on paper currency issued on April 10, 1777, and stayed in use at least to March 16, 1785. On March 2, 1809, the seal was "renewed" with the design to include the same elements as the old seal plus an olive branch, maize, a wreath and bald eagle. On the reverse side was the Goddess "Liberty" trampling a lion, the symbol of tyranny, with the motto "Both Can't Survive." Whether Liberty and the Lion were in the original seal or added in 1809 is not known. The Arms of Pennsylvania are the same as the "face of the seal" flanked by horses rampant, with a scroll in the eagle's beak and the motto "Virtue, Liberty and Independence."

No use of the seal or arms for the device of a Revolutionary standard is known. However, the standard of the 1ST PENNSYLVANIA REGIMENT OF 1775 does employ a hunter subduing a lion.

PENNSYLVANIA STATE NAVY

In July 1775 the Pennsylvania Provincial Assembly's Committee of Safety, of which Franklin was president, and George Ross and Robert Morris members, ordered a fleet of river gunboats of the galley type. A total of thirteen were quickly built, equipped and manned. The fleet eventually totaled forty-two vessels and 1400 crewmen.

In October 1775 the Committee adopted a Seal bearing a Cap of Liberty and the motto, "This is my right and I will defend it," and inscribed with "Pennsylvania,

111

Committee of Safety, 1775.'' The Committee's duties included military, naval, civil and executive matters.

Scharf and Wescott say without reference: ''. . . In Autumn, 1775, Philadelphia's floating-batteries used a white flag, tree in the field, motto, 'An Appeal to Heaven'. . .''. The author, while not claiming to have made a complete search, has not encountered any primary reference source for the above statement. Preble, p 227, also claims the Pennsylvania floating batteries carried the pine-tree flag in autumn of 1775; but, again, there is no reference cited. Possibly, he quoted Scharf and Westcott.

The first Continental Navy ships were outfitted in late 1775. According to the Day Book of a Philadelphia ship chandler, James Wharton, the ships ''Alfred,'' ''Columbus'' and ''Kitty'' were supplied with ''union'' flags, pendants and jacks. A surprisingly large number of flags were delivered, most being charged to the account of ''Committee of Congress,'' rather than to a specific ship. Included were a 13 stripe green and red ''union'' flag, a union jack of red, blue and white, and others (see Continental Navy). As pure hypothesis, it can be assumed that the Pennsylvania Navy officials were fully exposed to thirteen-stripe Union flags and could have adopted a version of the stripes as did the South Carolina Navy.

On May 8-9, 1776, the Pennsylvania State Navy aided by Continental ships repelled an attempt by the British 48-gun frigate, ''Roebuck'' and her sloop-of-war, ''Liverpool'' to penetrate the Delaware River defenses.

According to John W. Jackson in ''The Pennsylvania Navy, 1775-81,'' there is a receipt in the ''State Archives'' from a (Mrs.) Cornelia Bridges for ''£6/13s for making colors for the Floating Battery, Warren, and Bulldog, £2/3s for the former and £2/5s for the latter two.'' The receipt is dated May 25, 1776, which predates a payment to Betsy Ross for colors for the Pennsylvania Navy

(see below) by one year. Mrs. Bridges probably lived in Philadelphia.

The Provincial Assembly's Committee of Safety was responsible for navy matters. It can be hypothesized that Mrs. Bridges' colors were made to a design that was dropped when the Declaration of Independence was adopted. Otherwise, the letters from William Richards in August and October 1776 (see below) concerning the lack of a design for the flag would not have been necessary.

Captain William Richards wrote to the Pennsylvania Committee or Council of Safety, August 19, 1776, ''I hope you have agreed what sort of colors I am to have made for the galleys, etc., as they are much wanted''; and again on October 15, 1776, ''The commodore was with me this morning, and says the fleet has not any colors to hoist if they should be called on duty. It is not in my power to get them until there is a design fixed on to make the colors by.''

The first record noted by Preble of Pennsylvania State Navy Colors is in the minutes of the Navy Board, as follows: ''Present: William Bradford, Joseph Marsh, Joseph Blewer, Paul Cox. An order on William Webb to Elizabeth Ross for fourteen pounds, twelve shillings, and two pence, for making ship's colours, etc. put into William Richards store. £14.12.2.'' The date was May 29, 1777.

The Pennsylvania Navy and several Continental vessels were heavily engaged during the British invasion of Pennsylvania and the ensuing battle of the Delaware in September–November 1777. It was one of the most severe American naval engagements of the War. Following destruction of the forts at Mud Island and, eventually, Red Bank, the trapped Pennsylvania and Continental ships tried to sail upriver past the British guns at Philadelphia but were stopped by wind and tide. Most were burned, scuttled or captured. Despite the defeat, the Pennsylvania Navy and the river forts had served to prevent a direct British advance up the Delaware and delayed

Howe's supply ships for two critical months. There was also considerable damage inflicted on the British fleet, which included the loss of the 64-gun Augusta and 18-gun Merlin. Donop's force at Fort Mercer was also defeated.

Beyond the white flag with tree and motto, reportedly flown in autumn 1775, a description of the colors of the Pennsylvania Navy has not been found to the author's knowledge. Of course, Cornelia Bridges and Betsy Ross knew the design or designs as evidenced by the May 25, 1776 receipt, and the May 29, 1777 payment order. The author is confident that somewhere there must be a journal, letter, sketch, print, painting or receipt that would describe the flag.

Perhaps Benjamin Franklin indirectly provided a clue as to the colors of the Pennsylvania Navy and other State Navies in his oft-quoted October 9, 1778 letter to the Ambassador of the King of the Two Sicilies. In response to the Ambassador's inquiry, Franklin and Adams described the United States flag as having thirteen red, white and blue stripes with a small blue canton with thirteen white stars. Their joint letter goes on to say: "... Some of the States have vessels of war distinct from those of the United States. For example, the vessels of war of the State of Massachusetts Bay have sometimes a pine tree; and those of South Carolina a rattlesnake, in the middle of the 13 stripes; but the Flag of the United States, ordained by Congress, is the 13 stripes and 13 stars above described."

If Pennsylvania vessels of war had a distinct flag, Franklin would have probably said so. Eleven of the states had navies, but Franklin in 1778 said that only "some" had distinct colors and described only two. Therefore, it could be hypothesized that by 1778 or earlier, the Pennsylvania Navy was flying a version of the thirteen stripes or stars and stripes. Later, Franklin wrote to the President of the Continental Congress requesting descriptions of state navy ensigns.

PENNSYLVANIA STATE RIFLE REGIMENTS STANDARDS CAPTURED AT FT. WASHINGTON, N.Y., 1776

"2 Standards with a Rifleman on" were captured by the British at the surrender of Ft. Washington, August 27, 1776. Colonel Magaw of Pennsylvania was in command of Ft. Washington. There is also mention of Colonel Magaw's purple standard being captured.

STANDARD OF THE PHILADELPHIA LIGHT HORSE OF 1774-75 *(Plates 36, 37)*

The original standard and its lance, silver spearhead, and silver tassels are in the museum of the First Troop (now a unit of the Pennsylvania National Guard). The standard is the finest American Revolutionary flag still in existence and has complete documentation back to its origin in 1775. The original bills, dated September 1775, for designing and painting the flag are in the Troop's collection.

The yellow silk of the standard measures 33 (hoist) by 40 (fly) inches and is seamed at the horizontal midpoint. It has a metallic silver fringe, two inches in width. The present canton (9½ x 11½ inches) of thirteen alternate blue silk and silver painted stripes ¾ inches wide was applied over an original canton of the crosses of the British union (now faintly visible). In the center of the flag is a painted gold-bordered blue shield bearing in its center a golden knot from which radiates thirteen gold ribbon-like scrolls expressing the union. The head of a bay horse bearing a white star on his forehead appears as a crest to the shield. The supporters, one on each side of the shield, are the figures of "America," represented by an Indian holding a golden staff which is topped with a Liberty cap; and of "Fame," in the form of an angel with a staff in one hand and a golden trumpet in the other. Beneath the shield on

Drawing of the Standard of the Philadelphia Light Horse

114

a scroll is the motto "FOR THESE WE STRIVE". The extreme dimensions of the central device are 19 inches high by 23½ inches wide. Above the horse appear the intertwined embroidered letters "L H". Embroidered vines (laurel) border the three outer edges. Small thread-whipped eyelets are spaced at three and four-inch intervals, and a braided ¼ inch diameter cord is laced through the grommets. The staff has small metal eyelets to match the grommets.

The flag was presented to the Troop by its first commander, Captain Abraham Markoe, in 1775, and would have been carried at Trenton, Princeton, the Brandywine and Germantown. Captain Markoe resigned his commission late in 1775 in response to an edict of the King of Denmark forbidding his subjects to engage in the war.

Additional information on the Light Horse standard and on an eagle national standard of the 1790's is contained in the Notes.

STANDARD OF THE HANOVER ASSOCIATORS *(Plate 37)*

No original has survived.

Davis, in 1907, says that "this was a red flag with a hunter in buckskin and the motto 'LIBERTY OR DEATH'. As far as I have been able to ascertain, this flag no longer exists, but it is represented in colors in VOL. XIII (Second Series), Pennsylvania Archives. The authority for this print, I do not know."

The illustration depicts a crimson flag, bearing as a device a rifleman in green hunting shirt and buckskin leggings. He stands on guard with the motto, 'Liberty or Death' below on a yellow scroll.

The 1913 Flag Book of the Pennsylvania Society of Sons of the Revolution stated that: "The Hanover Associators (or Volunteers) originated at a meeting on June 4, 1774, of the inhabitants of Hanover, Lancas-ter (now York) County, Pennsylvania. Resolutions were there adopted: 'That in the event of Great Britain attempting to force unjust laws upon us by the strength of arms, our cause we leave to Heaven and our rifles.' The flag of the Hanover Rifleman was also adopted by the committee at the same time." No primary reference is quoted.

STANDARD OF THE WESTMORELAND BATTALION, PROCTOR'S BRIGADE OF 1775 *(Plate 38)* ALSO DESIGNATED THE 52ND INDEPENDENT BATTALION OF ASSOCIATORS

The original standard is at the William Penn Memorial Museum, Harrisburg.

The flag is described by Preble in 1880. The owner at that time was: "Mrs. Margaret C. Craig, daughter of General Craig [of Greensburg, Pa.], an officer of the Revolution, and now living in New Alexandria Pa.... The flag had been in Mrs. Craig's family for more than seventy years having been passed down to her father as the last surviving officer." Preble says that the flag was carried by "Colonel John Proctor's regiment all through the war and was at Trenton, Princeton, Ash Swamp, etc."

Davis described the flag in 1907 and says it was "now in the possession of Miss Jane M. Craig of New Alexandria, Pennsylvania.... The flag measures 6 feet 4 inches by 5 feet 10 inches, is of red silk, and has in the upper corner next the staff the English jack;... In the center of the flag is a coiled rattlesnake, its head directed toward the jack. Above the snake are the letters, I.B.W.C.P., and above that the monogram, J.P. These letters are said to mean 'John Proctor's 1st Battalion Westmoreland County Provincials'... Miss Craig very kindly had the flag photographed for me. In doing this she was assisted by Mr. Taylor, a direct descendant of Samuel Craig, the original color-bearer. The plate is from this photograph. The usual prints of this flag, it will be observed, are quite inaccurate."

The State of Pennsylvania acquired the flag in 1914. It is intact and in excellent condition.

John Proctor's Battalion was the 52nd on a list of fifty-three battalions of Associators existing in 1775.

The painted emblem with scrolls is quite large, measuring overall 36 inches high by 42 inches wide and appears on both sides. There is no fringe other than fraying on the outer edge. The flag is still intact, except for some small fragments of the emblem. The British Union is formed by employing white stripes and blue triangles of silk to outline a red St. George's cross and form a white St. Andrew's cross on a blue field. The canton is inset and measures about 20 inches high by 22 inches wide. The field displays a rattlesnake painted red, brown, white and blue and has thirteen rattles, with a fourteenth, budding (Canada). It has its head pointed in a striking attitude toward the staff. Below the snake, on a painted yellow scroll in large black painted letters is the motto, "DON'T TREAD ON ME."

A postcard published by the Westmoreland County Historical Society states that the Westmoreland Battalion was part of Proctor's Brigade and was raised in Hannas Town in 1775.

STANDARD OF THE PENNSYLVANIA RIFLE REGIMENT OF 1775, OF THE FIRST CONTINENTAL REGIMENT OF 1776 AND THE FIRST PENNSYLVANIA REGIMENT OF 1777 (Plate 39)

The original standard is at the William Penn Memorial Museum in Harrisburg, Pennsylvania. It was obtained about 1876 from descendants of Lt. Col. Thomas Robinson and displayed at Independence Hall during the Centennial. The standard's recorded history starts on 8 March 1776. The design dates back to Benjamin Franklin's Associators.

The field is of green silk with a crimson silk square in the center. Painted on the square is a device of a hunter with a spear striking a lion enmeshed in a net. The motto below is "Domari Nolo" (I refuse to be subjugated). The standard is described in a letter from Colonel Edward Hand to James Yeates of Lancaster, Pennsylvania, dated Prospect Hill (Boston) March 8, 1776.

The standard measures 53½ (hoist) by 61¼ (fly) inches including a 3¼ inch staff sleeve. The crimson center is 17¾ inches high by 21¼ inches wide. The field is made up of three horizontal strips, measuring from the top, 7 inches, 23 inches and 23½ inches; all are flat fell seamed.

Egle, the historian, says, "Within ten days ∴.. after news of the battle of Bunker's Hill had reached the Province of Pennsylvania, her first rifle regiment was officered and completed, many of the eight companies numbering one hundred men. It was commanded by Colonel William Thompson, of Cumberland county .... The Regiment ... at once marched to the relief of Boston, where they arrived about the last of July .... They were the first companies south of the Hudson to arrive in Massachusetts .... They were stout and hardy yeomanry, the flower of Pennsylvania's frontiersmen .... Two companies of this battalion were subsequently ordered to accompany General Arnold ... to Quebec. Their term of service was for one year."

According to Robinson family tradition, the standard was captured at Brandywine but retrieved by Colonel Thomas Robinson.

Thompson's Rifle Regiment or Battalion was reorganized as the First Pennsylvania Regiment of 1777. Thompson served as commander until March 1, 1776, and was succeeded by Colonel Edward Hand who, in turn, was succeeded by Colonel James Chambers, followed by Colonel Daniel Brodhead. Lt. Colonel Robinson was second in command during the Valley Forge Encampment and probably later.

Colonel Hand's letter of 8 March 1776 to James Yeates of Lancaster from Prospect Hill, Massachusetts says in part: "Every regiment is to have a standard and colours. Our standard is to be a deep green ground, the device a tiger partly enclosed by toils, attempting the pass, defended by a hunter armed with a spear (in white) on crimson field the motto Domari nolo."

The standard is discussed in detail in an article by Wendy M. Werner and John N. Armstrong, "1st Continental Regiment/1st Pennsylvania Regiment Flag," MC&H, Spring 1975. The standard was cleaned and remounted in 1975. When cleaned, the dingy dark field proved to be a light greenish-gold and not deep green as expected. Great care was taken during cleaning to remove only surface dirt. The conservation allowed both sides of the flag to be examined and disclosed that all prior illustrations of the flag's central emblem are in error. They should have depicted the obverse side of the flag with the lion to the left, staff side, and the unit's designation correctly arranged as P.M.

1st   R – – with the motto reading correctly. The shoulder of the hunter shows a later patch.

"THE STANDARD OF OUR REGIMENT," ENSIGN DENNY, YORKTOWN, 1781

Ensign Ebenezer Denny of a Pennsylvania Regiment was detailed to carry the standard of his regiment at the surrender ceremony at Yorktown. In his journal, Denny recorded the following for October 17-19, 1781:

"17th—In the morning before relief came, had the pleasure of seeing a drummer mount the enemy's parapet, and beat a parley, and immediately an officer, holding up a white handkerchief, made his appearance outside their works; the drummer accompanied him, beating. Our batteries ceased. An officer from our lines ran and met the other, and tied the handkerchief over his eyes. The drummer sent back, and the British officer conducted to a house in rear of our lines. Firing ceased totally.

"18th—Several flags pass and repass now even without the drum. Had we not seen the drummer in his red coat when he first mounted, he might have beat away till doomsday. The constant firing was too much for the sound of a single drum; but when the firing ceased, I thought I never heard a drum equal to it—the most delightful music to us all.

"19th—Our division man the lines again. All is quiet. Articles of capitulation signed; detachment of French and Americans take possession of British forts.

"Major Hamilton commanded a battalion which took possession of a fort immediately opposite our right and on the bank of York river. I carried the standard of our regiment on this occasion. On entering the fort, Baron Steuben, who accompanied us, took the standard from me and planted it himself. The British army parade and march out with their colors furled; drums beat as if they did not care how. Grounded their arms and returned to town. Much confusion and riot among the British through the day; many of the soldiers were intoxicated; . . . ."

The introduction to Denny's Journal by William H. Denny states that Denny received a commission of Ensign in the First Pennsylvania Regiment in early 1781. However, Denny's first entry in his Journal, at Carlisle, May 1st, 1781, says he was appointed an ensign of the 7th Pa. in August 1780 and that the 7th Pa. Regt was incorporated with the 4th in the consolidation (of 1 January 1781) under command of "Lt. Col Comt. William Butler." The Pennsylvania Line was reduced from thirteen to six regiments by the 1781 consolidation. Denny also recorded that all Pennsylvania recruits fit for service were formed at York into two regiments of eight companies each for the Virginia campaign. Berg states that there were three field battalions formed in 1781; the 1st commanded by "Col Walter Stewart," the 2nd probably by "Colonel Richard Butler", and the 3rd probably by "Colonel Thomas Craig." However the six regiments of '81 continued to exist administratively until 1783.

Following the surrender at Yorktown, Denny recorded that Wayne's Brigade was joined on October 20, 1781 by a "new raised regiment from Pennsylvania" and that on November 1, 1781 the "three regiments of Pennsylvania" commenced their march to join Green's army in South Carolina. By December 30, 1782, the Pennsylvanians had been so reduced by camp deaths and desertions that the surviving 600 men were formed into one regiment. Denny arrived back in Philadelphia on June 15, 1783.

In view of the 1781 organizational mergers and the manner in which the field battalions were formed for the Virginia campaign, it is not clear to the author as to which Pennsylvania Regiment Denny was actually assigned. Denny recorded that his company officers during the Virginia campaign, prior to Yorktown, were Captain Montgomery and Lieutenant Blauer. Montgomery was wounded at the battle of Jamestown on 6 July 1781 and, shortly after, Denny was transferred to "Irwin's company."

The basis for William H. Denny's statement that Denny was commissioned an ensign in the First Pennsylvania Regt is not given and does not apparently agree with Denny's Journal. William Denny also speaks of "the first action of the Pennsylva-

nia troops, under Lt. Col. Richard Butler, near Williamsburg", and that Butler's regiment was appointed to plant the first "American flag" upon the British parapet at the surrender; further, that Butler designated Ensign Denny to carry the flag. William Denny claims that Butler was offended that Steuben took the regimental standard from Denny and planted it himself. "Colonel Richard Butler" is listed by Berg as commander of the 2nd Pa. (Field) Battalion of 1781 for the Virginia campaign.

2ND PENNSYLVANIA REGIMENT OF 1777
(Plates 40, 41)

The standard of this regiment is pictured in a Charles Willson Peale portrait of Colonel Walter Stewart, who was commander of the regiment from July 1, 1778 to January 1, 1783. The full length portrait of Stewart in uniform is dated 1782. Based on correspondence, it was started in 1781 or earlier and finished in 1782. The companion portrait of Deborah McClenachan Stewart is dated 1782 and the receipt is dated 12/16/1782 for both paintings and two miniatures.

The encampment of Stewart's regiment is pictured in the background of the painting in extraordinary detail. Stewart's headquarters marquee, with red-trimmed scalloping similar to Washington's, is at the center rear. Also pictured are the tents of officers and men, rows of stacked rifles, field cannon, cooking fires, sentries and small groups of uniformed personnel. Espontoons are planted in front of the officers' tents, and the regimental standard on its staff is planted in front of Stewart's marquee.

The field of the standard is white. It bears in the center a large brown and light-red rattlesnake coiled to strike, with head extended and rattles erect. Below the snake is a large curving blue scroll extending across the field with touches of yellow at both tips, indicating painted fringe. Two tassels on cords are suspended from the staff head and hang about to the midpoint of the flag's hoist. The staff is tipped by a small formless touch of white. The painting, which is in a private collection, was closely examined for details with a magnifying glass by the author.

Judging by the height of a nearby sentry, the original flag would have been about five feet square. In the painting, the flag measures about 1 3/16 inch square which is too small to allow the artist to have inscribed any motto on the scroll, such as "Don't Tread on Me", which probably appeared on the original.

There is no indication of a canton or regimental designation. What could be assumed to be two ribbon-like streamers were found upon close inspection to be folds along the top edge of the flag. The full length of the brown-colored staff is visible, but this was probably required because of the small scale. The original standard was probably sleeved to the staff and would have been silk with the snake and scroll and motto painted directly on the field, as with similar standards, such as Proctor's Westmoreland Battalion and Webb's Additional Continental Regiment.

Stewart wears a dark blue coat with red lapels and cuffs as prescribed in general orders of 1779; gold or silver epaulets, silver buttons, white waistcoat and breeches, and black boots. His carefully detailed silver sword would be the one presented by Congress on November 19, 1776. His tricorn hat has a cockade and one of the black and red plumes brought from France by Lafayette and given to his Corps of Light Infantry during the Virginia and Yorktown Campaign of 1781.

Stewart commanded the 1st Battalion of Pennsylvania troops during the Yorktown campaign. Three field battalions were created by combining the new recruits and veterans of the six Pennsylvania Continental Regiments of '81 which were understrength. The thirteen Pennsylvania Continental Regiments of '77 had been consolidated into six

Standard of the 2nd Pa. Regt. of 1777 (Motto assumed)

Detail of Peale's portrait of Colonel Stewart (see color plates for full painting.)

by 1781; but none of the six existed as viable units. As was the practice, however, Stewart continued to be listed administratively as Commander of the 2nd. Following Yorktown, the three battalions were sent to join Greene's Southern Department Continental Army.

This is the only full contemporary rendering of an American Revolutionary regimental standard known to the author. The details of the painting show meticulous work by the artist. Also, Peale wrote Stewart on May 23, 1781 asking for 30 guineas payment and Stewart's approval of the sketch of the encampment.

FIFTH PENNSYLVANIA REGIMENT

The flag of the Fifth Pennsylvania Regiment included the rattlesnake symbol, according to Dr. Whitney Smith, "The Flag Book of the United States," 1970-1975. No original source is referenced.

*Original Color, 7th Pa. Regt. of 1776
Carried by Capt. Robert Wilson's
Company at Brandywine
—September 11, 1777*

DIVISION COLOR OF THE SEVENTH PENNSYLVANIA REGIMENT OF 1776 *(Plate 34)* (THE BRANDYWINE FLAG)

The original of this silk flag is at Independence National Historical Park.

The flag measures 54 (hoist) by 52 (fly) inches overall. The field is a faded red. There is no device or unit designation. The canton is a stars-and-stripes measuring 26 x 26 inches with red and white stripes and thirteen red silk, fat-bodied, eight-point, one and one-half inch diameter stars in the white silk canton—a canton within a canton—forming a 4-5-4 pattern. The canton's stripes, about one and three quarters inches wide, are formed by seven white silk stripes applied to the red field. The canton is inset, leaving a red border two inches wide along the top and one and one-half inches wide along the staff side. There are remnants of a red fringe along the flag's edge. Small, thread-whipped eyelets are spaced along the staff edge. The flag is labeled as being that of the "Seventh Pennsylvania Regiment." It was probably a Division Color of the regiment.

The flag was donated to Independence Hall in 1923 by Richard Wilson Harrison of Wilmington, Delaware. By family tradition, the flag was carried at the September 11, 1777 Battle of Brandywine by a Company commanded by Captain Robert Wilson, an ancestor of Mr. Harrison's. This Company was a part of the Seventh Pennsylvania Regiment raised in 1776. Colonel William Irvine was regimental commander at the time. Captain Wilson was wounded at the Battle of Paoli, nine days after Brandywine. According to Independence Park files, Mr. Harrison inherited the flag from his mother, Margarett Jane Wilson, whose father, John Wilson, was a grandson of Captain Wilson.

The stars and stripes canton could have been added at anytime after the June 14, 1777 flag resolution. Possibly the Color originally had a canton of stripes which was modified to include the stars. This 7th Regiment division color is quite similar to the Delaware militia color which was captured just before Brandywine.

4th BATTALION, PHILADELPHIA MILITIA THE HEADMAN COLOR

Gostelowe Standard No. 1 was traditionally carried by William Headman of the 4th Battalion of Philadelphia Militia. The Headman Color was donated to the Smithsonian by a descendant and is on display there (see Gostelowe Standards, Continental Army).

120

——16——

Rhode Island

RHODE ISLAND STATE SEAL

The present-day rope-entwined anchor seal of Rhode Island dates to 1647. This is the device on one of the two surviving colors of The Rhode Island Regiment of 1781. The anchor seal appeared on most issues of Rhode Island Colonial and Revolutionary-era currency and was always encircled with the Latin motto, "In te Domine Speramus" (In God We Hope). This motto in English was reported on other Rhode Island symbols during and after the Revolution but has now been shortened to the single word "Hope".

RHODE ISLAND MILITIA *(Plate 20)*
Red-White-Blue Stripes with Rattlesnake Canton
"General Sullivan's Command Standard"

This standard is covered in the section on continental and union colors.

NEWPORT LIGHT INFANTRY COMPANY *(Plate 42)*

Although no original survives, a detailed contemporary description and the insignia on a helmet allow accurate reconstruction of the standard.

The Rhode Island Historical Society *Collections* for January 1940 included an article on The Newport Light Infantry Company by Paul Francis Glesson which quoted original letters and news articles describing the colors of the company. The letters are self-explanatory and one is quoted below.

Hon. Henry Marchant, Attorney General of the Colony, wrote to John Hancock in Boston on November 15, 1774:

"Honorable Sir

"The publick you so honorably stand in throughout at least our American World will bring upon you some Inconvenience if not impertinent Applications. I am afraid mine will be One; but I make it to oblige others and in so doing to oblige myself.

"A Military Spirit is diffusing itself with the greatest Rapidity thro' every part of this Colony. Several Companies are formed and forming in this town. I am desired by one of those companies to enquire at Boston whether Sixty or Seventy neat good Arms can be purchased there and at what Price. It is desired their Colours should be made of the neatest, best Silk of a blue Ground with the Union at One Corner, and upon a Square in the Center it is my Idea to have a Female Figure representing the Genius of America Standing erect with a Staff in her Right Hand and the Cap of Liberty upon the Top of it. In her left Hand, either the Bible or America's Bill of Rights, and under her Feet, Chains, the Badge of Slavery. The following Motto in some proper Place: Pater Cara Carior Libertas. And, if a proper Place can be found, to have the Colony Arms, being no more than a plain Anchor.

"What is desired of Mr. Hancock is that he would inform me respecting the Fire Arms and apply to Mr. Copeley to know what he would undertake to furnish the Silk and to paint Them for (the Colours).

The response to the above letter is not known. Copley had left for London in June 1774. A contemporary news article described the finished flag when it was presented to its unit on April 3, 1775.

STANDARDS OF THE RHODE ISLAND REGT. OF 1781
(Plates 42, 43)

Two original standards of the Rhode Island "Corps" or "Continental Battalion" have been preserved in the collection of that state. The recorded history of the flags dates to February 28, 1784. At that time, the standards were presented to the Rhode Island General Assembly by the former commander of the Rhode Island Regiment of 1781, Lt. Colonel Jeremiah Olney, representing "the officers of the line" as being "the standards of their corps". The exact number of standards presented, and whether they were associated with any specific Rhode Island unit other than the "corps", was not stated. The Assembly replied to "To the Officers of the Line of this State's late Continental Battalion" and voted "that the standards should be carefully preserved under the immediate care of the governor, to perpetuate the noble exploits of the brave corps".

At the War's end, there was only *one* Rhode Island Regiment. It had been formed in 1781 by consolidating the First and Second R. I. Regiments which had been formed in 1776-7. Lt. Colonel Olney was Commander of the Rhode Island Regiment from May 1781 to November 1783 and had been second-in-command of the Second Regiment of 1777. Olney probably referred to the "Corps" rather than the "regiment" or "battalion" to make it clear that his unit had been formed by the consolidation and included personnel from both former regiments.

Newport Light Infantry Company
Painted leather mitre cap

Both standards are of white silk with a sewn-on blue silk canton bearing thirteen painted five-pointed stars. Each has a sleeve for its staff. There is no fringe. The central devices are a combination of painted and appliqued silk. The manner in which the flags are currently displayed unfortunately conceals some interesting areas. The following descriptions are taken from past records:

One of the colors, as described by the Rhode Island Secretary of State in 1871-2, measured 65 inches on the hoist by 90 inches on the fly. The central device is a blue silk anchor entwined by a white silk rope above which was a painted scroll. (The four sections of the scroll had fallen out by 1871.) The canton is of faded blue silk with thirteen gilt stars in a 3-2-3-2-3 pattern. Each star is outlined with a darker shade of blue and shadowed on its left side. Gherardi Davis illustrates this flag based on a photograph. He gives its size as about five by six and one-half feet. Davis' 1907 illustration indicates that portions of the outer and lower field were missing. The author suggests that the above standard could have originally been that of the First Rhode Island Regiment of 1777 and was carried by the combined regiment of 1781 as one of its two colors. The rope-entwined anchor appeared on Rhode Island Colonial and Revolutionary currency, and is the state symbol.

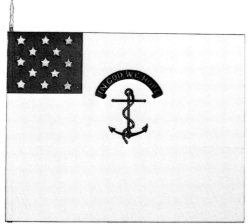

The anchor standard of the Rhode Island Regiment of 1781

1907 photograph of the anchor standard of the Rhode Island Regiment of 1781

In a letter to Admiral Preble, dated March 12, 1879, Hon. J. M. Adderman, the Rhode Island Secretary of State, wrote that in 1664 the anchor seal bore the motto ''Hope.'' This differs with the invariable use of the full motto in Latin on early Rhode Island currency.

The painted sections of the scroll had fallen out by 1871-2, according to letters from Hon. J. R. Bartlett, Secretary of State; who said in his letter to Admiral Preble that the scroll had carried the motto ''Hope''. This could only have been a guess. In the opinion of the author, the length and spacing of the holes left by the four painted missing sections of the scroll indicate strongly that it had carried the full colonial-era motto, ''In God We Hope.''

In accordance with Washington's General Orders of October 2, 1779 regarding Continental uniforms, the Rhode Island, New Hampshire, Massachusetts, and Connecticut regiments were to have white facings. It was also planned that the regimental colors would match those facings; and that the Rhode Island troops would wear entirely white uniforms. There is a sketch of a white uniformed Rhode Island soldier by one of Rochambeau's officers.

The second standard was described by the above Secretary of State, in 1871-2, as being torn, and measuring 51 inches on the hoist, by 45 inches on the fly. It probably was originally about the same size as its mate (65″ by 90″). This second flag was illustrated by Gherardi Davis in 1907 as the frontispiece of his book in which he states that the remaining fragment measured about four feet square. The 1907 Davis illustration, as well as the illustrations contained in the Society of the Cincinnati's reprint of H. M. Chapin's "Early Rhode Island Flags," clearly reveal that the scroll was located in the *center* of the field and not immediately adjacent to the canton—as has been incorrectly indicated in certain copies. The *central* device, which appears on both sides, is a foliated blue silk scroll with the inscription "R•ISLAND•REGT." The first part of the inscription "R•ISLAND R . . ." is visible on one side and the last part ". . . AND•] REGT" is visible on the other. The canton is light blue silk with thirteen small, painted, white, five-pointed stars in a 3-2-2-3 pattern.

The author suggests that the above "R•ISLAND•REGT" standard was probably made or modified for the Rhode Island Regiment of 1781. Both this and the anchor-symboled standards were probably carried by this Regiment from 1781 to 1783.

Each of the above standards has been conjecturally identified by various authorities over the years as that of the First Rhode Island Regiment. The anchor flag as displayed in 1925 was labeled as being that of the "First Continental Infantry," but there is apparently no documentary basis for this. In 1925, the Librarian of the Rhode Island Historical Society, Howard M. Chapin, in "Early Rhode Island Flags" reasoned that the "R•ISLAND•REGT" standard was probably that of the First Regiment. Davis and Schermerhorn identify the anchor standard with the First Regiment and the "R•ISLAND•REGT" with the Second, but apparently without any basis other than the above display label. The emblem of the anchor and the motto "HOPE" appear in the Rhode Island state flag, as adopted in 1877.

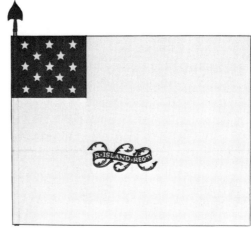

One of the two standards of the Rhode Island Regiment of 1781

1907 watercolor drawing of one of the original standards of the Rhode Island Regiment of 1781

Any attempt to distinguish which of the two standards was carried by the 1st and the 2nd Regiments of '77 ignores the fact that the two regiments had been combined in 1781 and this single Rhode Island Regiment served until the end of the War. Probably both standards were carried by the consolidated regiment. Olney refers, in 1784, to "the Standards of the Corps" and the Assembly replied to the "late Continental Battalion"—indicating one battalion or regiment with at least two standards. Of course, it is reasonable to assume that the two standards provide some clues as to the design of the standards of the regiments of 1777. If this assumption is made, then the most likely of the two that would have been carried by the 1st Rhode Island Regiment of 1777, the senior regiment, would have been the one bearing the state's anchor symbol and motto.

SECOND RHODE ISLAND REGIMENT

There is a description of a third Rhode Island regimental standard, bearing only the designation "SECOND RHODE ISLAND REGIMENT," in Edwin M. Stone's "Our French Allies." Stone simply states that "... The Standard that belonged to the regiment of Colonel Angell before the consolidation bears a legend as appears on the accompanying engraving..." The engraving shows a rectangular flag with the hoist and fly proportioned approximately in the ratio of five by six and one-half. This is about the same as for the two still existing Rhode Island regimental standards. The only device shown in Stone's engraving is a centered inscription in very large letters, as follows:

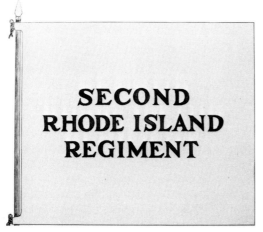

Standard of the 2nd Rhode Island Regiment of 1777 (Based on Stone's 19th-Century sketch.)

Stone's 1890 sketch of the Standard of the 2nd Rhode Island Regiment

SECOND RHODE ISLAND REGIMENT

No colors are stated or indicated in the sketch, although it could be assumed that the field was white and the letters black or blue. The flag has disappeared and no other reference to it is known. In Edward N. Field's "Diary of Colonel Israel Angell," 1899, the anchor flag is identified as being the standard of the Second Regiment. However, in 1871-72, the Rhode Island Secretary of State in his letters to Admiral Preble, apparently referred to the two flags simply as "No. 1" and "No. 2" without identifying either with a specific regiment; nor did he mention the "SECOND RHODE ISLAND REGIMENT" standard, as described by Stone in 1882.

COLORS OF A RHODE ISLAND ARTILLERY UNIT *(Plate 33)*

Two original colors of an early Rhode Island artillery militia unit are at The Rhode Island Historical Society. So far as the author has been able to determine, their recorded history starts with a description of the yellow field flag in an article by Howard

Yellow field Colors of a Rhode Island Artillery Unit —circa 1820's. Original

M. Chapin, *"Early Rhode Island Flags,"* which appeared in the October 1925 issue of the Rhode Island Historical Society Collections. Chapin refers to a February 21, 1861 letter requesting permission to parade the "flags of the company of 76." Since no description was given, however, this may not be the flag referred to. Traditionally, according to Chapin, the larger yellow field standard belonged to the United Company of the Train of Artillery of 1775. But no reference is known, and there is no information in the files of the Society on the origin or accession of the flag. Chapin wrote that the emblem on the flag is similar to the uniform buttons of the above artillery unit.

The yellow silk standard measures 40 (hoist) by 50 (fly) inches and is sleeved for its staff. There is an elaborate, finely painted, centered emblem of a coiled blue-and-gold rattlesnake below which is a pink, gold-edged scroll with the motto "DO NOT TREAD ON ME" in gold letters. Below is a blue, gold-edged scroll with "IN GOD WE HOPE," together with a blue, rope-entwined anchor and two brass cannon. A circle of thirteen blue-painted, gold-bordered, five-pointed stars (which are pasted on the flag) encircle the above emblem and mottos. The emblems and circle of stars apparently occupy the entire field of the flag, judging by Mr. E. Andrew Mowbray's photograph in his article *"14 Rhode Island Militia Flags"*. This flag is certainly Revolutionary in motifs

and spirit. However, on the fluke of the anchor is a tiny signature "Painted by John R. Penniman, Boston" who was active in 1826. This strongly evidences that the standard was either repainted in 1826, is a replica of an earlier original, or was the standard of a Rhode Island artillery unit of that date. Penniman's signature is visible in a black-and-white photograph sent to F. E. Schermerhorn, author of the 1948 flag book of the Sons of the Revolution.

The following advertisement appeared in the Massachusetts Spy, Worcester, Massachusetts, June 23, 1830, by this same John Penniman:

"Painting, John R. Penniman informs his friends and the public that he is removed from Boston to West Brookfield, where he has established himself in the business of Original Military Standard, Sign, Ornamental, and Portrait Painting in all the varieties formerly carried on by him at Boston.

"Also, accurate, Drawings of New Inventions designed to be Patented; Original Designs for Diplomas; Vignettes for Bank Bill Engravers, and Designs for Frontispieces and Title Pages to Books furnished as usual.

"J.R.P. respectfully solicits a continuation of the patronage heretofore so liberally bestowed on him while at Boston, by a generous public."

The second artillery standard of this pair is of blue silk with the identical emblems, mottos, and stars in the same arrangement as the yellow standard, but painted entirely in gold with black scrolls. The blue color now measures 39½ (hoist) by 32½ (fly) inches, but originally was probably the same size as the yellow standard. The emblem and circle of stars, based on Mr. Mowbray's photograph, now occupy most of the surviving part of the field. The emblem of the blue color is so similar to that of the yellow color that the same artist must have painted both, in which case the 1820's date would apply.

——17——

South Carolina

STATE SEAL OF SOUTH CAROLINA

The Boston Independent Chronicle and Universal Advertiser for October 9, 1777, described the seal of South Carolina as follows:

"A palmetto-tree, supported by twelve spears, which, with the tree, are bound together in one hand on which is written, 'Quis seperabit?' On the tree are two shields, the one inscribed 'March 26th,' the other 'July 4th'; and at the foot of the palmetto an English oak, fallen, its roots above the ground, and its branches lopt. In the exergon, 'MELOREM LAPSA LOCAVIT, 1776.' The legend, 'SOUTH CAROLINA,' immediately over the palmetto, and at the opposite part of the circle, 'ANIMIS EPIBUSQUE PARATI.'

"The reverse is Hope, advancing over a rock, which is rugged and steep behind her, but smooth and of gentle ascent before. The way is strewed with the arms of an enemy. She holds a laurel flower in her right hand, and has a view of the sun rising in full splendor. In the exergon, 'SPES.' The legend is 'DUM SPIRO SPERO.' "

The arms were designed by William Henry Drayton, and the original, executed by him with a pen, was in possession of his son and contained more devices. The reverse of the arms is said to have been designed by Arthur Middleton.

The Eutaw Banner
(1907 photograph
by Gherardi Davis)

THE EUTAW BANNER *(Plate 45)*

See 3rd Regiment, Continental Light Dragoons Colonel William Washington.

Continental Congress Silver Medal awarded to
Lt. Col. William Washington for his role at Cowpens

LIGHT INFANTRY OF THE SOUTHERN CONTINENTAL ARMY See Continental Army.

DEVICES OF THE SOUTH CAROLINA REGIMENTS

A letter from Captain Fitzhugh McMaster, dated July 25, 1978 offers the following information about the devices of South Carolina regiments.

First South Carolina Regiment

The device of this regiment was a pair of crossed scimitars and the motto "ULTIMA RATIO" (The Final Argument). The two colors were possibly blue and buff.

Second South Carolina Regiment

The device was a trophy of arms (drums, crossed flags, crossed muskets) and "LIBERTAS POTIOR VITA."

Third South Carolina Regiment

The device was a coiled rattlesnake; the motto is not known. The colors were probably blue and white.

Fourth, Fifth, Sixth Regiments

Devices and mottos are not known. The colors were probably blue and scarlet.

SOUTH CAROLINA NAVY

Rattlesnake Ensign (Plate 45)

No original has survived. There are, however, contemporary descriptions, an engraving and a number of references to such an ensign.

In the background of a 1776 English mezzotint of "Commodore Hopkins, Commander-in-Chief of the American Fleet," by Thomas Hart, 22 August 1776, are two ships, each flying an ensign. One ship flies the New England Pine Tree Ensign with the mottos "Liberty Tree" and "An Appeal to God." The second ship flies an ensign with a rattlesnake running diagonally across the thirteen stripes with the motto "Don't Tread Upon Me."

Benjamin Franklin and John Adams in a letter dated October 9, 1778 from Paris to the Ambassador of the king of the Two Sicilys wrote:

"... Some of the States have vessels of war distinct from those of the United States. For example, the vessels of war of the State of Massachusetts Bay have sometimes a pine tree; *and those of South Carolina a rattlesnake, in the middle of the 13 stripes ...*"

The above rattlesnake ensign of the South Carolina Navy may have resembled that shown in the Hopkins mezzotint illustrated in the section on Continental Navy ensigns. If so, it would have been flown on the Frigate "South Carolina" which had been built as "Le Indien" in the Netherlands for the Continental Navy. The ship had been promised to John Paul Jones. Due to protests from Britain, "Le Indien" was not turned over to Jones; instead it was sold to a French company which, in turn, "leased" it to South Carolina. Jones received the Bonhomme Richard, instead.

Preble illustrates two striped ensigns, one with red and white stripes and one with red and blue stripes. Both show a diagonally placed rattlesnake, and the motto "DON'T TREAD ON ME". The original source is not given.

Rice and Stars Ensign

On 19 July 1778, Rawlin Lowndes, President of South Carolina, wrote to Commodore Alexander Gillon of the South Carolina Navy that "... The Flagg which you are to wear and which is the flagg by which the Navy of this State is in the future to be distinguished, is a rich Blue field, a Rice Sheaf Worked with Gold (or Yellow) in the Center, and 13 Stars Silver (or White) Scattered over the field." No other mention of this flag is known to the author.

Crescent Ensign

Ships of the South Carolina Navy also flew the blue Fort Moultrie ensign with white crescent judging by the emblem on a South Carolina $8 note issued December 23, 1776, which shows a ship flying such a flag as an ensign and as a jack.

Ensign of the South Carolina Navy
13-Stripes and Rattlesnake
(present-day ceremonial version)

Stars and rice sheaf ensign of
the South Carolina Navy
(Based on a description)

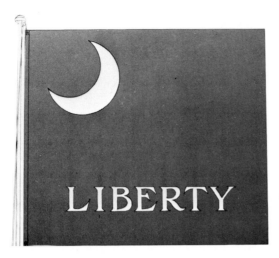

American provincial colors flown over Fort Johnson and the Fort on Sullivan's Island (Fort Moultrie) Charleston Harbor—1775–1776

FORT MOULTRIE FLAG
JUNE 28, 1776 *(Plate 45)*
FORT JOHNSON FLAG
SEPTEMBER 15, 1775
CHARLESTON BATTERIES
FLAGS—APRIL 3, 1780

No original flag has survived. Very creditable postwar accounts by participants described a blue field flag with silver crescent for Fort Johnson and the same flag with the added motto "Liberty" for Fort Moultrie. Colonel William Moultrie (later major-general and post-war governor of South Carolina) commander of the Second South Carolina Regiment of Foot of 1775, relates in his Memoirs (published 1802) of the seizure of Fort Johnson on James Island on the south shore of Charleston Bay on September 15, 1775. He wrote: "... A little time after we were in possession of Fort Johnson, it was thought necessary to have a flag for the purpose of signals; (as there was no national or state flag at that time). I was desired by the council of safety to have one made, upon which, as the state troops were clothed in blue, and the fort was garrisoned by the first and second regiments, who wore a silver crescent on the front of their caps; I had a large blue flag made with a crescent in the dexter corner, to be in uniform with the troops: This was the first American flag which was displayed in South Carolina: On its being first hoisted, it gave some uneasiness to our timid friends, who were looking forward to a reconciliation: They said it had the appearance of a declaration of war; . . ."

In January 1776, the South Carolina revolutionary forces started the erection of a large fort on Sullivan's Island on the north shore of Charleston Bay directly across from Fort Johnson. The sixteen-foot thick walls of the fort were constructed of two parallel rows of palmetto logs with earth between. Sullivan's fort was attacked on June 28, 1776 by a British fleet which was driven off only after a severe engagement. A British landing force, attempting to flank the fort, was also beaten back by forces commanded by Colonel Thompson and Colonel Daniel Horry. Moultrie does not describe the Fort Sullivan flag but does write that ". . . After some time our flag was shot away . . . Sergeant Jasper . . . brought it up through heavy fire, fixed it upon a spung-staff, and planted it upon the ramparts again: . . ." The fact that Moultrie does not describe the Fort Sullivan (Moultrie) flag could be interpreted as meaning that the same flag he had previously described for Fort Johnson was also flown over Fort Sullivan.

William Henry Drayton, son of the prominent South Carolina patriot of the same name (who died in 1778), published his fa-

130

ther's papers and memoirs in 1821. In Drayton's Memoirs the Fort Sullivan flag is described as follows, "... On the south-east bastion the flag staff was fixed, bearing a blue flag with a white crescent; on which was emblazoned the word "Liberty:..." Drayton writes of Sergeant Jasper's recovery of the flag as also does Ramsay in "History of the Revolution in South Carolina," published 1787.

Preble quotes the manuscript diary of Dr. John Jeffries, a Loyalist surgeon in the British army besieging Charleston who recorded on April 3, 1780 that he saw the "American Thirteen-stripes flag displayed" over one position, "two other flags displayed in their new works" and that "their great battery fronting Charleston harbor had the American flag of thirteen stripes displayed... This, up to this day, had been a blue flag with field and Thirteen stars. The other flag never hoisted until today." Preble also references J. Munsell, "The Siege of Charleston," published 1867, which quotes an eyewitness letter stating that on May 7, the Continentals marched out of Fort Moultrie and "the thirteen stripes were leveled with the dust ...." Therefore, it appears that the blue field Fort Moultrie flag was still in use in 1780 but with thirteen stars and no crescent. This would be a national union of stars as favored by Washington and flown by John Paul Jones in his 1779 fight with H.M.S. Drake.

COLORS OF THE FIRST SOUTH CAROLINA REGIMENT OF FOOT OF 1775

No original has survived, nor is there a specific contemporary mention or description known to the author. However, the South Carolina forces were well organized and equipped during the early years of the war and since the 2nd had a pair of colors, the 1st probably had a pair also.

The 1st and 2nd S. C. Regiments of Foot wore blue uniforms and had a crescent moon device on their caps, as did the North Carolina units. In June 1775, the uniforms of the 1st had buff facings which had been changed to scarlet by August 1775. The 2nd's facings were scarlet from its activation. On 2 October 1779, Washington issued general orders which specified blue uniforms with white facings for the North and South Carolina and Georgia regiments. The southern campaign of 1779-81, however, probably prevented any change to white facings.

The insignia of the 1st Regiment was crossed scimitars pointing upwards with the motto "ULTIMA RATIO" (The Final Argument). This device is shown in a portrait at the National Gallery on the crescent device worn on the cap of Captain C. C. Pinckney; it is also engraved on a surviving gorget.

If the 1st Regiment had a pair of silk colors, we can assume that one would have been blue and one red; or one blue and one buff. The design would have been similar to the pair presented to the 2nd in 1776. The device in the center of the colors would have been the crossed scimitars and the "ULTIMA RATIO" motto possibly in a wreath or on a crescent. The designation "I REGT." would have been placed in the upper quarter next to the staff.

The 1st Regiment took part in the siege of Savannah where the 2nd lost its blue color. The colors of the 1st were probably among the fifteen standards surrendered at the fall of Charleston in 1780. None of the captured standards are known to have survived. Moultrie, in his Memoirs, said the standards taken at Savannah and Charleston were possibly in the Tower of London.

Mr. Darby Erd, and Captain Fitzhugh McMaster, USN Ret., are the authors of a definitive article on the uniforms and insignia of the 1st and 2nd Regiments which was published in the Summer 1977 issue of the Journal of the Company of Military Historians. One of the drawings illustrating the article is of a gorget inscribed with the arms and motto that appear on the surviving blue color of the 2nd Regiment. The initials "A.H." and date "1776" are also on the gorget.

COLORS OF THE SECOND SOUTH CAROLINA REGIMENT OF FOOT OF 1775 *(Plate 44)*

The original of the blue color is at the Museum of The 60th Regiment, The King's Royal Rifle Corps, at Winchester, England. The red color of this pair of colors has disappeared. Their recorded history starts in 1776.

The Second South Carolina Regiment, Colonel Moultrie, Commanding, was ordered to Sullivan's Island in Charleston Harbor, on March 2, 1776, to take command of a "large fort sufficient to contain 1000 men" which was being built by a "great number of mechanics and negro laborers." This fort would be "the key to the Harbor," when the expected British naval expedition appeared, as it did on June 28, 1776—ten vessels, armed with over 250 guns, and carrying a landing force of nearly 3000.

The naval attack on the fort began between ten and eleven o'clock in the morning. "A most tremendous cannonade ensued ... Colonel Moultrie, with 344 regulars and a few volunteer militia, made a defense that would have done honor to experienced veterans." The fire was continuous until seven in the evening. By 9:30 P.M. the firing on both sides had ceased. The British did not return to the attack. After several weeks of repair, they sailed for New York. The British had lost two ships, and sustained great damage to its fleet and suffered 205 killed and wounded. The American loss was thirty-six killed and wounded.

On July 1, the wife of Bernard Elliott presented to the regiment in which her husband was a captain, "an elegant pair of colors ... one of a fine blue silk, the other a fine red silk, richly embroidered." She presented the colors in person saying: "Gentlemen-Soldiers! The gallant behavior in defense of liberty and your country, entitles you to the highest honors; accept of these two standards as a reward justly due to your regiment; and I make not the least doubt, under heaven's protection you will stand by them as long as they wave in the air of LIBERTY."

On October 9, 1779, during the American and French attempt to recapture Savannah, both colors were planted on the British redoubt and the blue color captured. The regiment was then commanded by Lieutenant Colonel Francis Marion. A Captain in the Royal American Regiment wrote that "at the assault on Spring Hill redoubt, Lieutenant Bush being wounded handed the blue colour to Sergeant Jasper. Jasper, who had already received a bullet, was then mortally wounded, but returned the colour to Bush, who the next minute fell, yet even in the moment of death attempted to protect the flag which was afterwards found beneath him. No one could have done more, and the colour hallowed by the blood of Bush and Jasper, deserves to be deposited under a consecrated roof ... After the action it was picked up under Bush's body by the Royal Americans and handed to their Colonel-Commandant, General Prevost, in the possession of whose grandson it remained as late as 1913." Lieutenant Gray, who carried the red color, was also killed but Sergeant McDonald planted the color on the redoubt, then either McDonald or Jasper succeeded in carrying it off to safety when the retreat was ordered. Moultrie's account of the capture of the colors is similar—four color bearers were killed on the rampart (see Notes).

Moultrie in his memoirs (1802) describes the loss of the blue color at Savannah and states that the red color was taken at the fall of Charleston (in 1780). Moultrie wrote, "I am told they are now in the Tower of London."

The flag is of blue silk—now netted and quite dark—and measures 57 (hoist) by 54 (fly) inches. The central circular device,

Device of the Regimental Color of the 2nd South Carolina Regiment of 1775

which is embroidered on both sides, is almost the same as the Seal of South Carolina of 1776. The objects in the device include a green-topped palmetto tree trunk, topped by a red liberty cap; a criss-crossed pair of staff-mounted flags, one of which is a faded blue, the other yellow (originally red); a horizontal log with lopped-off limbs (the shattered British oak); a white drum with a blue crescent device; a trumpet and various weapons (machete, sword, halberd, axe); a decorated quiver with twelve white feathered arrows (the South Carolina palmetto forms the thirteenth state); a green grass base with flowers; a circular gold lettered motto "VITA POTIOR LIBERTAS" and year "1775". All these are enclosed within a green-leafed wreath, bowtied with a red ribbon. One side of the wreath has oak leaves and acorns (a "civic crown.") The other side has narrower leaves and clusters of small white flowers, possibly laurel or oleander. The device measures approximately 17 inches in diameter. The unit's designation "II^D: REG^T: is lettered in gold in the upper inner corner. There is no sign of a fringe.

A watercolor illustration of the flag as it appeared about 1913 is included in a regimental history "The Annals of the King's Royal Rifle Corps." It shows one remaining blue tassel and two gold tassel cords. Also, the staff of the color is shown with a small, sharply-oval, solid-brass, spearhead fastened to the staff by an elaborate decorative brass ferrule.

The author examined and photographed the flag at the regimental museum in 1972. It was also examined by Captain Fitzhugh McMaster, USN Ret., when the standard was loaned to the South Carolina Triennial in 1970.

II^D:REG^T: designation on the Color

Device on the Color. This was the prototype of the arms of South Carolina

13 STRIPES AT CHARLESTON, SOUTH CAROLINA, MAY 1780

Upon the surrender of Fort Moultrie, Charleston, S.C. on May 7, 1780, the American garrison ''marched out, and Capt. Hudson marched in, took Possession, leveled the thirteen stripes with the Dust, and the Triumphant English Flag was raised on the staff...'' This was quoted from a letter dated May 19, 1780; the writer is unidentified.

Hough quotes an intercepted letter from Benjamin Smith to his wife, dated Charleston, 30th April, 1780, in which Smith sadly writes that ''the Thirteen Stripes will be levelled (sic) in the Dust...''

Hough quotes Rivington's Royal Gazette, as follows: ''Extract of a Letter, dated Charleston, Broad Street, May 22, 1780. 'On the memorable 12th of this month I had the pleasure to see the 13 stripes, with several white pendants, levelled to the ground, and the gates of Charleston opened...'' (The letterwriter is not identified.)

SURRENDERED AMERICAN REGIMENTAL COLORS CHARLESTON, S.C. May 12, 1780

Listed in the ''Return of Ordnance and Ammunition in Charleston when surrendered..., the 14th of May, 1780''...
''Stands of Regimental Colours—15''

These were the colours of the Southern Continental Army and state militia Regiments that formed the garrison.

—18—

Virginia

VIRGINIA STATE SEAL

Preble states: "In the convention of delegates held at Williamsburg, July 1, 1776, it was 'Resolved, that Mr. Richard Henry Lee, Mr. George Mason, Mr. Treasurer, and Mr. Wythe be appointed a committee to devise a proper seal for this Commonwealth'; and on the 5th of July the following entry appears on the Journal of proceedings; 'Mr. George Mason . . . reported . . . the following device . . . Virtus, the genius of the Commonwealth, dressed like an Amazon, resting on a spear with one hand, and holding a sword in the other and Treading on Tyranny, represented by a man prostrate, a crown fallen from his head, a broken chain in his left hand, and a scourge in his right.' " This is the same Declaration of Independence symbol as on the standard of Webb's Additional Continental Regiment of 1777.

Preble continues: "In the *exergon,* the word 'VIRGINIA' over the head of Virtus and underneath the words *'Sic Semper Tyrannis.'* On the reverse, a group; Libertas, with her riband and pileus. On one side of her, Ceres with her cornucopia in one hand and an ear of wheat in the other; on the other side, Aeternitas, with the glove and phenix. On the *exergon* these words *'Deus nobis pace olim fecit.'* " In October 1779, it was resolved that the motto on the reverse be changed to "Perseverando."

The above seal was probably borne on one or more standards of Virginia regiments during the Revolution. It appeared on Virginia Revolutionary War paper currency.

The "Liberty over Tyranny" symbol was borne on the reverse side of a white (silk) standard captured by the British in the Battle of Bladensburg during the War of 1812. The obverse carried the great eagle seal with what appears to be the designations "68 Regt" and "James City—Infantry." The Liberty symbol was described as follows: ". . .Upon it a female figure, with a helmet on her head and carrying a flag and cap of Liberty, rests her foot on a prostrate man—supposed to represent King George, whose crown is rolling off upon the ground—and stars, arranged in a circular form, surround these figures, with the word 'Virginia' on a blue band at top.'' The standard was displayed directly over the organ in the chapel of Chelsea Royal Military Hospital, London, in 1903.

A second standard with an indicated blue field bearing an eagle seal emblem was also captured at Bladensburg and was in the chapel in 1903. A snake is entwined along a scroll below the eagle and the scroll bears a partially legible designation ''FP (?)—HARTFORD (?) LIGHT (?)'' and ''TOUCH ME NOT.''

The facsimile copies of the 1903 sketches are not as clear as the actual sketches must be. These and other captured American colors including the 4th United States Infantry, captured at Fort Detroit, the 2nd Regiment captured at Fort Bayo near Mobile in Feb-

ruary 1815, and a New York Militia Regiment captured at Queenstown Heights were also at Chelsea Hospital in 1903. They were greatly disintegrated by the 1940's and were taken down and stored. The sketches are at Greenwich.

STANDARD OF THE CULPEPPER MINUTEMEN FIRST VIRGINIA REGIMENT OF 1775

No original survives. The earliest record is a description by a participant, George Slaughter, that appears in Dr. Phillip Slaughter's History of St. Mark's Parish. A description and sketch are also found in ''*The Pictorial Field Book of the Revolution*'' by B. J. Lossing. Lossing gives no reference and probably based his sketch on Slaughter's description.

Standard of the 1st Virginia Regiment of 1775 (Lossing's nineteenth century sketch)
The original would have been less rectangular

136

The flag served as the standard of a group of about one hundred minutemen from Culpepper, Fairfax?, Virginia. The group formed part of Colonel Patrick Henry's First Virginia Regiment of 1775. In October-November 1775, three hundred such minutemen assembled at Culpepper Court House and marched for Williamsburg. They were dressed in brown (Slaughter said ''brown'', Lossing said ''green'') hunting shirts with Henry's words ''LIBERTY OR DEATH'' in large white letters on the breast. They had bucks' tails in their hats and in their belts tomahawks and scalping knives. Their fierce appearance alarmed the people as they marched through the country. They participated in the Battle of the Great Bridge at Norfolk December 9, 1775 in which the Loyalists were defeated. The Culpepper Battalion was led by Colonel Stevens.

Lossing's sketch shows a rectangular flag but does not give dimensions. It would probably have measured four by five and one-half feet. There is a swallow-tailed, flying scroll across the top of the flag with the words ''THE CULPEPPER MINUTEMEN'' inscribed thereon. A spring-coiled rattlesnake is centered on the flag and divides the motto LIBERTY // OR DEATH. The words ''DON'T TREAD ON ME'' appear along the bottom. The color is not stated.

TALIAFERRO'S COMPANY ENSIGN

According to daybook records of the Williamsburg Public Store (Virginia State Library), Captain Taliaferro's Company was issued one and three-quarters yards of ''best white ditto (swanskin) for Ensign'' on October 25, 1775. Also, on an unspecified date during 1775, Captain Taliaferro bought a stand of colors and on the same date eight yards of ''white shalloon were received for camp colors for the army in Williamsburg.''

Later, on December 13, 1775 ''. . . 15 taffeta colors, 15 tassils and cords, 15 spears, etc. . . . were purchased . . .''

Regimental Standard of the VIII Virginia Regiment. Colonel Henry Muhlenberg (Present-day painting)

COLORS OF THE VIII VIRGINIA REGIMENT OF 1776 *(Plate 45)*

No original has survived. Henry A. Muhlenberg's biography of General Peter Muhlenberg, published in 1849, speaks of this flag as being in the writer's possession. He describes it as being of salmon-coloured silk with a simple white scroll in the center upon which is inscribed ''VIII VIRG:A REG:T.''

Colonel Peter Muhlenburg was Commander of the VIII Virginia Regiment of 1776.

Preble states: ''In the orderly book of the army, at Williamsburg, Va., under date, 'Head-quarters, April 8, 1776,' is found this entry: 'The colonels are desired to provide themselves with some colors and standards, if they are to be procured: it doth not signify of what sort they are.''' No reference is given.

ALEXANDRIA COMPANY IX VIRGINIA REGIMENT

No illustration is provided. The earliest and only record reports this standard was destroyed in the 1871 fire at the Alexandria-Washington Masonic Lodge. According to the list in Brockett's "The Lodge of Washington" (published 1876), among the relics destroyed there were three flags of the Revolution, including one "faded red, with yellow center, inscribed in black: "IX. Virginia Regiment, Alexandria Company; staff wood, stained red, with wooden lance." The "yellow center" could have been an emblem, scroll or wreath. There was a IX Virginia Regiment of 1777 and one of 1778, according to Berg.

XI VIRGINIA REGIMENT MORGAN'S RIFLE CORPS

Lossing illustrates a flag with the following inscriptions: "1776" (wreath encircled) below which is "XI. VIRG.. REGT" below which is "MORGAN'S RIFLE CORPS". Lossing states that he sketched this flag at the old Masonic Museum at Alexandria, Virginia. Neither the coloring nor the dimensions are given. The flag is pictured as being rectangular. Its design is similar to that of the Alexandria Rifle Company, XI Virginia Regiment, now at the Alexandria Washington Masonic Memorial Museum.

Nothing is known of the whereabouts or the history of "Morgan's Rifle Corps" flag, beyond Lossing's description and sketch. There are no records of its existence. The flag is not listed by Brockett as being among the relics destroyed in the fire of 1871. Brockett's list does include three Revolutionary flags, but none of Morgan's Rifle Corps or of the XI Virginia Regiment.

It is quite possible that Lossing might have seen and sketched the standard of the Alexandria Rifle Company, XI Virginia Regiment, 1776, which is now at the Alexandria Washington Masonic Museum. The painted words "ALEX.ᴬ" and "COMP.ʸ" are

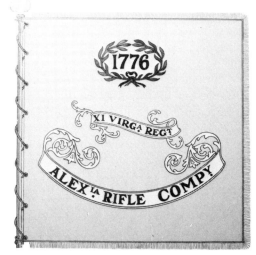

Standard of the Alexandria Rifle Company, XI Virginia Regiment (Painting)

badly deteriorated and most of the lettering is missing. This could have led to a misinterpretation by Lossing and others prior to the flag being carefully mounted and smoothed out.

ALEXANDRIA RIFLE COMPANY, XI VIRGINIA REGIMENT *(Plate 45)*

The original standard of this Company is in the collection of the Washington Masonic Memorial, Alexandria, Virginia.

The standard is of faded yellow silk measuring overall 42 (hoist) by 42 (fly) inches. There are remnants of a red fringe and eyelets for lacing to a staff. The symbols and scrolls are painted. At the top of the field is a laurel wreath of green leaves tied with a black ribbon encircling an off-white center on which "1776" appears. In the middle of the field is a waviform, foliated, painted white scroll with "XI VIRG.ᴬ REG.ᵀ" In the lower half of the field is a curved, foliated, white scroll with the remnants of "ALEX.ᴵᴬ RIFLE COMP.ʸ" All lettering is black and the foliation of the scrolls is white.

Most of the lettering of the lower scroll is

missing. This led to initial misinterpretation of the lettering on the scroll as ''MOR-GAN'S RIFLE CORPS.'' However, once the flag was properly mounted and smoothed out for display in recent years, sufficient portions of the lettering were made visible to allow for correct reading of the scroll, as stated above.

General Charles Lee's plan for colors for a regiment in 1775 provided for one regimental color and four company colors.

The commander of the XI Virginia Regiment of 1777 was Colonel Daniel Morgan, later commander of the Ranger or Rifle Corps. There were nine Virginia Continental Regiments in the formation of 1776.

XI VIRGINIA REGIMENT OF 1778

It is possible that the captured colors of this Regiment are pictured in a Reynolds portrait of British Lt. Col. Banastre Tarleton.

''The XIth Virginia Regiment and detachments of other regiments'' under Colonel Abraham Bulford, were defeated on May 29, 1780 at Waxhaws, South Carolina by the Loyalist British Legion, commanded by Tarleton. In Colonel Tarleton's May 30th report of the battle he lists ''Taken, 3 stand Of Colours, . . .''

The portrait of Tarleton, in uniform, shows three crumpled colors at his feet. One is buff with no visible device. A second is red with a small device of a crossed circle on white. The third has a buff field with a union of red and buff stripes.

In 1778, American regiments were being issued a stand of three colors—one regimental standard and two Division colors (see Continental Army—Gostelowe Return).

RICHMOND RIFLE RANGERS

The Masonic Museum in Alexandria, Virginia, was destroyed by fire on May 19, 1871. A list of the relics lost was included in Brockett's ''The Lodge of Washington,'' 1876. Four flags were listed, two of which were later found to have survived the fire. One of the flags lost was that of the Richmond Rifle Rangers, of white silk ''elegantly painted'' with a device and the motto ''NEMO ME IMPUNE LACES-SIT.'' No other information is known. The above motto ''No One Attacks Me With Impunity,'' is the national motto of Scotland.

Original Standard of the
Alexandria Rifle Company
XI Virginia Regiment

Lt. Col. Banastre Tarleton of the British Legion by Joshua Reynolds. The captured colors at his feet are possibly those of Buford's XI Virginia Regiment taken at Waxhaws. Georgia Major Jackson's account of Tarleton's defeat at Cowpens is in the notes to the Chapter on Maryland

Continental Congress Silver Medal awarded to Virginia Major Henry Lee for capture of the British Fort at Paulus Hook, August 19, 1779

—19—

French Forces in America

FRENCH ARMIES IN AMERICA

France sent a number of armies to America, including that of d'Estaing's 1779 expedition from the West Indies against Savannah, Rochambeau's premiere expedition to Newport in 1780 then to Yorktown in 1781, and Saint Simon's from the West Indies to Yorktown in 1781. The total number of French troops was about 3700 at Savannah and 7500 at Yorktown.

Reference sources differ as to exactly which French regiments or detachments of regiments were on American soil. Schermerhorn reports that "nineteen regiments or parts of regiments" are mentioned by one or more of the three principal authorities consulted, Davis, Balch and "Les Combattants." This number is increased to twenty-four when all detachments making up d'Estaing's 1779 Savannah expeditionary force are included, as listed by other sources. (see Notes and Comments Appendix).

FRENCH ROYAL NAVY

Among the major French fleets that were in American waters were the following: D'Estaing's, 1778-9, at the Delaware, Sandy Hook, Newport, and Savannah; Ternay's, 1780-81, transported Rochambeau's Army to Newport; DeGrasse's, 1781-82, Chesapeake campaign; Vaudreuil's, transported Rochambeau's Army back to France; the LaPerouse Expedition to Hudson Bay, 1782; and Des Touches Treville and DeTilly's.

French Royal Navy regulations for colors, flags and pennants, dated March 25, 1765, specified a square white flag for the ship of the Admiral, a white and blue flag for the ship of the Vice-Admiral commanding the second squadron, and a blue flag for the ship of the Rear-Admiral commanding the third squadron. The 1765 regulations go to considerable detail in specifying the color of the flag, dependent upon the size of a fleet or squadron, seniority of the commander, a particular ship's assignment within a squadron, etc.

For ceremonial occasions, Royal Navy ships could fly a blue flag sprinkled with yellow fleurs-de-lis.

The flag of the Grand Admiral of France was white with a central device which included a shield with three fleurs-de-lis, encircled by collars, surmounted by the Bourbon crown, and flanked by clouds and angelic heralds. However, in the opinion of Mr. Marcel Baldet, who supplied the above information, the Grand Admiral's flag was not flown in American waters.

There is a 1786 aquatint engraving of the Naval Battle of the Chesapeake, March 16, 1781 (reproduced in Rice and Brown, The Campaigns . . . , p 240) which pictures what is apparently a French naval ensign which has a white field divided by a darker colored cross (similar to a French regimental color).

Schermerhorn writes that the flag of "the French Navy in the period from 1778 to 1783" was white "with originally perhaps a white cross stitched upon it." He notes that 40,000 men of the French Navy were in American waters during the Revolution.

ROYAL STANDARD OF LOUIS XVI

The royal standard of the King of France at the time of the American Revolution had a white field bearing a large cartouche of the royal arms. The arms had a central blue field with three gold fleurs-de-lis encircled by orders of knighthood and by a wreath of palm branches or laurel and surmounted by the royal crown.

Traditionally, the royal standard would only be carried in the presence of the King. Schermerhorn notes that one authority stated that commanders of very high rank were at times authorized to carry the royal standard as representatives of the King. However, the general concensus is that the French royal standard was not carried in America. The French commanders who were here did carry white standards with gold fleurs-de-lis and other devices, but not their King's banner.

Standards of the ancient French kings displayed various objects and animals according to Preble. The blue "Chape de St. Martin" was the royal standard for about six hundred years of the Christian era—or at least through the reign of Charlemagne. The red or scarlet oriflamme of the abbey of St. Dennis succeeded St. Martin's banner and was carried until the battle of Agincourt in 1415. The royal blue shield sprinkled (semee) with many fleurs-de-lis came into use about the Twelfth Century. The number of fleurs-de-lis was reduced to three, symbolic of the Trinity, by Charles V in 1376. The white standard of the Bourbons was introduced with Henry IV in 1589; the white standard with fleurs-de-lis arms lasted until the French Revolution.

A map of the battle of Yorktown published in 1782 under the sponsorship of an American officer, Major Sebastian Bauman of New York, who was at Yorktown, has a decorative grouping of small scale flags flanking the explanatory notes. The topmost flag on one side (opposite the stars and stripes) is a white banner bearing a small, simplified cartouche of the French royal arms.

ROCHAMBEAU

No contemporary description of any banner which could be identified as "Rochambeau's command standard" is known to the author, nor was any known description quoted by Davis or Schermerhorn; nor, apparently, by the extensive references which they consulted.

Schermerhorn wrote that a colleague had seen in the Metropolitan Museum of Art a

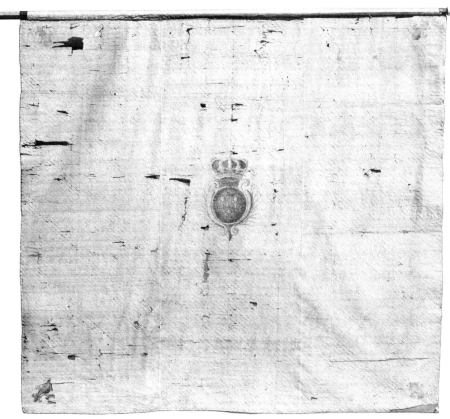

Early ceremonial banner with Royal Arms of France

ceremonial painted banner of heavy white silk with "the royal arms of France" in the center and a gold fleur-de-lis at each corner. The banner was purchased "from the dealer Kahlert of Berlin in 1913" and is believed to date from the last quarter of the XVIIIth Century. There is a narrow sleeve along the top edge to allow for horizontal display. Overall dimensions are about 61 by 62 inches. The arms consist of a near-circular blue shield ("about nine inches high") bearing three gold fleurs-de-lis (two over one) surrounded by a wreath of "palm branches" and surmounted by a crown bearing a cross. The fleur-de-lis at each corner are "about five inches high."

According to Schermerhorn there is no basis for linking this banner to Rochambeau, but he points out that the banner is probably representative of display banners of French royalty and noblemen. The use of fleurs-de-lis in the seals or arms of French noblemen was quite common and many such arms resemble the royal arms.

Rochambeau's seal (or arms) bore three six-pointed stars with holes or spur rowels (two over one) on an oval blue field encircled with various devices, collar and medal of St. Louis, nobleman's crown and mottos.

Mr. Marcel Baldet, French military historian, corresponded in 1960 with Captain Fitzhugh McMaster, USN Ret., concerning the French Flags illustrated in Schermerhorn's book. Mr. Baldet, who had access to the latest research of the Archives of the French War Department, noted that Rochambeau, as a lieutenant-general of a land army, would not have carried a flag with the royal arms. Also, he pointed out that the royal arms, if borne on a flag, would be very large, crowned, and encircled by Orders of Knighthood (see Lafayette-Girarden banner). Mr. Baldet stated that the banner illustrated by Schermerhorn was not representative of the French royal arms.

A 1781 British cartoon caricature of Rochambeau drilling his white uniformed troops is reproduced in The American Heritage's Book of the Revolution, published in 1972. The color bearer carries a large white standard bearing three or, maybe, four large fleurs-de-lis. There are two short tassels at the staff head. The standard is about the same height as the men which would make it about five feet square. The same design for a French standard was used by C. W. Peale.

LAFAYETTE-GIRARDIN BANNER

Harvard's Fogg Art Museum has a white silk armorial banner believed to have belonged to Lafayette. The framed size is three feet square. The banner bears a central circular cartouche, two feet in diameter, applied in waterbased paint.

The banner descended in the family of the Marquis de Girardin and was listed along with other Lafayette "objects and souvenirs" in an undated catalog prepared by some great-grandchildren of the Marquis. The Marquis de Girardin (1735-1808) and his son (1762-1827) were friends of Lafayette and formed the collection. The banner's association with Lafayette is evidently based on the above catalog.

The Fogg Museum catalog of their special Bicentennial exhibit "Harvard Honors Lafayette" contains an illustration of the above banner. (An excellent photograph and available information were kindly supplied by the Museum.) There is a central blue field with three gold fleurs-de-lis (seventeenth century fleur-de-lis design) encircled by the spiral chain and medal of the French Order

of St. Michael which, in turn, is encircled by the collar of the French Order of the Holy Ghost which, again, is encircled by a wreath of laurel. A medal of what appears to be the Order of Louis is suspended from the medallion of St. Michael. The French King's Bourbon crown with fleur-de-lis is at the top of the crest and is linked to the collar of the Order of the Holy Ghost. Louis XVI was a member of the Order of the Holy Ghost and, possibly, of St. Michael. It appears, therefore, that the banner bears the arms of the King of France, probably Louis XVI. If the banner was connected with Lafayette, it would have been displayed as a sign of allegiance *to* and authority *from* the King.

Lafayette, in the uniform of the Commander of the Parisian National Guard wears the "Cross of Saint Louis" in a 1790 portrait by Boze, which is also illustrated in the above Harvard catalog. Possibly Lafayette received the above royal banner when he was commander of the Guard and Louis XVI was still on the throne.

The banner of the French First Swiss Regiment of the Royal Guard (1820) has many almost identical features to those of the Girardin-Lafayette banner including the border, fleur-de-lis seal, crown, Orders of St. Michael and the Holy Ghost, Cross of Louis, wreath (but of laurel and oak) and the same proportions. The Guard's banner has, in addition, a collar of the linked arms of the twenty Swiss cantons staffing the Corps.

The author points out that Lafayette, while in America, was a major-general in the American army and in command of American troops and wore the American uniform. He identified strongly with the Americans and their cause. Lafayette would not have carried the above French royal armorial banner in America. However, the banner could have some connection with his career or family in France.

Lafayette recorded in his Memoires that he purchased a number of standards in France and distributed them to the battalions of his Corps of Light Infantry, prior to

Banner with French Royal Arms. Lafayette-Girardin Collection

the Virginia campaign of 1780-81. He partially described two of the standards (see the Corps of Light Infantry) and it is these standards which would have been most probably associated with Lafayette in America.

FRENCH REGIMENTAL COLORS *(Plates 46-56)*

The colors of a French regiment derived from the ancient heraldic banners of the barons and the banners of the knights whom they commanded. Eventually the barons evolved into colonels and the knights became the company captains. Gradually, as the country was nationalized, the banners became standardized as to size, shape and general design. Company standards were discontinued and at the time of the American Revolution there were only two distinct types of regimental colors carried: the col-

onel's color, which had a white field bearing a central white cross and gold fleur-de-lis, crowns and symbols; and the regimental "d'ordonnance" or regulation color, which was quartered by a central white cross into four cantons of distinctive combinations of colored silk. This orderly system of color-coding the flags was quite simple and, from a recognition standpoint, very effective.

There is some disagreement among reference sources as to the number of colors carried by a French regiment at the time of the American Revolution. Davis states that the number had been reduced to two per battalion, or four for each regiment, including the colonel's white field color and one to three identical regimental colors. Schermerhorn quotes Davis, but adds the opinion of Ernest Harot, at the time 1920-30's architect-in-chief of the historical monuments of France, that French Regiments were still following

145

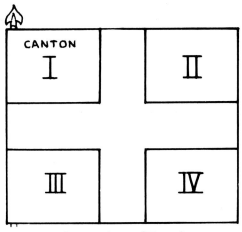

Proportions of French regimental standards

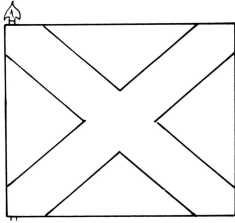

Diagonal cross (saltire) of a foreign regiment in French service

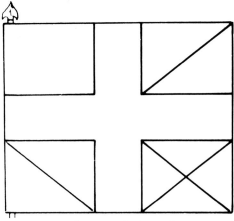

Typical triangulation of cantons

the tradition of carrying the colonel's color by the first company and a regimental d'ordonnance color by each of the other companions. To the author it appears that in America by 1781 each regiment was carrying only two, or, at times possibly three colors—the colonel's color by the first battalion and the regimental color by the second and third battalion. Possibly, if only the first battalion and the colonel were present, both colors were carried by the first battalion. The author bases this opinion on an examination of the paintings by a French War Ministry battle artist, Louis-Nicholas Van Blarenberghe (1716-1794) who painted "The Siege of Yorktown" in 1784, and "The Surrender at Yorktown" in 1785 for the King's collection. The paintings were done under the supervision of an officer on Rochambeau's staff, Louis-Alexander Berthier, who was at Yorktown. The paintings are at Versailles. Rochambeau liked the paintings well enough to order replicas which were painted in 1786 and are now in a private collection.

Van Blarenberghe's paintings are battlefield panoramas done in extraordinary detail, as was the custom. A number of colonels' and regimental d'ordonnance colors as well as the distinctive uniforms of various French regiments can be recognized. Also shown in the Surrender scene are a number of Continental Army national standards of the type favored by Washington—thirteen stars in a blue field without stripes—as in Washington's Headquarters Standard. The standards are spaced at regimental intervals among the American troops lining the roadside from Yorktown to the surrender field. Some of the standards have white fields rather than blue. All would scale to four or five feet square. There is one regiment with a stars and stripes in the Versailles copy, but none in the Rochambeau version.

French Old Regime flag history, including naval ensigns and regimental colors, was the subject of correspondence between Captain

Fitzhugh McMaster, USN Ret., and Monsieur Marcel Baldet, French military historian, in 1960. Mr. Baldet recommended use of the relatively recent (post-1930) research and findings of the Archives du Department de la Guerre which had significantly clarified much of French flag history and revealed errors in the older published reference sources. Mr. Baldet reviewed the French flags section of F. E. Schermerhorn's "American and French Flags of the American Revolution" (1948) and recommended a number of corrections which are incorporated herein.

The regimental colonel's color was of white silk, about five feet square, with a large central white cross outlined by seams sewn with white thread and blazoned with gold painted devices. According to eyewitness accounts and paintings there were three large (six to eight inches) golden fleurs-de-lis on the first canton. Two tassels woven of threads of the regimental colors were suspended by cords attached to the staff's spearhead. Recent research by the French War Department Archives, indicates there was no fringe; thus the lightweight silk could float more freely. The colonel's color was carried only when he was with his regiment and represented the King's commission, according to some sources. Davis and Schermerhorn state that a white scarf was tied to the spearhead of each color. Carefully made, full-scale replicas of the French Alliance regimental (d'ordonnance) colors were presented to Yorktown in 1976 by France; these copies have a white scarf knotted to the spearhead.

The regimental colors all followed the same basic design: about five feet square, of panels of silk, a central square white silk cross (for a few flags there was a diagonal cross) which divided the flag into four quarters. The individual quarters or cantons were formed of various colors of silk. With some colors the cantons were further subdivided into triangles of different colors. Some regimental colors bore painted gilt fleurs-de-lis on the arms of the cross; a few had painted crowns and mottos and, one, a harp. If painted devices were found on the regimental color they were also borne on the colonel's white field color. The regimental color also had two tassels suspended from the spearhead. There was no fringe.

The relative proportions of the width to the length of each arm of the cross is important. Davis correctly illustrates the width-to-length as being 1-to-4 for each individual arm (the free-standing portion), or 1-to-6 when the entire tip-to-tip length of either the horizontal bar or the vertical bar is considered. Mr. Marcel Baldet pointed out that the crosses illustrated by Schermerhorn are too narrow in their proportions.

Davis stated in 1907 that a number of original French colors of the period of the American Revolution still exist.

A French officer of Rochambeau's army, Jean de Verger, kept a journal of his experiences during the period of December 1781 to January 1784. Verger included a self-portrait as a frontispiece to his journal and is dressed in the uniform of the Royal Deux-Ponts Regiment. The portrait is flanked with decorative stands of flags. On Verger's right is a large white standard with three large, scaled eight inch, gold fleur-de-lys in the upper inner quadrant or first canton. On Verger's left is the stars and stripes with the red stripe at the top and the blue canton extending across five stripes vertically with hazily defined stars in irregular rows. Verger's journals and the above self-portrait are included in "The American Campaigns of Rochambeau's Army, 1780-83" by Rice and Brown, 1972.

A map of the battle of Yorktown was published in Philadelphia in 1782 by Major Sebastian Bauman of the New York or 2nd Regiment of Continental Artillery at Yorktown (and in 1783, commander of the Continental Corps of Artillery). As the topmost of a decorative grouping of small-scale flags, which flank the explanatory notes on the map, is shown a large white standard bearing in the first quarter the cartouche of a coat of arms—a central blue field bearing three gold fleurs-de-lis encircled by a gold wreath and topped by a crown bearing a cross. On the opposite side of the legend, and at the same level as the white standard, is the stars and stripes. Possibly the white standard was meant to represent the royal banner.

Brand Whitlock writes as follows of the surrender at Yorktown: "Far along the line that swept away to his (Lafayette's) left towards the York River were the French regiments, each with its two flags, the white banner of the King with the fleur-de-lis, and the regimental standard of its own colours, drooping from their staffs . . ."

The regimental colonels' colors were of while silk, according to a Yorktown eye-witness Hessian Sergeant and each bore three gold fleurs-de-lis.

Charles Willson Peale's portrait of Washington at Yorktown that is now at the Fogg Museum, is essentially a copy of his Washington at Trenton/Princeton. It was painted in 1784 for the State of Virginia to be sent to France as a model for Houden's statue of Washington. Houden, however, insisted on coming to America and modeling Washington from life. In the background of this painting, Yorktown is depicted; and in the near foreground are an American officer, Lt. Colonel John Laurens and a French officer, Viscount de Noialles, carrying unfurled colors and flanking two British officers with cased colors. Noialles carries a large white standard with three large (estimated eight to ten inches) gold fleur-de-lis (two over one) in the upper inner quadrant. The American officer carries the stars and stripes. In another version of this Yorktown painting, at the House of Delegates, Annapolis, Lafayette and Tilghman stand next to Washington and the white standard carried by Noialles again has the three gold fleurs-de-lis, but hazily depicted. A white silk banner with three gold fleurs-de-lis appears to have been typical of the colors of the colonels of the French regiments. Peale, knowing that his painting was to be sent to France, would probably have portrayed the French color carried by Noialles, accurately.

The descriptions of the regimental colors, which follows, have been kept brief; and those features given above, which are common to all the colors, are not repeated. The coloring of the four cantons is given in heraldic order; (1) inner upper-next to the staff, (2) outer upper, (3) inner lower, (4) outer lower. The staff is to the viewer's left in the illustrations. The spearhead of the staff was gilded iron or brass pierced with a fleur-de-lis.

Emphasis has been placed on describing and illustrating the colors, which is the main purpose of this book. Associated data on the regiment, its history and members have been kept to a minimum. There are available excellent publications on the military history of the French forces and personages in the American Revolution to which the reader is referred.

The colors of seventeen of the regiments are described, and typical examples illustrated. The colors of the remaining regiments are possibly to be found in "Les Drapeaux Francais," by Gustave Desjardins, 1874, but should be verified with the recent research of the Archives du Department de la Guerre. The colors of Lauzun's Legion are not known to the author, nor were any colors for this Legion found by Schermerhorn.

AGENOIS REGIMENT *(Plate 54)*

The regimental d'ordonnance color had a central white silk square cross forming four silk cantons. The first and fourth cantons were each divided into two triangles by a diagonal between the outer edges of the cross. The heraldic sequence of colors was as follows: 1st canton, outer triangle green, inner yellow; 2nd and 3rd cantons, purple; 4th canton, outer triangle green, inner yellow. The regimental colonel's color was of white silk with the cross outlined by seams and white thread and probably bore three

Agenois

Armagnac

Auxerrois

large gold fleurs-de-lis in the first canton.

The Agenois took part in the siege of Savannah in 1779 under its colonel, the Baron de Cadignan, where it incurred heavy losses in the assault of October 9. In 1781, the 1st and 2nd battalions were dispatched to Yorktown from the West Indies with the Gatinois and Touraine Regiments under Major-General the Marquis de St. Simon. The regiment took an active part in the siege of Yorktown under its commander, Comte d'Autichamp, including participation in the capture of the British redoubt on October 14.

Verger's Journal lists the Agenois Regiment as being at Yorktown. The regiment and its two colors are shown in Van Blarenberghe's 1785-6 paintings of the *"Surrender at Yorktown"*.

ARMAGNAC REGIMENT
(Plate 54)

The regimental color had a central white silk square cross forming four cantons all of feuille-morte (dead leaf or yellowish-brown) silk. The regimental colonel's color was white silk with the above cross outlined by seams and white threads and probably bore three large gold fleurs-de-lis in the first canton.

Two reference sources claim that a detachment of the Armagnac Regiment, stationed at the time on Guadeloupe, was with d'Estaing's army at Savannah in October 1779. Two other sources do not list the Armagnac as being in America, but one of these states that the regiment was sent to the West Indies in 1777.

AUXERROIS REGIMENT
(Plate 54)

The regimental color had a white silk square cross forming four silk cantons each divided into two triangles by diagonals between the outer edges of the cross and colored, as follows: (1) outer triangle green, inner blue; (2) outer blue, inner green; (3) blue, green; (4) green, blue. The regimental colonel's color was of white silk with the cross outlined by seams and white thread. It probably bore three large gold fleur-de-lys in the first canton.

Reference sources differ on the extent of service seen by this regiment in America. Certain references (Davis and Charles C. Jones (History of Georgia)), claim the Auxerrois Regiment was on Martinique in 1779 and that a detachment was with d'Estaing at Savannah in October 1779. Balch says the regiment left France in 1780 for the West Indies and was part of St. Simon's force transported from the West Indies to Yorktown in 1781 by de Grasse's fleet, but that the regiment's colonel (in 1778, Vicomte de Damas) did not reach America. "Les Combattants..." does not list this regiment among those in America.

onel's color was of white silk with the cross outlined by seams and white thread and probably bore three large gold fleurs-de-lis in the first canton. The regimental uniform was white with black facings.

The (13th) Bourbonnais was one of four infantry regiments which landed at Newport with Rochambeau in July 1780. The regiment was on the ships "Ardent" and "Jason" with D'Estouches fleet during the March 16, 1781 battle in the first French attempt to gain control of Chesapeake Bay. Later in 1781, the regiment marched from Newport and took part in the siege of Yorktown. The regiment and its colors are pictured in Van Blarenberghe's 1785-6 paintings of the "Surrender at Yorktown."

Colonel of the regiment was the Marquis de Laval de Montmorenci with the Viscount de Rochambeau, son of the Count, as second in command.

Champagne

CHAMPAGNE REGIMENT
(Plate 54)

The regimental color had a white silk square cross forming four cantons, all of pale green silk. The regimental colonel's color of white silk had the cross outlined by seams and white thread, and probably bore three large gold fleurs-de-lis.

Bourbonnais

BOURBONNAIS REGIMENT
(Plate 54)

The regimental color had a central white silk square cross forming four silk cantons colored, in heraldic sequence: (1) and (4), blue; (2) and (3), purple. The regimental col-

Some reference sources state that the Champagne Regiment was stationed on Martinique in 1779 and that a detachment was with the French Army at Savannah on October 9, 1779. There was a detachment with DeGuichen's fleet in 1780 and the entire regiment was with DeGrasse's fleet in the sea battle off Martinique on April 9-12, 1782. The regiment is not listed in "Les Combattante..." as having served in America.

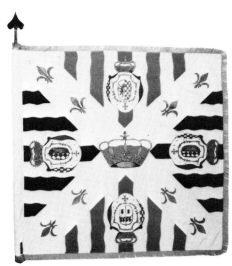

Deux-Ponts

ROYAL DEUX-PONTS REGIMENT *(Plate 54)*

The regimental color had a white silk diagonal (saltire) cross extending between corners forming four silk triangles. The upper and lower triangles were striped with six white and five red vertical wavy stripes. The right and left-hand triangles were striped with six white and five blue horizontal wavy stripes. Two gold fleurs-de-lis were borne on each arm of the cross and a crown was placed at the center. A heraldic shield with the arms of the Dukes of Deux-Ponts (Zweibrucken) was placed on each triangle. According to Gherardi Davis (who received his information from M. Edouard Detaille and M. O. Hollander) three "separated versions of the Deux-Ponts arms are

shown;... each with a mantling. The triangle next to the staff and the opposite triangle are charged with the following arms: per pale the Palatinate and Bavaria. The upper triangle bears: per pale Velding and Hohnstein; the lower triangle bears: per pale Rapzolstein and Holensack, a not very common but very artistic method of drawing the mantlings. The plate is an accurate copy of Mr. Hollander's drawing..."

The Deux-Ponts regimental colonel's color was of white silk without the diagonal cross and bore the gold fleurs-de-lis, the crown and coats-of-arms. The regimental uniform was blue with brilliant yellow facings and cuffs.

The above two colors can be seen with their regiment in Van Blarenberghe's 1785-6 paintings of the "Surrender at Yorktown".

The Regiment was from Zweibrucken, or Deux-Ponts, in the Bavarian Palatinate. It was the largest of the four infantry regiments in Rochambeau's army. Commanded by Count Christian de Forbach de Deux-Ponts, the regiment landed at Newport on June 11, 1780 and in the summer of 1781 marched and sailed to Yorktown. During the siege, a 400 man force made up of detachments from the Deux-Ponts, Bourbonnais, Gatinais, and Agenois regiments, led by Lieutenant-Colonel Viscount Guilliame de Deux-Ponts, assaulted and captured one of two key British redoubts. The French incurred heavy losses. The second redoubt was captured by an American force led by Alexander Hamilton. Verger's Journal lists the Royal Deux-Ponts as being at Yorktown.

DILLON REGIMENT *(Plate 55)*

The regimental color had a central crimson silk square cross edged with white silk forming four silk cantons which were colored in heraldic sequence: crimson, black, black, crimson. The cross bore in black letters the motto "IN HOC SIGNO VINCES." Davis places the "HOC" and "SIGNO" on the horizontal arms and the

Dillon

The Dillon Regiment was formed by the above Count Arthur Dillon's grandfather, from those Irish refugees who accompanied James II into exile to France in the 1690's. Count Dillon, his brother Robert and the Duc de Lauzun were guillotined in 1793. The French 87th Infantry Regiment traces its origin to the Dillon Regiment.

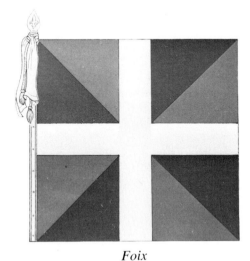

Foix

"IN" and "VIN/CES" on the vertical, evidently based on Desjardins' colored plate of 1771. Recent research of the French War Department Archives indicates that the above placement of the motto is correct. In the center of the cross is a large gold harp, crowned. Each canton is charged with a large diagonally-oriented crown with its cross pointing to the outer corner.

The regimental colonel's color was of white silk with a white cross and the crowns, harp and motto of gold. Irish and Swiss regiments in the French Army wore red coats.

Detachments or battalions of the Dillon Regiment fought in the West Indies, at Savannah in 1779, and at Yorktown in 1781. The regiment's colonel, Count Arthur Dillon, was wounded while leading a squadron of Lauzun's cavalry in a skirmish with Tarleton's forces near Gloucester. Robert Dillon, according to one source, led Lauzun's Legion on its return march to Newport. Verger's Journal lists Lauzun's Legion at Yorktown but not the Dillon Regiment specifically. The Regiment would have been across the river with Lauzun at the time of the surrender and is understandably not pictured in Van Blarenberghe's painting of the Surrender at Yorktown.

FOIX REGIMENT *(Plate 55)*

The regimental color had a white silk square cross forming four silk cantons, each divided into two triangles by a diagonal from the center to the outer corner and colored as follows: (1) upper triangle brown, lower green; (2) upper green, lower brown; (3) brown, green; (4) green, brown. The regimental colonel's color was of white silk, with the above cross outlined by seams and white thread; and, probably, with three large gold fleur-de-lys in the first canton.

The Foix Regiment was sent to the West Indies in 1777 and stationed on St. Dominique. A detachment fought at Savannah in 1779.

GATINOIS REGIMENT *(Plate 55)*

The regimental color had a central white silk square cross forming four silk cantons,

152

Gatinois

Franklin's Libertas Americana Gold Medal. In Commemoration of Saratoga and Yorktown. Engraved by Dupré in Paris in 1783. The head of Liberty, in various versions, was used on American coinage from the 1790's to the 1940's.

each divided into two triangles by a diagonal between the outer edges of the cross and colored, as follows: (1) outer triangle black, inner triangle marine blue; (2) marine blue, black; (3) marine blue, black (4) black, marine blue. The colonel's standard was white silk with the cross outlined by seams and white thread and probably bore three large gold fleur-de-lys on the first canton. The colonel was the Marquis de Rostaign who was promoted to Brigadier in December 1781.

The French military miniature color guard at Yorktown has the following sequence of canton triangle colors: (1) outer triangle green, inner blue; (2) blue, green; (3) blue, green; (4) green, blue.

The Gatinois Regiment took part in the combined French and American unsuccessful assault on the British garrison at Savannah in 1779 incurring heavy losses. The regiment was brought from the West Indies to Yorktown in 1781 with St. Simon's troops, where it took part in the capture of a British redoubt on the night of October 14. As a reward, the regiment was allowed to reassume its old title of the Royal Auvergne which had been lost in a reorganization in 1776. The regiment's motto "Sans Tache" was still in use by its military successor, the French 18th Infantry Regiment, during

World War 1. Davis states that the Auvergne Regiment had "two purple and two black cantons." Schermerhorn states that the Royal Auvergne cantons were red, blue, blue, red (Heraldic order, referencing Desjardins).

Verger's Journal lists the Gatinois as being at Yorktown. The regiment and its colors are pictured in Van Blarenberghe's 1786 painting of the Surrender at Yorktown.

153

Haynault

Rouergue

HAYNAULT REGIMENT
(Plate 55)

The regimental color had a central white silk square cross forming four silk cantons colored (in heraldic sequence): brown, blue, purple, green. The regimental colonel's color was of white silk with the cross outlined by seams and white thread and the first canton probably bore three large gold fleurs-de-lis.

The French military miniature color guard presented to Yorktown in 1976 has the following sequence of canton colors: olive drab, blue, green, purple.

The Hainault (or Haynault) Regiment was stationed on St. Dominique and a detachment (or battalion) fought at Savannah in October 1779.

ROUERGUE REGIMENT
(Plate 55)

Davis lists the Rouergue Regiment as having reached the United States, but too late to serve in the war. The regimental color had the central white cross with four dark green cantons, each charged with a red diamond. This regiment is not among the French military miniature color guards presented to Yorktown in 1976.

SAINTONGE REGIMENT
(Plate 55)

The Saintonge regimental color had a central white silk square cross forming four silk cantons, each divided by diagonals into four triangles colored blue, yellow, green and red. Authorities differ on the sequence of the colors. The latest research by the Archives of the French Department of War indicate the coloring was as follows: (1) upper triangle yellow, left triangle blue, right

Saintonge

triangle green, lower triangle red; (2) yellow, green, blue, red; (3) green, yellow, red, blue; (4) green, yellow, red, blue. The regimental colonel's color was of white silk with the cross outlined by seams and white thread and probably bore three large gold fleurs-de-lis in the first canton. The regimental uniform was white with green facings.

The French military miniature color guard presented to Yorktown in 1976 has the following sequence of canton triangle colors: (1) yellow, blue, green, red; (2) red, blue, green, yellow; (3) blue, red, yellow, green; (4) green, red, yellow, blue.

The Saintonge regiment was one of Rochambeau's four infantry regiments which landed at Newport in 1780 and marched and sailed to Yorktown in 1781. The commander from 1780 to November 11, 1782 was Comte de Custine, who was succeeded by Lieutenant-Colonel Vicomte de Rochambeau. Custine was guillotined during the French Revolution.

Verger's Journal lists the Saintonge Regiment at Yorktown. The uniformed regiment and its regimental color and colonel's color are pictured in Van Blarenberghe's 1785-6 paintings of the "Surrender at Yorktown".

The Marquis de Fleury, a young Captain of Engineers of the Saintonge Regiment, preceded his unit to America and joined the Continental Army in 1776. He was commissioned a lieutenant-colonel in 1777 and fought at Brandywine and Germantown. He was engineer-in-chief and wounded at Fort Mifflin during the 1777 siege. In 1778, he fought at Monmouth, then performed liaison with Conte d'Estaing's expeditionary force at Newport. On the night of July 15, 1779, de Fleury led one of the columns under Wayne which assaulted and captured the fort at Stony Point near West Point on the Hudson. Lt. Col. de Fleury was the first man to enter the fort and lowered the British colors. In recognition of his leadership and bravery at Stony Point, Congress awarded de Fleury a medal, one of a total of only twelve such awards made during the war, and the only

one to a foreign volunteer. He rejoined his Saintonge Regiment when it arrived with Rochambeau's army. At Yorktown he was made a Chevalier of St. Louis, for his part in the assault on British redoubts. In later years, de Fleury became a field marshal in the French army.

Continental Congress Medal awarded to Lt. Col. de Fleury for Stoney Point

155

SOISSONAIS REGIMENT
(Plate 56)

The regimental color had a white silk square cross forming four silk cantons, each divided into two triangles by a diagonal from the center to each corner and colored: (1) upper triangle red silk, lower triangle black silk; (2) black, red; (3) red, black; (4) black, red. The regimental colonel's color was of white silk with the cross outlined by seams and white thread and probably bore three large gold fleur-de-lys in the first canton.

The French military miniature color guard presented to Yorktown in 1976 has the following sequence of canton triangle colors: (1) black, red; (2) red, black; (3) red, black; (4) red, black.

The Soissonais was one of the four infantry regiments in Rochambeau's force. The colonel was the Comte de Saint Maisme and the lieutenant-colonel was the Vicomte de Noailles, brother-in-law of Lafayette. The regiment was at Yorktown, brigaded with the Saintonge Regiment under the command of Major-General the Viscount Viomenil. Vicomte de Noailles led the counter-charge on October 16, 1781 which recaptured two French redoubts.

The regiment's uniform was white with red facings and the hats were white with red

Rochambeau by C. W. Peale

Lt. Col. Armand, a French Volunteer, by C. W. Peale

plumes. The red had faded to a rose color by the time the regiment marched to Yorktown according to eyewitness accounts.

Verger's Journal lists the Soissonais at Yorktown. Van Blarenberghe's 1785-6 paintings of the "Surrender at Yorktown" picture the uniformed regiment together with its regimental color and colonel's color.

Soissonais

Lafayette by Houdon

Touraine

TOURAINE REGIMENT
(Plate 56)

The regimental color had a white silk square cross forming four silk cantons colored: (1) aurora (a yellowish red); (2) blue; (3) green; (4) red. The regimental colonel's color was white silk with the cross outlined by seams and white thread and probably bore three large gold fleurs-de-lis in the first canton.

The commander was either the Baron de St. Simon (according to Balch) or, from April 13, 1780 the Vicomte de Poudeux (according to "Les Combattants...''). This was the regiment of Lafayette's father who was killed by a cannon ball at Minden in 1759.

The regiment was transported from the West Indies to Yorktown by De Grasse's fleet. The Touraine, Gatinais, and Agenois Regiments established a battery of fourteen or more cannon and mortars, known as the Touraine Battery, on the left of the French line.

Verger's Journal lists the Touraine Regiment at Yorktown. Van Blarenberghe's 1785-6 paintings of the *"Surrender at Yorktown"* picture the Touraine Regiment together with its regimental color and Colonel's color.

WALSH REGIMENT *(Plate 56)*

Schermerhorn points out that the Desjardine 1771 colored plate of the regimental color of the Walsh Regiment has a white square cross forming four cantons colored: red, pale yellow, pale yellow, and red. This differs from the illustration given by Gherardi Davis which has a red Greek cross edged with white, four white cantons, the British Royal crest at the center topped with a crowned lion statant, guardant.

The author believes that the Davis illustration (taken from a print in M. Mouillard's work) is the correct version, because the Walsh Regiment was manned by exiled

Walsh

Irishmen, as was the Dillon Regiment, both of which also had a red cross and crown(s). Mr. Marcel Baldet agrees with Davis and, further, says the devices are gold and the crest features a leopard rather than a lion.

The regimental colonel's color would have been of white silk with the above red cross (edged with white), the gold crown, and the gold crowned leopard. Irish regiments in the French army wore red coats.

Reference sources differ as to whether this regiment saw service in America. "Les Combattants..." lists one battalion as being at Savannah in October 1779. Balch says that the 2nd battalion of the regiment was sent to the West Indies in 1780 and that it did not go to Yorktown.

de BRIE, CAMBRESIS, LA SARRE, VIENNOIS, and ROYAL CONTOIS REGIMENTS

In commemoration of the Bicentennial, twenty-two, full-scale, hand-crafted copies of French regimental standards were presented by France to the Yorktown battlefield park museum. Also presented, were twenty-one sets of French miniature soldiers in their respective regimental uni-forms. Each set forms a color guard consisting of the color bearer and two flankers. There are no colonel's colors of white silk among the sets, only the regimental color. None of the standards has fringe, except for a pink dragoon guidon. A white scarf and two tassels worked in the colors of the regiment are fastened at the spearhead of each regimental color except for the guidon. All except one of the flag copies are represented by the miniature color guards and are therefore identified as to their unit. The one standard not so identified is a pink guidon which is believed to be that of the Belzunce Dragoons.

In addition to the regiments covered up to this point, the French miniature color guards include the Regiments de Brie, Cambresis, La Sarre, Viennois, and Royal Contois. The miniatures do not include the Regiments de Rouergue, Auxonne (Artillery), and Grenoble (Artillery).

de Brie — Square white cross with narrow diagonal yellow cross on a red field.

Cambresis — Square white cross, each canton divided into two triangles by diagonals from outer tips of cross. Canton colors, as follows: (1) outer triangle yellow, inner blue, (2) blue, yellow, (3) yellow, blue, (4) blue, yellow.

La Sarre — Square white cross, canton colors, as follows: (1) red, (2) black, (3) black, (4) red.

Viennois — Square white cross, each canton divided into two triangles by a diagonal from outer corners of cross. Canton color sequence, (1) outer triangle purple, inner red, (2) red, purple, (3) purple, red, (4) red, purple. A detachment of this regiment was at Yorktown.

Royal Contois — Diagonal red "raguly" cross, beige-pink or salmon-colored

158

field. Each triangularly-shaped canton or quarter bears thirty-six gilt fleurs-de-lis.

LAUZUN'S LEGION

No description of any colors for Lauzun's Legion are given by the references consulted. Possibly, there was no specific color for the Legion which was formed of various detachments in 1780, just before departure from France.

Lauzun's Legion of Foreign Volunteers consisted of about 300 to 600 light infantry and 300 hussars. It may also have included a battalion from the Dillon Regiment. Verger's Journal lists the "Light Infantry of the Lauzun Legion" and "400 huzzars of the Lauzun Legion" as being at Yorktown. Van Blarenberghe's 1785-6 paintings of the Surrender at Yorktown do not picture the Lauzun Legion, because at that time the Legion was across the river at Gloucester, accepting the surrender of the British units under Tarleton.

Lauzun's Legionnaires formed part of Rochambeau's army which sailed for America on May 2, 1780. The Legion was part of the force that invested Gloucester during the siege of Yorktown and skirmished with Tarleton's Legion outside Gloucester on October 3, 1781. The unit's official designation was Lauzun's Foreign Volunteers. It had been created in March 1780 from the 2nd Legion of the Foreign Volunteers of the Navy, apparently an early version of the French Foreign Legion. The Legion left America for France in March 1783.

No description or mention of a standard of Lauzun's Legion is given by any of the sources consulted, nor does the French national Musee de l'Armee have any record of such a standard. Probably there was no specific standard for the Legion, as it was formed of various detachments.

The uniform of the Legion, perhaps specifically of the mounted troops, was a light blue jacket, Hungarian-style yellow breeches, plumed shako and fur-trimmed cape.

Lauzun joined the French revolutionary forces and commanded one of its armies in 1789. But after all this in the cause of liberty, Lauzun was guillotined by order of the French Revolutionary Tribunal as were many of his comrades of the American War. When the tumbril came for Lauzun, he invited the driver to join him in a glass of wine while he finished his meal of oysters.

Belzunce Dragoons

BELZUNCE DRAGOONS
(Plate 56)

Among a set of some twenty full-size regimental standards presented to the Yorktown battlefield park museum by France in 1976 is a pink silk swallow-tail dragoon guidon which bears the motto "NEC PLURIBUS IMPAR." The symbol is a radiating sun with basic facial features. There is heavy gold fringe. This guidon, of which there is only the one example, is not identified. The guidon's device and the motto were associated with Louis XIV.

Colonel Martel, Conservator, Muses de l'Armes, Hotel National de Invalides, in correspondence with the author in 1977 suggested that the pink guidon is that of the Belzunce Dragoons. Colonel Martel mentioned that two detachments of dragoons served in the United States during the premiere expedition, the Belzunce-Dragoons and the Conde-Dragoons, and that the standard of the Conde-Dragoons was identical to the Belzunce but with a "chamois" field.

AUXONNE REGIMENT *(Plate 56)*
ROYAL CORPS OF ARTILLERY

The regimental color had a central silk square cross forming four silk cantons: (1) and (4), orange-yellow; (2) and (3), gorge de pigeon (reddish purple with irridescent green tints). A number of gold fleurs-de-lis were painted on each arm of the cross. Davis shows five to eight on each arm in a staggered pattern; Schermerhorn shows four on each arm in a single line. The regimental colonel's color was of white silk, with the above cross formed by seams and white thread; each arm of the cross bore four to nine gold fleurs-de-lis.

The second battalion of this regiment was with Rochambeau at Newport and Yorktown. A detachment manned a battery on the Hudson just above Peekskill in the summer of 1781, and damaged a British squadron on July 18, 1781. The principal officers were Nadal and DeBuzelet. One source gives the strength of the "Royal Corps of Artillery of Auxonne" as being 500 artillerymen and 26 artificers.

Verger's Journal lists one battalion of the Auxonne as being at Yorktown. Also, some units and the regimental colors of the "Royal Artillerie" are pictured in Van Blarenberghe's 1785-6 paintings of the "Surrender at Yorktown."

GRENOBLE REGIMENT
ROYAL CORPS OF ARTILLERY

The regimental color (according to Schermerhorn) had a central white silk square cross forming four silk cantons col-ored: (1) green, (2) yellow, (3) yellow, (4) green. The arms of the cross bore painted gold fleurs-de-lis. The regimental colonel's color was of white silk with the cross outlined by seams and white threads, with gold fleurs-de-lis on the arms of the cross.

One company of this regiment was with Rochambeau in America according to "Les Combattants..." Verger's Journal does not list any units of the Grenoble Regiment at Yorktown. Van Blarenberghe's 1785-6 paintings of the "Surrender at Yorktown" picture "the regimental color of the Royal Artillerie (blue coats again)" according to Rice and Brown's "The Campaigns of Rochambeau's Army in America, 1780-83".

METZ REGIMENT
ROYAL CORPS OF ARTILLERY

The regimental color had a central white silk square cross forming four silk cantons, colored: (1) and (4) "gorge de pigeon" (reddish purple with irridescent green tints); (2) and (3) orange-yellow. Four gold fleur-de-lis were painted on each arm of the cross. The regimental colonel's color was of white silk with the cross outlined by seams and white thread, with the gold fleur-de-lis on each arm. The Metz color is the reverse of the Auxonne color.

The commander was the Count d'Aboville who (according to Stone) was in command of all the artillery at Yorktown. d'Aboville became a lieutenant-general in the French Revolution, and later a senator and officer of the Legion of Honor.

The Metz Artillery Regiment was with Rochambeau in America from 1780 to 1783 including Yorktown. Davis lists the Metz Regiment as part of the French force at Savannah. Verger's Journal lists two companies of the Metz Regiment at Yorktown as part of the Royal Artillerie. Van Blarenberghe's 1785-6 paintings of the "Surrender at Yorktown" picture blue-uniformed troops and the regimental color of the Royal Artillerie.

160

—20—

British and Loyalist Colors

BRITISH ARMY AND NAVY COLORS *(Plates 57-59)*

By the time of the American Revolution, British colors had evolved into a half dozen basic designs, standardized throughout the army and navy. A British regiment carried a pair of colors: The first a King's color and the second a regimental color. For a line regiment of foot, the King's color was the "Great Union" or "Grand Union," covering the entire surface with the broad, square, red cross of St. George of England, edged in white, and the diagonal, narrow, white cross of St. Andrew of Scotland, both centered on the blue field. The regimental color had a solid-colored field, which usually matched the facings of the regimental uniform, and featured a Great Union in the first canton. For a Foot Guard Regiment, or Battalion, the above arrangement was reversed, the King's color was crimson, with a union canton; and the regimental color was the Great Union throughout.

"Royal" regiments had blue facings; therefore, they carried a blue field regimental color. There were also regimental colors with yellow, green and buff fields. Foot regiments with red or white facings carried a regimental color with a white field quartered by the red cross of St. George, with the union in the first canton. Regiments with black facings, such as the 64th Foot, which fought at Camden, had a regimental color with a black field quartered by a red cross.

The regimental badge (either of royal or provincial significance) was placed at the center of the colors and the regiment's designation in gold Roman numerals was placed in the first canton. Those regiments which had not been assigned a badge,

161

British National Ensign with Grand Union Canton

Royal Navy Ensign

placed their unit designation in Roman numerals at the center of the colors, and on their regimental color surrounded the numerals with a wreath of roses and thistles. The badges were compactly designed heraldic emblems, or devices assigned by royal warrant.

British colors were made up of panels of silk and measured 72 by 78 inches. Judging by those which survived, the badges, numerals and wreaths were embroidered. Each had a pair of tassels of red and gold. Spearheads were possibly all of the same design—a pointed oval with an open work cross.

The author has direct information on only two surviving original British colors carried during the American Revolution. One is at West Point, the other at Sandhurst. Since there were fifty-seven British regiments that fought in America, there are possibly other surviving originals in British museums and private collections. The colors which are described here are representative of the various regulation types carried during the war.

More detailed descriptions of the badges and colors of specific British regiments can be found in such comprehensive works as "The Records and Badges of Every Regiment and Corps in the British Army" by H. M. Chichester and G. Burges-Short, London, 1895, and "Standards and Colors of the Army" by Milne, London, 1893.

The British Royal Navy ensign was, and still is, a white field quartered by the red cross of St. George with the Great Union in the first canton. There were also red field (first squadron) and blue field (last squadron) ensigns. Warships flew the national Grand Union at the bowsprit jack, and the Royal Navy ensign at the stern. British merchant shipping flew the familiar red ensign with the union in the first canton.

Loyalist forces were, for the most part, organized and equipped in ways similar to British units, and flew their own colors. The total American population at the time of the Revolution was about 2,500,000. Of these, an estimated 500,000 to 800,000 opposed independence, and at least 200,000 of these openly fought their fellow Americans with words and weapons. A large part of the population tried to remain neutral and many crossed over the Alleghenys to avoid the strife. Some historians consider the Revolution to have been more of a civil war between rebels and loyalists and that this internal conflict lasted from 1775 through the War of 1812. Of course, both sides considered themselves to be the true patriots. At the close of the Revolution, about 70,000 loyalists left the United States, most settling in Canada, Britain, the West Indies and Florida.

In addition to such American-manned regular British army units as The 60th, or "The Royal American Regiment," there were many provincial loyalist battalions, regiments and legionary corps. These included: Allen's Pennsylvanians; Chalmer's Maryland Loyalists; Arnold's American Legion; Bayard's Rangers; the British Legion (Lt Col Banastre Tarleton, commanding); Browne's American Volunteers; Delancey's New York Volunteers; Diemar's Corps; Emmerich's Corps; Fanning's Corps; Ferguson's Rifle Corps; Queen's Rangers; Robinson's Loyal American Regiment; Skinner's Brigade; Col Benjamin Thompson's, or The King's American Dragoons; and others. Twelve Loyalist regiments were raised in or near New York, alone, according to F. V. Greene.

THE KING'S AMERICAN DRAGOONS (Plate 58)

The original regimental standard of the King's American Dragoons—a guidon—is in the New Brunswick Museum. It bears a number of embroidered devices, and is heavily fringed. The standard is in excellent

King's Colors
33rd Regiment of Foot

Regimental Colors
33rd Regiment of Foot

163

Original Regimental Standard, The King's American Dragoons

condition, and the painting, shown here, is based on a photograph furnished by the above Museum. This regiment was commanded by Loyalist Colonel Benjamin Thompson, later known, in England, as Count Rumsford.

The standard of the King's American Dragoons is in excellent condition. It compares favorably with that of the Philadelphia Light Horse as to artistic quality and detail. A colored picture of the standard appeared in "The National Geographic," April 1975.

"The width from top to bottom (excluding the fringe) is 59 cm. The length of the flag (excluding the fringe) from edge to edge is 73½ cm. The length of the flag (excluding the fringe) from the unfringed end to the V-shaped cut out is 55½ cm. The fringe is of gold covered twine, 5 cm. long. The front and back are stitched together, about 6½ cm. from the unfringed edge, to form a sleeve. Both the front and back do not have any seams, and since these two pieces are stitched together with the fringe, along the edge, the edgeseam and selvage cannot be seen.

"The background of the standard is of blue silk (now faded to a blue-grey) with five circular pieces of scarlet silk appliqued to it. Around the edge and in the centre of each piece of silk is an intricate embroidery design in both gold and non-metallic thread. Enclosed is a photocopy of a picture of the standard, and the individual designs can be seen.

"Near the unfringed end are attached two braided gold and scarlet cords, one is about 35½ cm. long (from the fringe) the other is about 47 cm. long, and each cord is attached to one tassel, about 13½ cm. in length. The standard seems to be backed with fairly stiff cotton."

THE FOOT GUARDS *(Plate 59)*

The various Guards Regiments or Battalions in America were formed of companies detached from their home Guards Regiments. A typical battalion was formed of companies from the Coldstream and Scots Guards. The Union colors, if carried, would have been the crimson field ensign with a company badge at the center and the Grand Union in the first canton. The battalion color would have been one of the company colors—the union throughout with a company badge at the center. Within a regiment, the badges were rotated by rule of the company seniority as the colors were retired and replaced.

The IIId Foot Guards (Scots Guards) contributed ''the 1st and 2nd companies of the regiment'' which ''in battalion with a like number of Coldstream fought all through the American Campaigns, from 1776 to 1783 . . .'' according to Chicester and Burges-Short. The Grenardier Guards also contributed its quota to the American War. Baurmeister wrote of the ''regiments of Foot Guards numbering eleven hundred men'' with Howe's Army, and refers to the ''Brigade of Foot Guards'' just before Brandywine.

THE SEVENTH REGT. OF FOOT
THE ROYAL FUSILIERS
(Plates 58, 59)

An original King's color, the Great Union of this regiment, still survives and is among the national trophys at West Point. One set of colors of the Seventh was captured at Fort Chambley during Montgomery's invasion of Canada in 1775; and a second set when Morgan defeated Tarleton at Cowpens, South Carolina in 1781. The regimental colors have disappeared, as have all other British colors captured during the War. All had apparently disappeared within the first forty years following the Revolution—probably to

King's Color, Third Foot Guards
(Scots Guard)

Regimental Color, Third Foot Guards
(Scots Guard)

King's Color, VII Regiment of Foot
The Royal Fusiliers

Regimental Color, VII Regiment of Foot
The Royal Fusiliers

souvenir hunters. A Congressional Committee reported in 1814 that it was able to locate only one or two of the British colors captured during the Revolution. Since about thirty-five or forty were captured, their loss must have been due to souvenir hunters and neglect.

The King's color of the Seventh is of red, white and blue silk panels, and bears the Great Union of the crosses of St. George and St. Andrew throughout. The embroidered regimental badge is at the center. The badge is a royal device featuring the white rose, joined with the red rose (Lancaster and York) on a crimson field. The field is encircled by a purple and gold Garter bearing the motto "HONI, SOIT, QUI. MAL.Y. PENSE" with a gold crown above. The Roman numeral "VII" in gold appears as a reversed "IIV" on the obverse, and is placed near the upper inner corner on an arm of St. Andrew's cross.

The regimental color of the Seventh, according to Chichester and Burges-Short, and assuming that there was no change, was blue silk, with the numeral VII in the first canton, and the White Horse of Hanover in each of the other three cantons displaying the motto "NEC ASPERA TERRENT." The regimental badge was at the center.

The Royal Fusiliers served throughout the Revolution and saw much action. During the War of 1812, the regiment was with

Packenham's army at the battle of New Orleans.

THE NINTH REGIMENT OF FOOT *(Plate 59)*

The original "Regimental Colors" of the regiment is at Sandhurst. The "King's Colors" was the Union throughout, with the numeral "IX" at the center; but no surviving Revolutionary War original is known.

The regimental color, much disintegrated, is of yellow silk with the union in the first canton. The numeral "IX" is at the center encircled by a large wreath of roses and thistles. The staff spearhead is identical to those on the original colors of the 2nd New Hampshire Regiment.

King's Color, IX Regiment of Foot

Lt. Col. John Hill, commander of the Ninth, saved his regiment's colors, when Burgoyne surrendered at Saratoga, by ripping them from their staff and packing them in his personal baggage, which was exempt from search. The surrender or "convention" terms did not call for the surrender of colors, but only of "arms and artillery". Hill was exchanged in 1781 and presented the colors to King George who appointed him "Aide-de-Camp" and promoted him to Colonel.

Regimental Color,
IX Regiment of Foot

Colonel Hill also sent or brought back to England two captured American regimental colors which still survive. These are assumed to be those of the "2nd New Hampshire" Regiment taken at the July 8, 1777 battle near Fort Anne. Hill's regiment reportedly did capture a color at Fort Anne, but its description does not fit either of the two surviving colors, and the 2nd New Hampshire was not at the battle of Fort Anne.

The following appears in a British periodical "The Navy and Army Illustrated" January 24th, 1903, p 490, as a footnote to an article on the "War Trophies (Colors) at Chelsea, IV": " . . . There is an interesting history attached to the colours of the 9th Foot. When General Burgoyne was compelled to surrender at Saratoga, the 9th Foot (now the Norfolk Regiment) was included in his force. The colonel of the regiment, reluctant to let the colours pass into the hands of the enemy, removed them from their staves and secreted them. When the regiment returned home in 1781 the colours were remounted and presented to the King, who returned them to the colonel to be retained as an heirloom. Passing through many hands, they finally descended to the chaplain of the Royal Military College, Sandhurst. He presented them to that institution, where, on their reception, they were trooped by a battalion of the regiment. They were afterwards placed in the college next to a pair of colours borne by the 9th during the Peninsular War. Those carried in America are distinguished from the later ones by the absence of the St. Patrick's Cross in the King's colours."

Some British regiments burned their colors at Saratoga. Baroness Riedesel in her "Memoirs" said she hid the colors of her husband's Hessian battalions in her bed. Later, the Baron sent them home with an exchanged officer, Capt. O'Connell, who left them in Rhode Island, from where they were subsequently carried to Canada by Lt. Col. Specht.

The defeated regiments secreted or burned their colors at Saratoga because of the liberal terms of the "Convention," which did not specifically call for surrender of the colors, but only referred generally to "arms." Congress siezed on the non-surrender of the colors as one of their pretexts to nullify the Convention, and hold Burgoyne's army as prisoners for four years. Gates in a letter to Henry Laurens, dated Albany, December 3rd, 1777, said, " . . . Respecting the standards, General Burgoyne declared upon his Honor, that the Colours of the Regiments were left in Canada . . ."

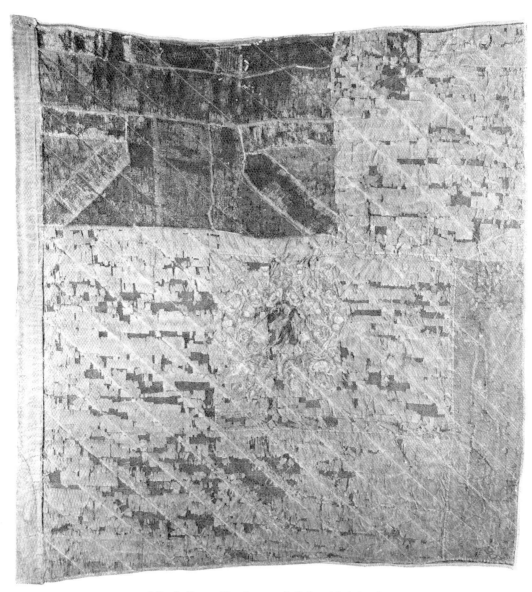

Ninth Foot, Regimental Color (Original)

—21—

German Colors

REGIMENTS AND DESIGN OF COLORS

There were thirty German regiments in America during the Revolution, according to the military historian, F. V. Green. The six German states that sent nearly 30,000 troops to America were Hesse-Cassel, Hesse-Hanau, Anspach-Beyreuth, Brunswick, Waldeck, and Anhalt-Zerbst. Only 18,000 returned home. Of the 12,000 casualties, 5,000 were deserters who elected to stay in the New World. Hesse-Cassel supplied more than half the German force. Brunswick sent 4,300.

Britain's use of mercenaries did as much to alienate the colonists as did her alliance with the Indian tribes. The Germans were disciplined, well-equipped and ably officered. They fought well but gained a reputation for ruthlessness, atrocities and plunder. Their attitude mellowed with time and battles. A continuing barrage of propaganda by the colonists, offering citizenship and land, also helped to soften some.

Davis wrote that: "It is probable that all of the German regiments which served in America had one color for each company." With thirty regiments, each with four or five companies, there must have been many colors—though the artillery and Yager regiments did not carry colors, and only four of the Brunswick regiments had colors.

Despite the large number of originals, only four German colors carried in America are extant—all are war trophies in this country in national museums. Two are at West Point, a third at the Smithsonian, and the fourth at Yorktown. The four are of Anspach-Beyreuth regiments. No Revolutionary War German colors were located in Germany by Davis during his research in the early 1900's. There is a fragment of an unidentified Hessian color at the Philadelphia First Troop museum. Since there were "no less than twenty-two German colors captured" and they were of heavily embroidered, brocaded silk, their loss can only be attributed to souvenir hunters and neglect. Actually, there were probably thirty-three or more German

169

colors captured. Hessian General Heister, on January 5, 1777, reported fifteen lost at Trenton (versus the four to six which reached Congress).

Judging by the four surviving originals, and by paintings, descriptions and photographs of four or five others, German colors had certain similar features. They were generally about four feet square and made of two layers of heavyweight silk. The fields were elaborately decorated with embroidered and painted symbols, with marked differences between the symbols on the obverse and reverse sides. Colors were sleeved and nailed to their staffs and had tassels on cords about four feet long. Staff spearhead finials were quite large and of intricate, pierced designs. There were no national or union colors. However, each color bore some common symbol identifying the particular German State to which the regiment belonged. Hessian colors bore "a red and white striped lion (the arms of Hesse)." Brunswick standards were distinguished by "a white horse in a red field (the arms of Brunswick)." The Anspach-Beyreuth regiments bore "a red eagle (Brandenburg) and the letters M.Z.B. (Markgraf zu Brandenburg)."

Davis wrote that he had been unable to find out anything about the Waldeck or the Anhalt-Zerbst colors.

HESSIAN COLORS *(Plate 60)*

Although no Hessian colors are extant, we have accurate depictions of four or five. There are Davis' 1907 photographs of two green field colors which were at the Historical Society of Pennsylvania, and, even more exact, Charles Willson Peale's painting of Washington shows one green and two black field Hession colors in considerable detail. Also, Davis quotes Ellery's description:

"On December 31, 1776, William Ellery, writing from Baltimore to the Governor of Rhode Island, described a Hessian color with great accuracy as follows: 'Among other things that fell into our hands by the victory at Trenton, were four standards, one of which is now in the room where Congress is held, and directly before me. It is a Hessian silken standard. The battalions which were surprised and subdued were the regiments of *Landspatch, Kniphausen* and *Rahl.* I would describe it, if I were acquainted with heraldry, and if it were important enough to engage your attention. In the centre of a green field of about four or five feet, is a decorated gilted circle, which encloses a lion rampant, with a dagger in his right paw, and this motto in the upper part of it: 'Nescit Pericula.' The crest is a crown, with a globe and cross upon it. In the corners are gilted decorated circles, with crowns and globes, and crosses, on their tops; and in the middle 'F.L.' in cyphers. A broad blaze extends from the corners to the piece in the centre, and three small blazes are placed in the field; one in the middle of the side next staff; one in the opposite side; and one in the midst of the lower side or bottom.*** (R. I. Col. Rec., Vol. VIII, p. 170)."

Davis illustrated and described the two Hessian flags and a small remnant from a black field Hessian flag which were at the Historical Society of Pennsylvania in 1907. The remnant (among the Clymer papers) "shows a part of the monogram 'F.L.' (Friederich Landgraf) and of the wreath on white silk, and a very little piece of a black field." Davis pointed out that the same monogram appeared clearly on one of the two green field flags at the Historical Society.

Davis described the two flags as follows: "The field of both these flags is a faded green, the corner blazes brownish white, the centre blue with traces of a red and white striped lion. The oddly shaped "blazes," which appear in the corners of the flags, are still not uncommon on flags in the Prussian Army. The flags were painted in gold and colors, the gold being sharply outlined in black: the wreaths, monograms and crowns are gold. Where the two green flags were

*Color of a Hessian Regiment.
Probably, Knyphausen's
Regiment. See Peale's
Washington at Trenton
(Present-day painting)*

*Two original green-field Hessian colors of unidentified regiments. Probably
captured at Trenton. Photographed in Philadelphia in 1907. Present
whereabouts unknown*

*Fragment of a black field Hessian Color.
Photographed 1907 in Philadelphia*

captured or to what regiment they belonged is not positively known. I will only add, that on the better preserved flag the sword and the lion's paw can be seen distinctly. . . . It would seem as though the lion as well as the corners had been deliberately torn out of each of these flags."

The above remnant and the two flags disappeared some time between the time of Davis' photographs, around 1900-1907, and the mid-1970's, when they were found to be missing. It has been conjectured, based on a cryptic entry on an accession card, that the flags were loaned out, possibly during the Sesquicentennial of 1926, and not returned. Possibly, they are stored away in some cabinet with the holder unaware of their identity or historical value. Hopefully by means of this book they might be located. Additional reports on the captured Hessian flags are in the paragraphs that follow.

Hessian Adjutant General Major Baurmeister reported, "... on the 26th (December) an hour after sunrise, Lossberg's, Knyphausen's and Rall's Regiments were surprised in Trenton by more than ten thousand rebels. They were badly treated and made prisoners, losing their guns, colors, and all equipage..."

General Heath wrote to Govenor Trumbull on December 30, 1776 that four standards were taken.

William Buehler wrote to Admiral Preble on November 18, 1881 that "two flags out of the six captured... at Trenton are in the department on the hill at Harrisburg". The colors have since disappeared. Staff members of the William Penn Museum at Harrisburg have no knowledge as to the whereabouts of any surviving remnants there.

Some fragments of a "Hessian flag captured at Trenton" are in the First City Troop Museum, Philadelphia. The fragments total about twenty by seven inches and consist in the main of black brocaded silk seamed to a narrow strip of white and are decorated with small elements of brown and yellow painted designs. (Not the same as 1907 fragment.)

Another account says that six of the Hessian colors, and nine hundred prisoners taken at Trenton, were paraded in the streets of Philadelphia on December 30, 1776. The prisoners were on their way to Lancaster. The colors, or some of the colors, were sent on to the Continental Congress in Baltimore; to which place the Congress had fled upon occupation of the east bank of the Delaware by British and German units.

ANSBACH-BAYREUTH REGIMENTS *(Plate 61)*

Four original colors of two Anspach-Bayreuth regiments, *Von Seybothen* and *Voit*, are extant. They were taken at Yorktown according to Davis, who referenced Doehla's diary that eighteen German colors were captured. The other fourteen have disappeared. Davis wrote that ten of the eighteen belonged to the two Ansbach-Bayreuth regiments of five companies each, and that eight belonged to the two Hessian regiments, *Erb-Prinz* and *von Bose*.

The four colors were at West Point during 1905-1907 where they were photographed for Davis' book. One of the four was at the

Obverse   *Reverse*

Original Colors of an Ansbach-Bayreuth Regiment Captured at Yorktown

Alexandria Masonic Museum in the 1840's, where it was sketched by Lossing. It had originally been presented to Washington by Congress.

The four colors are of the same design, except that two bear the date "1775" and one "1770". All are of two layers of heavy white silk damask, figured with a pattern of a small spray of flowers and leaves. The damask pattern figure of the 1770 color is of a "different pattern from the others."

The four colors have been repaired and mounted since Davis' photographs were taken. However, his description is still applicable and is quoted here:

" . . . The nailing of the flags to the staves is a common German custom, but it will be observed that the three flags are not nailed in the same manner. The embroidery is of colored silk much faded. On one side of each flag is an eagle, now dull reddish brown, but originally red (the Brandenburg eagle), and a scroll with the motto PRO PRINCIPE ET PATRIA (gold on silver), now badly tarnished. On the other side of the flags are palm and laurel branches of green, tied together by a pink ribbon now quite pale in color, together with a large monogram, a crown and the letters M.Z.B. and the date, all of bullion. The spear-head is shown in detail with the French and English spearheads and on the same scale. I am informed by Dr. Julius Meyer, Secretary of the Mittel-Franken Historical Society at Ansbach, that the large monogram should be read as follows: S.E.T.C.A., and that the first four letters stand for: SINCERITER ET CONSTANTER (the motto of the order of the Red Eagle, then of Ansbach, now of Prussia). The fifth letter is the initial of ALEXANDER, the reigning Prince, whose complete monogram appears in the spear-head. . . . —C.F.C.A., Christian Friedrich Carl Alexander. The only remaining cord and tassel are silver and black.

Two of these flags are clearly shown in Peale's smaller picture of Washington at the Metropolitan Museum . . . where the bullion is shown as apparently sewed down with red silk, and the eagle is painted bright red. . . ."

173

Colors of the Von Riedesel Infantry Regiment of Brunswick

BRUNSWICK COLORS *(Plate 60)*

Davis described the colors of the Brunswick regiments, as follows:

"By a letter from Director Walter (April 15, 1907) of the Vaterländisches Museum in Brunswick, I am informed that, while the Brunswick flags which were saved by Madame von Riedesel and brought back to Brunswick, were deposited in the Arsenal there, they are no longer in existence. Only four of the Brunswick regiments had flags. All were of the same pattern, but of different colors, namely: The *Prince Frederick* regiment had a black flag with a yellow cross; the *Riedesel* regiment's flag was yellow with a blue cross; the *Rhetz* regiment's flag was green with a white cross; and the *Specht* regiment's flag was red with a white cross. The centres of all the flags were red with a white horse (the horse of Brunswick) and the decorations, monograms, crowns, mottoes, etc., were painted in gold and color. The print I have had made of such a flag is from a large water-color sent me by the Ducal Museum in Brunswick. The motto, "NUNQUAM RE-TRORSUM," is still on one of the colors of the *92nd Regiment* (Brunswick). The cypher in the corners, a double C, is for "Carl," the reigning duke.

The *Brunswick Dragoons* brought with them to Canada four small swallow-tail standards, but did not carry them in the field, as the regiment fought on foot. These standards were blue with decorations painted in gold and colors. The two sides were not the same; on one side was the Brunswick horse, in white, standing on green grass; on the other side were the large Brunswick arms emblazoned in their proper colors."

174

Post-War Colors

ORGANIZATION, CAMPAIGNS, AND COLORS *(Plates 60, 61)*

Following the Revolution, the United States Navy, once it was reactivated, continued to fly the stripes and stars as well as the stripes with an eagle canton. Also, ships flew the stars, alone, as well as the eagle and stars, alone, as a jack. Prints and paintings indicate that stripes, alone, also continued in use well into the Nineteenth Century. There is an early striped ensign extant in a private collection which bears two large stars indicating it was the standard of an admiral.

Post-war Army colors are comprehensively covered by Mr. Detmar H. Finke in the Fall, 1963 issue of *Military Collector and Historian* to which the reader is referred. The author drew heavily on Mr. Finke's work for reference guidance.

The United States Army was reactivated as a single regiment in 1784 from the company size unit to which it had been reduced at demobilization. Several types of colors and standards were flown over the next several decades. The thirteen stripes and stars was hoisted over forts and served as a garrison flag. The single Army regiment created in 1784 carried a "standard" and had four camp colors. However, the designs are not specifically known. The standard and colors were made in Philadelphia in October 1784 by Rebecca Young who sewed the "standard" and by John Henderson who painted devices on the standard and colors. That a flag painter was needed indicates that the standard was not a stars and stripes. Probably, it was the eagle and stars on a blue field. Also, it could have been the stripes with an eagle canton such as descended from General Philip Schuyler and also such as pictured on the Society of Cincinnati diploma. That a new standard was needed also indicates that either all of the War-time standards had disappeared or that none were of the desired design, including the fifty standards made in mid-1782 and delivered to Washington at Verplanck's Point in February-March 1783.

The First Regiment under General Joseph Harmar carried its standard on the unsuccessful expedition against the Indians of the old northwest territory in the fall of 1790. The Indians, allies of the British, refused to accept the fact they had lost the War and were not parties to the peace treaty by which Britain ceded the territory to the United States. The territory had been conquered during the War by George Rogers Clark.

Following Harmar's expedition, the Army was increased to two regular regiments and two regiments of levies. Another Revolutionary War veteran, Major General Arthur St. Clair, replaced Harmar. Brigadier General Richard Butler commanded the regiments of levies. In June and July 1791, Secretary of War Henry Knox in Philadelphia ordered four silk standards for the regiments. The standards and their linen cases were sewn by Nancy Nash. Henry P. Pearson provided the poles; John Wucherer, the mountings, metal butts and points (finials); and Wood and Thornely, the silk tassels. Mr. Wright painted the devices of the standards and also painted the poles.

The four standards were sent to St. Clair's army at Fort Washington (Cincinnati, Ohio) but arrived too late for his expedition in Fall 1791 which ended in a second defeat by the united Indian tribes backed by their Tory, British and Canadian allies.

The Army was again increased in size, this time to 5,120 men, and Wayne was placed in command. In Fall 1792, he organized the Army into a "Legion of the United States" with four Sub-Legions, each with infantry, riflemen, cavalry and artillery. Wayne asked Secretary Knox for standards, battalion and camp colors. Knox replied that with changes the four silk regimental standards sent to St. Clair and stored at Fort Washington could be used as sub-legionary standards. For the Legion's standard, Knox suggested the device be a life-size silver eagle. Wayne instituted strict training and discipline standards and moved his Army from Pittsburgh to an isolated campsite twenty-two miles away which received the name Legionville. The present day veterans organization, the American Legion, takes its name from Wayne's Legion.

On 23 September 1792, Wayne ordered his Quartermaster General to make up sixteen camp colors each two feet square. There were to be four each of white, of red, of yellow and of green and they were to be painted on each side, respectively, 1st, 2nd, 3rd, and 4th S.L.U.S.

In March 1793, Wayne inquired again as to "a Legionary Standard, Sub-Legionary and Battalion Colors," and was again referred to the four colors at Fort Washington. However, Knox did include a funding request for twelve battalion colors in his 1793 budget. Stillé implies that Wayne received his requested standard and colors but gives no reference.

Wayne had the designations on the four, 1791, St. Clair "Division Standards" changed from 1st to 2nd Regiment and 1st and 2nd Levies to 1st Sub-Legion, 2nd Sub-Legion, 3rd and 4th. Also they were to be equipped with cords, tassels and cases.

On 20 August 1794, Wayne's Legion defeated the combined forces of the united Indian tribes and their Canadian allies at the Battle of Fallen Timbers on the Miami River, southwest of Toledo.

POWEL STANDARD

A well preserved example of a blue standard with an eagle device is that presented to the Philadelphia Light Horse by Mrs. Powel in the mid-1790's and described in the notes to the section on the Light Horse standards. There is also a large regimental standard of beige colored cloth bearing an eagle seal and seventeen stars at the Masonic Museum in Philadelphia. Two beautiful examples of the blue-field, eagle-deviced army national standard of the circa-1800 period are at West Point and Independence National Park.

Color Plates

*Charles Willson Peale portrait of Washington at the Battle of Trenton.
Painted in 1779. Note blue-field standard with circle of six-pointed stars.
There are no stripes. Captured British and German flags are at
Washington's feet.*

179

Plate 1

LIBERTY AND UNION FLAGS

LIBERTY FLAG (top left); UNION FLAG: Ship Alfred, December 1775—Cambridge, January 1, 1776 (middle left); UNION FLAG: Brigantine Lexington, September 1777—John Paul Jones Coat of Arms (bottom left); SONS OF LIBERTY (top right); UNION FLAG: "The Rebel Stripes" (middle right); UNION FLAG: Fort Stanwyk, August 1777—Fort Mifflin, October 1777 (bottom right)

*Red-White-Blue Striped
Ensign of the Continental
Brigantine Lexington.
Captured by HMS Alert,
September 19, 1777*

British Lt. Col. Simcoe's sketch of Yorktown, October 1781. Note Stars and Stripes

STRIPES WITH UNION OF STARS

Trumbull, 1780–90's (top left); Abel Buell Map, 1783 (middle left); Division Color—7th Pa. Regt. September 1777 (bottom left); Peale, 1780's (top right); Fort Mercer, October 1777 (middle right); Mondhare Flag Sheet, 1781, Lotter Flag Sheet, 1793 (bottom right)

White-Blue Stripes, Red Canton, Fort Mercer, Red Bank, N.J.,
October 1777

Red-White-Blue Stripes, Fort Mifflin, Philadelphia, October 1777

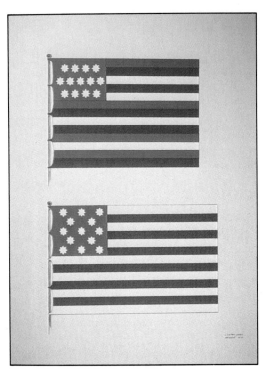

Serapis, The Texel, October 5, 1779 (top);
Alliance, The Texel, October 4, 1779
(bottom)

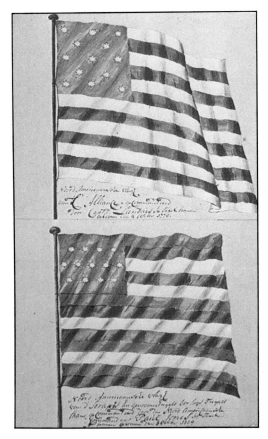

John Paul Jones
Harbor of the Texel, Holland, October 4
& 5, 1779
Continental Frigate Alliance (top);
Captured HMS Serapis (bottom)

Arthur Lee, September 20, 1778 (top);
Franklin and Adams, October 9, 1778
(bottom)

Yorktown—1781—John Trumbull, painted circa 1790

Surrender at Yorktown—1781—by John Trumbull, painted 1787

185

Plate 7

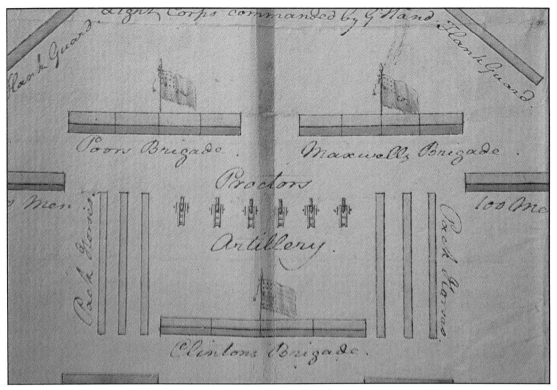

Order of Battle, Maj. Gen. Sullivan's army—1779. Sketch by New Jersey Major John Ross.   Note stars and stripes and regimental standards with stars

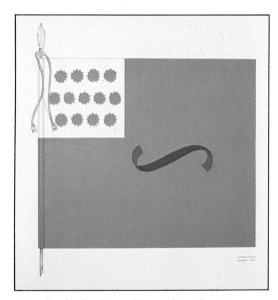

Standard of a New Hampshire Regiment, General Poor's Brigade—1779. Major General Sullivan's Order of Battle. Major John Ross' sketch

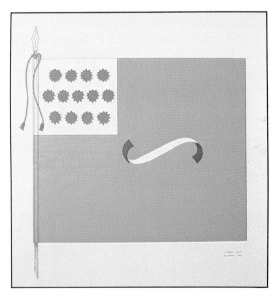

Standard of a Regiment of Maxwell's New Jersey Brigade—1779. Major Ross' sketch

186

Plate 8

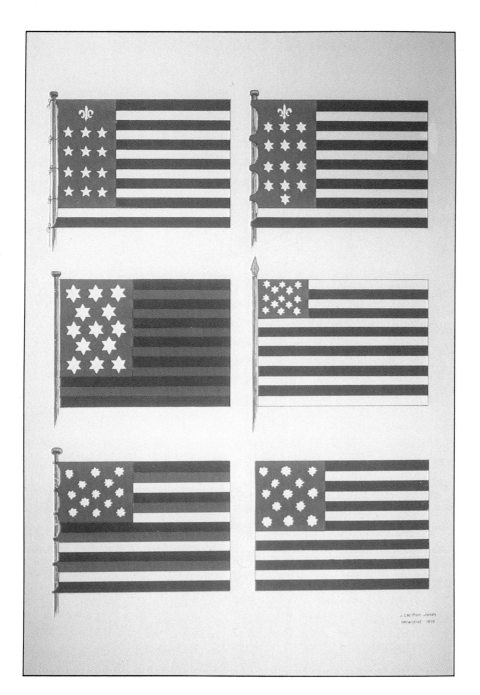

STRIPES WITH UNION OF STARS

*Mondhare Flag Sheet, 1781 (top left); British Lt. Col. Simcoe, Yorktown,
October, 1781 (middle left); Matthias Sprengel, British Almanac, 1784
(bottom left); Lotter Flag Sheet, ca. 1782 (top right); Major Bauman's
map of Yorktown, published 1782 (middle right); John Wallis Map,
London, 1783 (bottom right)*

Yorktown—
Charles Willson Peale.
Note Eagle Canton and
Stripes National Standard

The Seal of
the United States.
Painted Panel above
Washington's Pew,
St. Paul's,
New York,
ca. 1789

Plate 10

Original Eagle and Stripes. General Philip Schuyler, circa 1780's

Original Eagle and Stripes. Painted Blue Silk Canton. Arms of the United States. Descended in the family of General Philip Schuyler

189

Plate 11

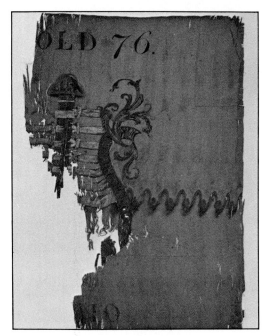

Original of The Headman Color
Gostelowe Standard No. 1

Gostelowe Standard No. 1
The Headman Color

Gostelowe Standard No. 2

Gostelowe Standard No. 3
Harmonious Union

190

Plate 12

Gostelowe Standard No. 4
America Triumphant

Gostelowe Standard No. 5
Sustain or Abstain (Help or Stay Neutral)

Gostelowe Standard No. 6
Death or Honor

Gostelowe Standard No. 7
Perseverance

191

Plate 13

Gostelowe Standard No. 8
Fight Back—The Outcome is in Doubt

Gostelowe Standard No. 9
Honorable Remembrance

Gostelowe Standard No. 10
Armed Resistance

Gostelowe Standard No. 11
American Defence

Gostelowe Standard No. 12
Defeated—We Rise Again

Gostelowe Standard No. 13
United We Stand

Reverse   *Obverse*

Standard of Pulaski's Legion of 1778. (Painting)

193

Plate 15

Blue Color of the 2nd Regiment, Continental Light Dragoons

Blue Color of the 2nd Regiment, Continental Light Dragoons (Original)

194

Plate 16

Red Color of the 2nd Regiment, Continental Light Dragoons (painting)

Red Color of the 2nd Regiment, Continental Light Dragoons (Original)

195

Plate 17

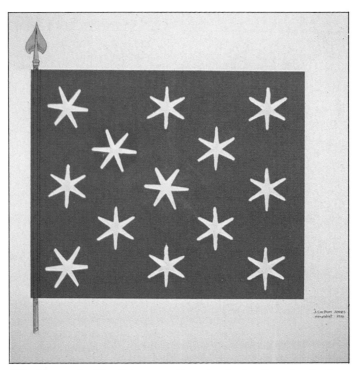

Washington's Headquarters Standard, the Standard of the Army in 1781. Present-day copy

Washington's Headquarters Standard (Original)

196

Plate 18

Detail of the Battle of Princeton by William Mercer. Note Washington's Headquarters Standard

Original silk standard of Washington's Life Guards. The scenic emblem depicts the Spirit of Liberty handing the Commander's Standard to an officer of the guard

197

Plate 19

Matthias Sprengel, Berlin Almanac—1784

Lossing's 1849 Version of the Standard of the Commander-In-Chief Continental Navy. The "Gadsden Flag"

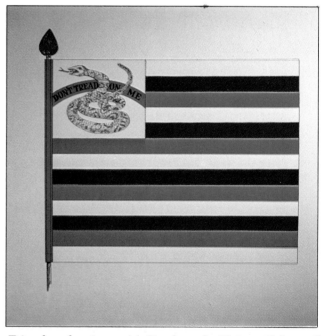

Tri-colored stripes with Rattlesnake Union, Colors of the Rhode Island Militia Standard of General Sullivan's Guard

198

Plate 20

Continental Frigate Bonhomme Richard vs. HMS Serapis, September 23, 1779

Battle Of Lake Champlain, 11-13 October 1776.

199

Plate 21

John Paul Jones Coat of Arms—1776-77. Four Flags are shown. British Union Red Ensign. Red, White, Blue Stripes with British Union. Red, White, Blue Stripes with Pine Tree Union. Commodore's Blue Pennant

200

Plate 22

Red, Blue,
White Stripes
with The
British Union

British Union
Red Ensign

Commodore's Blue
Command Pendant

Red, White,
Blue Stripes
with Pinetree Union

Coat of Arms—1776-77. From the original at The Masonic Library—Boston

201

Plate 23

*Standard of the Third Connecticut Regiment of 1775 (top); Standard of the
II Battalion, II Connecticut Regiment (Artist's Rendition) (middle); Colors of the
1st Grand Subdivision—Webb's Additional Continental Regiment of 1777 (bottom
left); Original colors of the 1st Grand Subdivision (bottom right)*

202

Plate 24

Standard of Webb's Additional Continental Regiment of 1777. Later the 9th Connecticut Regiment of 1780, then the 3rd Connecticut Regiment of 1781 (Present-day Painting)

Original fragment and reconstruction of Webb's Additional Continental Regiment of 1777

Detail of the Standard of Webb's Additional Continental Regiment of 1777

*Standard of the Thirteenth
Continental Regiment of 1776*

*Colors of a Newburyport Independent
Company*

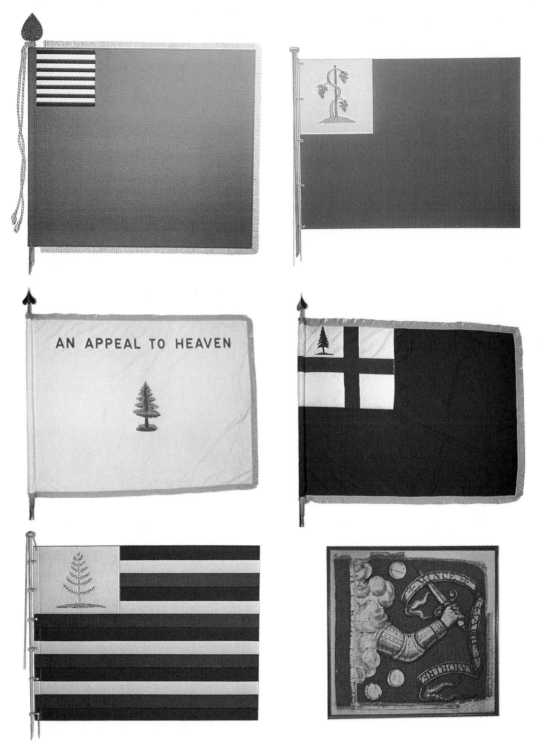

Delaware Militia Color—1777 (top left); Massachusetts State Navy Ensign and Ensign of Washington's armed vessels—1775 (Present-day Ceremonial Version with Fringe) (middle left); Red, White, Blue Stripes with Pine Tree Union—John Paul Jones Coat Of Arms 1776-77 (bottom left); Blue Ensign of the Connecticut State Navy (top right); Lossing's version of the Bunker Hill Flag; Original Standard of the Bedford Minutemen—1775 (bottom right)

205

Plate 27

The Battle of Bunker Hill by John Trumbull

Bunker Hill Color—1775,
John Trumbull's version

The Battle of Bunker Hill by Howard Pyle. Grenadiers of the 52nd Regt. are in
the foreground. Note their colors

The Battle of Germantown, 1777. Troops of the 7th Pennsylvania Regiment storm the Cliveden house. (Painted by Howard Pyle)

207

Plate 29

Present-day Painting of the Standard of the 2nd New Hampshire Regiment of 1777

Original Blue Standard of the 2nd N.H. Regt. of 1777

Original Buff Color of the 2nd New Hampshire Regiment of 1777

Painting of the Buff Color of the 2nd New Hampshire Regiment of 1777. The symbol is a union of 13 links—Benjamin Franklin's design

209

Plate 31

*Standard of Stark's
New Hampshire Militia Brigade —1777
(Modern-day ceremonial version)*

*Fragment
of the original color
of Stark's New Hampshire
Militia Brigade*

*Standard of the
3rd New York Regiment of 1777
(Present-day Painting)*

"Guilford" Stars and Stripes
Evidence of 14 to 16 stripes
and 15 stars originally

Yellow field Colors
of a Rhode Island Artillery
Unit—circa 1820's
(Present-day Painting)

211

Plate 33

*Original of a Division Color,
7th Pa. Regt. of '76*

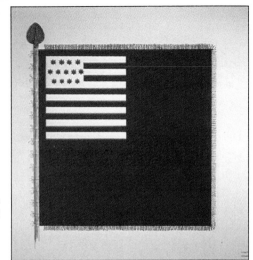

*Division Color,
7th Pa. Regt. of '76*

*"The Monmouth Color"
Descended from Capt. William
Wilson, 1st Pa. Regt.*

212

Plate 34

Blowing up of the British Frigate HMS Augusta. Battle of the Delaware, October 22–23, 1777. Fort Mifflin and vessels of the Pennsylvania State Navy are in the left background. Postwar painting by a British Naval officer—probably an eyewitness

Fort Mifflin, October 22–23, 1777. Detail of HMS Augusta painting. Note stars and stripes over Fort. One flag has tri-colored stripes

213

Plate 35

Original Standard of the Philadelphia Light Horse, 1775. Note British union beneath striped union

Symbols on the Standard of the Philadelphia Light Horse. Designed by John Folwell and painted by James Claypoole

214

Plate 36

Lance Finial and Tassels. Philadelphia Light Horse Standard

Hanover Associators Standard (19th Century artist's interpretation)

215

Plate 37

Standard of the Independent Battalion, Westmoreland County, Pa.,
John Proctor's 1st Brigade (Present-day Painting)

Original Standard of the
Independent Battalion.
Westmoreland County, Pa.

216

Plate 38

Original Standard of the 1st Pa. Regt. Reverse side with the top and staff (to right) edges folded under.

Symbol of the Standard of the 1st Pa. Regt.

217

Plate 39

A Continental Regiment in Summer Encampment. Colonel Walter Stewart, Commander of the 2nd Pennsylvania Regiment of 1777 and 1781, by Charles Willson Peale. The regimental encampment is in the background.

218

Plate 40

Commander's Marquee
with Regimental Standard,
Officers' Tents with Spontoons.
Enlisted Men's Tents
with Muskets

Regimental Standard,
Marquee and Sentry

Present-day Interpretation
of the Regimental Standard

219

Plate 41

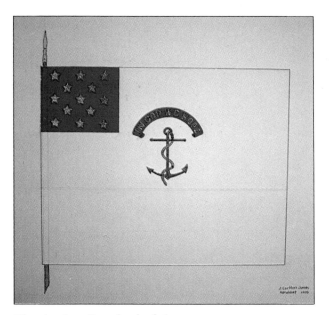

*The Anchor Standard of the
Rhode Island Regt. of '81*

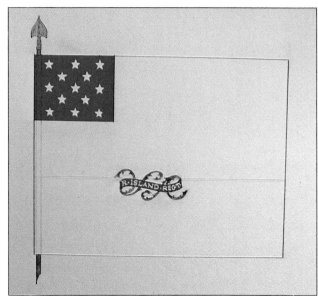

*One of the standards of
the Rhode Island Regiment of '81*

*1907 watercolor drawing of one
of the original standards of the Rhode
Island Regt. of 1781*

*Standard of the
Newport Light Infantry Company—1775*

220

Plate 42

Early Rhode Island Colors, State House, Providence. The two original Standards of the Rhode Island Regiment of 1781 are centered

221

Plate 43

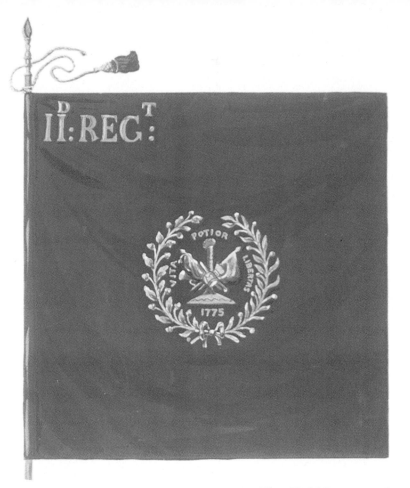

Blue Field Regimental
Colors of the
2nd South Carolina Regiment of 1775

Circa 1900 painting
of the Regimental Colors,
2nd S.C. Regt.

222

Plate 44

American provincial colors flown over Fort Johnson and the Fort on Sullivan's Island (Fort Moultrie) Charleston Harbor—1775-76 (top left); Regimental Standard of the VIII Virginia Regiment. Colonel Henry Muhlenberg (middle left); Standard of the Alexandria Rifle Company, XI Virginia Regiment [present-day copy] (bottom left); South Carolina State Navy (top right); The Eutaw Flag (middle right); Original Standard of the Alexandria Rifle Company, XI Virginia Regiment (bottom right)

223

Plate 45

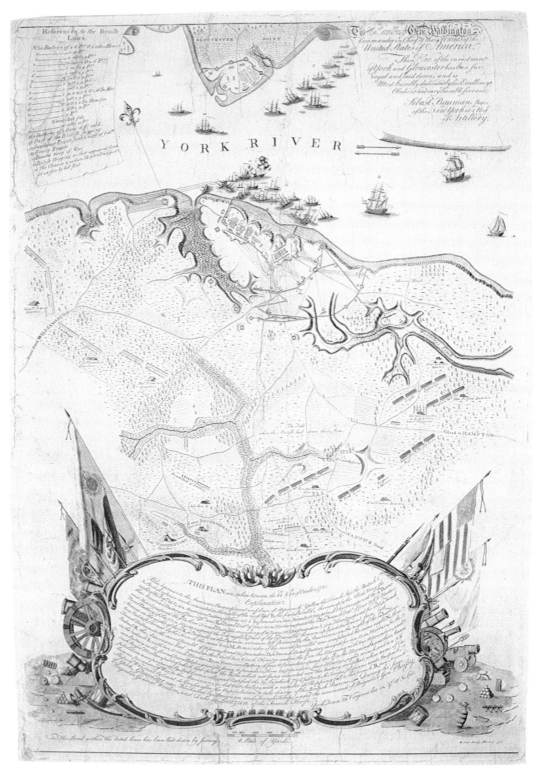

The Continental and French Armies at Yorktown—October 1781. New York Artillery Major Sebastian Bauman's Map; Phila. 1782. The oblong blocks indicate the position of regiments grouped by brigades, state lines and army divisions. American and French flags flank the explanatory notes.

224

Plate 46

Flagstaff Finials

R.I.	*Phila.*	*British*	*German*	*French*		*R.I.*	*2nd S.C.*
Regt.	*Light*	*Regt.*	*Regt.*	*Regt.*		*Regt.*	*Regt.*
of '81	*Horse*		*Comp'y*			*of '81*	*of '75*

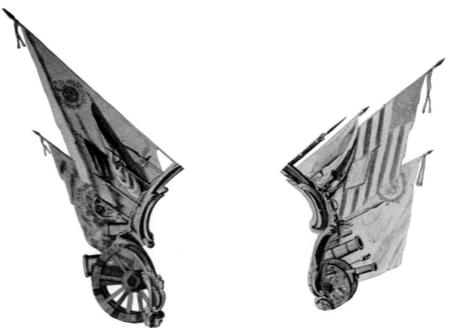

Colors flanking the title notes on Major Bauman's map of Yorktown.
Engraved by R. Scot, Philadelphia, 1782

225

Plate 47

Detail from Van Blarenberghe's "Siege," 1786

Detail from Van Blarenberghe's "Siege," 1786

226

Plate 48

The Siege of Yorktown, by Louis-Nicolas Van Blarenberghe, Rochambeau Replica, 1786. The "covered way," or trench along which Pennsylvania Captain Duncan carried his regiment's colors is at the far right

227

Plate 49

Detail of The Surrender of Yorktown, by Louis-Nicolas Van Blarenberghe, painted 1786. Note French colors and Washington's blue standard

Detail of the Surrender of Yorktown, by Louis Nicolas Van Blarenberghe, painted 1786. British and German regiments are grounding their arms and cased colors in the surrender field

228

Plate 50

The Surrender of Yorktown, by Louis-Nicolas Van Blarenberghe, Rochambeau Replica, 1786. Note the blue field and white field standards with stars along the American line.

229

Plate 51

Detail of Van Blarenberghe's Surrender of Yorktown. Note Deux Ponts regimental standard and Washington's national standard of the army with blue field and stars (no stripes)

Detail of Van Blarenberghe's Surrender of Yorktown showing the standard of the Colonel of the Deux Ponts Regiment

230

Plate 52

Detail of Van Blarenberghe's Surrender of Yorktown showing a French colonel's and a regimental standard and an American regimental standard of stars on a white field

Detail of Van Blarenberghe's Surrender of Yorktown showing French regimental standards and an American regimental standard of stars on a white field

231

Plate 53

FRENCH REGIMENTAL STANDARDS

*Agenois (top left); Armagnac (middle left); Auxerrois (bottom left); Bourbonnais
(top right); Champagne (middle right); Deux-Ponts (bottom right)*

232

Plate 54

FRENCH REGIMENTAL STANDARDS

Dillon (top left); Foix (middle left); Gatinois (bottom left); Haynault (top right);
Rouergue (middle right); Saintonge (bottom right)

233

Plate 55

FRENCH REGIMENTAL STANDARDS

Soissonais (top left); Touraine (middle left); Walsh (top right); Auxonne (middle right); Belzunce Dragoons (bottom)

234

Plate 56

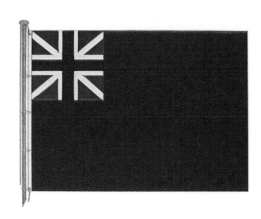

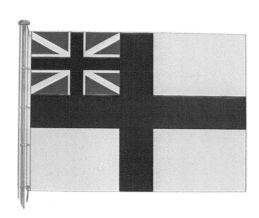

BRITISH STANDARDS

British National Ensign with Grand Union Canton (top); Royal Navy Ensign
(middle left); King's Colors, 33rd Regiment of Foot (middle right);
Regimental Colors, 33rd Regiment of Foot (bottom)

235

Plate 57

Regimental Standard, The King's American Dragoons

Original of the King's Color, VII Regiment of Foot

236

Plate 58

KING'S COLOR; REGIMENTAL COLOR

Third Foot Guards [Scots Guard] (top left); IX Regiment of Foot (middle left);
VII Regiment of Foot, The Royal Fusiliers (bottom left); Third Foot Guards
[Scots Guard] (top right); IX Regiment of Foot (middle right); Regimental Color,
VII Regiment of Foot, The Royal Fusiliers (bottom right)

237

Plate 59

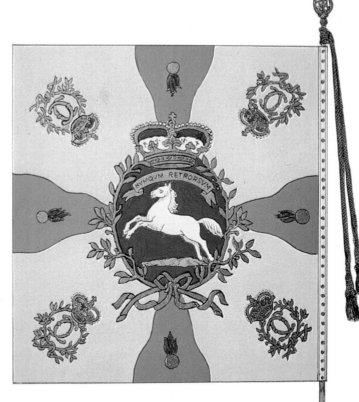

Colors of the Von Riedesel Infantry
Regiment of Brunswick

Colors of a Hessian Regiment.
Probably Knyphausen's Regiment.
See Peale's "Washington at Trenton"

238

Plate 60

Colors of an Ansbach-Bayreuth Regiment. Captured at Yorktown

239

Plate 61

The Powel Standard. National Standard of the Philadelphia Light Horse (First City Troop), circa 1797. The field was originally blue. There are fifteen 8-pointed stars. The shield bears the arms of Pennsylvania. The motto "AD ASTRA" translates "TO THE STARS"

240

Plate 62

"General George Washington Reviewing the Western army at Fort Cumberland (Maryland) the 18th of October, 1794," by Frederick Kemmelmeyer. Note various standards and colors

National Standard of the 1st Regiment, United States Army, ca. 1790's.

241

Plate 63

Original Color of the 3rd Battalion, Ist Sub-Legion, ca. 1793. Descended in the family of Colonel Hamtramck, who commanded the left wing of the Legion at Fallen Timbers. (Reverse side. Hoist 56 inches, Fly 40 inches. Intact)

A VIEW of the AMERICAN MERCHANT SHIP PLANTER, beating off a FRENCH NATIONAL PRIVATEER of 22 Guns July 10th 1799.

242

Plate 64

Appendix I

Chronological Summary of George Washington Correspondence, Orders and Events and Other Documentation Relating to Continental Army Standards and Colors.

Feb.–July, 1775	*Maj. Gen. Charles Lee's Plan for Colours* One Regimental and four Divisional Colours. All with the motto "LIBERTY".	Ford, Corres. & Journals of S. B. Webb, Vol. 1, pp 85–87
July 3, 1775	*Washington takes Command* of Provincial Troops before Boston.	Baker, Itinerary, 1, p 8
July 4, 1775	*General Orders, Cambridge* All troops inducted into the service of the United Provinces of North America.	Baker, Itinerary, 1, p 9
July 18, 1775	*Scarlet Color, Prospect Hill, Mass.* Hoisted scarlet color of the 3rd Conn Regt. (Putnam)	Baker, Itinerary, 1, p 12
Oct. 18–24, 1775	*Plans for New Army for 1776* — Cont. Cong. Comm. meets with representatives of the New England colonies (Oct. 18–22) and G. W. (Oct. 23–24). — No mention of any flag in G. W. "Writings" or Committee's Reports. — Uniforms to be brown with regiments distinguished by facings.	Writings, V4 p 35, 37, 41, Force, AA, 4th, V3, p 1155
Oct. 20, 1775	*Ltr., Col. Reed to Col.'s Glover & Moylan* Suggests white flag with tree and Motto "An Appeal to Heaven" for armed vessels.	AA, 4th, V3, p 1126
Dec. 31, 1775	*G. W. to Pres. of Congress* Estimate for Tents, Drums, Colours . . . £15,000.	Writings, V4, p 199
Dec. '75–Jan. '76	*Continental Navy Outfitted (which see)* St. George's ensign with stripes. 13-stripes red and white jack.	Nav. Doc. of Rev., V3, App. D
Jan. 1, 1776	*General Orders, Cambridge Mass.* Commencement of new army.	Writings, V4, p 203

Jan. 4, 1776	*Ltr., G. W. to Joseph Reed*	Writings, V4, p 210
	Hoisted "union flag" on Jan. 1, 1776 in honor of new army and United Colonies.	
Jan. 17, 1776	*Ltr., British Transport Captain at Boston*	Preble, p 218, referencing Force, AA
	The rebels' colors, a little while ago, were entirely red but on receipt of the King's speech they hoisted the union flag.	
Jan. 5, 1776	*General Orders, Cambridge, Mass.*	Writings, V4, p 213
	Regimentals (uniforms) ready for issue.	
Feb. 20, 1776	*General Orders, Cambridge*	Writings V4, p 341
	— Each Regiment must have a Standard (or Regimental Colours) and Colours for each Grand Division.	
	— To be small and light.	
	— The number of the Regiment and a Motto to be marked on "the Colours".	
	— Colonels to select the Motto and a color that relates to uniforms.	
	— Qr. Mr. Gen. to provide Colours as soon as possible.	
Mar. 8, 1776	*Ltr., Lt. Col. Hand to J. Yeates*	Preble, p 206 (Pa. Arch)
	1st Pa. Regt., Prospect Hill, Mass. Every regiment to have a standard and colours. Our standard to be a deep green ground, the device—a tiger, etc. The Motto—.	
May 28, 1776	*Ltr., G. W. to Putnam (from Phila.)*	Writings, V5, p 88
	Colonels to hurry on Colours.	
May 31, 1776	*General Orders, New York*	Writings, V5, p 91. AA, 4th, VI, p 637.
	Colonels to complete Colours immediately.	
Aug. 27, 1776	*Battle of Long Island*	
	— Hazlett's Delaware Battalion fought with "colours flying".	"76", C & M, p 435
	— Eleven "Liberty" flags captured— Hessian Adj. Gen. Baurmeister.	Uhlendorf, Revol. in Amer., p 41
Sep. 16, 1776	*Battle of Harlem Heights*	
Oct. 28, 1776	*Battle of White Plains*	
Nov. 16, 1776	*Battle of Ft. Washington*	
	American colours captured. Col. Magaw's purple standard. Yellow, white and light blue colours taken by Knyphausen.	G. Davis, Regt. Colours, p 13
Dec. 26, 1776	*Battle of Trenton*	
	Six to fifteen Hessian Colours captured.	

Jan. 3, 1777	*Battle of Princeton*	
June 14, 1777	*13 Stars and Stripes Adopted* Continental Congress "the flag of the United States" (Marine Committee).	Jour. Cont. Cong.
June–Oct., 1777	*Burgoyne Invasion from Canada*	
Aug.–Dec., 1777	*Howe Invasion from the Chesapeake*	
Dec. '77–June '78	*Valley Forge*	
Jan. 15, 1778	*Ltr., G. W. to E. Cheever, Comm. Mil Stores* Requests report on arms and accoutrements at Springfield.	Writings, V10, p 308n
Jan. 15, 1778	*Ltr., G. W. to Knox* — Requests report on Arms in Mass., N.H., Boston. — Col. Flowers to make return of all magazines under his immediate direction. — Commissary at Springfield to do likewise.	Writings, V10, p 208
Apr. 2, 1778	*Ltr., G. W. to Ezekiel Cheever, C.M.S.* Acknowledges report on Ordnance, Arms, and Military Stores at Springfield.	Writings, V11, 198-9
June 28, 1778	*Battle of Monmouth*	
Aug. 28, 1778	*Ltr., G. W. to Heath* Gen'l. Patterson's request for silk "for a set of Colours."	Writings, V12, p 365
(Aug. ?) 1778	*Board of War and Ordnance* Adopts Seal which bears a pair of colours— one, a stars and stripes, the other plain— and the rattlesnake and motto.	
July–Aug., 1778	*Col. Benjamin Flowers & Maj. J. Gostelowe* Commissary General of Military Stores, Continental Army. A Return of Mil Stores for July–Aug. 1778, including; "Return of New Standards & Division Colours for Ye Use of Ye Army of Ye United States of America in the Possession of Major Jonathan Gostelowe, Comy Mily Stores" (location not stated, but apparently Phila., Pa.).	Nat. Archives, Rec. Gp. 93
Sep. 2, 1778	*General Orders, White Plains* To report on Colours; the several Regiments tomorrow.	Writings, V12, p 388-9
Sep. 5, 1778	*Scammel's Report* Number and condition of Colours of the several Brigades.	Writings, V12, p 389, 470

Sep. 6, 1778	*Ltr., G. W. to Heath* Gen'l. Patterson to choose devise for his Colours.	Writings, V12, p 407, 408
Dec. 18, 1778	*Ltr., G. W. to Schuyler* Refers to Lt. Col. Flowers, C.G.M.S., and to Mr. Rensselaer, C.M.S. at Albany.	Writings, V13, p 429-4
Mar. 23, 1779	*Continental Uniforms* Congress authorizes G. W. to prescribe uniforms.	Lefferts, p 10
April, 1779	*Steuben's Regulations* — Two Colours to a Regiment (one for each Battalion). — Discussed with Board of War (Peters). — Regulations printed post-June 1779.	Steuben Steuben's "Blue Book" See below ltr. May 10, 1779
May 10, 1779	*Ltr., Board of War (R. Peters) to G. W.* — Steuben and G. W. to define plan for Colours. — Every regiment to have two Colours, one the Standard of the U. S., the other a Regimental Colour . . . (to match) the facings of the Regiments. — Not settled what is the Standard of U. S. — G. W. to recommend design. — Congress will establish a Standard. — Sufficient will be ordered for Army. — G. W. to define uniforms, then Board can plan for Regimental Colours.	Writings, V15, p 50 n G. Davis, p 11 Quaife et al, p 33, 34
May 12, 1779	*Ltr., G. W. to Knox* Requests comments on Peters' letter.	Writings, V 15, p 50
May 13, 1779	*Ltr., Knox to G. W.* — Comments on Peters' ltr. of May 10. — "Standards of the regiments". — Two would be sufficient—a continental and a regimental or state. — Wait for uniforms.	Writings, V15, p 50 n
May 14, 1779	*G. W. to Board of War* The arrangements respecting Colours is not yet made.	Writings, V15, p 82
June 11, 1779	*Board of War* Estimate of blue, crimson, white, and buff silk to be imported from France.	PCC, Item 147, Vol III p 417, 419 Nat. Arch. (Peterson, Continental Soldier).

Sep. 3, 1779	*Board of War to G. W.* — Enclosed drafts of a Standard for the Army. — Will be made, once you approve. — Prefer Union and Emblems in the Middle—variant from Marine Flag.	Writings, V16, p 283 n Davis, p 11
Sep. 14, 1779	*G. W. to Board of War* — Agree that Union and Emblems should be in the centre. — The number of the Regt. and the State in the curve of the serpent.	Writings, V16, p 283
Oct. 2, 1779	*General Orders* — Uniform regulations. — Blue with different colored facings (crimson, blue, white, buff).	Writings, V16, p Lefferts, p 10
Feb. 23, 1780	*Ltr., G. W. to Board of War* Great deficiency of drums, fifes, and standards. Presume they are being procured.	Writings, V17, p 46
Feb. 28, 1780	*Ltr., Board of War to G. W.* — Colours shall be provided by Com. Gen. of Mil Stores. — Awaiting articles from France. — Standards to conform to the plan. — Two for every Regiment. — One, the Standard of the U. S. — The other, the Regimental Standard—the Ground to match the Facings.	Writings (Ref) V18, p 75 G. W. Papers, LC, No. 94, Folio 209 Davis, (Whitney ed) p 12
Mar. 6, 1780	*Ltr., G. W. to Board* Pleased that supplies from France are expected.	Writings, V18, p 75
Oct. 6, 1781	*General Orders* — Headquarters before York[town]. — All the troops will march with Drums beating Colours flying. — The standard bearers will plant their standards upon the Epaulments.	Writings, V23, p 177–185
Oct. 27(–29), 1781	*Ltr., G. W. to Congress* 24 standards taken at Yorktown.	Writings, V23, p 294
June 20, 1782	*Continental Congress* Adopts eagle seal of the U. S.	
July 2, 1782	*Commissary General of Mil Stores* Samuel Hodgdon Estimate for procurement of 100 silk standards for the Continental Army.	*(Peterson, Cont. Soldier,* p 249. War Dept. Coll. of Revol. War Records, Vol 148, Nat. Archives.

July ? 1782	*Comm. Gen. of Mil Stores (NB: on above)* Estimate cut to 50 standards.	Same as above.
Aug. 2, 1782	*Ltr., G. W. to Secr. of War* Requests Colours be forwarded. Informed they are purchased.	Writings, V25, p 454
Aug. 8, 1782	*Board of War to G. W.* Colours are ready. Will be sent immediately. Also drums and fifes...	(Quaife, Weig, Appleman, p 35)
Sep. 5, 1782	*General Orders, Verplanks Pt.* Turn in Light Infantry Colours presented by Lafayette.	Writings, V25, p 131
Sep. 6, 1782	*Adj. Gen. Hand to Col. Webb* Sends two Lt. Inf. Colour	Ford, "Webb Corres" (see Webb's Regt.)
Feb. 17, 1783	*Queries, G. W. to Secr. at [sic] War* Should not the Colours be sent on? (Answer: The Colours will be sent on. I wish they were better than they are.)	Writings, V26, p 140
Mar. 1, 1783	*Secr. at War (Lincoln) to G. W.* The standards are in the hands of the Q Master at Camp and have been there for some time.	Writings, V26, p 205 Quaife et al, p 35
Mar. 10, 1783	*G. W. to Colonel Pickering* Requests explanation on receipt of Standards.	Writings, V26, p 205
Mar. 10, 1783	*Col. Pickering to G. W.* The Field Commissary of Mil Stores has not picked up the Standards.	Writings, V26, p 205
Mar. 11, 1783	*G. W. to the Secr. of War* The Standards are in the care of Mr. Richard Frothingham, F. C. of Mil Stores.	Writings, V26, p 206-207
Mar. 14, 1783	*General Orders* Regiments without regimental Colours will immediately apply for them to Mr. Frothingham, C.M.S.	Writings, V26, p 222
Mar. 23, 1783	*Ltr., G. W. to Lafayette* General military situation. British garrisons reinforced.	Writings, V26, p 254
Mar. 27, 1783	*Ltr., G. W. to Knox* Receipt of news of definitive peace.	Writings, V26, p 269

A Plan for Regimentary and Company Colours for use by Battalions in America as proposed by Mr. Charles Lee (later Major General of the Continental Army) in early 1775.

Mr. LEE'S PLAN

A Battalion consisting of one Colonel, one Lt. Colonel, Two Majors, four Captains, four Captain Lieutenants, sixteen Lieutenants, eight Ensigns, Thirty two Sergt's, Thirty two Corporals, six hundred and fivety eight Private, sixteen Drummers or Musick Men, 24 Colour Guards, one Adjutant, one Sergt; Major, one Musick or Drum Major. There must likewise be annex'd a Company of light infantry, of a Capt. Lt., three L'ts, four Serj'ts, four Corporals, two horn or Conch Sounders and seventy six Privates. The whole will consist of seven hundred and 48 rank and file. This Battalion is to be form'd into four Companies. Each is to have a Standard and an equal number of officers. There is likewise to be one Regimentary or Great Colour, by which the four Standards of the four Companies are to regulate their advances, their retreats, their Conversions and all their Movements. The four Standards must be of different Colours—for instance, the first or right hand may be red; the 2d or left hand white; the 3d or right hand center blue; the 4th or left hand center green. The colour of the Regiment may give the name of the Regiment; if it is orange, the Reg't may be call'd orange. This Colour must be much larger and shou'd be much more showy than the Standards. If the Reg't is the Orange all the men of the Battalion must have an orange colour'd cape to their jacket, and an orange Cockade; but an epaulette on one shoulder of the Colour of the standard of his respective Company. This will distinguish the Reg't and particular Company he belongs to. In the Colour and the standards must be embroider'd the word liberty.

The Colonel should be distinguish'd by some mark in his Cap or hat—as a feather or tuft dy'd of the Colour of his Reg't. The other field officers the same but with some difference in their size—the Capt's a tuft of the Colour of their particular Standard, the Capt. Lt's the same, but smaller than the Capt's. The subalterns must have likewise some badge to specify their rank. The Sergt's and Corporals must have likewise some.

2 of ye Lt must be rang'd in the intervals of the Front; two (   ) in the rear; ensigns posted in the rear behind the Standards. The Corporals to be divided in equal files on the two flanks of the respective Companies. Serj'ts half to be in the interval of the front, and half in the rear at proper distances. The Drums or Musick men to be half behind their respective Colours in the rear; the other half of the whole behind the Reg'ts Colours. A major to be on each Flank. The Adjutant with the Colonel, the Serj't Major with the Lt. Colonel—the Majors to be allow'd two each of the most alert and intelligent light infantry to be orderly on their Persons. Twenty four men or twelve file of men of the most esteem'd valour are always to compose the grand Colour'd Guard, which is to be posted

This Battalion on the Parade, form'd two deep-

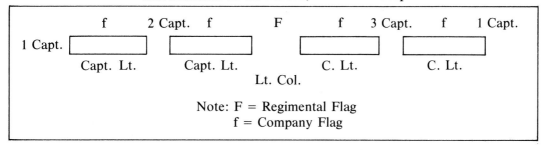

in their Center. Some extraordinary pay or exemptions ought to be allow'd to these Colour Guards—and they must be sworn never to abandon it, as may each Company with respect to its proper standard bearers, of which there are to be four to each Company.

The light infantry Company may either be subdivided on the wings of the Battalion, or scatter'd along the Front as the General or Colonel directs. In short, they can have no fix'd station. The chief things to learn are to load and fire without confusion, to march in front or retreat without crowding or opening their files too much; to wheel and change their front. This will be done well, of course, if those who carry the standards are practiced to know the necessary distances; for which reason all of the Standard bearers, as well as colour guards, are to be soldiers of capacity and judgment. There must be four to each Company, who must have the same distinctions and exemptions. With the Colour Guards, the ensigns being in the rear will be able to assist 'em much.

Ref: "Mr. Lee's Plan" is quoted in "Correspondence and Journals of Samuel Blatchley Webb," by W. C. Ford, N.Y. 1892, Vol 1, pp 84–87. The "Plan" is quoted in association with a letter from Lee to Silas Deane (Webb's stepfather and a commissioner to France) datelined Cambridge, July 20, 1775. The letter does not refer to the "Plan". Both Lee and Webb were in Cambridge at the time. This basic plan as to Colours appears to have been adopted by Webb for his regiment. The plan is endorsed by Deane "Gen'l Liegh's Plan."

Washington to Joseph Reed

Cambridge, January 4, 1776.

Dear Sir: Since my last I have received your obliging favours of the 19th and 23d ulto, and thank you for the articles of intelligence therein contained, as I also do for the buttons which accompanied the last letter, al-though I had got a set better, I think, made at Concord. I am exceeding glad to find that things wear a better face in Virginia than they did some time ago; but I do not think that any thing less than the life or liberty will free the colony from the effects of Lord Dunmore's resentments and villainies.

We are at length favored with a sight of his Majesty's most gracious speech, breathing sentiments of tenderness and compassion for his deluded American subjects; the echo is not yet come to hand; but we know what it must be, and as Lord North said, and we ought to have believed (and acted accordingly) we now know the ultimatum of British justice. The speech I send you. A volume of them was sent out by the Boston gentry, and, farcical enough, we gave great joy to them, (the red coats I mean,) without knowing or intending it; for on that day, the day which gave being to the new army, (but before the proclamation came to hand,) we had hoisted the union flag in compliment to the United Colonies. But, behold, it was received in Boston as a token of the deep impression the speech had made upon us, and as a signal of submission. So we learn by a person out of Boston last night. By this time I presume they begin to think it strange, that we have not made a formal surrender of our lines. Admiral Shuldham is arrived at Boston. The 55th and the greatest part, if not all, of the 17th regiment, are also got in there. The rest of the 5 regiments from Ireland were intended for Halifax and Quebec; those for the first, have arrived there, the others we know not where they are got to....

I fear your fleet has been so long in fitting, and the destination of it so well known, that the end will be defeated, if the vessels escape. How is the arrival of French troops in the West Indies, and the hostile appearance there, to be reconciled with that part of the King's speech, wherein he assures Parliament, "that as well from the assurance I have received, as from the general appearance of affairs in Europe, I see no probability that the measures, which you may adopt, will be interrupted by disputes with any foreign power''? I hope the Congress will not think of adjourning at so important and critical a juncture as this. I wish they would keep a watchful eye to New York. From Captain Sears' account, (now here) much is to be apprehended from that quarter.

A fleet is now fitting out at Boston, consisting of five transports and two bomb-vessels, under convoy of the Scarborough and Fowey men-of-war. Three hundred, some say, others more, troops are on board, with flat-bottomed boats. It is whispered, as if designedly, that they are intended for Newport; but it is generally believed that they are bound either to Long Island or Virginia; the other transports are taking in water and a good deal of bisquet is baking, some say for the shipping to lay in Nantasket Road, to be out of the way of ice, whilst others think a more important move is in agitation. All, however, is conjecture. I heartily wish you, Mrs. Reed and family, the compliments of the season, in which the ladies here and family join.*

Preble wrote: "An anonymous letter, written Jan. 2, 1776, says: 'The grand union flag of thirteen stripes was raised on a height near Boston. The regulars did not understand it; and as the king's speech had just been read, as they supposed, they thought the new flag was a token of submission.', and further; "The captain of a British transport, writing from Boston to his owners in London, Jan. 17, 1776, says: 'I can see the rebels' camp very plain, whose colors, a little while ago, were entirely red; but on the receipt of the king's speech, which they burnt, they hoisted the union flag which is here supposed to intimate the union of the provinces.' "

General Orders (Washington)

January 5, 1776.
Head Quarters, Cambridge,
Parole Hancock, Countersign Adams

The Majors of Brigade, to order the Adjutants to be exact and punctual, in making their Weekly Returns of the Strength of each regiment; Also a separate Return of the Numbers in-listed in the course of last week, at Orderly time tomorrow—The weekly Returns to be according to the Form lately sent by the Adjutant General.

The Regimentals, which have been made up, and drawn for, may be delivered to the respective Colonels by the Qr. Mr. General, to the Order of those Colonels, who drew them at such prices, as they have cost the Continent, which is much cheaper than could otherwise be obtained—As nothing adds more to the Appearance of a man, than dress, and a proper degree of cleanliness in his person, the General hopes and expects that each Regiment will contend for the most Soldier-like appearance: He is also very desirous of having the Men instructed, as speedily as possible in all parts of their duty, and recommends it to all the Colonels, to be very careful in the choice of their Non-Commissioned Officers, and to their Captains, to divide their Companies into small Squads, appointing a Serjeant and Corporal to each, from whom the utmost diligence is expected—Those Serjeants and Corporals are by no means to suffer the Arms, and Accoutrements of any man in their Squads, to be dirty, or unfit for use, and as far as in them lies, to make the men appear neat, clean, and soldier-like—Neglect of duty in these Instances, they may rely upon it will reduce them to the Ranks—These Orders are not intended to exempt the commissioned Officers of the Companies from the strictest attention to these things. . . .

General Orders

February 20, 1776.
Headquarters, Cambridge,
Parole Manchester, Countersign Boyle

As it is necessary that every Regiment should be furnished with Colours, and that those Colours should, if it can be done, bear some kind of similitude to the Uniform of the

---

*The text is from Ford.

251

regiment to which they belong, the Colonels with their respective Brigadiers and the Qr. Mr. Genl. may fix upon such as are proper, and can be procured. There must be to each Regiment, the Standard (or Regimental Colours) and Colours for each Grand Division, the whole to be small and light. The Number of the Regiment is to be mark'd on the Colours, and such a Motto, as the Colonel may choose, in fixing upon which, the General advises a Consultation amongst them.

The Colonels are to delay no time, in getting this matter fix'd, that the Qr. Mr. Genl. may provide the Colours as soon as possible; they are also to consider what Camp Equipage may be further necessary, that no time may be lost in providing it, as the season is fast approaching for taking the field.

The Genl. cannot again help urging it in the strongest terms to the Colonels the necessity of the strictest attention to the discipline of their Men—learning them to march and perform all the different Evolutions and Manoevures; which is of more essential service, then dwelling too long upon the Manual Exercise—He also recommends to the Colonels a proper attention to the Cloathing of their Officers and Men, that they may appear in a soldierlike manner.

The General desires that the Brigadiers, who have not complied with the Orders of the 6th Instant concerning the Ammunition; and that of the 7th respecting the Arrangement of Chaplains; may be informed, that he expects an immediate report from them.

Lieutenant-Colonel Hand, to Jasper Yeates, "Prospect Hill, March 8, 1776

"I am stationed on Cobbles Hill, with four companies of our regiment. Two companies—Cluggage's and Chamber's—were ordered to Dorchester on Monday. Ross's and Lowden's relieved them yesterday. Every regiment is to have a standard and colors. Our standard is to be a deep green ground, the device a tiger, partly enclosed by toils, attempting the pass, defended by a hunter armed with a spear (in white) on a crimson field. The motto, 'Donari Nolo.'" Quoted by Preble, p 206. Also see Pa. Archives.

Washington to Major General Israel Putnam

Philadelphia, May 28, 1776.

Sir: I received yours of the 24th, Inst. with its several Inclosures, and the Letter and Invoice from General Ward, giving Intelligence of the fortunate Capture made by our armed Vessels, on which Event you have my Congratulations. . . .

. . . P.S. I desire you'll speak to the several Colls. and hurry them to get their colours done.

General Orders

May 31, 1776.

Head Quarters, New York,
Parole Portsmouth. Countersign Georgia

. . . The Provost Marshal to make a report in writing, every morning, at Head Quarters, of the prisoners he has in charge, specifying their names, regiments, companies, by whom confined, crimes, numbers of nights confined, tried or not tried.

Edmund Britt of Capt. Butler's Company, and Col. Nixon's Regiment, tried at the General Court Martial whereof Col. Nixon is President for "Desertion"—is found guilty, and sentenced to receive Thirty-nine lashes.

Ahimaas Sherwin of Capt. Butler's Company, of Col. Nixon's Regiment, tried at the above Court Martial for "Desertion" is also found guilty, and sentenced to receive Thirty-nine lashes.

The General approves of the sentence, on the above two prisoners, and orders it to be put in execution, to morrow morning, at guard mounting.

After Orders

General Washington has wrote to Genl. Putnam, desiring him in the most pressing terms, to give positive orders to all the Colonels, to have Colours immediately completed for their respective regiments.

General Orders

Wrote as follows; "Colonel Rud. Ritzema addressing the members of the New York Congress, May 31, 1776, says that, the day before, it was given out in general orders that General Putnam had received a letter from General Washington, requesting all the colonels at New York to immediately provide colors for their several regiments; and he asks that Mr. Curtinius may have directions to provide a pair for his regiments, of such a color and with such devices as shall be deemed proper by the Congress, i.e., New York Provincial Congress." (Preble, p. 226)

> American Archives, 4th series, vol. vi. p 634, and on page 637 is the order he refers to, viz.:-
> "After Orders, May 31, 1776.
>> "General Washington has written to General Putnam desiring him the most pressing terms to give positive orders to all the colonels to have colors immediately completed for their respective regiments."
> In a letter to General Putnam, dated May 23, 1776, Washington adds, in a postscript, "I desire you'll speak to the several colonels, and hurry them to get their colors done," Washington Letters, B, vol i. p. 316.

Washington to Brigadier General Henry Knox

January 15, 1778.

Head Quarters, Valley Forge

Dear Sir: Should it be thought expedient to draw a Body of Men together early next Spring, it will be necessary for us to know previously what number of Arms we could have ready for such an emergency. I have desired Colo. Flowers to make me a return of all at the Magazines under his immediate direction, and have wrote to the Commissary at Springfield to do the like. You will be pleased to make the proper inquiry for such as may be in Boston and any other places in Massachusetts and New Hampshire, have them collected and properly deposited and a Return of them made to me as soon as possible. There may probably be quantities of Arms laying up and down useless at present for want of repairing; be pleased to endeavour to have them collected and put into a way of being fitted up.

I shall be glad to hear what steps are taking to recruit the Army, and of any other matters that relate to the Service, I am. etc.

1. Commissary General of Military Stores.
   Note: A letter was sent to Ezekel Cheever, Commissary of Military Stores.

To Ezekel Cheever

April 2, 1778.

Head Quarters, Valley Forge

Sir: I yesterday received yours of the 15th. March with a general Return of the Ordnance, Arms and Military Stores at Springfield. I beg you will be as industrious as possible in getting the New Arms cleaned and put in order, and having all the old that are worth repairing made fit for service. You need not wait until the whole are completed, but keep sending them forward as they are finished.

Washington to Major General Heath

August 28, 1778.

Head Quarters, White Plains

(acknowledges letters and General Patterson's request for silk "for a set of Colours").

RETURN OF COLOURS BELONGING TO THE SEVERAL BRIGADES PRESENT

Brigades	Standards		[?] Regimental		Grand Division	
	Good	Bad	Good	Bad	Good	Bad
N. Carolina		2				
Woodford's	1					
Muhlenberg		4				
Scott		1				
Smallwood						
2nd Maryland						
Wayne	2	2			4	4
2nd Pennsylvania		3				
Clinton	1	2			4	8
Parson		2			8	
Huntington						
Nixon	3				11	
Paterson						
Larned	1	1			4	
Poor	1		1		4	
Total	9	17	1	—	35	12

NB. One Standard & 4 Division Colours belonging to the first Pennsylvania Brigade are in Lancaster and one Standard in Philadelphia.

Alex Scammell Adj. Genl.

Orderly Office Septem 5th, 1778 (Ref: Wash Writings, Fitzpatrick, Vol 12, p 470)

General Orders

Wednesday, September 2, 1778.
Head Quarters, W. Plains,
Parole Jedburgh. Countersigns June, July.

The Court of Enquiry whereof Colo. Marshall is President will assemble at ten o'Clock tomorrow morning at the Presidents quarters and take into consideration a Complaint exhibited by Mr. Kean, Assistant Commissioner of Issues against Lieutt. Seldon of the 4th Virginia Regt; both Parties to attend.

A return of Colors in the several Regiments to be made tomorrow at Orderly time.

Author's Note:

A return of the colors belonging to the several brigades in camp was made by Adjt. Gen. Alexander Scammell on September 5. It shows three classes of colors; Standard, regimental and grand division. Also it shows that in the 15 brigades listed there were 45 good flags and 29 others in bad condition. This return is in the Washington papers. See G. W. Writings, V12, p 470.

The above inventory indicates that about half the regiments had standards since there were approximately fifty regiments in the above brigades based on strength reports near the above date, as follows:

Brigade	Regiments	Reported As of
North Carolina	1st through 9th N.C. Regts.	(VF 1777–78)
Woodford's	7th, 11th Va. Regts	(VF 1777–78)
Muhlenberg's	1st, 5th, 9th, 6th and 13th Va. and the German Regt	(VF 1777–78)
Scott's	8th and 12th Va.; Grayson's Continental Regt	(VF 1777–78)
Smallwood's 1st Md	1st, 3rd, 5th, 7th Md Regt	(Sept 13, 1779)
2nd Maryland	4th, 6th Md Regts	(Oct 27, 1779)
Wayne's	1st, 2nd, 7th, 10th Pa. Regts	(VF 1777–78)
2nd Pa.	4th, 5th, 8th, 11th Pa. Pegts	(VF 1777–78)
Clinton's	New York Regts (1st and 3rd?)	
Parson's	3rd, 4th, 6th, 8th Conn Regts	(Fall 78)
Huntington's	1st, 2nd, 5th, 7th Conn Regts	(Fall 78)
Nixon's	Mass Regts (4 ?)	
Peterson's	10th, 11th, 12th, 14th Mass Regts	(VF 1777–78)
Learned's	7th, 8th, 9th Mass Regts	
Poor's	1st, 2nd, 3rd N. H.; 2nd, 4th N. Y. Regts	(VF 1777–78)

Ref. Berg p 146–148.

255

Washington to ___
Major General William Heath

September 6, 1778.

Head Quarters, White Plains

Dear Sir: I have been favd' with yours of the 26th, and 30th. August, and 1st and 2nd instants. I am glad to find that your sentiments, respecting the reception that ought to be given to the Count D'Estaing and his Officers, corresponded with mine and that you had taken proper steps to prepare for refitting his fleet, previous to the receipt of my letter. As the Rhode Island expedition is now at an end, I can see no objection to Mr. Commissary Clarkes' going thither, and if he should have occasion to go from thence to New York to settle his accounts and procure Mondy, he may do it without any disadvantages to us.

I do not know what device Genl. Patterson will chuse to have upon his Colours. I will speak to him and desire him to inform you. . . .

Author's Note:

During July-August 1778, Major Jonathan Gostelowe, of Philadelphia *Commissary of Military Stores* (probably for the Main Continental Army) made an inventory or "return" of regimental standards and colors in his stores ready for issue. A total of thirteen regimental standards, each with a unique emblem, and twenty-six division colors, two per standard, are listed. However, there is no hint as to which regiments the standards were to be issued to. Gostelowe's Return is discussed under the section on Continental Units. Perhaps there was some relationship between Gostelowe's inventory and Scammell's report, since they are so close in date.

Scammell makes an interesting and, to the author, puzzling distinction between *Standards* of which he lists nine "good" and seventeen "bad" (condition) and *Regimental Colours* of which he lists only one. Perhaps some colonel insisted that his regiment had a "regimental colour" rather than a "standard," preferring to reserve that term for the union or national standard when and if they were supplied.

Scammell's *Grand Division Colours* must be equivalent to Gostelowe's *Division Colours* which were colors apparently smaller and of plainer design than the regimental standards. *Several Grand Division Colours* of Webb's Additional Continental Regiment still exist. The author believes that Scammell's list of *Standards* are the regimental standards of the brigades similar in design to Gostelowe's standards and not national standards. There would have been one such standard authorized for each regiment. In 1779 and possibly earlier, Washington and the Board of War of the Continental Congress started a four year long exchange of letters concerning the design and supply of a suitable national standard for the army regiments which was to be different from the *marine flag*, i.e., the stripes and stars.

Steuben's Regulations—May 1779

Gherardi Davis wrote as follows:

"Steuben's Regulations for the Order and Discipline of the Troops of the United States (1779), Chapter IV, a regulation relating to colors, namely: 'A regiment is to consist of two battalions, if of over 160 files, and one color shall be posted in the centre of each battalion. If the regiment is of less than 160 files, it shall consist of one battalion and both colors shall be in the centre.' In the chapter on Instructions, it is provided in regard to Ensigns, that 'As there are two colors to a regiment, the ensigns must carry them in turn.' The diagrams on Steuben's Plate 1 show how the colors are to be posted." The diagrams are extraordinarily detailed, finely drawn prints by L'enfant. Reproductions of Steuben's Regulations do not do justice to the prints which should be examined in the original edition.

256

Board of War to Washington

War Office, May 10th, 1779.

The Board have been frequently applied to on the Subject of Drums and Colours for the several Regiments. It is impossible to comply with all the Requisitions for these Articles, as we have not materials to make either in sufficient Numbers. We hope however to have in short Time a competent Number of Drums. So soon as they are made we send them to Camp as we find many Irregularities and Inconveniences arise from delivering them or any other Articles here.

As to Colours we have refused them for another Reason. The Baron Steuben mentioned when he was here that he would settle with your Excellency some Plan as to the Colours. It was intended that every Regiment should have two Colours one the Standard of the United States which should be the same throughout the Army and the other a Regimental Colour which should vary according to the facings of the Regiments. But it is not yet settled what is the Standard of the U. States. If your Excellency will therefore favor us with your opinion on the Subject we will report to Congress and request them to establish a Standard and so soon as this is done we will endeavor to get Materials and order a Number made sufficient for the Army. Neither can we tell what should be the Regimental Colours as the Uniforms were by a late Resolution of Congress to be settled by your Excellency.

> We have the Honour to be with the greatest Respect Your very obedient Servants
>
> Richard Peters

His Excellency the Commander in Chief. By Order.

Ref: G. Davis, *Regt Colors*, p 11 (crediting W. C. Ford)

Washington to Brigadier General Henry Knox

Middlebrook, May 12, 1779.

Dear Sir: The Inclosed letters respecting the rank of Officers in Proctors Regiment, and Colo. Flower's pretensions, are this moment come to hand. I wish you to consider them attentively, and give me your Sentiments in writing, fully, upon every matter and thing contained in them. The amusements of Phila. have such preferable charms to the dangers and hardships of the field, that I shall not be surprized at finding a thousand difficulties enumerated by the above Corps to prevent their Marching. I wish therefore as far as is consistent with the rights of others, that every obstacle may be removed, and complaints done away.

The letter to the Council of the Massachusett's bay is under a flying Seal for your perusal. Please to take the necessary, and most speedy measures to bring on the Cannon therein required to the Posts in the Highlands. I am, etc.　　　(N.Y.P.L.)

Knox's answer (May 13) states, among other things; "With respect to the Standards of the regiments, mentioned in Mr. Peters's letter, I think two would be sufficient; a continental and a regimental or State. As I understood the ground of the Uniform of each State will be the same, the Standards of the State ought to be one ground; the standards of each regiment to be distinguished by its number, and such other emblems as shall be pointed out. These might be agreed on immediately, but I should suppose the execution ought to be deferred until the Troops were uniformed." Knox's letter is in the Washington Papers.

Washington to the Board of War

May 14, 1779.
Head Quarters, Middle Brook

Gentlemen: I have been honored with your Letters of the 7th and 10th, instant. . . .

... I will issue the order you request to prevent applications for supplies at Philadelphia. The arrangement respecting colors is not yet made. I have the Honor, etc....

Estimate of Articles to be Imported in the Department of the Board of War and Ordnance (June 11, 1779)

Powder.....
Lead.....
Field Artillery.....
Muskets with bayonets.....
Brass Bullet moulds.....
Fusees.....
Blunderbusses.....
Copper.....
Block Tin.....
Sheet Copper.....
Sheet Lead.....
Tin Plate.....
Bugle Horns.....
Drum Heads.....
Trumpets for the horse.....
Setts of Musical Instruments....

Plain Strong Silk for regimental colors

of crimson	300	
deep blue	1100	1760 yards
wite	280	
buff	80	

Tassils & Cords of dccp bluc silk and gold mixed for the colors—400

400 yds White & 400 yds yellow silk fringe for Ditto—800 yds

(Ref: Papers of the Continental Congress, Item 147, Vol. III, pp 417 and 419, National Archives)

Washington to the President of Congress

August 23, 1779.
Head Quarters, West Point

Sir: I have the honor to inclose your Excellency Major Lee's report of the surprise and capture of the Garrison of Powles Hook. The Major displayed a remarkable degree of prudence address enterprise and bravery upon this occasion, which does the highest honor to himself and to all the officers and men under his command. The situation of the Post rendered the attempt critical and the success brilliant: It was made in consequence of information that the garrison was in a state of negligent security, which the event has justified.

I am much indebted to Major Genl. Lord Stirling for the judicious measures he took to forward the enterprise, and to secure the retreat of the party.

Lieut. McCalister who will have the honor of delivering these dispatches, will present Congress with the standard of the garrison which fell into his possession during the attack. Major Lee speaks of this Gentlemen's conduct in the handsomest terms. I have the honor, etc.

P.S. The report not having been received 'till this day prevented a speedier transmission. Major Lee mentions twenty men lost on our side. Capt. Rudolph informs that since the report was concluded several of the missing had returned which will lessen the supposed loss near one half.

[The original of Lee's report, dated Aug. 22, 1779, is not now found in the Washington Papers, but a copy by Tilghman is filed with this letter from Washington in the Papers of the Continental Congress.]

Washington to Major Henry Lee

Head Quarters, August 23, 1779.

Sir: I have received your report of the attack of Powles Hook transmitted by Captain Rudolph, which I have forwarded to Congress by Lieutenant McCallester. I shall be sorry if this should be contrary to your wish or Captain Rudolph's expectation, as I have the best opinion of this Gentlemens merit. My motives for sending Mr. McCallester with the dispatches were that he

General Orders, Oct. 2, 1779

On October 2, 1779, blue was officially fixed as the basic color for the Continental Army uniforms with linings and facings to be as follows:

Artillery and Artificers	— Scarlet facings and linings.
Light Dragoons	— White facings and linings.
Infantry	— White linings.
New Hampshire, Mass., Conn., Rhode Island	— White facings.
New York and New Jersey	— Buff facings.
Pa., Del., Md., Va.	— Red facings.
N. C., S. C., Georgia	— Blue facings.

Ref: Washington, General Order of Oct. 2, 1779, Lefferts, p 10) (Varick, Transcripts of Washington's General Order, Lib. of Congress).

commanded one of the forlorn hopes and got possession of the standard. As custom required the sending this to Congress, I thought the bearer of it ought to be the Person who had the good fortune to gain possession of it, especially as you had forwarded it by him to me; nor would it have been warranted by precedent to have sent one with the dispatches and another with the standard. You will find my sense of your conduct and of that of the officers and men under your command, expressed in the General order of yesterday and in my letter to Congress. I congratulate you on your success. You will send a small escort of dragoons with Lt. McCallester, I am, etc.

P.S. You will be pleased to order Capt. Handy with the detachment under his command to join his Brigade as soon as the Soldiery has recd. their shoes.

Washington to the Board of War

September 14, 1779.

Head Quarters, West Point

Gentlemen: I have been honoured with yours of the 31st August and 3d instants. Hallet was safely delivered to me by Lt. Colo. Washington and I sent him up to Govr. Clinton, with an account of his conduct, similar to that which you have transmitted to me.

I agree with you in opinion, that the Standard, with the Union and Emblems in the Centre, is to be preferred; with this addition the number of the Regt. and the State to which it belongs inserted within the curve of the serpent, in such place, as the painter or designer shall judge most proper.

Lt. McCallister, who brought me your favr. of the 3d, informs me that you desired him to tell me, that you had recd. an Acct. after sealing, that the Vessel with powder had arrived in the Delaware. This is a most agreeable piece of intelligence, and General Knox will inform the Board what quantity of the powder it will be necessary to have sent forward immediately to the Army.

Inclosed you have the Return of Major Gibbs Corps of Guards agreeable to the Resolve of 15th March last. I have the honor, etc.

The Commander in Chief's Guard. . . .

Footnote: The Board had written (September 3); "the enclosed Drafts of a Standard for the Army are sent for your Approbation, Rejection or Alteration. The Officers will be by and by pressing for Colours and if Materials can be procured they shall be made when you send us your Ideas of the Plan of the Standard. The one with the

Union and Emblems in the Middle is preferred by us as being variant from the Marine Flag." The Board's letter is in the Washington Papers.

(Writings, v. 16, p 283; G. Davis, p 5 referencing "Washington Correspondence," p 93, 94.)

General Orders

Saturday, January 22, 1780.

Head Quarters, Morristown

Parole Sacharissa. Countersigns Saint, Simple....

...Brigade returns, regimentally digested, are to be made to the Adjutant General on wednesday next of the arms, ammunition, accoutrements, drums and fifes in possession of the respective regiments; and on the same day the brigade Conductors (or Quarter Masters where there are no Conductors) are to make a return of all those articles in their possession.

The officers commanding brigades will take care to have the men completed with bayonets as speedily as possible.

Washington to the Board of War

February 23, 1780.

Head Quarters, Morris Town

Gentlemen: By the regulations the non-commissioned officers are to be armed with swords as a mark of distinction and to enable them the better to maintain the authority due to their stations. This necessary arrangement has not yet been carried into execution. By some returns I have seen there appears to have been a considerable number of Hessian hangers at Albany, though I find no mention of them in the last returns of The Commissary of Military stores. I presume the Board know where they are and I should think it would be adviseable to have these and any others that may be brought to the army distributed.

There is a great deficiency of drums, fifes and standards. I presume the necessary measures are taking to procure them with other articles of similar kind. I have the honor, etc.

Board of War to Washington

Feb. 28, 1780.

Sir: We have been honoured with your Excellency's Letter of the 23d. I have given Orders to the Commissary General of Military Stores in Consequence. As many Colours as possible shall be provided but until we receive the Articles from France, of which we have lately had agreeable Accounts, we cannot have the Standards prepared agreeably to the plan proposed viz: to have two for every Regiment—one, the Standard of the United States, the other, the Regimental Standard, the Ground whereof to be the Colour of the Facing. The Regiments must shift with what Colours can now be given them until the Arrival of our expected Supplies.

We have the Honour to be with the greatest Respect & Esteem,
Richard Peters.

Ref: G. W. Papers, L. C. No. 94, Folio 209 (quoted by G. Davis; W. Smith ed.)

General Orders

Monday, March 6, 1780.

Head Quarters, Morristown
Parole Newnham. Countersigns Gratton, Recorder.

Two men, one from the 1st. Pennsylvania brigade and one from the second, are to be sent to Mr. Gambles', the Commissary in Morristown, to assist in securing the hides and tallow.

Returns of Drums, Drum heads and cords, fifes and fife cases on hand and wanting in the several brigades, and of those in the hands of the Conductors and Commissary of Military Stores to be made to the Adjutant General as soon as possible.

To the Board of War

March 6, 1780.

Head Quarters, Morris Town

Gentlemen: I have been honored with yours of the 28th Ulto. It gives me great pleasure to find by your letters and by one which I recd. a few days ago from Mr. Lovell that we have favorable accounts from France on the subject of supplies of Cloathing and other stores. I have directed the Adj. General to call for an exact return of the drums and fifes wanting which shall be transmitted to the Board as soon as they are brought in.

General Knox informs me that the Hessian swords which were at Albany were ordered down to Fishkill with an intention to deliver them out to the non Commd Officers of the Artillery and Infantry, but that on their arrival they were found stripped of their mountings which having been brass, had been taken off to cast into Gun Mountings and for other purposes. He says they may be remounted again with Iron, and that he will order part of them to be fitted up again. I have the honor, etc.

General Orders

Saturday, October 6, 1781.

Headquarters before York,
Parole York.
Countersigns Viomenil, Lincoln.

Officers of the day Tomorrow
  Brigadier General Clinton
  Colonel Vose
  Major Olney
  B. M. Fullerton

.... Regulations for the Service of the Siege

1 The service of the siege will be performed by Division alternately; the Fatigue men will first be detailed out of the Division and the remainder will form Battalions under their respective Commanders to guard the Trenches; the first night there will be an exception to this Rule; the first regiment of each Brigade will that Night form a Division, Commanded by Major General Lincoln.

. . . .

17 The Trenches shall be relieved every Twenty four hours unless a particular order to the contrary by the General in which case the relief shall be in the rear of the others.

. . . .

21 The Drums are to be equally distributed in front and rear of the brigade. One only will March with each Picquet that may be detached in the Trenches.

. . . .

25 All the troops either relieving or relieved will March with Drums beating Colours flying and carry Arms to the place from whence they are to file off when they will support their Arms.

26 When the Troops shall have taken there post in the trenches the standard bearrers (sic) will plant their standards upon the Epaulments and sentries will be posted with proper intervals, with orders to give Notice of whatever they may see coming out from the place and of the shells that may be thrown by the Enemy, but no notice to be given or any movement to be made for Cannon shot.

27 The sandbags will be deposed on the Epaulments of the Trenches to cover the sentries.

.... 55 Besides the fatigue men of the trenches a sufficient detachment shall be given to the superintendent of the Deposit in the Trenches whose service shall be for twenty four hours: this officer is to employ them in collecting the tools, in making the different distributions, in going with the Litters, and bringing the wounded to the hospital of first dressings.

Some Rum being arrived an issue of one Jill pr man to all noncommissioned officers and privates will be made this afternoon at three o'clock near Major General Steuben's Marquee on Return signed by the officers commanding brigades, and one week's allowance of Spirits to officers agreeably to the General Orders of August 1780 will be issued tomorrow morning at eight o'clock on regimental returns to be signed by the respective Colonels or officers commanding regiments at the Magazine near the Commissary General's tents; those who neglect sending proper returns will have only themselves to blame if they lose their dividend on this occasion.

Washington to the President of Congress

Head Quarters, October 27, (–29), 1781.

Sir: I do myself the Honor to inclose to your Excellency, Copies of Returns of Prisoners, Artillery, Arms, Ordnance and other Stores, surrendered by the Enemy in their posts of York and Gloucester on the 19th instant, which were not completed at the Time of my last Dispatches, (and but this Moment handed to me). A Draft of these Posts with the plan of Attack and Defence is also transmitted, and 24 Standards taken at the same Time, are ready to be laid before Congress....

Feltman's Journal
"The Journal of Lt. William Feltman of the First Pa. Regt., from May 26, 1781 to April 25, 1782, embracing the Siege of Yorktown and the Southern Campaign". Collections of the Historical Society of Pennsylvania, Vol. 1, publ. 1855. (Lt. Feltman was a native of Lancaster Co.)

p 319–20 (siege lines at Yorktown)

12th Octr, '81

".... This day at 12 o'clock we were relieved by Gen. Lincoln's Division, when our division marched off with drums beating and colours flying...."

p 320–321 (siege lines at Yorktown)
15th Octr, '81

".... This day 12 o'clock our Troops were relieved by Genl. Lincoln's Division when we marched off with drums beating and colours flying, after a very fatiguing night...."

p 316
"Lt. Col. Huntington [3rd Conn] of Col. Scammel's Regt" (actually a battalion of light infantry)

p 317
"5th Oct'r '81-
".... In the evening we were relieved by Col. Duey, commanding the Rhode Island Reg't."

p 321
"17 Oct'r-
".... This day flags (parley flags) passing and repassing. Lord Cornwallis proposed ... surrender...."
".... Lord Cornwallis sent a flag;..."

"18 Oct'r—Flags passing and repassing this whole day...."

"19th Oct'r '81—At one o'clock this day Major Hamilton with a detachment marched into town and took possession of the batteries and hoisted the American flag...."

Feltman (Author's Note)

Organization of the American Army at Yorktown on 28 Sept'r, 1781. Feltman states there were six brigades but lists only five, as follows:

"Brig. Gen Muhlenberg
    Col. Vons's [Vose's] Battalion of Infantry
    Lt. Col. Barber's Battalion of Infantry
    Lt. Col. Gemot's [Gimat] Battalion of Infantry

Brig. Gen. Harem [Hazen]
    Col. Scammall's Reg't

Lt. Col. Hamilton's Battalion of Infantry
Harem's [Hazen's] Regt

Brig. Gen. Wayne
Col. Gaskin's Virginia Regt
The two Battalions of Pennsylvania's

Col. Dayton
The two Jersey Battalions
The Rhode Island Reg't

Brig. Gen. Clinton
Third Maryland Regt
Fourth Maryland Regt"

Estimate for Procuring One Hundred Standards for the Army of the United States.

Philadelphia, 2 July 1782

100 Standards at L 12 .. each = L 1200 ..

To be made of the best materials. The Silk estimated at 25 p[s?] per yard. Each colour to contain 4¼ yards. The name of the State & the number of the Regiment to be done in a garter of blue with pure gold leaf. Two silk Tassels to each standard & the ends of the staff mounted with brass—

Hon'ble Secretary   Sam'l Hodgdon
    at War   CGMS

NB:
50 Only was admited
at this time

Ref: Volume No. 148, War Department Collection of Revolutionary War Records

Author's Note

The number of standards to be furnished was subsequently reduced to fifty apparently matching the reduction in the number of regiments that was occurring by consolidations and furloughs.

Four and one-fourth yards of silk, assuming a selvage width of 28½ inches and allowing for two horizontally seamed panels and six inches for the staff sleeve, would provide a standard measuring 57 x 69 inches, which is equivalent to the standard of Webb's Additional Continental Regiment.

To the Secretary at War

August 1, 1782.

Head Quarters, Newburgh

Sir: As it is highly essential to the Discipline, as well as the Appearance of the Troops that they should be furnished with Colours, I could wish they might be forwarded as soon as possible for I am informed they are already purchased. There is a Deficiency of about 30 Drums and 20 Fifes (as you will perceive by the Inspection Returns) which should likewise be supplied.

The Bearer is charged with the General Return of the Army, the Inspection Returns and Musters for the Month of June. I have the Honor, etc.

General Orders

Thursday, September 5, 1782.

Head Quarters, Verplanks Point,
Parole Sussex.
Countersigns Easton, Bethlehem.

For the Day tomorrow
    Major General Heath
    Colonel Cortlandt
    Major Woodbridge
    Brigade Major Cushing
For duty tomorrow 3d.
    Connecticut and 9th. Massachusetts regiments.

All the Colours presented by Major Gen. the Marquis de la Fayette to the Light infantry are to be immediately lodged at the Orderly office.

Adjutant-General Hand to Colonel S. B. Webb

Camp Verplanks Point
6 September, 1782

Dear Sir

By direction of the Commander-in-chief I

send you two of the Lt. Infantry Standards, one for the use of your own and the other for Col. Jackson's Regt.

I am very sincerely yours

Edw. A. Hand
A. Gen

Ref: Ford, "Webb," II, p 416.

Washington to Lincoln

Quiries Submitted to the Secretary at War

February 17, 1783.

.... 1st Is the reduction of the Lines of New Hampshire, Rhode Island and New Jersey to take place on the 1st March?

2. In that case shall the Troops of New Hampshire be organized into one Regiment of 500 Rank and file and the residue formed into one complete Battalion of four Companies and the Troops of Jersey the same? or what mode shall be adopted.

3d Will it not be best to reform Hazen's Regiment immediately and put it upon the same Establishment as the rest of the Army.

.... 4th Should not every possible effort be made to furnish Scarlet cloth for facings and other Materials for turning the present Coats of the Army?

5 The German Armourers Cartridge Boxes, colours etc should be sent on?

6 It seems necessary that something should be done towards regulating the Issues of Provision to the Canadian Refugees And is Colo. Antills family entitled to draw, under that denomination.

Lincoln to Washington
(In Reply to above letter)

#4 The answer was: "I will leave no measure untried to effect it."

#5 The answer was: "The German armorers have been sent for, cartridge boxes are being made and repaired and colors will be sent on. I wish they were better than they are."

Washington to Colonel Timothy Pickering

Head Quarters, March 10, 1783.

Sir: In Answer to a Letter written by the Comr in Chief a Week or two ago (several havg been written before on same Subject) to the Secty at War, respectg the Standards for the Army. The followg reply has been made.

"The Standards are in the Hands of the Q Master at Camp, and have been there fore some Time." The Commander in Chief requests your Explanation of this Matter. Yours Sc.

Pickering answered the same day (March 10) that the standards came to the store at camp in a box with other articles. The field commissary of military stores removed the other articles, "but left the standards, saying he would send for them: however, there they are yet set." Pickering's letter is in the Washington Papers.

Washington to the Secretary at War

Head Quarters, March 11, 1783.

Sir: I am honored with your several Letters of 26th feby, 1st, 4 and 4th of March.

.... The Standards, I have found, by examining, to be in the Care of Mr. Frotingham, F. C. of Military Stores. Your Intimation in your last, was the first Notice, I had, of their being near me. I am &c.

General Orders

Friday, March 14, 1783.

Parole Darby. Countersigns Epsom, Fez.

For the day tomorrow Major Scott, Brigade Qr. Master from the Hampshire brigade.

For duty the Jersey Battalion.

The regiments which are not furnished with regimental Colours will immediately make application for them to Mr. Frothingham, Commissary of military stores.

Appendix II

PHILADELPHIA FLAGMAKERS AND FLAGPAINTERS

The author has found references to a number of Philadelphia flagmakers and flagpainters in original Revolutionary War records and related sources. They are discussed in the paragraphs that follow. There were undoubtedly others beyond those included here.

JAMES CLAYPOOLE AND JOHN FOLWELL— FLAGPAINTERS, SEPTEMBER, 1775. WILLIAM BARRETT—BETSY ROSS' FLAGPAINTER.

Two Philadelphia painters of military standards are identified in contemporary Revolutionary War records.

James Claypoole was paid on 8th September 1775 for painting the silk standard of the Philadelphia Light Horse which bears a Union symbol of thirteen ribbons tied together. John Folwell was paid on September 16th, 1775 for having drawn and designed the Light Horse "Coulours." The above two receipts are in the collection of the Philadelphia First Troop.[1]

A William Barrett was named by Mrs. Rachel Fletcher, one of Betsy Ross' daughters, as having painted a watercolor of the American flag design which Betsy was to make and who later was employed by Betsy to paint coats of arms of the United States and of Pennsylvania on silk flags.[2]

MARGARET MANNY
DECEMBER 2, 1775

Margaret Manny made an "ensign" for the flagship *Alfred* (originally the merchantman *Black Prince*) of the Continental Navy in November or very early December 1775.

The reference to Margaret Manny is found in the Day Book of a Philadelphia ship chandler, James Wharton, who supplied naval stores and other items to those Continental Navy vessels being outfitted at Philadelphia in December 1775. The original Day Book is at the Historical Society of Pennsylvania and is discussed under Continental Navy.[3] Wharton's entries for December 2, 1775 for deliveries to the "Ship Alfred" included the following:

"Cr Margaret Manny for making an Ensign £1.2.8. . ."

There is also a record of payment to Margaret Manny for flagmaking in other records according to Theodore Gottlieb.[4]

A Loyalist identified only as "B. P." reported in a letter dated December 20, 1775, that on ". . . . the 3d instant, the Continental flag on board the *Black Prince* opposite Philadelphia was hoisted." (see Continental Navy).[5]

John Paul Jones who was appointed First Lieutenant on the *Alfred* and who supervised her outfitting stated in a letter to Robert Morris, dated October 10, 1783, that ". . . . It was my fortune, as senior of the first lieutenants, to hoist, myself, the flag of America the first time it was displayed." Jones made the same claim in a letter to Baron Van der Capellan and gave "the Delaware" as the location.[6]

Subsequently, as the Continental Navy squadron prepared to sail, Commodore Hopkins, aboard the flagship *Alfred*, issued his signaling instructions dated February 14, 1776 which listed one of the Alfred's flags as "the ensign" and again as "a St. George's ensign with stripes."[7]

On the basis of the above, it appears strongly evidenced that Margaret Manny's "ensign" was the Continental stripes with a British Grand Union canton and was the one hoisted by Jones on December 3 and the one flown by the flagship *Alfred* during the first cruise of the Continental Navy in Spring 1776.

Nothing about Margaret Manny, other than the above, is known to the author. There probably are records that would further identify her. Margaret apparently made the first, or one of the first, ensigns that symbolized the Union of the American Colonies. The Continental Grand Union was definitely the recognized ensign of the United Colonies and, after the Declaration, of the United States. It was recognized as the "Union" or "American" flag by the Continental Army, Navy, Congress and by the thirteen colonies and their state forces and by the British and other nations. It continued in use until the stars were introduced as the Union along with the field of thirteen stripes by the Congressional Resolution of June 14, 1777. The author acknowledges that the Continental Grand Union was not officially adopted by Congress as is clearly evidenced by John Jay's letter to Colonel Alexander MacDougall of New York, dated March 23, 1776, in which Jay stated that the Congress had made no order concerning colors.[8]

The document which names Margaret Manny also lists a "Committee of Congress", apparently the Naval or Marine Committee, that was purchasing ensigns, jacks and pendants for the newly formed Continental Navy in December 1775 and January 1776. Probably, the Committee by directly controlling the flags was insuring uniformity in the design of colors furnished the thirteen Continental vessels being outfitted in Philadelphia and other ports.

It could be conjectured that one of the striped union flags was sent to Washington at Cambridge and was hoisted there on January 1, 1776. This is not idle conjecture.

Lt. Col. Joseph Reed, Washington's secretary in 1775, had returned to his native Philadelphia in late 1775. He had been with the Congressional Committee which conferred with Washington on needs and budgets for the Army in October 1775. It was to Reed that Washington wrote his often quoted January 4, 1776 letter which mentioned the hoisting of the "Union" flag before Boston on January 1, 1775. Washington did not describe the flag to Reed. He speaks of it only as "the union flag" which indicates that Reed knew the design. [9]

CORNELIA BRIDGES
MAY 1776

The reference to Mrs. Cornelia Bridges is a receipt dated May 25, 1776 in the Pennsylvania State Archives for "£ 16.13s. for making colors for the Floating Battery, Warren & Bulldog. £ 2.3s. for former & £ 2.5s. for later [sic] two." [10]

ELIZABETH ROSS—MAY 1777
ANNE KING—MAY 1777
REBECCA YOUNG
ANNE WARD

The reference to Elizabeth Ross is an entry in the Pennsylvania State Navy Board Minutes on May 29, 1777 for payment to Mrs. Ross of £ 14.12s. 2d for making ship's colors. [11]

Family tradition credits Betsy Ross with also having made the first stars and stripes to the design of a "Committee of Congress." She is so well known that the author had initially planned to just refer to the family story without comment, however, he eventually succumbed and researched Betsy's story as detailed later.

Jackson wrote that Anne King was paid for "colors" for the fireship of the Pennsylvania State Navy in May 1777. [12]

Theodore Gottlieb, who did considerable research on the Betsy Ross family tradition,

wrote that Rebecca Young advertised as a flagmaker in the Philadelphia newspapers and that records show she was paid "at least thirty times" for flags. Gottlieb also wrote that there was a record of an Anne Ward being paid for flags. [13]

The presence of so many other Philadelphia women flagmakers could be taken as support for the Betsy Ross story, particularly for the odd little detail quoted by her daughter that the "Committee" had ordered sample flags from other flagmakers as well as from Betsy. [14]

POSTWAR FLAGMAKERS
1784-1799

In the postwar period, several Philadelphia flagmakers and flagpainters are identified and they could have made flags during the Revolution. Rebecca Young was paid for sewing the standard and John Henderson for painting the devices (the design is unknown) on the standard and on four camp colors for the First United States Regiment, commanded by Lt. Col. Josiah Harmar, in October 1784. [15]

In June and July 1791, four silk regimental standards and their linen cases were supplied to the two regular and two militia regiments of the Army. Nancy Nash did the sewing, Henry P. Pearson made the poles, John Wucherer made the mountings, metal butts, and points. The silk tassels were purchased from Wood and Thornely. A Mr. Wright painted the devices of the standards (believed to have been the great eagle seal of the United States) and he also painted the poles. [16]

In 1798, a "Chrs Gullergy" was paid for painting an eagle seal on a blue silk standard for the Philadelphia First City Troop (the Light Horse). In 1799, John Myers was paid for a set of mountings and a spear for the "Colour staff" and Thomas Jacquet and George Hicks were paid for the pole, silver tassels, ribbon, thread, a case and for sewing the silk and fringe. [17]

267

All of the above clearly establish that Philadelphia was well equipped with seamstresses, painters, and other artisans required to design and make flags, poles, spearheads, and mountings.

Possibly, one of the above flag painters (Claypoole ?) painted the elaborate devices on the thirteen silk regimental standards for the Continental Army described in Major Johnathan Gostelowe's Return of July-August 1778 which listed military stores in Philadelphia at the time. Major Gostelowe's Return is discussed under that heading.

BETSY ROSS

William J. Canby, a grandson of Elizabeth (Griscom) Ross-Ashburn-Claypoole, read a paper before the Historical Society of Pennsylvania on March 14, 1870 entitled "The History of the Flag of the United States." The original paper was apparently not published at the time, at least not by the Historical Society, but a facsimile copy of Canby's manuscript is available there. Canby did author a version of the paper which was published in 1882. The original manuscript is at the Huntington Library, San Marino, California. [18]

Canby's paper evidences careful preparation, good penmanship and reflects that he was an articulate, serious, well-read individual. Although its title is rather broad, the paper's main topic is a family tradition that Canby's grandmother, Betsy Ross, made the first stars and stripes. He said the design for the flag was specified to her by a Continental Congress Committee composed of George Washington, George Ross and Robert Morris who came to her upholstery shop on Arch Street in Philadelphia. Canby does not give a date for the committee's visit or the making of the flag in his March 14, 1870 paper. A subsequent affidavit, dated July 31, 1871, which Canby obtained from one of his aunts states that the committee called on Betsy in "June 1776 or shortly before the Declaration of Independence." [19]

Betsy, according to Canby, made several unrecorded suggestions concerning the design which were incorporated on the spot by Washington including one specific suggestion that five-point stars be used rather than the committee's six-point stars which Betsy said were "wrong". She also noted that the design was "unsymmetrical." Betsy told the committee that she had never made a flag before but agreed to try. She set to work using an artist's painting of the committee's design and an old ship's color as a pattern. When Betsy finished the flag it was trial-hoisted "over a ship at the wharf", received the "unanimous approval of the committee" and on "the same day was carried into the State House and laid before Congress with a report from the committee" and was "adopted by Congress".

Betsy was then given a standing order by George Ross, the uncle of her deceased husband, for as many stars and stripes as she could turn out and he helped in financing purchases of cloth. Betsy and then her eldest daughter continued to make flags until 1857.

Canby's paper acknowledged the need for some documented record of his grandmother's story. He describes his search, which must have extended over a number of years, for such a record or any records as to the flag's origin. He searched "every book, pamphlet or newspaper" in the Philadelphia area libraries and the unpublished records in the archives of the State Department. He found nothing to support the family tradition. Of original records on the flag's origin, he found only the well known flag resolution of June 14, 1777 and Washington's letter on hoisting of a "Union Flag" at Cambridge on January 1, 1776.

Although lacking documented proof, Canby pointed out that such traditions as his grandmother's story should be preserved, particularly in view of the apparent lack of any recorded history on the flag's origin. He acknowledged the encouragement and help of the officers of the Society, particularly for the letter of introduction which gained him access to the State Department's Archives.

Canby's 35-page paper devotes only about three pages to recounting his grandmother's story. The balance is concerned with a description of his search, the rationale for his paper, and comments on the June 14, 1777 flag resolution, on flag design, family genealogy, Betsy's life, her three husbands and her children. Although his manuscript does not give even an approximate date for the committee's visit and Betsy's making of her first flag, he notes that almost a year elapsed after the Declaration before a national flag was adopted by the Congress.

Canby's paper triggered much debate and interest and challenges. He therefore obtained affidavits from one of Betsy's three surviving daughters and from a granddaughter and a niece. Canby and his relations expended considerable effort over the next several generations defending and researching the story. Probably the most important piece of data to come to light is a record of "an order on William Webb to Elizabeth Ross" for "ship's colours, etc." in the Pennsylvania State Navy Board Minutes for May 29, 1777.[20]

Records of Betsy's three marriages, the births of her children, military service and civilian occupations of her husbands, shop and home addresses and other genealogical data have been compiled—remarkably detailed and complete. However, nothing has been found to directly prove the family story about the visit from the committee, the existence of such a committee, Betsy's making of the flag, its hoisting, its display or its adoption in June 1776 "before the Declaration." Betsy left no written record of the flag story nor was it publicly told until 1870. She died in 1836 at 84 when her grandson was eleven. He recorded the story in 1857 as told him by Betsy's eldest daughter.[21]

Canby's paper does not claim that Betsy designed the stars and stripes nor does it even mention the circle of stars design. However, according to the July 31, 1871 affidavit of Betsy's daughter, Rachel Fletcher, Betsy said the committee's design for the flag was square and the stars were scattered promiscuously over the field. Her affidavit, as quoted by Ray Thompson in "The Story of Betsy Ross," does not mention any stripes. As Mrs. Fletcher recalled her mother's story, Betsy told the committee the stars "should be in lines, or in some adopted form, as a circle, or a star, and that the stars were six-pointed in the drawing, and she said they should be five-pointed. Betsy reportedly also said a flag should be one-third longer than its width, not square.[22]

The flag resolution of June 14, 1777 did not prescribe the number of points or the arrangement of the stars, nor did it call for a rectangular flag rather than a square one. Flagmakers, including Betsy, were left free to choose whatever number of star points and arrangement and flag proportions suited them and their clients as is amply evidenced by prints, drawings and paintings of the variety of the stars and stripes designs at the time, and for the next century. The circle of stars was used in a purely imaginary painting of Betsy Ross by C. H. Weisberger in the 1890's. This painting has received wide circulation and is the primary reason that the circle of stars has been identified with Betsy Ross.

Charles W. Peale employed a circle of six-point stars in his 1779 portrait of Washington at Princeton and the circle of stars was used on a 1778 issue of Continental currency designed by Francis Hopkinson. L'enfant placed the stars in an oval in his 1783 initially proposed diploma for the Cincinnati and the circular arrangement became quite popular after the War. However, there were few instances of the use of the circle of stars during the Revolution. Most eyewitness drawings of the union of stars show the

269

stars in rows. Washington's personal or headquarters standard, which has survived to this day, has an all blue field with thirteen six-point stars in a rectilinear 3-2-3-2-3 pattern. Six-point and eight-point stars were more often used than five-point, and six-point stars appeared on American coinage well into the 20th Century. Heraldically, six- and eight-point stars were more frequently used than five-points. The Seal of the United States, adopted in June 1782, has thirteen six-point stars.

As to Mrs. Fletcher's recollection that the Committee's flag design was square, it should be noted that flags used by land troops are of squarish proportions while those intended for marine or garrison use are rectangular. It would have been only reasonable, with Washington present, for the ''committee'' to have shown Betsy an army-type square flag design. However, the family tradition claims that she was given an old ship's colour to use as a pattern. This tends to support the many historical indications (not connected in anyway with Betsy Ross) that the stars and stripes was intended primarily for the navy and not the army. Naval flags are very different in their material, stitching, grommeting and proportions from the silk, painted or embroidered, sleeved, squarish-proportioned banners of army field units.

The affidavit of Mrs. Fletcher claims that William Barrett, a Philadelphia artist, made a water-color drawing of the committee's design as a guide for Betsy's use and that Barrett was often employed thereafter by Betsy to paint coats-of-arms of the United States and of the State on silk flags. This indicates that Betsy made army as well as navy type flags in the subsequent years and must have been familiar with the design of each type.

Both Canby and his aunt recall that Betsy Ross said that the delegation included George Ross, Robert Morris and George Washington, representing a ''Committee of Congress.'' There is no record of any committee specifically responsible for flags. However, there was a committee appointed in July 1776 to design a seal of the United States.

According to Scharf & Westcott, George Ross was a delegate to the Continental Congress of September 4, 1774 and of 1775 but not, initially, of the Congress of 1776. He was not a delegate on July 4, 1776 but was appointed on July 20, as one of five new delegates to replace those Pennsylvania delegates who abstained or voted against the Declaration. He and the other delegates signed the formal parchment copy of the Declaration on August 2. Ross was evidently not a member of the Continental Congress in June 1776 at the time of the claimed visit to Betsy Ross.

Ross was a member of the Pennsylvania Committee of Safety in 1775 and 1776 and of the Constitutional Convention of 1776. The Committee's duties were assumed by the Council of Safety in mid-1776 and then by the newly elected Supreme Executive Council in March 1777 which immediately appointed a Pennsylvania State Board of War and a Navy Board. George Ross was not a member of either Board. Ross was appointed Judge of Admiralty for Pennsylvania in mid-1776.

Robert Morris was a delegate to the Continental Congress in 1775, 1776 and on, and was a member of the Secret Committee responsible for procuring arms and ammunition and other military stores.

Various writers have conjectured that it might have been the Secret Committee that Ross, Morris and Washington represented when they reportedly visited Betsy Ross with their design since there was no specific committee on flags established. The author has not encountered any record indicating that the Secret Committee was responsible for establishing the design or procuring flags. However, there are records that a ''Committee of Congress'' was procuring ensigns, jacks and standards for the newly formed Continental Navy in December 1775 and January 1776.

The Day Book of a Philadelphia ship chandler, James Wharton, who was involved in fitting out some of the vessels, lists the flags furnished to individual ships but also separately lists various flags charged to and apparently delivered to an unidentified "Committee of Congress." Also, a few sundry articles were debited to the account of "Committee of Congress." All of the hundreds of other items furnished were debited to individual ships and the total bill sent to the "Honorable Continental Congress." This Day Book and its entries are discussed under the "Continental Navy." The point that has caught the author's attention is that only flags, specifically, were debited to this "Committee of Congress."

There had been a Naval Committee established to direct the formation and operations of the Continental Navy. The Naval Committee was responsible for seeing that the ships were purchased, converted and outfitted, including all items furnished by the ship chandler. However, the ship chandler differentiated between items, including flags, delivered to the ships and the flags delivered to the "Committee of Congress." Probably, the Naval Committee was purchasing flags through the ship chandler for use on other Continental Navy ships being outfitted in other colonies to assure that the flags were all to a prescribed design. It could be conjectured that such a committee could have drawn up a new national ensign design or designs: the stars—or the stripes and stars—a few months later in May-June 1776 or in May-June 1777 and had samples made by various Philadelphia seamstresses.

As concerns the date and the presence of Washington, as claimed by Canby's aunt in her affidavit, it is of interest that Washington was in Philadelphia from May 23 to June 5, 1776 conferring with Congress on the impending British attack on New York. [23]

Washington was Commander-in-Chief of the Continental Army and not a member of Congress after June 1775.

The Board of War and Ordnance was established during his visit and went into operation on June 12, 1776. However, Washington and the Board of War apparently considered the stars and stripes to be primarily a marine flag. They corresponded from 1779 to 1783 on the design and supply of a "standard of the United States" for the regiments of the army that would be "variant" from the "marine flag" (the stripes and stars). Their initial design placed the "union" in the center and included a rattlesnake emblem. The rattlesnake was used on the seal of the Board of War and Ordnance adopted in 1778 which is still in use today by the Department of the Army. The seal also includes a pair of standards one of which is the stars and stripes, the second is plain. However, Army regiments were not authorized to carry a stars and stripes until the 1830's. Washington, as noted above, employed thirteen six-point stars on a blue field (the union) as his headquarters standard. At times, the stars and stripes was hoisted over an American army. For example, Hamilton hoisted the stars and stripes at Yorktown, and General Clinton's New York Brigade of Sullivan's Army carried a stars and stripes in August 1779.

On May 28, 1780, Francis Hopkinson, a New Jersey delegate to the Continental Congress and an artist-heraldist who had designed a number of seals, wrote to the Board of Admiralty and requested recognition for having designed the "Flag of the United States of America," or as he later named it, "the great Naval Flag of the United States." His claim, initially well received, was eventfully rejected and Hopkinson angrily resigned as Treasurer of Loans. A Congressional committee investigated and on August 23, 1781 reported that Hopkinson's claim should not be recognized because he was not the only person who had worked on design of the flag. Hopkinson chaired the Marine Committee at the time of the June 14, 1777 flag resolution.[24]

The verifiable aspects of the Betsy Ross tradition can be summarized as follows:

— She was a life long native of Philadelphia and was a seamstress and flag-maker during the Revolution. Surviving records establish that she was paid for making colors for the Pennsylvania State Navy in May 1777. She had a shop and residence on Arch Street and, later, at other nearby locations.
— Genealogical records on Betsy are quite complete. She married three times, had a number of descendants and died in 1836 at the age of 84. She was a member of the Society of Free Quakers (the church still stands at Fifth and Arch) and was patriotic, honest, resourceful and respected. Her first two husbands were casualties of the war and her third husband was a veteran of land and sea service.
— She continued to make flags, according to her children, well into the Nineteenth Century with help from her daughters.
— She told her daughters she had made the first stars and stripes to a design brought to her shop by a delegation from the Continental Congress and that she had suggested the use of five point stars and an orderly arrangement of the stars.
— Her daughters told their children and in 1870 a grandson prepared and delivered a paper on his grandmother's story.

The following facts bear on the Betsy Ross tradition and, circumstantially, tend to support it as to the presence and probable interest of the three men who reportedly made up the delegation or committee, the June 1776 date of their visit, and the involvement of the Continental Congress and Philadelphia flagmakers in any newly designed national standard:

— Washington was in Philadelphia in the latter part of May and early June 1776, leaving for New York on the morning of June 5. Robert Morris and George Ross were not members of the Congress in June 1776 but were later. However, the two men were closely connected to the activities of both State and Continental Congresses at the time. All three men, especially Washington, would have been strongly interested in the design of any proposed national standard. The impending Declaration of Independence was being discussed by leaders of the Continental Congress at the time and it seems plausible that there would have been some thought given to a national standard.
— A "Committee of Congress" (the Marine Committee) was purchasing ensigns for the Continental Navy in December 1775-January 1776.
— Washington wrote from Philadelphia on May 28, 1776, to Gen. Putnam urging the Army to get flags.
— A number of Philadelphia women flagmakers are identified in the records as having made flags during the Revolution. The Continental Congress and Philadelphia seamstresses would certainly have been involved in the design and making of the first national standard. For instance, Francis Hopkinson, a delegate, submitted a bill for having designed the "great naval flag of the United States" and the response from his fellow delegates was that others had also been involved and that credit should not go to him alone.

There are elements of the Betsy Ross story which simply are not supported by recorded history. For instance, Betsy's suggestions as to the design and arrangement of the stars and the proportions of the flag do not appear in any record, nor was there any recorded action by Congress as to such detailed design of the flag in June 1776.

In the author's opinion, the Betsy Ross family tradition probably became clouded with a number of embellishments and inaccuracies which is a typical problem with most unrecorded and with some recorded history dependent on human memory and interpretation. Such details as the five point stars, specific star patterns, and flag proportions could have been unconsciously added to the tradition by Betsy or her daughters and represented the flagmaking guidelines they developed over the years.

PHILADELPHIA FLAGMAKERS—REFERENCES

1. Jos. Lapsley Wilson, ed, "Book of the First Troop, Philadelphia City Cavalry, 1774-1914, "Phila 1915, p 243.
2. Ray Thompson, "The Story of Betsy Ross," Bicentennial Press, 1775, p 6.
3. William Bell Clark, ed, "Naval Documents of the American Revolution, Vol 3, 1775-76," Washington, GPO, 1968, p 1380.
4. Theodore Gottlieb, "The American Flag," New Jersey Hist. Society, Proceedings, LV11 (1939), 240-244 (reference from Hugh F. Rankin, "The Naval Flag of the Revolution," Wm. & Mary Quarterly, July 1954, p 347).
5. Clark, "Nav Docs," V 3, p 186-7.
6. Charles W. Stewart, ed, "John Paul Jones, Commemoration at Annapolis, April 24, 1906," Washington, 1907, p 162.
7. Rhode Island Hist. Soc., Mss, Vol 8, 4. Also, Hopkins Papers (RIHS). Clark, "Nav Docs", V 3, p 1287-9.
8. Henry P. Johnston, ed., "The Correspondence and Public Papers of John Jay" (New York, 1890), Vol 1, pp 46, 47, 49 (reference from Hugh F. Rankin, see (4), above). McDougall wrote to Jay on March 6, 1776 requesting a description of the "Continental Colours". Jay replied on March 23, 1776 that Congress "had made no order concerning them, and I believe the captains of their armed vessels have in particular been directed by their own fancies and inclinations."
9. Fitzpatrick, "Writings of George Washington," V 4, p 210.
10. John W. Jackson, "The Pennsylvania Navy, 1775-1781," Rutgers Press, p 17, 408, 409 (referencing Penna Mss, RG-4, Various, Box 1, Committee of Safety Receipt Book B, May 23 to July 3, 1776).
11. Ibid, pp 17, 408 (referencing P.A., 2nd Series, Vol 1, p 164).
12. Ibid, pp 408, 409 (referencing Pa MSS, RG-4, Mil Accts, Box 2, re. W. Webb and J. Nicholson).
13. Hugh Rankin in *The Naval Flag of the American Revolution* references Theodore Gottlieb's report that the records of the Quartermaster Department of the Continental Army or of the Pennsylvania State Navy list a Rebecca Young of Philadelphia, who was paid "at least thirty times for flags" and that these records also list Anne Ward and Margaret Manney as having been paid for flags. Further, that Rebecca Young advertised herself as a seamstress and flagmaker in the "contemporary Philadelphia press. (Hugh F. Rankin, "The Naval Flag of the American Revolution," The William and Mary Quarterly, July, 1954; referencing Theodore Gottlieb, "The American Flag," New Jersey Historical Society, Proceedings LVII (1939) p 178).
14. Thompson, "Betsy Ross," p 6.
15. Detmar H. Finke, "United States Army Colors and Standards, 1784-1808," MC & H (The Journal of the Company of Military Historians) Fall 1963, pp 69-72.
16. Ibid.
17. Ibid.
18. Wm. J. Canby, read a Paper before the Historical Society of Pennsylvania, March 14th, 1870, entitled, "The History of the Flag of the United States." A facsimile of Canby's manuscript is at the Historical Society of Pennsylvania. The

Philadelphia, Pa. Press, page 6, March 15, 1870 reports on Canby's story. A Philadelphia Times booklet by Canby, "The First American Flag and the Family History of Betsy Ross," was published in 1882.

19. Thompson, "Betsy Ross," pp 5, 6.
20. Jackson, "Pennsylvania Navy," p 17, 408
21. Thompson, "Betsy Ross," gives a biography.
22. Thompson, "Betsy Ross," pp 5, 6, for Mrs. Fletcher's affidavit.
23. W. S. Baker, "Itinerary of General Washington," Phila. 1892, p 40.
24. Hugh F. Rankin, "The Naval Flag of the Revolution," Wm. & Mary Qtrly, July 1954, p 346, 347.

NOTE: Also of reference value for those researching Betsy Ross is an article, "Face to Face with Betsy Ross," by Whitney Smith, Ph.D., published in the *Flag Bulletin*, Vol. XIV:I, The Flag Research Center, Winchester, Mass.

Glossary

ARMS, COAT OF ARMS, ACHIEVE-MENT OF ARMS: a heraldic design which consisted mainly of a shield, supporters and crest with stylized symbols, colors, arrangements, and identified a personage, corporation, political organization, state, city, county or nation. Arms were placed on the cloth coat drawn over a Knight's armour. They were used as an official seal and emblazoned on standards. The "Logo" of a present-day business corporation is a descendant of the ancient coat of arms.

ARTIFICIER: an artilleryman who prepares shells.

ASSOCIATORS: Colonial militia provincial forces. "Pennsylvania Associator Battalions".

BADGE: A distinctive symbol or device or emblem placed on military colors and standards to identify the unit. The badge of the Rhode Island Regiment of 1781 was an anchor entwined with rope.

BANNER: (French, banniere). A flag of a personage, saint, commander or organization usually bearing a symbol and motto. Originally, the standard under which a band of men united. In the Middle Ages, the right to carry a banner was restricted to knight-bannerets and higher ranks. A banner was emblazoned with the coat of arms of its owner. The union jack of Great Britain is a religious banner.

BANNERET: The senior rank of knighthood, almost equivalent to a baron. In England, a Knight-banneret ranked below a knight of the garter, but was senior to a common knight, who, in turn, outranked an esquire.

BANDEROLE, BANNEROL, BANNER ROLE, BANDROLE: "A small banner about a yard square, generally, but not always, rounded at the fly, several of which were carried at funerals. They displayed the arms and the matches of the deceased's ancestors..." At Cromwell's funeral were displayed: four elongated triangular, notched Standards (England, Scotland, Ireland, Wales); a Guydon (rounded fly); and eight banners (including the Union, St. George, St. Andrew, King David, Cromwell and Allied families). (Ref. Preble).

CAMP COLORS: Small, sturdy, square flags flown in camps to identify a unit and mark boundaries. They were about eighteen inches square. British camp colors were also termed BANDCROLES.

CANTON: One quarter or less of the field of a flag. Usually the upper inner quarter and bearing the national symbol or other device. For flags the upper inner quarter is the first quarter or canton, the upper outer the second, the lower inner the third, and the lower outer the fourth.

CHIEF: A heraldry term for the upper third of the shield of a coat of arms. The seal of the United States has a shield with a blue chief symbolizing Congress with thirteen vertical red and white stripes below the chief symbolizing the states.

COLORS, COLOR: The unit or national flag of a military organization or combatant ship. More applicable to ground forces than to naval units. The term "colors" applies to one or more flags. Military colors generally bear some relation to the color of the unit's uniforms, frequently matching the cuffs and lapels.

The flags of infantry or foot regiments are known as "colors" and the term applies to one or more flags, e.g., the "colors of the First Pennsylvania Regiment," included the regiment's regimental standard and its subdivisional (two or more companies) "colors". When necessary for grammatical ease and meaning, the term "color" is used in the singular sense although "colors" is the primary military term. Washington, in 1776, called on the regimental commanders to "fix" on designs for "The Standard (or Regimental Colours) and Colours for each Grand Division" for their regiments.

In 1779, General Knox wrote to Washington that "two Standards" would be sufficient for each regiment, "a continental and a regimental or State." Later in 1779, Washington and the Board of War corresponded on a design for a "Standard for the Army" that would be variant from the "Marine Flag."

Infantry (foot) units carried COLORS. Cavalry carried a STANDARD or GUIDON.

COLOR GUARD: The color bearers and their armed guards. During the Revolution, the colors of a military unit had a primary role in battle-field control of troops and provided a visible rallying point. Color bearers were prized targets, therefore, were assigned a guarding force. Picked troops were assigned, and given extra pay and perquisites (see Charles Lee's plan for Colours). As an example of what could happen to color bearers, read Moultrie's account of the capture of the colors of the 2nd S. C. Regiment.

CORNET: The junior commissioned officer of a dragoon regiment. He carried the colors or standard.

CORPS: A specialized subdivision of the military forces. During the Revolution, a Corps consisted of a number of regiments, at times organized into two brigades. The Corps of Rangers or the Rifle Corps, The Corps of Light Infantry. Today, the Marine Corps.

CREST: The uppermost symbol above the shield in a coat of arms.

DRAGOONS: Lightly equipped cavalry, essentially, mounted foot soldiers.

ENSIGN: (Latin insigne) Also known as an "Ancient." The principal flag of the king, chieftain, commander, military unit, ship, state or nation. Its bearer was also known as the "ensign" and the rank was employed in American Revolutionary War regiments. The army "ensign" is now a second lieutenant. The rank still exists in the Navy.

EMBLEM: A symbolic device conveying an idea, goal, or attitude placed on the field of a flag.

FIELD: The principal area of a flag. Ground.

FINIAL: The decorative spearpoint or other ornament at the top of a flag pole, staff, pike or lance.

FLAG: (Anglo-Saxon meaning "to fly"). An all-inclusive, generic term for a lightweight piece of cloth usually decorated or emblazoned with a symbol and/or motto and serving to identify a group, organization, state, nation, leader, commander, military or naval unit. Also used as a verb, "to signal." The term "flag" is loosely used to cover all types of such specific flags as banners, standards, colors, guidons, ensigns, pennants, jacks, and streamers. Such use is roughly the same as speaking of all wheeled vehicles as "cars" rather than differentiating the various types, such as racers, trucks, passenger cars, emergency vehicles and so forth.

FLY: The free length of a flag measured from the hoist or staff edge out to the free edge.

FOOT REGIMENT: Infantry

FUSILEER: Soldier equipped with a fusil-type musket.

GONFANON: Religious banner. In the Middle Ages, the standard of the commander-in-chief; "barons had gonfanons, knights had pennons." William the Conqueror's gonfanon had three tails.

GRENADIER: Grenade thrower.

GROUND: See Field.

GROMMET: A reinforced fastening hole or eyelet along with hoist edge of a flag. Revolutionary era grommets were thread whipped. Metal grommets were introduced in the Nineteenth Century. Marine and garrison flags generally have grommets. Military colors have sleeves or closely spaced lacing eyelets.

GUYDON OR GUIDON: (French: guide-homme) The standard of a company of soldiers and borne by their cornet. Similar to a banner in form and emblazonment but one-third less in size and the fly rounded off. Carried by mounted troops. (Preble).

HORSE: Heavily equipped cavalry.

JACK: A flag attached to a jackstaff and flown at the bow of a ship. Generally, a jack bears a union symbol. Also used as a term for a union flag—union jack.

LANCE: The stave or staff for the standard or guidon of a cavalry or dragoon unit.

LEGION: A military unit made up of mounted troops and foot soldiers on a ratio of about one to two.

LIGHT-INFANTRY: Lightly-equipped, fast-moving foot soldiers used to maneuver and fight in a more independent open style than foot regiments. Usually, no flag was carried.

OBVERSE: The front side of a flag with the staff or hoist to the viewer's left. For the REVERSE side the staff is to the viewer's right.

ORGANIZATIONAL TERMINOLOGY:

LINE: The combatant forcés of the army or navy. The "Connecticut Line."

ARMY: A major, fully-equipped land military force capable of conducting independent operations. There was a Northern, a Main and a Southern Continental Army. Two or more WINGS.

WING: Two or more DIVISIONS. The first major organizational subdivision of an army.

CORPS: A specialized major subdivision of the armed forces, e.g., the Rifle Corps.

DIVISION: Two or more BRIGADES.

BRIGADE: Two or more REGIMENTS.

LEGION: A fast-moving tactical unit consisting of foot and mounted infantry.

REGIMENT: The basic organizational element of the army. Responsible for administration, supply, recruiting, training, quarters. About six to seven hundred officers and men.

BATTALION: The field formation of a regiment during a campaign. At times the two terms, battalion and regiment, were used interchangeably.

GRAND SUBDIVISION: During the Colonial and Revolutionary eras, the temporary combination of two companies for tactical reasons during campaigns and battles to provide greater coordination or firepower. (see below)

COMPANY: The basic tactical unit. Usually there were eight to ten companies to a regiment or battalion.

TROOP: A unit of cavalry. A division of a squadron. Equivalent to a company.

SQUADRON: Two or more troops of cavalry. The term also applies to a division of a naval task force.

PAVON: "A peculiar-shaped flag, somewhat like a gryon attached to a spear" (Preble). A triangular flag of the Middle Ages.

PENNANT, PENDANT: A long, streamer-like naval flag, usually triangular and swallow-tailed.

PENNON or PENIONE: (French) A small streamer half the size of the guydon, of a swallow-tailed form and attached to the shaft of a spear or lance. Carried by knights.

PENONCELS or PENSILS: A small narrow pennon usually borne on a knight's helmet or horse.

PIKE: The stave or staff for the standard and colors of a military infantry unit.

POLE: STAFF, STAVE. A long mastlike shaft from which a flag is flown. A pole is usually fixed. A staff is meant to be carried.

RANGER: Rifleman. Scout.

SEAL: A small device bearing the arms of a personage, state or nation and so made as to leave an impression on wax or paper.

SELVAGE or SELVEDGE: The "self edge" of a length of woven cloth. Silk weavers of France in the Eighteenth Century incorporated a distinctive combination of different color threads in the selvage to identify the cloth's weaver.

STANDARD: The principal flag of a commander or military unit, usually bearing a device and motto. Originally, a standard was borne by a commander of noble rank. "A BANNER was always charged with the arms of its owner; but on the standard only the crest or badge and motto were exhibited. In the Middle Ages, a king's standard was eight or nine yards long; a duke's seven; a marquis's six and a half; an earl's, six; a viscount's, five and a half; a baron's, five; a banneret's, four and a half; and a knight's, four." (Preble). These early standards because of their size were not carried but were fixed (stand) in the ground.

SUPPORTERS: The figures placed one each side of the central shield in a coat of arms.

TAFFETA: A fine, smooth, glossy silk.

TASSEL: A pendant ornament ending in a tuft of loose threads and, for flags, suspended from the finial by a heavy, decorative cord. The use of TASSELS and

FRINGE stem from ancient religious customs.

UNION: A symbolic representation of a political union of colonies, provinces, states or nations. A flag symbolizing the union by its basic design, such as thirteen stripes, or by bearing a symbol of the union, such as thirteen stars. The canton (of a flag) which is emblazoned with a symbol of the union. At times, "union" was loosely used to identify the canton.

VEXILLOGY: (From Latin "Vexillarius") The study of flags.

REGIMENTAL GRAND SUBDIVISION—"DIVISION"

The term "division" or "grand subdivision" was employed to designate two or more companies of line infantry temporarily pooled to maneuver, fight or parade as one unit. The term extends back into the Colonial era. A Continental Regiment was usually undermanned and the troops were joined into subdivisions to provide sufficient massed firepower. The Gostelowe Return of 1778 lists thirteen sets of new regimental standards, each with two "division colors" ready for issue.

Typical references as to the use of such subdivisions follow:

Colonel John Glover wrote that Colonel Shepherd's regiment "fired by grand divisions" (i.e., by two companies at a time) when opposing the British at Pell's Point during the skirmishing prior to White Plains. (Ltr from Col. John Glover at Miles Square, October 22, 1776. Force, American Archives, 5th Series, II, 1188-9).

When marching through Philadelphia on Sunday, August 24, 1777 on their way to Brandywine the Continental troops were instructed "to march by subdivisions at half distance, the ranks six paces asunder..." (S. & W., Vol I, p. 344).

ORGANIZATION OF THE ARMED FORCES

The various elements of the American Revolutionary armed forces were similar in many ways to the armed forces of today. There were Minutemen, State Troops (militia), the Continental Army, Navy, and Marines, State Navies, State Marines, and Continental and State Privateers. There were also independent troops and companies such as the Philadelphia Light Horse. Only the Privateers do not have a parallel in the present-day forces.

In addition to their different military functions, there were good reasons for this diversity of units. Foremost among these was geographical separation and autonomy of each colony, plus the need for some public or private source to recruit, equip, train, pay and maintain men and provide ships. There was also an abiding distrust by Americans of any sort of standing army. And, finally, there was the strong desire for short enlistments—an arrangement that would allow the troops to return to farms or business, or simply to protect their families in a more personal way.

The Minutemen (similar to Britain's homeguard of WW II) stayed close to home until called upon to repel invaders. They provided their own weapons and were organized along town, parish or county lines. Their main strengths were in their availability for active duty, as needed, and their ability to sustain themselves between callups. Their weaknesses were found in lack of training, poor weapons, slowness in mobilization, and a natural unwillingness to leave their homes unprotected. Their overall contribution, however, was significant, as testified by their action at Boston, Bennington, Saratoga, King's Mountain, Cowpens and Eutaw Springs. "Militia" replaced "Minuteman" as the war progressed.

The State Troops or militia (today's national guard) were better organized, trained

279

and equipped than the Minutemen, but their primary mission was the defense of their home state. They strenuously objected to marching beyond their state borders, and sometimes refused to join or even take orders from the Continentals. Even so, they served well in augmenting the regulars, and also as a training-ground for men who were later recruited into the Continentals.

The "standing militia" was a collective term applied to the bulk of able-bodied men who formed the reserve pool for organized active units.

The Continental Army was divided into the Northern (Schuyler, Gates, Stark, and others), Main (Washington), and Southern (Howe, Lincoln, Gates, Greene) Departments. These were the "regulars" with each state providing its quota of line regiments of foot, artillery and dragoon support. Most men and officers had prior experience as militia and state troops. The Continental regiments were basically state units, in the service of Congress. Also, there were some specific continental units raised "at large." They operated as a standing army, trained, equipped and disciplined to the rigors of campaigns and the shock of battle.

Privateers were financed by private sources; State Navies and Marines by state governments; and the Continental Navy and Marines by the Continental Congress.

The Continental Navy was the least attractive service because of pay, little chance for prize money, long cruises and a high degree of danger.

The Privateers, of which over three thousand five hundred were commissioned, did significant damage to the British merchant fleet and captured supplies badly needed by the Americans. When such men were captured they were treated harshly. Over 11,000 captured American seamen and soldiers died of disease on a half-dozen British prison ships in New York Bay.

Each Army's Lines, Wings, and Divisions were commanded by Major-Generals; its Brigades by Brigadier Generals, and the Regiments by Colonels. The regiments were the basic organizational unit and were, in turn, composed of four to ten foot-companies or dragoon troops or artillery companies.

The terms "regiment" and "battalion" were used interchangeably, at times; with the basic difference that a regiment was the administrative unit responsible for recruiting, training, and other support functions. The regiment was formed into battalions for campaigns and battles. Depending upon the number of companies and men available, a regiment formed itself into one or two or more battalions when it took to the field. However, there were some regimental-type units that were identified only as "battalions."

"Legions" were a mix of both mounted and foot soldiers. The designation "corps" was generally used for a large unit composed of a number of companies, or troops or regimental detachments of a special skill. Examples were the Corps of Light Infantry, which was formed as the situation demanded by calling together the highly trained infantry companies of each regiment. Morgan's Rifle Corps, or Corps of Rangers, was composed of companies of frontiersmen specially skilled at marksmanship and wilderness fighting. Lafayette commanded the Corps of Light Infantry when maneuvering against Arnold and Phillips, and then against Cornwallis in the Virginia campaign leading to Yorktown. William Washington commanded the 3rd Legionary Corps (of 1781) formed from the remnants of the detachments from the 1st, 3rd and 4th Continental Light Dragoons in the Southern Campaign of 1780–81. Pulaski was initially placed in command of the Corps or Brigade of Continental Light Dragoons (four regiments) but soon requested reassignment. He was then authorized to form an independent corps, Pulaski's Legion, in March 1778, consisting of 68 cavalrymen and 200 light infantrymen from the Baltimore area.

Artillery and dragoon units started out as local and state organizations, but logistics soon forced them to combine into Continental units which were spread across the various colonies.

Staff functions included the Adjutant General, Quartermaster, Commissary, Commissary of Military Stores, Artillery Artificer, Hospital, Medical, Engineer, Inspector General, Judge Advocate, Paymaster, Provost and Geographer.

Terms of enlistment started off at six months, but were soon increased to three years or "the duration." This did not always work either, because men frequently were kept beyond their agreed term without being paid, fed or clothed. Consequently, there were a number of mutinies.

The regular American forces did not, as a rule, fight woodsmanstyle, despite popular belief. Using French and British smoothbore muskets, they formed in ranks, fired by volleys, and charged with bayonets—provided they had been properly trained, equipped and battle hardened. There were, of course, riflemen (or rangers) who played an important part, but their slow rate of fire limited them to sniping—deadly accurate but not sufficient to stop a British charge as at Monmouth, or to take a fort by bayonet as did Wayne's light infantry at Stoney Point.

State Navies, of which there were eleven, and the Continental Navy were successful primarily as cruisers and raiders. They were no match for the numerous British men-of-war which maintained a close blockade. There were, of course, some brilliant individual ship-to-ship engagements, such as that of the BonHomme Richard and Serapis. But mainly, it was a matter of long periods in port, trying to recruit and refit. And when off to sea, dodging blockaders, making daring hit-and-run raids, and chasing prizes. Privateer service proved so attractive that it became difficult to man Continental ships with volunteers.

At last, entry of the French Navy into the War provided a match for the British fleet and led to capture of Cornwallis' army and victory.

ARMY REORGANIZATIONS

As the war progressed, the Continental Army underwent a number of reorganizations. All of the colonies had authorized regiments or battalions by 1775, and many had sent units to Boston; but there was no central cohesive command to coordinate activities. To remedy this, Washington was appointed Commander-in-Chief in June 1775. He arrived at Boston shortly after Bunker Hill.

On July 4, 1775, a proclamation was read inducting all troops at Boston into the Army of the United Provinces of North America. But enlistments were good for only six months (or until the end of the year), so by January, 1776, Washington's army was reduced to a skeleton force! Fresh regiments, however, had been authorized in November, 1775, by the Continental Congress. Each state was to furnish a specified number, and these new regiments arrived at Boston in early Spring.

It is interesting to note that the 1st, 2nd, 3rd, 4th, 5th and 6th Connecticut Regiments of 1775 existed as organizations only from May 1, 1775 to mid-December 1775. They were succeeded by the newly formed and manned Continental Regiments of 1776.

Another reorganization was ordered during the winter of 1776–77, including the authorization of sixteen additional regiments to be raised at large—that is, beyond the established state quotas. This 1776–77 organization called for a Continental Army almost as large as that of the entire British Army; but with only one-third the population resources! This quota could not be met; therefore, most units operated below their authorized strength and some existed only as a handful of officers and men.

Early in October 1780 the Continental Congress established a new organization for the Army known as the "Consolidation of

1781.'' The number of foot regiments (88 + 16) authorized in 1777 exceeded the capacity of the country; therefore, most regiments never reached their proper strength. According to Hollister, the 1781 consolidation called for the following:

> All new enlistments to be for the duration of the war.
> 50 Regiments of foot
> 4 Regiments of artillery
> 2 Corps of rangers (under Armand and Lee)
> 1 Regiment of artificers
> 4 Legionary corps, 2/3 horse, 1/3 foot

The quotas for foot regiments were:
States

Massachusetts ....11 Regiments
Virginia ....11 Regiments
Pennsylvania .... 9 Regiments
Connecticut .... 6 Regiments
Maryland .... 5 Regiments
North Carolina .... 4 Regiments
New York .... 3 Regiments
South Carolina .... 2 Regiments
New Hampshire .... 2 Regiments
New Jersey .... 2 Regiments
Rhode Island .... 1 Regiment
Delaware .... 1 Regiment
Georgia .... 1 Regiment
58

The Corps of Armand, Lee, and Hazen to be recruited at large.

After the victory at Yorktown in 1781 and the signing of a preliminary peace in 1782, the troops began to press for discharge. By mid-1783, most units were furloughed, except for those watching the last British garrisons. In November 1783 the remaining force was reduced to 1,000 men. In June 1784, this was further reduced to a total of eighty privates and a few officers who guarded the military stores at West Point.

ENLISTMENTS AND CASUALTIES

The actual number of men who served under arms in the Revolutionary forces has never been accurately established. Enlistments totaled 395,058 but most men enlisted two or more times. A recent "guess," by a team of historians who conducted an extensive study of the number of casualties suffered, is that about 200,000 men served at one time or another. The majority would have been in the militia—state troops, levies, minutemen, or irregulars. This is seven percent of the total white and black population of 2,750,000 in 1780.

The above study established that there were 1,331 military engagements, large and small, and 215 naval engagements resulting in "verifiable minimums" of 5,992 American revolutionists killed, 8,445 wounded, 18,152 captured, 1,426 missing, and 100 eventual deaths from wounds. These figures are stated as minimums, and that the number killed was probably closer to 7,000. In the opinion of this author, the number of wounded is unrealistically low compared to the number killed.

Of those captured, an estimated 7,500 died in prison; but again this is believed to be low. It's more plausible that 11,000 or more died in prison. The total number of camp deaths is estimated conservatively at 10,000. The total number of "probable deaths in service" is therefore estimated at least at 25,324, which would represent 12½ percent of those under arms. This has been exceeded only during the Civil War where the Union Army death rate was 13 percent. The above estimates do not include many unreported casualties, both military and civilian, resulting from skirmishes, guerilla warfare, Indian raids, and Loyalist-Rebel blood feuds. In the final count, the Revolution was probably our most costly war in the proportion of deaths and property loss.

Fred Anderson Berg's ''Encyclopedia of

Continental Army Units" speaks of a post-war report by General Knox which estimated the number of Continental Troops as follows:

1775	27,443
1776	45,891
1777	34,820
1778	32,899
1779	27,699
1780	21,615
1781	13,292
1782	14,256
1783	13,476

If the militia, state troops, privateers, state navies and Continental navy were included, the above figures would probably double.

By comparison, Berg quotes the total number of British, Loyalists and German troops "in the American Theatre (including Canada, Florida, and the West Indies)" as follows:

June	1777	28,000
March	1778	33,750
August	1778	34,000
November	1778	22,550
February	1779	26,750
May	1779	25,600
December	1779	29,600
May	1780	31,600
August	1780	35,000
December	1780	38,200
September	1781	35,600
November	1781	29,400

References and Notes

PAGE 2

Flag resolution: Attributed to the Marine Committee because it immediately precedes (in the Journal of the Cont. Congress) a resolution appointing John Paul Jones to command the *Ranger.*
Union in the center: See Appendix I.
1834, 1841: Quaife, Weig, & Appleman, pp 87–90.
Ross sketch: Du Simitiere Papers, HSP.
Simcoe sketch: Colonial Williamsburg.

PAGE 3

Commanders' standards: See Washington's Hq. standard; Gates' (James Peale painting, ca. 1800. MHS).
Eagle with stars: See page 12.
Resolutions 1777, 1795, 1818: U.S. Congress.
100 regiments: Greene, pp 289, 290.
3,500 privateers: Coggins, p 74.
July–August 1778 inventory: See Gostelowe Colors.

PAGE 4

1814-captured colors: Preble, pp 328, 334.
N.Y. invoice: F. C. Knight, "New York in the Revol.," Sup. 1901, (cited by Schermerhorn, p 57).
Williamsburg Public Store: Div. of Archives, VSL.
Rodney's green silk: Preble, p 289; (see Notes, Chapter 7).

Estimate-1760 yds: NA, PCC, Item 147, Vol III, pp 417, 419.

PAGE 5

100 standards: NA, Vol 148, War Dept. Coll., Revol. War Records; NA, PCC, Item 147, Vol III, pp 417, 419.
Paper currency symbols: E. P. Newman.

PAGE 9

Standards—state arms: See chapters on states.
Washington—Board of War: See Appendix I.

PAGE 10

General references: Preble, "The Flags of the U. S. . . ." Cambridge, 1880; Patterson & Dougall, "The Eagle and the Shield," Dept. of State, Wash., D.C., 1976.
July 4, 1776, Committee: Patterson & Dougall, p 6.
Du Simitiere's design: Ibid., p 16.

PAGE 11

Franklin's words: See Gostelowe No. 10.
March 25, 1780, committee: Patterson & Dougall, p 32.
Massachusetts seal, 1780: Preble, p 609.
May 2, 1782, committee: Patterson & Dougall, p 44.
Barton and Thompson: Ibid., pp 56, 71.
June 20, 1782: Ibid., p 83.

PAGE 12

Thompson's report: Ibid., pp 83–86.

PAGE 13

Sheathed in iron: Preble, pp 193–194.
Taunton: Harrison, p 24.
Vertical striped: Mastai, Boleslaw, D'Otrange, (no primary reference); Cresswell, "The Amer. Revol. in Drawings and Prints," Lib. of Congress, 1975, p 299.

PAGE 15

Liberty flag—Concord: John Barker, "The British in Boston," Cambridge, 1924, p 32.
"Liberty colours"—Georgia: Nav. Docs. of Revol., Vol 6, pp 103, 108 (P.R.O. Colonial Office, 5/556. 731–734).
"Liberty" flags—Long Island: Uhlendorf, pp 41, 56.
"Liberty" flag—Schenectady/Scotia, N.Y.: The Glen-Sanders house dates to the early 1700's and still stands.

PAGE 17

North Carolina $7.50: Newman, p 228.
Ensign of East India: Quaife, Weig, & Appleman, p 27, fig 16; Rankin, "William and Mary Quarterly," Vol XI, No. 3, p 341; Preble, pp 220, 221; C. Fawcett, "The Striped Flag . . . ," "Mariner's Mirror," Vol XXIII (1937), pp 459, 460.

PAGE 18

Jan. 1, 1776: See Appendix I.
Three-man committee: Fitzpatrick, "Papers of Washington," Vol 4, pp 17, 35, 41.

PAGE 19

Surrendering: See G. W.'s letter; Appendix I.
1779—national standard: See Appendix I.
McGraw's powder horn: Grider drawings, NYHS.
Jones' coat of arms: Masonic Library, Boston; S. E. Morison, "The Arms and Seals of John Paul Jones," The American Neptune, Vol XVIII, 4 (Oct. 1958), pp 301–305.

PAGE 20

Franklin's letter: J. Sparks, "Dipl. Cor. of Amer. Revol." Vol I, p 469.

PAGE 21

June 14, 1777: "Journals of Cont. Congress."

PAGE 22

Hopkinson flag: Patterson & Dougall, pp 42, 43.
$40 seal: Newman, p 46.
Eagle seal: Patterson & Dougall, pp 32–39.
A. Lee's letter: Mastai, p 64 (possibly quoted in Sparks or Wharton).

PAGE 23

Ft. Stanwyx, general references: William M. Willett, "A Narrative of the Military Actions of Colonel Marinus Willett, taken chiefly from his own manuscript," New York, Carvill, 1831; Lee Hanson and Dick Ping Hau, "Casements and Cannonballs" (Ft. Stanwyx archeological investigation), U.S. Dept. of Int., Park Service, 1975.
Garrison standard: F. J. Hudleston, p 138.
Soldier's account: Journal of William Colbraith as quoted by Max W. Reid, "The Story of Old Fort Johnson," G. P. Putnan & Sons, N.Y., 1906.
Forts Mifflin and Mercer, general reference: S. S. Steele, "Fight for the Delaware," Philip Frenau Press, N.J., 1970.

PAGE 24

Lt. Digby: J. P. Baxter, ed., "The British Invasion from the North," Albany, 1887, pp 234–235.
Capt. Hughs: E. A. Berian, ed., "A Journal by Thomas Hughs," London, 1947, pp 80–81.
Tarleton: A colored illustration of Reynolds' painting is in Ketchum's "The World of George Washington," Amer. Heri., 1974, p 138.
Trumbull: T. Sizer, "The Works of Colonel John Trumbull," Yale, 1950.
Peale: C. C. Sellers, "Portrait and Miniatures

by Charles Willson Peale," Philadelphia, 1953.

PAGE 26

Union flags—Phila.: F. Moore, Vol II, p 213.

PAGE 27

7th Pa. Regt.: All information from INHP, Philadelphia.
Rev. Trout: Colls. of the HSP, Vol I (1853), p 70.
Dearborn's journals: F. Cook, "Journals of the Mil. Exped. of Sullivan," 1887, pp 66, 67.

PAGE 28

Jones—the Texel: Also see Continental Navy.
St. Patrick's Day flag: F. Moore, Vol I, p 464.
Butler's letter: H. P. Johnston, "The Yorktown Campaign . . . ," Harper, 1881, p 202.

PAGE 29

Simcoe: Colonial Williamsburg.
Bauman's map: NYPL, I. N. Stokes Coll.; John Carter Brown Libr., Brown Univ.
Mondhare and Lotter flag sheets: John Carter Brown Libr., Brown Univ.

PAGE 30

Weatherwise Almanack: G. R. Cooper, p 4.
Wallis maps: Libr. of Congress. Also NYPL, I. N. Stokes Coll.

PAGE 31

Bowles flag sheet: Cooper, p 4.
L'enfant—Cincinnati: Society of the Cincinnati, Wash., D.C.
Berlin Almanac: J. C. Brown Libr., Brown Univ.; Libr. of Congress.
Stripes on the Thames: Preble, p 292; P. D. Harrison, pp 128–129.
Buell map: HSP; New Jersey Hist. Society.

PAGE 32

Militia Standard—Easton: F. Moore, Vol I, p 269.

PAGE 34

Eagle and Stars: See Appendix I and page 12.
Eagle, Stars and Stripes—Schuyler: Accession Records, INHP, Philadelphia.

PAGE 36

L'enfant—Cincinnati Eagle and Stripes: Society of the Cincinnati, Wash., D.C.
Peale—Washington at Yorktown: House of Delegates, Annapolis.

PAGE 37

Putman's Third: See Appendix I.
J. Reed: See Appendix I.
Feb. 20, 1776: See Appendix I.
1st Pa.: See Appendix I.
May 1776: See Appendix I.
Baurmeister: Uhlendorf, pp 41, 56.

PAGE 38

Scammell: See Appendix I.
Lee: See Appendix I.
Webb's Regt.: MC & H, MUIA Plate No. 78 by H. McBarron & F. P. Todd.

PAGE 39

Gen. orders: See Appendix I.
Facings: See Appendix I.
Peters: See Appendix I.

PAGE 40

Corresponded: See Appendix I.
Seal—1778: Preble, p 698.
Estimate, June 11, 1779: See Appendix I.
Estimate, July 2, 1782: See Appendix I.
Washington letters and orders: See Appendix I.

PAGE 41

Lincoln letter: See Appendix I.
Morgan's and Jones' medals: The gold medals awarded by Congress to General Daniel Morgan for Cowpens and to John Paul Jones show flags with the eagle canton. The medals were engraved in France in 1789,

and the artist used a flag design popular at that time. Thomas Jefferson approved the design of the medals and, apparently, wanted the eagle and stripes shown.

Standard of 13th Regiment: Force, "Amer. Archives," Vol II, p 244, no date, no heading, or signature. Placed among letters dated Sept. 8, 1776. (Preble, p 209).

13th Regiment: F. A. Berg, p 34.

PAGE 42

Gostelowe Return: War Dept. Coll. of Revol. War Records, NA, Record Group 93, MC 859, No. 28012.

Author's note: In the author's opinion, the thirteen sets of regimental standards, each with its two grand-subdivision colors, were probably made in Pennsylvania for the thirteen Pennsylvania Continental regiments authorized in 1777. However, it is known that some of these regiments already had colors, i.e., in 1776 the color of the 1st Regiment was green. Therefore, it is possible that some or all of the standards went to regiments from other states or to Pennsylvania state militia units.

The apparent lack of any specific design feature, other than the union of stars common to all the standards, is an intriguing part of the puzzle. Whether there is correlation between the color of the standards and the facings of Pennsylvania regiments should be investigated.

The device for Standard No. 9, a memorial wreath on a tomb and the motto "Si Recte Facies" (if you live righteously you will be honored, or "Immortal Honor"), is an ancient symbol taken from Camerarius' book and used on Continental $30 bills.

According to Gherardi Davis in "Regimental Colors of the War of the Revolution" (1907), the following regulations for regimental colors in the Connecticut line was adopted September 10, 1780; "The ground of each to be different—each to bear the number of the Regt. in large characters:— the device on one side, the Connecticut Arms on the other, the device and motto of the 30 Dollar Bills. If the ground of two colours should be so alike as not to be distinguishable [within] 300 or 400 yards, a

small field of 13 stripes in the Lower Quarter of one of them may serve as a distinction." Set No. 9 has the seal and motto of the Continental $30 bill and possibly was issued to a Connecticut regiment.

The accompanying illustrations of the thirteen Gostelowe regimental standards are the work of J. Carlton Jones of Philadelphia, who has studied and practiced the art of heraldry for the past forty years. Mr. Jones and the author based their interpretations of Standards 2 through 13 on the assumptions that: (1) all thirteen standards were of the overall dimensions of the Headman Color, the surviving original; (2) the devices and motto scrolls of all had the same general artistic approach and proportions as the Headman Color and occupied the middle of the flag; (3) the symbols and mottos on the seven denominations of Continental currency associated with Sets No. 3, 5, 6, 7, 8, 9, and 12 would have been adapted to the larger scale required by the flags; (4) the design of the motto scrolls would have resembled the Headman Color and other surviving Revolutionary Colors; and (5) the figures of Britannia, the Indians, armored arm, sword, Liberty cap, and other devices would have followed the design of similar devices found on other known Colonial and Revolutionary flags.

The color of the fields for Sets No. 12 and 13 was possibly buff, since no color is listed; however, the colors, used for the illustrations herein, were selected by the author after considering the colors of the other eleven sets. Further, the author selected the rectilinear pattern for the Union of Stars on the basis that it was more representative of the period, as evidenced by the Rhode Island, Stark, Washington Headquarters, and other standards.

Also included in the Gostelowe Return are columns listing the number of "Old Division Colors" on hand, of which there were 8, followed by a column for "Regimental [Ditto]" (colours) totaling 6, then for "Standards & Division Colours Poles" totaling 28 and "Camp Colour Poles" totaling 128. There are four columns of equipment "Taken from the Hessians" including "Camp Colors unfit for Service" totaling 32. Gostelowe's Re-

turns for March 1778 and for September
1778 are in the Archives, and the September
Return lists the total number of standards
and colors on hand.

The author is indebted to Dr. Stuart Lee
Butler and Dr. Frederic A. Greenhut of the
National Archives for their assistance in
locating and providing copies of the
Gostelowe Return and of Samuel Hodgdon's
estimate of silk cloth required for 100
standards for the Army (2 July 1782) and the
estimate for French silk dated June 11, 1779.

In a letter to the author in 1980, Dr.
William Francis Headman of Knoxville,
Tennessee, who donated the Headman Color
to the Smithsonian, wrote that the flag was
intact up until 1862 when it was ripped by
strong winds during a parade. He knows of
no other fragments but does have the
original flag staff.

PAGE 45

Holt's newspaper: B. J. Lossing, Vol II, p
796 n.

PAGE 46

Schaeffer's Company: Pa. Archives, 6th
series, Vol I, pp 225, 280.

PAGE 47

Standard No. 2: According to Gostelowe's de-
scription, a second motto, "We are always
Ready," was also on the flag.
Duncan's journal: See Hazen's Regiment.
Duncan wrote that Hazen's and Muhlen-
berg's brigades composed Lafayette's Light
Infantry.

PAGE 49

Resistance to tyrants: Bartlett gives two possible sources for this motto: The first is
Benjamin Franklin (who slyly, as was his
wont, credited it to Oliver Cromwell). The
second is reportedly an inscription on a cannon at the burial place of the ashes of the
regicide, John Bradshaw, on a hill overlook-
ing Martha Bay in Jamaica.

Acanthus plant: The symbol is from Joachim
Camerarius, "Symbolorum . . . ," Mainz,
1702 (in Franklin's library). The legend behind the symbol involves the death of a child
in ancient Greece and a faithful nurse who
places a basket of toys on the grave and
weighs the basket lid down with a rock. An
acanthus plant, though crushed under the
basket, still sends out its leaves, which gave
rise to the motto. The sculptor of the
Corinthian-style column took his inspiration
from the sight of the basket enveloped in
acanthus leaves.

PAGE 51

Third color: In 1907 Gherardi Davis illustrated
this third color which was pink. It is mark-
edly similar to the "pink standard" now in
the Smithsonian (Emily Howell Wilkins
Collection), but there are definite differences
between the two in the detail configuration
of the thunderbolts. Attempts by Schermerhorn in 1943 to locate the pink standard of
Davis' book were not successful. Mr. Morgan B. Brainard of Hartford, Connecticut,
wrote to Schermerhorn in 1943 that the blue
standard at the Connecticut State Library,
as well as a pink one, had been owned by
his uncle, Senator Morgan G. Bulkeley, and
that the pink one had mysteriously disappeared. The pink standard illustrated by
Johnston in 1904 and by G. Davis in 1907
was owned by Mr. F. E. Harper of New
York City. The blue standard illustrated by
Johnston in 1904 was owned by Mrs. J. H.
Knox of Troy, N.Y., and is the same one illustrated by Davis in 1907. It appears to be
identical to the one at the Connecticut State
Library.
Red and blue colors: The author has not been
able to find a primary reference for the claim
that a red and blue standard was at the head
of the squadron of 2nd Continental Light
Dragoons when it left Wethersfield, Connecticut, on June 21, 1777, (J. T. Hayes, p 11).
Hayes cites Swain who, in turn, cites H. P.
Johnston, ed., "Memoir of Colonel Benjamin Tallmadge," 1904, published by the
New York Society of Sons of the Revolution. Johnston illustrates the extant red
(pink) and blue standards, but Tallmadge's

memoir makes no mention of them, although the departure from Wethersfield is described.

Six troops: H. P. Johnston, editor, "Memoir of Colonel Benjamin Tallmadge," 1904, N.Y. Society of Sons of the Revolution, p 25. Also J. T. Hayes, "Connecticut's Revolutionary Cavalry, Sheldon's Horse," Pequot Press, 1975, pp 10, 11.

Standard—captured: J. T. Hayes, p 29.

PAGE 52

The Eutaw standard: A photograph of the standard as it appears today and a descriptive brochure were kindly furnished by the Washington Light Infantry. The standard no longer has the heavy fringe that is present in the G. Davis 1907 photograph. No exact dimensions were furnished, and the "eighteen inches" is an estimate by the author."

Miss Elliott: Dr. R. Wilson, "Half Forgotten Byways of the Old South," edited by R. Lathan, the State Co, Columbia, S.C., 1928.

Pulaski's Legion: Photographs and some description and history were kindly furnished by the Maryland Historical Society. G. Davis described the standard in 1907, and it has since been covered by other authorities. Berg gives a summary of the Legion's history. McCrady provides information on the Legion's southern campaign. Information on Captain Bentalou's association with the standard, its parading in 1824 and placement in Peale's (Baltimore) Museum the same year, was provided the author by Mr. James V. Murfin, National Park Service, Harper's Ferry. Mr. Murfin listed the following references: an article by Brantz Mayer, President, Maryland Historical Society, "Concerning the Pulaski Banner," March 6, 1845 (it is assumed the publication was by the MHS). See "Niles' Register," Oct 16, 1824, for deposit of the standard in the museum. It is believed that Edmund Peale, son of Raphael who founded the Baltimore Museum, presented the standard to the Historical Society in 1845. The flag was given conservation treatment in 1975–6.

PAGE 54

Stoney Point, British standards: C. J. Stillé, "Maj Gen Wayne . . . ," J. B. Lippincott,

1893, App. III, pp 404, 405, 406 (postscript to Washington's Official Report to Congress, July 21, 1779).

PAGE 55

Webb: Ford, "Corres. of Samuel B. Webb . . . ," Vol II, 1778–82, pp 414–416, 427, 430–431.

Lafayette—helmet & plumes: Brand Whitlock, "Lafayette," D. Appleton, 1929, Vol I, p 210.

Lafayette—flags: Whitlock, Vol I, p 210 (no primary reference); Charlemagne Tower, "The Marquis de Lafayette . . . ," Lippincott, 1895, II, p 158 (see Lafayette's Memoirs, vol I, p 261—but not apparent when checked by the author).

PAGE 56

Laurens' Lt. Infantry: George C. Rogers, Jr., of the Dept. of History, Univ. of So. Carolina, in personal correspondence with the author (received after the main text had been typeset) provided clarification on the portrait. It was painted by Charles Fraser many years after the Revolution as a companion piece to a Fraser copy of Copley's Henry Laurens. The face was copied from Charles Willson Peale's miniature. Mr. Rogers is editor of "The Papers of Henry Laurens."

PAGE 57

Washington's Headquarters Standard: Harry Emerson Wildes in "Valley Forge," published in 1938, writes; "Historians of the Valley Forge Park Commission, while admitting that the banner is undoubtedly an authenticated record of the encampment, hold that the flag was more probably a regimental standard. Their own researches, based largely upon a Charles Willson Peale painting, indicate that Washington's personal flag had its stars arranged in circular form." Wildes does not identify the historians of 1938 or give the rationale for their several conclusions.

The author cannot agree with the historians referred to by Mr. Wildes. There is nothing recorded, to the author's knowledge, to associate the flag with Valley Forge other than that Washington was there and the union of stars had been adopted in June 1777. Washington's correspondence does indicate, however, that he preferred the union (of stars), alone, as a national standard for the army, and it is possible that he flew this flag at Valley Forge.

The flag is not large enough, nor of the proper proportions, to be an infantry regimental standard, but it is too large and rectangular to be a canton union cut from a large silk stars and stripes or regimental standard as has also been suggested. It is the same size and proportions as a Light Dragoon standard and is meant to be carried by a mounted color bearer.

While Peale used the circle of stars, there were two other artists who depicted an all-blue standard with the stars in rows. The two paintings were done shortly after the Revolution under the supervision of participants and eyewitnesses. The artists were Wm. Mercer, son of General Mercer, and Louis-Nicholas Van Blarenberghe, a French military artist. It can be inferred that their paintings show the basic design Washington recommended as a national standard for the army.

Wm. Mercer's painting of the January 3, 1777, "Battle of Princeton," where his father was killed, pictures a very large (by proportion about five-by-five feet), blue-field standard with thirteen stars in a rectilinear pattern being carried next to Washington. Wm. Mercer studied under Peale. The painting is at the Historical Society of Pennsylvania and is illustrated in Ketchum's "The World of George Washington," Amer. Heritage, N.Y., 1976. Since the union of stars was not adopted until June 1777, it is very unlikely that such a flag was carried at Princeton. However, the point is that Wm. Mercer and his teacher, Charles Willson Peale, associated Washington with such a flag.

The French military artist, Van Blarenberghe, under the supervision of one of Rochambeau's staff officers, Quartermaster General Louis-Alexandre Berthier, painted official panoramas of "The Siege of Yorktown" and of "The Surrender" in 1784–86.

The various American, French, and British units involved are rendered with meticulous detail, so that uniforms and regimental colors of French units are recognizable. A blue standard with rows of stars is shown prominently in the American line in the replica of the painting done by Van Blarenberghe in 1786 for Rochambeau. There are similar starry standards at intervals along the American line. The Rochambeau replicas differ in some details from the originals done in 1784–85 for the King's Collection at Versailles, which also depict such standards. Rice and Brown's "American Campaigns of Rochambeau's Army," provides good illustrations of Van Blarenberghe's paintings.

Close examination of the 1786 Rochambeau replica reveals that there are three, possibly four, similar starry standards spaced at intervals along the American line stretching to Yorktown. Two have white fields, two light blue. The closest three have ten to twenty dots (for stars). In the far distance, outside the ramparts at Yorktown and just before the line of troops, is a group of uniformed, mounted men in blue. One is on a white horse and is probably Washington.

Following the above discovery in the 1786 Rochambeau replica, the 1785 Versailles original was examined closely. First, a stars and stripes was noted in the American line with a canton of nine dots (stars) on white and fifteen blue and white stripes. There are six square standards (three with all-white fields and three with blue), each with about thirteen or so dots. The standards are spaced at regimental intervals along the American line. This strongly indicates that in 1781 American regiments were carrying blue- or white-field standards with thirteen stars (in rows) but no stripes. They were similar to, but larger and squarer than, Washington's Headquarters Standard. The author believes this was the design Washington had in mind for the national standard for the army when he wrote to the Board of War in 1779 suggesting that the union and emblems be in the center.

There is yet another drawing of a thirteen-star flag (no stripes) associated with the Continental Army. This is an undated and unsigned pen-and-ink sketch of a proposed seal for the Board of War and Ordnance found among the papers of General Anthony Wayne. The emblem of the seal includes a square flag with the thirteen starlike crosses in rows. There is no date or signature. It was apparently a proposed design for the army's seal sent to Wayne by a correspondent.

Charles Willson Peale painted many portraits of Washington in the pose he originated for his "Washington at Trenton." In most of the paintings in this group that have been viewed by the author, Peale shows only the blue union with a circle of stars and has deliberately blocked off the edges of the union, so that the stripes, if present, are not visible. In one painting, the blue field stands alone. While Peale occasionally did allow the stripes to appear in his paintings, his main theme was to associate Washington with an all-blue flag with stars. This is in accord with Washington's indicated preference as discussed in the section on a national standard for the army. Whether the artist placed the stars in rows or a circle is secondary; apparently both patterns were used.

In addition to Peale, Wm. Mercer, and Van Blarenberghe, there was a fourth artist, an unknown flag painter, who associated Washington with an all-blue flag with stars. The standard of the Commander-in-Chief's Guard or Washington's Life Guards at the Washington Masonic Memorial in Alexandria has as its central motif a woman, symbolizing "Liberty" or "Fame," presenting a blue flag with an oval of stars to an officer—the Guard's commander. The flag, logically, would have been Washington's personal standard. Scaling by height of the officer, the actual blue flag would have been about 22 by 36 inches. There is an eagle and shield included in the symbolic scene, a fact which dates the flag after June 1782 when these symbols were adopted as part of the Seal of the United States. Lossing describes and includes a print of the Life Guards' standard in his "Pictorial Field Book of the Revolution." Since Washington was usually mounted while in the field, his standard bearer would also have been mounted and his standard sized for mounted carriage, which is the case for the standard now at Valley Forge and that depicted as the Life Guards' standard.

Washington's commission reappointing him commander-in-chief of the army in the 1790's pictures, in the decorative cartouche of flags and arms, a medium-sized (by proportion about three feet square), staff-mounted, fringed standard with a full circle of fourteen stars with a fifteenth in the middle. This was probably the standard of the commander-in-chief of the army at the time (ref: R. M. Ketchum, p 270).

Based on the above and after examining the original flag with the kind assistance of Mr. John Reed, this author is of the opinion that the Washington Headquarters Flag at Valley Forge is exactly what Miss Lovell claimed it to be—Washington's Revolutionary-era command or headquarters standard. It was possibly succeeded in the 1780's or 90's by the version with a circle of stars.

PAGE 59

Floating batteries: Nav. Docs., Vol II, pp 248, 538.
Armed vessels: Nav. Docs., Vol III, p 1077; Vol II, pp 565, 567.
Broughton: Nav. Docs., Vol I, p 1287 (letter, G. W., 2 Sept 1775); Vol II, pp 474, 565.
Blaskowitz: D. H. Cresswell, "The Amer. Revol. in Drawings and Prints," Libr. of Congress, 1975, p 905.
Reed: Nav. Docs., Vol II, pp 537, 538, 571–572, *passim.*
Moylan to Reed: Nav. Docs., Vol II, p 565.

PAGE 60

Duncan's Journal: "A Yorktown Journal," Pa. Archives, 2nd series, Vol XV, p 744, and ("Hazen's Regt.") Vol II, p 99.

PAGE 61

General reference: H. Rankin, "Naval Flag of the Amer. Revol.," "William and Mary Quarterly," Vol XI (July 1954) pp 339–353.
Additional references: Captain Hyde Parker, Jr., RN, reported on Thursday, 4 January 1776, as follows: "Hopkins Commands the *Alfred,* she has yellow sides, her head the figure of a Man, English Colours but more

striped . . ." (Nav. Docs., Vol III, p 615).

Gordon Saltonstall wrote to the Connecticut Committee of the Pay Table from New London, 23 December 1775, that, "She was heretofore called the *Black Prince*, mounts 32 Guns and on Board the *Alfred*, Commodore Hopkins hoists his Flagg . . ." (Nav. Docs., Vol III, p 215).

Delegate Benjamin Harrison was sent to Baltimore, Maryland, in December 1775 to assist in obtaining equipment for two Continental vessels, the *Wasp* and the *Hornet*, being outfitted there. He returned to Philadelphia shortly before December 20 (Nav. Docs., Vol III, pp 186, 208, 209).

The fleet sailed against New Providence, British West Indies. It was a successful expedition, but Hopkins did not capture his main objective—the two hundred barrels of gunpowder stored there, which were spirited away.

Committee: Nav. Docs., Vol III, pp 209, 720.
Adams: Nav. Docs., Vol III, pp 205–210.
"B. P.": Nav. Docs., Vol III, pp 186–187; Force, "Amer. Archives," 4th series, Vol IV, pp 358–363.
Barkley: Nav. Docs., Vol III, p 721; Pa. Mag. of Hist., Vol LXXXV, pp 28–30 (Sir Henry Barkley Papers).

PAGE 62

Lt. James Josiah: Nav. Docs., Vol III, p 615.
Flags, signal, Hopkins: Mss, Vol IV and VIII, RIHS; Nav. Docs. of Revol. Vol III, pp 1287–1289.

PAGE 63

Signal flags, Whipple: Preble, p 233; (no primary reference).
Pendants: Preble, p 245, quoting Journal of Congress, Vol I, p 531 (edition of Way & Gideon, Wash., D.C.).
Col. McDougall to John Jay: Nav. Docs., Vol IV, p 216.
Wm. Lux to York County Committee: Nav. Docs., Vol IV, p 313.
Day Book, Wharton: HSP.

PAGE 66

Brigantine "Lexington": Preble, p 242; Capt.

F. McMaster, USN (Ret.), M C & H, (Winter 1974), p 225.
Frigate "Trumbull": "The Remembrancer; or Impartial Depository of Public Events," London, 1775–1784, Vol X, pp 142, 225 (as quoted by Commager and Morris, "The Spirit of 'Seventy-Six'" Harper & Row, pp 256–259).
Gadsden: Jour. of the Prov. Congress of S. C., pp 21–24; Nav. Docs., Vol III, p 1190; Drayton's "Memoirs of the Amer. Revol.," Vol II, pp 71–72.
Marine committee: Nav. Docs., Vol III, p 101 (citing Ford edition, J.C.C., Vol III, pp 427–428); Nav. Docs., Vol III, pp 805–807 (Hopkins' Papers, RIHS).
Jay's letter: Hugh Rankin, "The Naval Flag of the Amer. Revol.," William and Mary Quarterly (July 1954), p 343 (citing H. P. Johnston, "The Corr. and Papers of John Jay," N.Y., 1890, Vol I, p 49 (letter of Jay to Colonel Alexander McDougall, 23 March 1776). Jay's letter also says that Congress had made no order "concerning [Continental] colors and I believe the captains of their armed vessels have in particular been directed by their own fancies and inclinations."
Strong evidence: Hopkins' signal flag order speaks of "the standard" at the main topmast head. Also, a letter from Timothy Matlach to Hopkins, Philadelphia, January 7, 1776, says that "Captain [John] Hazard . . . brings with him also the standard." At the time, Hopkins' fleet was frozen in the river south of Philadelphia (Nav. Docs., Vol III, p 671 [Hopkins Papers, RIHS]).

PAGE 67

Continental Ensign: S. E. Morison, "The Arms and Seals of John Paul Jones," Amer. Neptune, Vol XVIII, No 4 (Oct. 1958), pp 301–305; Hugh F. Rankin, "The Naval Flag of the Amer. Revol.," W. & M. Qtrly, July 1954.

PAGE 68

General references: See Morison, Rankin, Sherburne, de Koven; (disregard Buell).

Lt. Jones to Morris: R. de Koven,
"... Jones," Vol II, pp 23–34.

PAGE 70

"B. P.": Nav. Docs., Vol III, pp 186–187.
Salute, Quiberon Bay: R. de Koven, Vol I,
pp 262, 263.
"Ranger" —American stars: R. de Koven,
Vol I, pp 293, 333.

PAGE 71

Fly American colors: R. de Koven, Vol I,
p 404.
Gunner: R. de Koven, Vol I, p 454.
General reference: C. R. Smith, "Marines in
the Revolution" USMC, 1975 (GPO).
Standard, 19th century: Quaife, Weig & Appleman, p 92.

PAGE 72

Rattlesnake: Force, "Amer. Archives," 4th
series, Vol IV, p 468.
Additional references: The "London Public
Advertiser" for November 14, 1776, reported the following: "Captain Reveniss
who arrived at Southampton from Oporto,
says, Captain Squires, of the 'Ceres' who is
arrived at Oporto from Bilboa gives an account of sixteen Sail of American armed
Vessels being at Bilboa; one of which had
taken five English ships on her passage
thither . . . in the Harbour of Ferrol four
American Privateers, supplying themselves
for a Cruise. The same Day the Post from
Lisbon brought Advice, that a Schooner of
eighteen Guns, sailing extraordinary fast had
taken several Vessels near the Rock; the
Colours are a red Field with thirteen Stripes
where our Union is placed, denoting the
United Rebellious Colonies" (Nav. Docs.,
Vol VII, p 740).

The English publication, "Low's Astronomical Diary" (1777), reported that, "An
American privateer was some time since
taken by one of our frigates. She carried the
continental colors, which are thirteen red
and white stripes . . ." (Preble, p 243).

The "London Chronicle" for January 1776
reported, "There is in the admiralty office
the flag of a provincial privateer. The field is
white bunting. On the middle is a green
pine-tree and upon the opposite side, is the
motto, 'An appeal to Heaven!' " (Preble,
p 203).

There are other quotations by Preble
regarding captured vessels flying the above
pine tree ensign, which was the ensign of
Washington's Navy and of the Massachusetts State Navy and was apparently flown
also by Massachusetts privateers. It should
be noted that Washington's cruisers and the
State Navy vessels were commissioned combatants and not privateers.

The author was not successful in locating
the reference by Preble quoted in earlier flag
books as to a "Naval privateer flag" of alternate yellow and black stripes. However,
such a striped flag would have been a Continental Union. The labeling is also wrong for
the ensign of the Continental Brig *Reprisal*
at Martinique, "in September 1776," described as a flag with thirteen stripes, whose
field was yellow and white, and supposedly
that of a privateer. This is not so. The *Reprisal* was a fully commissioned combatant
ship of the Continental Navy. Further, the
Reprisal was not at Martinique in September
1776, having sailed from that port on 26 August after a month's layover for repairs. The
Reprisal's colors were described on July 27
by Captain John Chapman, R N, in his report to Vice Admiral James Young, July 29,
1776 (Nav. Docs., Vol V, p 1278), as being
"red and white striped, with a Union next
the Staff." This would have been the Continental Union.

Preble (p 204) also quotes a news article
(without citing the publication) datelined
Halifax, Nova Scotia, June 10, 1775, that reports the arrival of a privateer brig, Captain
Tracy's *Yankee Hero,* captured by the Milford frigate. "Her colors were a pine-tree on
a white field."

The American Heritage Magazine describes a painting at the National Museum,
Greenwich, England, signed "F. Holman,
1778," which pictures four captured American merchantships, each with the British
ensign flying over the American ensign of
red-white-blue stripes, without canton. The
captured ships are guarded by a British brig.

PAGE 73

Seal: Preble, p 612.
Colony arms: Ford, "Webb," Vol I, p 55.
Device—$30 bill: J. P. Johnston, "Record . . . of Conn. Men . . . Revol.," Adj. Gen., Hartford, 1889.
Brig "Defence": Middlebrook, Vol II, pp 16, 45.

PAGE 74

"Defence" tammie: Ibid., p 4.
Standards, 1775: G. H. Hollister, "Hist. of Conn.," 1857, Vol II, p 50 (quoting R. R. Hinman, "Amer. Revol.," pp 172, 173); Preble, p 197.
Colors, 1780: H. P. Johnston, "Record . . . Conn. Men . . . Revol.," Adj. Gen., Hartford, 1889.

PAGE 75

Conn. Assembly: Preble, pp 196, 197.
Hollister: Vol II, p 231 (citing Humphrey's "Life of Putnam," pp 100, 101).
New England Chronicle: Preble, p 201.
Lt. Lunt: Preble, p 201.

PAGE 76

Ninth-Third: Berg, p 22.
Two original flags: "Proceedings," Pa. Soc. of Sons of the Revol., pp 1905–1906.

PAGE 77

Eight companies: H. P. Johnston, "Record . . . Conn. Men . . . Revol.," Adj. Gen., Hartford, 1889.
Condition—1876: Preble, p 205.

PAGE 78

Two additional colors: Accession records of N-YHS.

PAGE 79

Lee's system: See Appendix I.
Webb's service: Ford, "Corres. of Samuel B. Webb," 3 vols, N.Y., 1893, and "Family Letters of . . . Webb," 2 vols, N.Y., 1912.

Additional notes on Webb's regimental standard and colors: The men and units that formed Webb's Third Regiment of 1781 had seen action at Saratoga, Whitemarsh, Valley Forge, Monmouth, at Forts Clinton and Montgomery, and at the August 19, 1778, Battle of Rhode Island. A part of S. B. Webb's regiment was with Wayne during the capture of Stoney Point. Detachments were also with Lafayette's Light Infantry Corps in the Virginia Campaigns of 1780–81 and at Yorktown. Webb commanded his Additional Regiment, then the Ninth and then the Third, until it was deactivated in 1783. He continued to be listed as the nominal commander of his regiment even while a prisoner on parole. During Webb's absence, Lt. Col. Ebenezer Huntington was in charge and is pictured in Trumbull's painting of the "Surrender at Yorktown." Detachments of the regiment marched through Philadelphia with Washington's Army on the way to Yorktown.

Webb was Commander of the Main Army's Corps of Light Infantry in 1782–83. The Corps was not a permanent standing unit, but was formed by detaching the light infantry companies from each of the various regiments. Therefore, Webb was Commander of the Third and of the Corps simultaneously. Adjutant General Edward Hand, on September 6, 1782, sent Colonel Webb "two of the Lt. Infantry Standards, one for the use of your own, and the other for Col. Jackson's Regt." The two standards sent by General Hand were two of those provided by Lafayette to the battalions of his Light Infantry Corps. These had been recalled on September 5, 1782, and two were issued to Webb and Jackson. Of the five battalions composing Webb's Light Infantry, four were grouped into two regiments. The fifth battalion was under Major Forman.

Webb's Additional Continental Regiment, according to Mr. Fred Berg, was "perhaps the most successful of all the additional regiments . . . was always in uniform . . . wore scarlet coats [British uniforms captured by John Paul Jones] . . . well trained and effective in battle. It even had a band. . . ."

Such a well-equipped regiment would certainly also have had colors. Their scarlet coats decoyed one of the British couriers trying to reach Burgoyne at Saratoga in the famous silver bullet affair. Washington objected to scarlet coats for obvious reasons, but reluctantly allowed their use. Most of the regiment's troops were in rags by 1779–80, according to a letter from Lt. Col. Huntington to Colonel S. B. Webb. Excellent descriptions and an illustration of the uniforms of Webb's Regiment appear in "Uniforms of . . . American Revolution," MUIA series, MC & H, (Plate 78), Co. of Military Historians.

It is believed that the regimental standard and division colors were carried initially by the members of Webb's Additional Continental Regiment of 1777, then by the Ninth and (after the merger with the Second) by the Third Connecticut Regiment of 1781. The regimental commander would have been presented with the standard and colors at the close of the war. Webb moved to New York after the Revolution. The colors were held by his descendants until donated to the above societies. One descendant founded Shelburne Village Museum in Vermont.

PAGE 81

Col. John Mix: Preble, p 197.

PAGE 83

Arms: Preble, pp 621, 622.
Delaware Militia color: Accession data, DHS.

PAGE 84

Del. colors—Long Island: Commanger & Morris.
Rodney's flag: Preble, p 289 (citing a letter from Dr. Rodney King of Philadelphia in 1875. Dr. King said he had a bill, dated 1783, from the papers of Gov. Daniel Rodney. The bill refers to "materials for a Continental Flag," one item of which was "for a piece of Green silk").

PAGE 85

Seal: Preble, pp 630–632.

Union flag, Savannah: C. C. Jones, "History of Georgia," 1883, Vol II, pp 176–7; Preble, p 201.

PAGE 86

Floating battery: Nav. Docs., Vol VI, pp 103, 108.
1st Regiment and Habersham's gorget: Marko Zlatich, "Two Georgia Revolutionary War Officers' Portraits," MC & H, Vol XXXII, No 2, (Summer 1980).

PAGE 87

Seal: Preble, pp 622, 623.

PAGE 88

State Navy: Nav. Docs., Vol III, p 1375.
3rd Md. Regt.: Berg, pp 65, 67.
Cowpens Battle: [Morgan to Green]

Camp near Cain Creek,
Jan. 19th, 1781.

Dear Sir: The troops I have the honor to command have been so fortunate as to obtain a complete victory over a detachment from the British army, commanded by Lieut. Col. Tarleton. The action happened on the 17th inst, about sunrise, at the Cowpens. It, perhaps, would be well to remark, for the honor of the American Arms, that although the progress of this corps was marked with burning and devastation, and although they waged the most cruel warfare, not a man was killed, wounded, or even insulted, after he surrendered. Had not Britons during this contest received so many lessons of humanity, I should flatter myself that this might teach them a little. But I fear they are incorrigible.

To give you a just idea of our operations, it will be necessary to inform you, that on the 14th inst, having received certain intelligence that Lord Cornwallis and Lieut. Col. Tarleton were both in motion, and that their movements clearly indicated their intentions of dislodging me, I abandoned my encampment on Grindall's Ford on the Pacolet, and on the 16th, in the evening took possession of a post, about seven miles from the Cherokee Ford, on Broad river. My former position subjected me at once to the operations of Cornwallis and Tarleton, and in case of a defeat, my retreat might easily have been cut off. My situation at the Cowpens enabled me to improve any advantages I might gain, and to provide better for my own security should I be unfortunate. These reasons induced me to take this post, at the risk of its wearing the face of a retreat.

I received regular intelligence of the enemy's movements from the time they were first in motion. On the evening of the 16th inst, they took possession of the ground I had removed from in the morning, distant from the scene of action about twelve miles. An hour before daylight one of my scouts returned and informed me that Lieut. Col. Tarleton had advanced within five miles of our camp. On this information, I hastened to form as good a disposition as circumstances would admit, and from the alacrity of the troops, we were soon prepared to receive him. The light infantry, commanded by Lieut. Col. Howard, and the Virginia militia under the command of Maj. Triplet, were formed on a rising ground, and extended a line in front. The third regiment of dragoons under Lieut. Col. Washington, were posted at such a distance in their rear, as not to be subjected to the line of fire directed at them, and to be so near as to be able to charge the enemy should they be broken. The volunteers of North Carolina, South Carolina, and Georgia, under the command of the brave and valuable Col. Pickens, were situated to guard the flanks. Maj. McDowell, of the North Carolina volunteers, was posted on the right flank in front of the line, one hundred and fifty yards; and Maj. Cunningham, of the Georgia volunteers, on the left, at the same distance in front. Cols. Brannon and Thomas, of the South Carolinians, were posted in the right of Maj. McDowell, and Cols. Hays and McCall, of the same corps, on the left of Maj. Cunningham. Capts. Tate and Buchanan, with the Augusta riflemen, to support the right of the line.

The enemy drew up in single line of battle, four hundred yards in front of our advanced corps. The first battalion of the 71st regiment was opposed to our right, the 7th regiment to our left, the infantry of the le-

gion to our centre, the light companies on their flanks. In front moved two pieces of artillery. Lieut. Col. Tarleton, with his cavalry, was posted in the rear of his line.

The disposition of battle being thus formed, small parties of riflemen were detached to skirmish with the enemy, upon which their whole line moved on with the greatest impetuosity, shouting as they advanced. McDowell and Cunningham gave them a heavy and galling fire, and retreated to the regiments intended for their support. The whole of Col. Pickens' command then kept up a fire by regiments, retreating agreeably to their orders. When the enemy advanced to our line, they received a well-directed and incessant fire. But their numbers being superior to ours, they gained our flanks, which obliged us to change our position. We retired in good order about fifty paces, formed, advanced on the enemy, and gave them a fortunate volley, which threw them into disorder. Lieut. Col. Howard observing this, gave orders for the line to charge bayonets, which was done with such address, that they fled with the utmost precipitation, leaving their fieldpieces in our possession. We pushed our advantages so effectually, that they never had an opportunity of rallying, had their intentions been ever so good.

Lieut. Col. Washington having been informed that Tarleton was cutting down our riflemen on the left, pushed forward, and charged them with such firmness, that instead of attempting to recover the fate of the day, which one would have expected from an officer of his splendid character, broke and fled.

The enemy's whole force were now bent solely in providing for their safety in flight—the list of their killed, wounded, and prisoners, will inform you with what effect. Tarleton, with the small remains of his cavalry, and a few scattering infantry he had mounted on his wagon-horses, made their escape. He was pursued twenty-four miles, but owing to our having taken a wrong trail at first, we never could overtake him.

As I was obliged to move off the field of action in the morning, to secure the prisoners, I cannot be so accurate as to the killed and wounded of the enemy as I could wish. From the reports of an officer whom I sent to view the ground, there were one hundred non-commissioned officers and privates, and ten commissioned officers killed, and two hundred rank and file wounded. We have now in our possession five hundred and two non-commissioned officers and privates prisoners, independent of the wounded, and the militia are taking up stragglers continually. Twenty-nine commissioned officers have fell into our hands. Their rank, &c, you will see by an enclosed list. The officers I have paroled: the privates I am conveying by the safest route to Salisbury.

Two standards, two fieldpieces, thirty-five wagons, a traveling forge, and all of their music are ours. Their baggage, which was immense, they have in a great measure destroyed.

Our loss is inconsiderable, which the enclosed return will evince. I have not been able to ascertain Col. Pickens's loss, but know it to be very small.

From our force being composed of such a variety of corps, a wrong judgment may be formed by our numbers. We fought only eight hundred men, two-thirds of which were militia. The British, with their baggage-guard, were not less than one thousand one hundred and fifty, and these veteran troops. Their own officers confess that they fought one thousand and thirty-seven.

Such was the inferiority of our numbers, that our success must be attributed to the justice of our cause and the bravery of our troops. My wishes would induce me to mention the name of every sentinel in the corps I have the honor to command. In justice to the bravery and good conduct of our officers, I have taken the liberty to enclose you a list of their names, from a conviction that you will be pleased to introduce such characters to the world.

Maj. Giles, my aid, and Capt. Brookes, my brigade-major, deserve and have my thanks for their assistance and behavior on this occasion.

The Baron de Glaubuch, who accompanies Major Giles with these dispatches, served with me in the action as a volunteer, and behaved in such a manner as merits your attention.

I am, dear sir, your obedient servant,
Daniel Morgan.

Our loss was very inconsiderable, not having more than twelve killed and about sixty wounded. The enemy had ten commissioned officers and upwards of one hundred rank and file killed, two hundred rank and file wounded, and twenty-seven officers and more than five hundred privates which fell into our hands, with two pieces of artillery, two standards, eight hundred stand of arms, one traveling-forge, thirty-five wagons, ten negroes, and upward of one hundred dragoon horses.

Although our success was complete, we fought only eight hundred men, and were opposed by upwards of one thousand British troops.

(Graham, ''Life of General Morgan,'' p 467).

A list of the commissioned officers in the action of the 17th of January, 1781, of the Light Infantry.

John Howard, Lieutenant-Colonel commandant.
Benjamin Brookes, Captain and Major of brigade.

Capt. Robert Kirkwood	Delaware
Capt. Anderson	Maryland
Capt. Dobson	"
Lieut. Ewing	"
Lieut. Watkins	"
Lieut. Hanson	"
Lieut. Barnes	Virginia
Lieut. Miller	"
Ensign King	"
Ensign Smith	Maryland
Ensign Dyer	"
Lieut. Anderson	Delaware

Of the third Regiment of Light Dragoons.

Lt.-Col. Wm. Washington	Virginia
Major Richard McCall	"
Captain Barrett	"
Lieut. Bell	"
Cornet Simmons	South Carolina

Of the [Virginia] State Regiment.

Edward Giles, Major and acting Aid-de-Camp of the Virginia militia.
Major Triplett
Capt. Buchannan   Virginia militia

Capt. Tate	Virginia militia
Capt. Gilmore	"
Ensign Comus	"
Ensign McCoskell	"
Ensign Wilson	"

Colonel Pickens and all the officers in his corps behaved well; but from their having so lately joined the detachment, it has been impossible to collect all their names or rank, so that the general is constrained not to particularize any, least it should be doing injustice to others.

By orders B. Gen. Morgan,
(copy)   Edward Giles, A.D.C.
Jan. 19th, 1781.

Note: The Baron de Glaubuch served as a volunteer in Gen. Morgan's family, and Mr. Andrews with Colonel Washington's regiment.

(Graham, "Morgan," p 311).

[Greene to Morgan]

Camp near the Iron Works
10 miles from Guilford C. H.,
March 20th, 1781.

Dear Sir: Since we crossed the Dan, we have made many manoeuvres and had much skirmishing. I have not time to give you the particulars. Until the 11th, our force was inferior to the enemy's, which obliged us to act cautiously. But forming a junction with a body of North Carolina and Virginia militia, and Col. Campbell coming up with a detachment of eighteen months men from Virginia, I determined to give the enemy battle. It was fought a little west of Guilford C. H. . . .

. . . The bearer of this, one of Lee's legion, waits upon you to get the colors, taken at the Cowpens, to convey them to Congress, there to be deposited as a lasting monument of your gallantry and good fortune.

Marquis de Lafayette is coming to Virginia, with a detachment of light infantry from the Northern army. Arnold must fall. I have not time to be more particular. God bless you with better health.

With esteem, I am, &c.,
To Gen. Morgan   N. Greene.

[To this letter Morgan replied:]

Saratoga, 11th April, 1781.

Dear Sir: I was honored with your letter of the 28th of March. I assure you, sir, it gave me very great satisfaction, both from the intelligence and the mode of conveyance. I have been particularly happy in my connections with the army, and am happy to tell you, sir, you are among the number I esteem. . . .

. . . I was not at home when the express arrived, nor did he await my coming. But I sent the standards on to Congress, and informed the President by your order. . . .

. . . I am directed by our assembly to send their thanks to the officers and men that fought with me on the 17th of January last; will be much obliged to you to put it out in orders.

The pain in my hip has left me; but I believe the same kind of pain has taken me in the head, which makes me blind as a bat two or three times a day. But the cold bath seems to help me; and I am in hopes ere long to give you some little assistance.

Please to make my compliments respectfully to the gentlemen of your family.

I have the honor, &c.
Hon. Maj. Gen. Greene.   Daniel Morgan.

(Graham, "Morgan," pp 372, 377)

[Hon. Samuel Huntington to Gen. Morgan]

Philadelphia, April 11th, 1781.

Sir: Your letter of the 28th ult. hath been duly received, with the standard of the 7th British regiment which fell into your hands in the battle of the 17th of January. This will be deposited with other trophies in the War Office, to remain a lasting evidence of the victory that day obtained with so much gallantry and bravery.

I am sorry to find your health so much impaired; hope by your present retirement and relaxation from the toils of the field that it may be perfectly restored, and your country reap signal advantages from your future service.

I have the honor to be, &c.,
Brig. Gen. Morgan.   Samuel Huntington.

(Graham, "Morgan," p 320)

299

Author's note: Two standards were captured, two sent off by Morgan, but Huntington acknowledges receipt of only one.

[Gen. James Jackson to Gen. Morgan]

Senate Room United States,
Philadelphia, Jan. 20, 1795.

Dear General: Since I last saw you in Philadelphia, which I think was in 1791, a gentleman has undertaken to write the history of Georgia. Your address to the Georgia refugees, published at Pacolet, in South Carolina, being in my hands, I gave it to him among other materials for insertion. The same gentleman, a Mr. Langworthy, has applied to me for other documents, and particularly to know if any Georgians were at the Cowpens. None of the authors who have written, have mentioned them in that action, nor did the account given by your aid-de-camp, Maj. Giles, to Congress, notice them, or any officer belonging to the State, although the officers of the other States were very generally mentioned, and their militia applauded. The Georgians have imputed this to the loss of your dispatches, and not of any intention of yourself, who have always been one of their favorite commanders; but they think hard of the silence respecting them in that celebrated action, and which did you the honor of turning the tide of affairs in favor of the United States.

My object in writing at present is to request, if you see no impropriety in it, your giving a certificate under your hand to their being present—three companies. The detachment was small; but, if you recollect, you placed them in front of the whole; and they strictly obeyed your orders in keeping up a warm fire and gradually retreating. I could wish your expressing that they behaved as well as the other militia in the field. The officers commanding, if you choose to say anything of them, were Maj. Cunningham and Capts. Samuel Hammond, George Walton, and Joshua Inman, who all behaved well; and the latter was particularly serviceable to you in advertising you of the enemy's approach and skirmishing with their advance. The detachment was under my immediate command and direction, although I acted also as brigade-major to all the militia

present. It is with difficulty I mention myself; but having the honor of introducing Maj. McArthur, the commander of the British infantry, a prisoner on that occasion, taken by myself, and having run the utmost risk of my life, in an attempt to seize the colors of the 71st regiment in the midst of it, on their attempt to form after they were broken, being saved by an exertion of Col. Howard's and for which I had the honor of your thanks on the field of battle, I think it a duty to my children, as the history of my State is to be told, to have some insertion, even of my conduct, in that well-fought battle. You, sir, were rendered immortal by the action. My ambition is, to let my descendants and the citizens of Georgia know that I was present, and contributed my mite to your glory. Gen. Pickens has already certified to the requests of this letter fully. But whilst you are alive, his certificate is not the best evidence, and your testimony will be grateful to the citizens of Georgia.

I am sorry to break in upon the important business of your present command, and should have waited until the next session of the Federal Legislature, where we hope to see you a member, but for the pressing request of Mr. Langworthy to have the necessary papers.

I am, dear general, with the highest respect and esteem.

Your old fellow-soldier and most
obedient servant,
James Jackson

If you could favor me with an answer, previous to the rising of Congress about the 1st of March, it would highly oblige me.

Brig. Gen. Morgan.
(Graham, "Morgan," p 471)

[Gen. James Jackson to Gen. Morgan]

Philadelphia, Feb. 9th, 1795.

Sir: I did myself the honor of writing you about a fortnight since, respecting the service of the Georgians under you at the Cowpens. Lest two observations of mine in that letter should be misunderstood, I beg leave to correct them. The first was, that I was brigade-major to all the militia present. I since recollect that you had militia from Virginia. The second, that I had your thanks. I meant not by this, your thanks in orders, but verbally for my conduct, which a hundred living evidences could prove was creditable to myself, and deserving of your approbation. Colonel McDowell, now in Congress, and who commanded the North Carolina militia on that day, is one of them. General Pickens's written testimony, I informed you, I was possessed of, and under him I was acting. A circumstance I will take the liberty of mentioning will serve to revive your memory. You had placed a sergeant over a cask of wine. After my return with General, then Major McArthur, and who I had left in custody of Col. Washington, I came across this man, and found him dealing the wine out to all in his way. A wounded militia-man at some distance requested me for a drop to revive him, which the sergeant refused on my application, and I then ordered the men with me to drive him off and take possession of the cask. He went and complained to you, and you came very angry, and I expected would have struck me. Feeling myself injured, I explained to you the conduct of the fellow, and could not help adding that my conduct had deserved a better return, mentioning to you my leaving the British officer commanding their infantry with the Colonel (Washington). It was then that you made the sergeant beg my pardon on his knees, and gave me your verbal thanks, which were repeated when we stopped on the borders of North Carolina, and where we (Gen. Pickens and brigade) took the prisoners under charge, and you parted from us. Maj. Giles mentioned at Charlotte, on his tour to Congress, my name, as one who had distinguished himself; and considering the responsibility of my station, and the risks I ran that day, I had some right to expect to be named. I confess I was chagrined when the account came. I, after this, ran the utmost risk of my life at Torren's when the British crossed the Catawba, and believe, that in some measure, owing to my exertions with a few officers and men, the slaughter was not so great as it otherwise would have been. At Salisbury, where you had reached, it was believed by Gen. Pickens and yourself, that I was killed. When I arrived, I had

the honor of being received by you and him with friendship and satisfaction. At the Yadkin we parted, and I had the happiness after, to have my conduct signally approbated by that great officer Gen. Greene, who appointed me to the command of a State legion.

I have been thus particular, lest so long a lapse of time should have made these circumstances escape your memory; and which, not being necessarily connected with the principal events, and only concerning an individual officer, are not likely to be retained. I had the honor, however, in 1791, to have the principal circumstances recognized by you.

I shall leave this in about a fortnight for Savannah. Should you not see it proper to give a certificate as to myself, I shall be happy to have your approbation of the conduct of my countrymen.

I am, sir, &c. James Jackson

Feb'y 9th, 1795. (Graham, "Morgan," p 472)

Author's note: Major James Jackson, author of the above letters, was aide to Colonel Pickens and brigade major of the Georgia and Carolina State Militias that formed the forward skirmish lines at Cowpens. He later commanded a battalion under General Anthony Wayne during the successful 1782–1783 campaign to free Georgia from the British, Loyalists, and their Indian Allies. Daniel Morgan, who achieved his greatest fame as a leader of militia, became a strong critic of the militia concept after the war. The running national debate on whether a regular army was needed probably influenced Morgan's attitude and opinions and led to his playing down the militia's role at Cowpens.

PAGE 89

Seal: Preble, pp 609–611.
Currency—1775: E. P. Neuman, ". . . Paper Money of America," Whitman, 1967, pp 146, 150.

PAGE 90

An appeal: P. Harrison, "The Stars and

Stripes . . ." Little, Brown & Co., 1906, p 25.

Pine tree ensigns: See Washington's Armed Vessels, Chap. 4. Preble, p 228.

PAGE 91

April 1776, Mass. Council: Preble, p 204.
London Chronicle, Jan 1776: Preble, p 203.
English newspapers, Jan 6, 1776: Preble, p 204.
Joseph Webb: Preble, p 270.
Bedford: Also see A. E. Brown, "Hist. of Bedford," 1891, p 23; H. C. Lodge, "The Story of the Revol.," 1898, Vol I, p 45; Preble, p 124.

PAGE 92

Banners—Parliamentarians: A. Fraser, "Cromwell . . .," Knopf, 1973, illus. following p 202.

PAGE 93

Bunker Hill: Dr. E. V. Mittlebeeler, "What Flag Flew at Bunker Hill," "The Flag Bulletin," XVII; T. Sizer, "Works of . . . Trumbull," Yale, 1950; Lossing, Vol I, p 541; Preble, pp 198, 199; John Clarke, 1st Lt. of Marines, "An Impartial and Authentic Narrative of the Battle Fought on the 17th June, 1775," London, 1775.

PAGE 96

Newburyport Company: Preble, 1880, pp 204, 264.
Forster colors: (Unit unknown).
Intact color: Copy of an unidentified news article kindly provided by Dr. Whitney Smith, The Flag Research Center, Wilmington, Mass.

PAGE 97

Canton of second color: Information kindly furnished by the Essex Institute. There is a copy of a notarized note by Emma R. Tenney, granddaughter of Major Forster, which states that the "remainder of the flag was white silk and was cut off by a member of

the family in 1862 and used for dress trimming." Mrs. Peggy Holsten, Registrar of the Essex Institute, located two men by that name living in Manchester at the right time, but neither is listed in the multi-volume "Massachusetts Soldiers and Sailors of the Revolution." There are two listings for "Israel Foster"—one a private from Bolton, the other "belonged" to Marblehead (no rank given). There are three "Samuel Forster" listings, all privates, and quite a number of "Samuel Foster," listings, one a private from Manchester and the other a lieutenant in Captain Marster's company on April 19, 1775. There is also an Israel Forster listed in the Essex Inst. Hist. collections as the owner of the schooner *Hawke* in 1770 and 1774.

The author notes that the use of the white silk field for dress trimming some eighty years after the Revolution does not speak well of the user but does speak well of the durability of eighteenth-century silk. In the 19th century, a crystalline sizing solution was used to give silk more sheen and weight. This caused rapid deterioration of the fabrics with the result that most silk flags and clothing of the period from roughly 1820 to recent years have disintegrated.

PAGE 99

Seal: Preble, pp 606, 607.
2nd N.H. Regt.: G. Davis, p 18 (traditional history); Accession records, NHHS; O. G. Hammond, "History of the Seal and Flag of . . . New Hampshire," 1916; Otis G. Hammond, "Flags of the U.S. & of New Hampshire in the Colonial & Revolutionary Period," Catalog No. 9299, H227 NHHS, 17 March 1914.
Lt. Digby's journal: J. P. Baxter, "Invasion from the North: The Campaign of General Carleton and Burgoyne from Canada, 1776–1777, with the Journal of Lieut. William Digby, of the 53rd, or Shropshire Regiment of Foot," (Albany, N.Y., 1887), pp 234, 235 (cited by Quaife, Weig & Appleman).

PAGE 101

Franklin's design: Newman, pp 32, 46.
2nd Regt. history: Berg, p 80.

2nd N.H. colors: The author has not been able to resolve certain questions on the 2nd New Hampshire colors—their exact identity and where captured. Such information as has been gathered is presented herein to help in future research. The answers are worth seeking because it is possible the flags are the regimental colors of two American regiments rather than a pair of colors of the 2nd New Hampshire alone.

Of course, the blue color is obviously the regimental standard of a "2nd N.H. Regt." whose designation it bears, and very probably it is the 2nd N.H. of 1777 commanded by Col. Nathan Hale (Berg, p 80). However, the buff color with Franklin's 1776 circle of thirteen links (Neuman, "Early Money," pp 32, 46) appears to be too distinctive to be the second color of a regiment. Possibly the buff color might be the standard of the 11th Massachusetts Regiment of 1777 or of Seth Warner's Continental Regiment. Both regiments were defeated at the battle of Hubbardstown on July 7, 1777 along with part of Colonel Hale's regiment. Circumstances strongly indicate that the 2nd's colors were taken at Hubbardstown, not at Ft. Anne.

There is also the possibility that one or both colors were captured the previous year when Carleton's force drove the American Northern Army from Canada and down Lake Champlain. Hill's Ninth had arrived in Canada in spring 1776 and took part in Carleton's 1776 campaign.

The presence of Americanized versions of British Union cantons on the two colors indicate they date to the early years of the war. Such British Union cantons were gradually replaced with stripes after the Declaration in 1776; then after June 1777, some colors displayed stars in the canton. Such transitions were slow, however, and it is not unreasonable that regimental colors should still display the British Union in summer 1777.

The 2nd New Hampshire Continental Regiment of 1777 under Colonel Nathan Hale was part of General Barry St. Clair's garrison holding Fort Ticonderoga when Burgoyne's army swept down Lake Champlain and invested the fort on July 2, 1777. On July 5, St. Clair decided to abandon the fort rather than see his army entrapped. The garrison slipped out the night of July 5. At 4:00 A.M. on July 6, the rearguard, Colonel Francis' 11th Massachusetts Continental Regiment, left the fort.

In the morning, Burgoyne immediately set out in pursuit, sending General Frazer and Baron Riedesel after the main American army and leading his fleet after the second column down Lake Champlain. The main part of the American army led by St. Clair was retreating overland via Hubbardstown and Castleton. St. Clair stationed Col. Seth Warner's Continental Regiment of 150 men at Hubbardstown to wait for Colonels Francis and Hale, while the main force went on another six miles and encamped at Castleton on July 6.

The remainder of the Ft. Ticonderoga garrison consisted of Colonel Pierce Long's New Hampshire Regiment. Together with some non-combatants and the army's baggage, they were hurriedly loaded on small boats and galleys the night of the fifth and sailed down Lake Champlain to Skenesborough, arriving about noon on the sixth. Long's flotilla was closely pursued by Burgoyne's fleet. Within two hours after reaching Skenesborough, the Americans were forced to set fire to boats, stores, buildings, and baggage and retreat to Fort Anne, twelve miles to the south. Long's column reached Fort Anne about 5:00 A.M. on July 7, where they were reinforced by 400 New York militia under Col. Henry Van Renselaer (Carrington, p 315; Greene, pp 104–105).

On the Sixth, Burgoyne dispatched Lt. Col. Hill and 190 men of the Ninth to Fort Anne. The Ninth encamped the night of July 6 (or July 7, depending on the source) near the fort.

At 10:30, the morning of July 7, Long and Van Renselaer attacked the Ninth "with a heavy and well directed fire" and were pushing them badly when British and Indian reinforcements arrived. The Americans, short of ammunition, returned to Fort Anne, fired it on July 8, then retreated to Fort Edward on the Hudson twenty miles south. The Ninth, badly mauled, rested on the field, then pulled back to Skenesborough, where Burgoyne spent two critical weeks regrouping his army for the push south (Carrington, p 315; Greene, p 105; Hudleston, p 161; Stone, I, 118; Lossing, I, pp 141–142). Sergeant Roger Lamb of the 9th Regiment was in the thick of the fight and was left to tend the badly wounded. They stayed for about a week in a woodcutter's cabin and could hear the Americans all around them felling trees across the streams and trails, but they were not attacked. Lamb wrote his memoirs in the early 1800's. He said nothing about any flags being captured ("An Original and Authentic Journal of Occurences During the Late American War from the Commencement to 1783," by a Late Sergeant in the Royal Welsh Fusilier's, Dublin, Wilkinson & Courtney, 1809; R. Graves in his historical novel, "Sergeant Lamb's America," Random House, 1940, includes a statement that the Ninth captured the 2nd's colors at Ft. Anne, but Lamb's actual Journal does not say that).

At the July 7th battle near Fort Anne, the Ninth did capture a flag, but its description does not fit either of the surviving 2nd New Hampshire colors. Lt. William Digby of the 53rd Shropshire Regiment of Foot recorded in his Journal on July 24; "We marched from Skenesborough, and tho but 15 miles to Fort Anne, were two days going it, as the enemy had felled large trees over the river. . . . We saw many of their dead unburied, since the action of the 8th [sic], which caused a violent stench. One officer of the 9th regiment, Lieut Westrop, was then unburied, and from the smell we could only cover him with leaves. At that action, the 9th took their colours, which were intended as a present to their Colonel Lord Ligonier. They were very handsome, a flag of the United States, 13 stripes alternate red and white, in a blue field representing a new constellation . . ." (Baxter, pp 234–235).

Quaife, Weig, & Appleman, in "History of the U.S. Flag," pointed out that the nineteenth-century historian James P. Baxter, who originally quoted Digby's Journal in his "Invasion from the North . . .," inserted the bracketed words, "with thirteen stars," just before Digby's words "in a blue field" (pp 48–49). Thereby, Baxter erroneously transformed

the flag into a stars and stripes from the typical regimental or grand subdivision colors. It had a solid-blue field and a striped red-and-white canton, as described by Digby. Similar striped-canton colors include the Delaware militia color of 1777 and the Philadelphia Light Horse standard. Of course, Baxter was undoubtedly struck by Digby's use of wording so similar to that of the Congressional flag resolution of June 14, 1777. However, Digby could not have known of the resolution at the time, since it was not published until September 2, 1777, when it appeared in Dunlap's Pennsylvania Packet (ibid.). Hopefully, Digby's original Journal can be located and checked on this point. The coincidence of the wording is remarkable. Quaife suggested that Baxter might have seen a copy of Digby's Journal at the "British Museum."

What became of the above color captured at Fort Anne and intended for Lord Ligonier is not known. It was probably a color of Colonel Long's or Colonel Van Renselaer's unit. It may have reached Lord Ligonier and still be with his descendants. Regardless, Digby's description of the color does not match either of the two now identified with the 2nd New Hampshire, except for the blue field. Further, on July 7, the 2nd was at the battle of Hubbardstown, thirty miles northeast of Fort Anne, or rather its Colonel and some of his men were there. Maybe a detachment of the 2nd was at Fort Anne and carried a blue field "Grand Subdivision" color.

At Hubbardstown, the regiments of Warner and Francis, together with Colonel Hale who was escorting the invalids, were encamped as the rearguard of St. Clair's army. They were decisively defeated by Frazer and Riedesel's pursuing force on the morning of July 7, 1777. Hale, who was sick himself, together with, reportedly, his regiment (or part of it), and other men broke and fled when the British charged but were quickly captured on the field, plus Hale and his men—possibly 500 to 600 casualties (Carrington, pp 316–371; Greene, p 104; Lossing, I, pp 144–147; Berg, pp 74, 80, 134; Stone, I, pp 114–116, 118; Kidder, p 109).

The fighting was intense while it lasted.

Lord Balcarres, commanding Frazer's light infantry, received thirty bullets through his clothing but escaped serious injury (Hudleston, p 160). Carrington quotes Gordon (II, p 484) that British casualties amounted to 183 in killed and wounded and that Riedesel's Brunswickers lost twenty-two, a total of 205.

Francis and Warner initially pushed the British back by fighting woodsman-style and were close to victory when Riedesel's three battalions reached the field and charged. The Americans were completely routed and scattered. Lossing reported that rows of muskets dropped by the fleeing Americans were found in the woods (Lossing, I, p 146n).

It is generally during such fierce actions and decisive defeats as at Hubbardstown that colors are taken—either surrendered or picked up later from the field. Although heavy seesaw fighting marked the later battles with Burgoyne, there was no rout or capture of American regiments other than at Hubbardstown during Burgoyne's campaign.

Riedesel recorded that as Burgoyne's Army approached the American position at Bemis Heights (Freeman's Farm) on September 18, 1777, "toward four in the afternoon, four regiments of the enemy, with banners, could plainly be seen. Three were hidden behind the hills, and two behind some woods on the plain. . . ." and on September 19, 1777, Riedesel wrote ". . . the 20th, 21st, and 62d English regiments were forced to remain under fire without intermission for four hours. The 9th Regiment was kept as a reserve . . ." (Stone, "Memoirs, Letters and Journals of Major General Riedesel," 1868, I, pp 25, 144).

Some of Hale's regiment must have survived Hubbardstown or been elsewhere, because the 2nd N.H. Regiment was in the thick of the fighting as part of Poor's Brigade at Freeman's Farm where the regiment's Lt. Col. was killed (Kidder, p 35; Berg, p 74). Also Warner and eighty of his men rejoined St. Clair on July 9, and this regiment reinforced Stark's New Hampshire militia brigade at Bennington on August 16, 1777. Colonel Benjamin Tupper took command of the 11th Massachusetts on July 7, 1777, and the regiment served until the consolidation of January 1, 1781. Hale denied

allegations of misconduct, demanded a court martial, and was cleared in absentia. He died still a prisoner of the British in 1780 (Carrington, pp 331–333).

It is evident that Lt. Col. Hill had great respect for military colors. He not only carried or sent the color captured at Fort Anne as well as the 2nd New Hampshire's colors to England, but also saved the Ninth's colors at Saratoga. He "ripped" his regiment's colors from their staffs and packed them in his personal baggage at the surrender (Hudleston, p 265n; "The Navy and Army Illus.," Jan. 24, 1903, p 490n). By terms of the "Convention of Saratoga," the surrender of colors was not specifically called for and personal baggage was exempt from search.

Hill was exchanged in 1781 and presented his regiment's colors to the King who appointed him aide-de-camp with a promotion to Colonel (Hudleston, p 265n). The regimental color of the Ninth is now at Sandhurst. The King's color of the Ninth has disappeared (see section on British Colors).

The 2nd New Hampshire apparently did lose one or more colors before or early in July 1777 ("colors" of a regiment could mean one or more flags). According to Preble, p 606 (no original reference), "In July 1777, the Committee of Safety of New Hampshire ordered the Receiver-General to pay Lieutenant Noah Robinson £ 30 18s. 9d, in full for Captain Samuel Blodgett's account for a suit of colors for Colonel Hale's regiment of continental troops; and, Feb 4, 1779, ordered him to pay Samuel Sawyer £ 19 4s. for taffeta to make colors for Colonel Cilley's regiment."

Following the July 6–7 battles, the British army spent about two weeks regrouping at Skenesborough, where orders were issued that the officers were "to send all their personal baggage to Ticonderoga . . ." (Carrington, p 328). It is probable that any colors captured at Fort Anne or Hubbardstown would have been started to England at that time.

Since there were only 190 men, the equivalent of about three companies, of the Ninth Regiment at the Fort Anne Battle on July 7, there is a question as to the whereabouts of the remainder of the regiment. They might have been left at Ticonderoga or at Skenes-borough but more likely were part of the "twenty companies" of General Frazer's division and, thereby, took part in the battle of Hubbardstown, where they could have captured the 2nd's colors.

W. H. Crockett, in "A History of Lake Champlain," McAuliff Paper Co., Burlington, Vt., p 188, briefly describes the evacuation of Fort Ticonderoga and the battle of Hubbardstown. He wrote that "the American standard" of the Fort was taken and that, later, the standard was recovered when Colonel Brown's force recaptured Mount Hope (p 135).

History of Stark's Brigade: Accession records, Bennington Historical Society.
Battle of Bennington: Riedesel, Vol I, pp 127–133; Lossing, Vol I, pp 294–298; Carrington, pp 329–374.

PAGE 102

Stark's commands: Berg, pp 32, 79; Lossing, Vol I, p 394n. General John Stark in his August 22, 1777, report to General Gates on the battle of Bennington (August 13) mentions the following militia units: Lt. Col. Greg's, Col. Williams', Col. Herrick's, Col. Brush's, Col. Simons' of Berkshire County, Col. Nichol's, Col. Hubbard's, and Col. Whitney's. He also describes the part taken by Col. Seth Warner's Continental Regiment (Green Mountain Boys). (Gates Papers, NYHS, Box VII, No. 33). The green standard probably was carried by one of the above militia units or as a brigade command standard.
History of Bennington '76: Accession records, Bennington Hist. Soc.
Textile historian: G. R. Cooper, "Thirteen-Star Flags," Smithsonian, 1973, pp 29–30.

PAGE 103

Seal: Preble, pp 617, 618.
Currency: Newman, pp 192, 193
Monmouth color: Monmouth County Historical Society accession records.

PAGE 104

To be American: D. Holst, MC & H.
Du Simitiere's sketch: HSP.
Regiments: Sullivan's Expedition (op. cit.), pp 315–329; Berg pp 81, 82.

PAGE 105

Seal: Preble, pp 616, 617.
Commission: Guthman Americana (adv.), Antiques Magazine (Mar. 1978), p 504.
Long Island flag: Preble, p 246 (citing "Hessian Account of the Battle of Long Island," Memoirs of Long Island Historical Society, Vol II, pp 434, 435). Also, E. J. Lowell, "The Hessians . . . in the Revolutionary War," 1884, p 65, quoting General von Heeringen.
Red damask liberty flag: Scheer & Rankin, "Rebels and Redcoats," World Publ Co., N.Y. 1957, p 187. Also, Max Von Eelking, translation in Memoirs of L. I. Hist. Soc., Vol II, pp 431–438.

PAGE 106

Eleven flags: B. A. Uhlendorf, trans., "Revol. in America, Ltrs. . . . of Adj. Gen. Maj. Baurmeister," Rutgers, 1957, p 41.
White Plains flag: Preble, p 246.
Colonel Van Shaik: Berg, p 84.

PAGE 107

3rd N.Y. Regt.: Accession records, Albany Inst. of Hist. and Art; Preble, pp 614, 615.
Regt. dates and commanders: Berg, pp 84, 85.
Emblem: G. Davis, pp 13, 14.

PAGE 108

Petitioned for color: Preble, p 614.
Knight-silk: E. C. Knight, "New York the Revol.," Sup. 1901, (as cited by Schermerhorn, p 57).
Author's Note: New York regiments were each to be equipped with a pair of colors in 1776 in response to Washington's orders (of May 13, 1776), according to records of the New York Provincial Congress. "Colonel Rud. Ritzema, addressing the . . . New York

Congress, May 31, 1776, says that the day before, it was given out in general orders that General Putnam had received a letter from General Washington, requesting all the colonels at New York to immediately provide colors for their several regiments; and he asks that Mr. Curtinius may have directions to provide a pair for his regiment, of such a color and with such devices as shall be deemed proper by the [New York] Congress,'' (Preble, p 226). The main Continental Army was at New York City at the time.

PAGE 109

Seal: Preble, pp 627–628.
Early flags: Wheeler, ''History of N. C.,'' as cited by Preble, p 627.
Guilford flag: See accompanying letter from Mr. Brandon, Nat. Park Service, to F. E. Schermerhorn, dated Feb. 10, 1941; and letter from Miss M. E. Edwards, N. C. Hist. Comm., to F. E. S., Feb. 13, 1941.

UNITED STATES
DEPARTMENT OF THE INTERIOR
NATIONAL PARK SERVICE

February 10, 1941

Mr. Frank E. Schermerhorn,
Proctor and Schwartz, Inc.,
Seventh Street and Tabor Road,
Philadelphia, Pennsylvania.

My dear Mr. Schermerhorn:

Your enquiry as to the ''Guilford Flag'' is most interesting. I am very happy to be able to provide some of the information which you need, and at the same time I must express my regret that I am unable to supply more, and cannot solve one or more of the questions which the very information that I can supply raises.

I shall begin by attempting to answer your specific questions in their numerical order.

1. The Guilford Flag is now in the ''State Hall of History'' at Raleigh, North Carolina. This is an historical museum of sorts and one of the phases of activity connected with the North Carolina Historical Commission, a state agency.

2. The present dimensions are: Hoist 3 feet 5 inches; Fly: 8 feet 4 inches; Dimensions of Canton; Hoist 2 feet 3 inches; Fly: 5 feet 6½ inches; Canton covers the hoist end of the first 8 stripes of the flag.

The color arrangement is as follows: Stripes alternating from top to bottom Blue, Red, Blue, Red: Canton White with 13 Blue stars; Stars show 8 points and are approximately 8 inches in extreme width. The Stars are in three rows of which the first and third have four stars each and the second three. The stars in the second row are placed opposite the intervals of the first and third rows. The remaining two stars are at the extreme right of the Canton opposite the intervals between the first and second and second and third rows, respectively. Only twelve stripes are present in their entirety.

3. So far as I know there is no pamphlet dealing solely with the flag in existence. A brief recitation of the known history of the flag is contained in an address by Marshall DeLancy Haywood which was published in the *North Carolina Booklet* vol. xii, No. 1, July 1912. This however deals primarily with a personality connected with the flag, the man who according to tradition brought it home from the Revolution.

4. The flag first appears in authentic records in *The Proceedings of the Grand Lodge of Ancient, Free and Accepted Masons, 121st Communication* held at Raleigh, January 14–16, 1909 (Oxford, N.C. 1909). On pages 124 to 126 in the minutes of the afternoon session of Jan. 15, 1909, there is recorded the presentation to the Grand Lodge of the Flag. (At some subsequent date the Grand Lodge deposited the flag in the Hall of History where it now is.)

In the remarks of presentation are the following words:

''This flag is presented by . . . the two oldest living male descendants of Micajah Bullock, who brought it home from the battlefields of North and South Carolina about the close of the War of the Revolution. . . . This flag was brought home by our ancestor, and the family tradition says was carefully preserved in his home until the dedication of the lodge at Mt. Energy in April 1854. At this Masonic festival his son, Major Edward

Bullock, then eighty-one years old carried this flag in the Masonic procession and left it at the lodge. Here it was carefully preserved with other Masonic paraphernalia until Mt. Energy Lodge was moved to Creedmore in the year 1904." There is further implication in very strong terms, though not a definite statement, that the flag remained in the possession of the Creedmore Lodge from 1904 to 1909.

It should be noted that there is no definite statement that the flag was at Guilford Courthouse. It could have been, but the statement as to its use is general: "The battlefields of North and South Carolina." The North Carolina Militia was in this Battle, and in others. I am inclined to regard it as possible, or even probable, but by no means as certain. . . .

Sincerely yours,
William P. Brandon,
Acting Superintendent.

The North Carolina Historical Commission
OFFICE OF THE SECRETARY
RALEIGH

February 13, 1941

Mr. Frank E. Schermerhorn
416 South 45th Street
Philadelphia, Pennsylvania

Dear Mr. Schermerhorn:

Dr. Charles Lee Smith has referred to us your letter of January 24 requesting information concerning the flag which is said to have been carried by the N. C. Militia at the battle of Guilford Courthouse. This flag is now in our museum. We have no pamphlet on it, but I am enclosing on a separate sheet a description of the flag and its history so far as we know it. . . .

Sincerely yours,
(Miss) Mattie Erma Edwards
Collector, The Hall of History

THE SO-CALLED GUILFORD BATTLE FLAG

A flag said to have been carried at the battle of Guilford Courthouse is now preserved in the Hall of History, which is under the administration of the North Carolina Historical Commission, in Raleigh, N. C.

The entire length of the flag is 8 1/2 feet and the present width is 3 feet, 3 1/2 inches. There are fragments tacked to the staff in a way that indicates that part of the flag is missing. The top fragment is blue and is attached to the last red stripe by a seam similar to the seams joining the red and blue stripes; this seam runs the entire length of the red stripe, and the torn blue edge is visible along the entire length. At the staff there is only enough material left to show slightly beneath the leather strip which holds the flag to the staff. Joined to this blue fragment at the staff, by a seam similar to the other seams in the flag, is a small fragment of the red material used in the flag. This likewise is tacked to the staff in the position it would have if it were part of a stripe. Five or six inches below this is another fragment of red, not connected with the rest of the flag except that it is held to the staff by the leather strip and tacks holding the flag proper. It too is in a position as to indicate that it was once part of the bottom edge of the flag. The distance from the edge of the last existing stripe to the bottom edge of the last fragment is a little over 13 inches, which is about the width of four stripes. It seems fairly certain that there were originally at least 14 stripes, and possibly 16. It is possible that instead of two blue and two red stripes, there were one blue and one red, the red stripe being ten inches wide.

It appears that the missing part was deliberately removed, for the torn edge is too even to have been torn accidentally. Why it was removed, when, or by whom is not known.

The flag has 13 blue stars averaging 8 inches in diameter in a white field. Each star has 8 points. The field measures 6 1/2 feet by 2 feet 1 inch. There are 6 blue stripes and 6 red stripes showing with 2 blue stripes and 2 red stripes apparently cut off.

The flag is hand sewn of heavy cotton material, with the red stripes having a self-colored figure.

There are evidences of age in that the flag is faded, stretched, slightly dirty with several small tears.

PAGE 111

Seal: Preble, pp 620, 621.

PAGE 112

In-batteries: Scharf & Westcott (S&W), Vol I, pp 299, 300.
Matters: Ibid., pp 301, 305.
An appeal: Ibid., p 346.
Day book: Clark, Nav. Docs. of the Revol., Vol III, App. D.
On-defenses: S&W, Vol I, pp 306, 323, 338, 339.
Receipt: J. W. Jackson, "The Pa. Navy 1775–81," Rutgers, p 17.
Richards: Pa. Arch., Vol V, pp 17, 46 (cited by Preble, p 246).
Ross receipt: Pa. Arch., 1st series, Vol V, p 46 (as cited by Preble, p 270).
Delaware: Smith, "Fight for the Delaware," Philip Freneau Press, 1970.

PAGE 113

Franklin's letter: Wharton, "Revol. Dipl. Corres. of the U.S.A.," Vol II, 1887, pp 759–760.
Pa. Rifle Regt.: "Notes and Queries," Pa. Mag. of Hist. & Bio., Vol VI (1882), pp 514–515.
Magaw: Holst, MC & H (Fall 1960), p 69; Berg, p 42.
Phila. Lt. Horse: The following description of the Philadelphia Light Horse Troop standard is quoted with the kind permission of the First Troop, PCC, from S. Lapsley, "The Book of the First Troop, Philadelphia City Cavalry, 1774–1914," Philadelphia, 1915. (See Chapter 22 Notes for description of the Powel Standard, 1797):

"The exact date of the invention of the Troop flag seems impossible of discovery. The only documents are two bills of account, found among the papers of Captain Markoe and given to the Troop in 1874 by his great-grandson, Lieutenant William Camac (561) which are here reproduced:

September 16th, 1775
Mr. Marchoo Dr.
To John Folwell

To Drawing & Designing the Coulours for the Light Horse,
£ 1.15.-
Ten shillings paid in part.
Recd. 22d of Sep. of Abram Markoe Above in full
John Folwell

Philada. 8th Sept. 1775
Captain Markoe
To James Claypoole, Dr.
To painting, gilding & silvering a Device, Union & Motto on 2 Colours for the Troop of Light Horse @£4   £8.00
Received the Contents in full from
Mr. Mitchell   James Claypoole

"A description of the standard is to be found in the Donnaldson Mss. already referred to in this book, as follows:

"The standard is of yellow lustring or taffety silk very fine & double, 39 inches by 34 inches, bound with two inch silver lace all round and a vine worked in silver on both sides of the border. In one corner in a square are 13 stripes blue & white, on both sides an antique shield, cerulean, in the centre of which is a star d'or with 13 points, the shield supporters are two figures, on the right a female with wings, blowing a trumpet held by the right hand & by the left a wand representing Fame. On the left the figure of an Indian warrior with bow & arrow & a pole with cap of Liberty d'or. The shield is mounted with a crest, a horse's head on which are worked in silver the letters LH—under the shield is the motto—For these we strive—It is mounted on a pole 8 feet 8 inches long with a silver spear head. The flag is much tattered & preserved with great care in a tin case at the commander's quarters being exhibited only on particular occasion. A note to this description says that the supporters represent 'Liberty and Fame.'"

Charles J. Lukens, a writer on heraldry, a member of the Historical Society of Pennsylvania and editor of the Architectural Review, wrote a paper describing the Troop standard. This paper of Mr. Lukens, as furnished Admiral Preble for his book, reads:

"The flag of the light horse of Philadelphia

is forty inches long and thirty-four inches broad. Its canton is twelve and one-half inches long and nine and one-half inches wide. The armorial achievement in its centre occupies the proportional space in the drawing; both sides of the flag exhibit the same attributes. The left side shows everything as if the material were transparent, giving the right side entirely in reverse, except the cyphers L.H. and the motto, 'FOR THESE WE STRIVE.' The cyphers, the running vine on both sides, the cord and tassels, and the fringe are of silver bullion twist. The spear-head and the upper ferrule, taken together eight inches in length, are of solid silver. The staff is of dark wood, in three carefully ferruled divisions screwing together. Ten screw rings at irregular intervals from two and one-half to three-fourths inches, are used to attach the flag to the staff by means of a cord laced through corresponding eyelets in the flag. The flag is formed of two sides very strongly hemmed together along the edges, each side being of two equal pieces attached together by means of a horizontal seam, the material of the flag being a light bright yellow silk. The canton of the flag is 'Barry of thirteen azure and argent.' The azure being deep ultra marine, the argent silver leaf. The achievement in the centre of the flag is azure, a round knot of three interlacings, with thirteen divergent, wavy, bellied double foliated ends or; whereof two ends are in chief, and one in base. The scrolled edging of the shield is gold, with outer and inner rims of silver.

"The crest (without a wreath) a horse's head bay, with a white star on the forehead, erased at the shoulders, maned sable, bitted and rosetted, or, and bridled azure. Over the head of the charger is the monogram L.H. Beneath the shield, the motto 'FOR THESE WE STRIVE,' in black Roman capitals of the Elizabethan style, on a floating silver scroll, upon the upcurled ends of which stand the supporters, DEXTER, an Indian with a bow or, the loosened string blue floating on the wind, in his left hand, and in his right, a gold rod upholding a liberty cap, with tassel azure, the lining silver, head dress and kilt (or ga-ka-ah) of feathers of dark red, and gold, with fillet of crimson.

*** The quiver is a gold supported over the right shoulder by a blue strap, its arrows are proper. The moccasins are buff with feather tops, I think alternated dark red, and gold. The Indian approaches the shield in profile as does also the sinister supporter which represents an angel of florid tint, roseate cheek, with auburn curly hair, and blue eyes, blowing a golden trumpet, held with his right hand, and holding in his left a gold rod. His wings are a light bluish gray with changeable flashes of silver. His flowing robe from the right shoulder to the left flank is purple. These supporters not being heraldic in position and motion for human or angelic figures, their left and right action have the natural and not the heraldic significations."

Hanover Assoc.: The Pennsylvania Associators were militia units formed voluntarily in response to Benjamin Franklin's appeal published (during the French and Indian War) in a pamphlet entitled, "Plain Truth." The Quaker-dominated Pennsylvania Assembly had refused to pass a militia law, and Franklin appealed directly to the people, who responded enthusiastically. In his autobiography, Franklin said: "The women, by subscriptions among themselves, provided silk colours, which they presented to the companies, painted with different devices and mottos, which I supplied." ("The Autobiography of Benjamin Franklin," Garden City Publ. Co., New York, 1939, p 131). Some of the Associator flags are described in "The Pennsylvania Gazette" for January 12 and April 16, 1748 (Schermerhorn, p 100).
Westmoreland battalion: Preble, pp 205, 206.

PAGE 116

Proctor's battalion: J. P. Clarke "Official Hist. of the Militia and Nat. Guard of Pa.," 1909, Vol I, p 88.
1st Pa. Regt.: Preble, p 206.

PAGE 117

Regt. history: Berg, p 94; W. H. Egle, "Hist. of . . . Pa.," 1877, p 154.
Hand's letter: Pa. Arch., 5th ser, Vol II, p 13.

Conservation: Werner & Armstrong, ''1st Cont. Regt. Flag,'' MC & H, (spring 1975).

Denny's Journal: HSP Proc. 1860, pp 243, 249, 253, 256.

Pa. battalions: Berg, pp 94–96.

2nd Pa.: Berg, pp 94, 95.

Peale correspondence: C. C. Sellers, ''Portraits and Miniatures by Charles Willson Peale,'' Vol 42, Part 1, Trans. Amer. Philo. Soc., Phila., 1952, pp 201, 202, 827–830, plts 106–108.

Receipt: Private collection.

PAGE 119

Sword: JCC, Nov. 19, 1777.

Plumes: Whitlock, ''Lafayette,'' Vol I, p 210.

PAGE 121

Seal: Preble, p 611.

R.I. Militia: Letter to author from Thomas G. Brennan, Registrar, RIHS Apr. 13, 1977.

Newport Lt. Inf.: P. F. Gleeson, ''The Newport Lt. Inf.,'' Collections of RIHS, Jan. 1940, pp 1–13.

Lt. Inf. helmet: Courtesy of William Guthman, Westport, Conn. Photograph courtesy of Smithsonian Institution. Advertised in Antiques Magazine, May 1978. Formerly in collection of Royal United Service Museum, Whitehall Place, London. The cap is described by W. L. Claver, ''Newport Lt. Inf. Co. Insignia,'' RIHS Collections, Oct. 1934.

PAGE 122

Contemporary news article: The first public appearance of the Company was on April 3, 1775. Four companies of the Newport militia, totaling 250 men, and the Light Infantry of 47 men marched to the house of Henry Marchant who presented the battalion commander, Colonel Jabez Champlin, with ''a suite of colors'' for the new command. The ''pair of colors'' consisted of the Newport Light Infantry colors and the ''King's Colours'' (Quoted by P. F. Gleeson from a copy provided by Miss Susan S. Brayton, authoress of the MSS. biography of Henry Marchant).

Mr. Marchant made the following address:

''Gentlemen of the Newport Light Infantry: From a sincere desire of promoting and encouraging the military spirit diffusing itself through this town, colony, and America, I here present you the colours to be borne by your Ensign; and I shall esteem myself highly honoured by your acceptance of them.

''I have endeavored to throw such figures and devices into them as may lead you on to the great objects which ought to possess the mind of every American soldier, every friend to his country.

''By the female figure, you have AMERICA, your native country, presented to your view, which will justly demand your protection when in danger—by the CAP OF LIBERTY, upon the staff, which she holds in her left hand, and points at with her right, you will be led to contemplate the importance of liberty, civil and religious, to man: An existence without liberty cannot be wished for; every other possession, nay, our country itself, would lose every enchantment, deprived of her all enlivening principle: Therefore adopt the motto, 'Patria, Carior Libertas.'

''The BROKEN CHAINS AND SWORD under her feet may intimate to you that the principles of true liberty diffused through America will ever prevail over violence and oppression.

''Carrying these principles into practice, the ANCHOR, the Arms of our colony, placed over America, will lead you to a well grounded HOPE, that, by adding thereto unanimity, wisdom, firmness, and virtue, we shall succeed in the righteous struggle, and secure to ourselves and posterity the invaluable rights, liberties, privileges, and happy constitution, which the God of nature hath transmitted to us, through our pious and venerable ancestors.

''Adopt with a Christian sincerity the motto placed above the anchor, IN GOD WE HOPE,——act worthily your part for God and your country, and you have the God of your fathers with you, and who then can be against you.

''Let loyalty to your King, a love to your country and its laws, a zeal for liberty, and a full faith and confidence in Heaven, actuate you through life, so will you gain the love, veneration and esteem of your country, and the world of mankind for your admirers.

"Permit me to say, I cannot but feel myself concerned and interested in every part of your duty—that it may be discharged to the public acceptance, and thereby to your own honor and approbation: To this great end nothing can more contribute than an entire confidence in and high respect for, the officers of your country:—And I am sure those gentlemen, elected by yourselves, cannot fail of affording every proof of the wisdom of your choice, since they will meet in return, with every satisfaction that a generous officer can wish, from a company of gentlemen, delighting in military order, and filled with the noble sentiments of liberty, honor and friendship" ("Newport Mercury," April 17, 1775).

The Light Infantry fired a volley, paraded the colors, then adjourned to a public house for dinner where seventeen or eighteen toasts were called for—the first to the King, the last to America. They included a toast to Henry Marchant "who generously presented the Newport Light Infantry with their colours."

The description of the device on the colors is very similar to the insignia on the metal frontispiece of a military cap which had been captured in America and was in the collection of the Royal United Service Institute at Whitehall, London in 1934 (RIHS Collections, Oct. 1934, "Newport Light Infantry Company, Insignia" by W. L. Calver; and "Emblems of Rhode Island," p 29). This was evidently a Newport Light Infantry cap. The device on the cap has somewhat different features such as an olive branch and liberty cap in the left hand of America and sword in her right. The motto is inscribed on a garter encircling America and was translated by W. L. Calver as "Country is dear, but Liberty is dearer." At the crest are the initials C. R. (Colony of Rhode Island) and a ribbon-like scroll which once carried some now indecipherable writing which Calver surmised was originally the word "Hope" but under special lighting appears to be "In God We Hope." At the foot of the device, on a ribbon scroll, is "Newport Light Infantry."

The illustration of the colors in this book follows the device on the cap to a considerable degree, and it therefore differs in some details from Henry Marchant's description of the final design of the actual colors.

The painter for the original flag is unknown. It was not Copley, of course. The illustrator of the colors has assumed that the field was blue and bore a British Union canton as called for in Marchant's letter to Hancock.

It would appear that the Light Infantry Company was uniformed and made "a fine appearance" (Literary Diary of Ezra Stiles, Vol I, p 544). On May 25, 1775, Captain Topham's company of Newport militia marched for the army at Roxbury (Boston, Mass.) and was escorted on its first day by a number of Light Infantry.

Calver states that the Newport Light Infantry Company was probably scattered during the British occupation of Newport. He refers to a census of 1777 that lists Jabez Champlin in Charlestown.

The cap is now in the collection of William Guthman, Westport, Connecticut, having been sold by the above Royal United Services Institute. It was advertised for sale in the May 1978 issue of Antiques Magazine (p 950). Mr. Guthman kindly authorized a photograph by the Smithsonian Institute through Mr. Donald Kloster. Mr. Kloster, in personal correspondence with the author, pointed out that the initials are to all appearances "C. R.," not "G. R.," as had been previously assumed. Also, that the motto appears to be "In God We Hope," not "Hope" alone. The "C. R." would have probably been the cypher for "Colony of Rhode Island." The Rhode Island Assembly directed that "C. R." be stamped on some muskets they ordered during the war (this information was kindly provided by Mr. Kloster).

R.I. Regt. of '81: Preble, pp 286–287, citing R.I. Colonial Records, Vol X, pp 14, 15. G. Davis also cites "Col. Isaac Angell's Diary" and a "Report by Col. Asa B. Gardiner to the Adj. Gen. of R.I., Jan 4, 1897."

One R.I. regt: Berg, pp 105, 106.

PAGE 123

R.I. Secr. of State: Letters to Preble, pp 287, 288.
R.I. currency: Newman, pp 267, 297.

PAGE 124

H. M. Chapin: "Early R.I. Flags," RIHS Coll., Oct. 1925, pp 129–131.

PAGE 125

2nd R.I. Regt.: E. M. Stone, "Our French Allies," Providence, 1884, p 453. Also, Edward Field, "Diary of Colonel Israel Angell," 1899.
R.I. artillery unit: H. M. Chapin, "Early R.I. Flags," RIHS Coll., Oct. 1925; E. Andrew Mowbray, " 14 R.I. Militia Flags," MC & H, Vol XIX, No. 2.

PAGE 126

Penniman: Photograph, courtesy RIHS (F. E. Schermerhorn files).

PAGE 127

Seal: Preble, pp 628, 630; Drayton, "Drayton's Memoirs," Vol II, p 372.
Advertisement: See Antiques Magazine, Feb. 1978, p 447.

PAGE 128

Devices of regts.: Letter to author from Captain Fitzhugh McMaster, USN Ret., dated July 25, 1972; MC & H, (spring 1980), "Brigantine-of-War Notre Dame, S.C. Navy, 1776–1780," p 25; J. Drayton, "Memoirs of the . . . Revol.," 1821, Vol II, pp 281, 281n, says that the caps of the 1st Regt. and 2nd Regt. had a crescent with the words "Ultima Ratio" and "Liberty" engraved, respectively.
Hopkins: Engraving by T. Hart: Library of Congress (and others).
Franklin & Adams letter: J. Sparks, "Dipl. Corres. of the Amer. Revol.," Vol I, p 467. Also F. Wharton, "The Revol. Corres. of the U.S.A.," 1889, Vol II, pp 759, 760.

PAGE 129

Rice sheaf & stars: Letter of R. Lowndes to Commodore A. Gillon, 19 July, 1778, in Peter Force Transcripts, S.C. Misc., 1667–1788, Ms. Div., L.C. Annex, Wash, D.C.
Crescent ensign: Wm. Moultrie, Gen. Orders, HM681, MS., Henry Huntington Library, San Marino, Calif. (inside front cover).
S.C. $ 8 bill: So. Carolina Libr., U.S.C., Columbia, S. C.

PAGE 130

Ft. Moultrie flag: Moultrie, "Memoirs," Vol I, pp 90, 91.
Sgt. Jasper: Moultrie, p 179; J. Drayton, "Memoirs of the . . . Revol.," Charleston, 1821, Vol II, p 298.
Flag: J. Drayton, "Memoirs," Vol II, p 290, says the flag was on the southeast bastion of the fort and that it was blue "with a white crescent; on which was emblazoned the word LIBERTY. . . ."
Blue field flag with three white crescents: Drayton, "Memoirs," Vol I, p 45, says such a flag was hoisted over Fort Johnson (in Charleston harbor) by a group of Americans protesting the Stamp Act in 1765.

PAGE 131

Jeffries manuscript diary: Cited by Preble, p 284; and by G. Canby, "Evolution of the Amer. Flag," 1909, p 77.
1st S.C. Regt.: Crescent 2nd motto, Drayton, "Memoirs," Vol II, pp 281, 281n.

PAGE 132

Sullivan's Island: Moultrie, "Memoirs," Vol I, pp 124, 174, 175.
Mrs. Elliott: Moultrie, Vol I, p 182.
Savannah: Moultrie, Vol II, pp 40, 41; L. Butler, "The Annals of the King's Royal Rifle Corps," London, 1912, pp 216, 217.

PAGE 133

Capt. Fitzhugh McMaster: "Flag of the 2nd S.C. Regt. . . . ," MC & H (winter 1970), pp 137–139; Capt. F. McMaster & D. Erd, "1st and 2nd S.C. Regt. 1775–1780," MC & H (summer 1977), pp 70–72.

PAGE 134

13 Stripes: May 19, 1780 letter, J. Munsell, "Siege of Charleston," 1867 (as cited by Preble, p 284).

F. F. Hough, ed.: "Journal of the Investment of Charleston on the Land Side," pp 84, 167, and quoting Rivington's Royal Gazette, No. 387, June 21, 1780.

Surrendered colors: Lt. Col. Tarleton, "Campaigns," London, 1787, p 67.

PAGE 135

Seal: Preble, pp 623–625; Lossing, Vol II, pp 505, 506.

Captured colors: "War Trophies at Chelsea, Part IV," The Navy and Army Illustrated (British periodical), Jan. 24, 1903, pp 489, 490.

PAGE 136

Culpepper standard: B. J. Lossing, Vol II, p 505 (sketch, no ref.); R. T. Green, "Gen. & Hist. Notes on Culpepper Co., Va., Embracing a Revised & Enlarged Edition of Dr. P. Slaughter's Hist. of St. Mark's Parish," Culpepper, Va., 1900, Part Second, p 13.

PAGE 137

15 taffeta colors: "Mil. Uniforms in America, the . . . Revol.," Comp. of Mil. Historians, Col. J. R. Elting, ed., Presidio Press, 1974.

VIII Va. Regt. colors: H. A. Muhlenberg, "Life of . . . Gen. Peter Muhlenberg . . . ," Phila., 1849, pp 338, 339. The actual quote is as follows: "The regimental colour of this corps is still in the writer's possession. It is made of plain salmon-colored silk, with a broad fringe of the same, having a simple white scroll in the centre, upon which are inscribed the words, 'VIII VIRG—REGᵀ.' The spear head is brass, considerably ornamented. The banner bears the traces of warm service, and is probably the only Revolutionary flag still in existence."

PAGE 138

Alex. Co., IX Va. Regt.: Brockett, "The Lodge of Washington . . . ," Alexandria-Washington Lodge #22, A.F. & A. M., Alexandria, Va., 1876 (& 1928), p 87.

XI Va. Regt. (Morgan's Rifle Corps): Lossing, Vol II, p 637.

Alex. Rifle Comp'y, XI Va. Regt.: Collection of Alexandria-Washington Masonic Lodge No. 22, Alexandria, Va.; letter to author from Mr. Harold R. Cumbee, Lodge Archivist, May 12, 1975.

PAGE 139

Regt.'s commander: Berg, p 130.

XI Va. Regt. of '78: For a color illustration of Reynolds' portrait of "Tarleton," see Ketchum's "Life of Washington," Amer. Heritage, 1974, p 138. The original painting is at the National Gallery, London. Lt. Col. Tarleton, "Campaigns," London, 1787, p 84; D. W. Holst, "Regimental Colors of the Continental Army," MC & H (fall 1968), pp 70–71.

Richmond Rifle Rangers: Brockett, "The Lodge of Washington," Alexandria, Va., 1876 (& 1928), p 87.

PAGE 141

General references: G. Davis, "Regt'l Colors in the . . . Revol.," NYC, 1907, pp 23–29. He, in turn, cites: General L. Susane, "Histoire de l'Ancienne Infanterie Française," 1849–1853; M. Mouillard, "Les Regiments sous Louis XV;" de Bouille, "Les Drapeaux Français," Paris, 1874; G. Desjardins, "Recherches sur les Drapeaux Français," Paris, 1874. F. E. Schermerhorn, "American & French Flags of the Revol.," Phila., 1948, pp 103–144. He cites: G. Davis; Desjardins; "Les Combattants Français de la Guerre Americaine 1778–1783," compiled by the French Ministry of Foreign Affairs, 1903; T. Balch, "The French in America," 1885; A. Forbes & P. Cadman, "France and New England," 1925; E. M. Stone, "Our French Allies," 1884.

G. Davis supplemented his references, above, with personal correspondence with two French military historians, M. Edward

314

Detaille and M. O. Hollanger. F. E. Schermerhorn wrote that his French flag descriptions were taken from Desjardins or Davis. He also corresponded with H. M. Chapin of the Rhode Island Historical Society.

For descriptions of French colors, the author has depended mainly on G. Davis with specific reference, at times, to Schermerhorn and others. Particularly useful has been the fine work by Rice & Brown ("The American Campaigns of Rochambeau's Army, 1780–81," Princeton Univ. Press, 1972) and C. C. Jones, "Hist. of Ga.," Boston, 1883, Vol II, pp 404, 405. Also very helpful were letters, dated (Paris) 22 August 1960 and 14 September 1960 from Monsieur Marcel Baldet to Capt F. McMaster, USN Ret., commenting on Schermerhorn's French flags and on French naval and army flags in general.

French forces in America: Comte d'Estaing's Expeditionary Force against Savannah in 1779 was described in an account published in "The Paris Gazette" of January 7, 1780: ". . . . The French Troops consisted of 2,823 Europeans, draughted from the Regiments of Armagnac, Champagne, Auxerrois, Agenois, Gatinois, Cambresis, Haynault, Foix, Dillon, Walsh, le Cap, la Guadeloupe, le Martinique and Port au Prince, including a Detachment of the Royal Corps of Infantry of the Marine, the Volunteers of Vallelle, the Dragoons and 156 Volunteer Grenadiers, lately raised at Cape Francois. The coloured troops consisted of 545 Volunteer Chasseurs, Malattoes and Negroes, newly raised at St. Domingo . . ." (as quoted in Franklin B. Hough, "The Siege of Savannah," 1866, Univ. of Georgia).

Davis listed the following regiments as being represented (most, if not all, by detachments) at Savannah; Agenois, Champagne, Armagnac, Auxerrois, Foix, Haynault, Metz (artillery), Dillon (Irish), Walsh (Irish).

Davis listed the following regiments as being represented at Yorktown: Gatinois (Royal Auvergne), Saintonge, Touraine, Bourbonnais, Soissonnais, Auxonne (artillery), Royal Deux-Ponts.

According to "Military Uniforms in America," edited by Colonel John R. Elting, USA Ret., MC & H, 1974, page 112, and "French Regiments at Savannah, 1779," by Eugene Leliepvre and Marcel Baldet, the following detachments were assigned from regiments stationed in the West Indies to Admiral Comte d'Estaing's fleet for the October 1779 siege and assault on British-occupied Savannah: *Martinique:* A total of 750 men drawn from the Viennois, Champagne, Auxerrois and La Martinique Regiments together with some artillerists. *St. Dominique:* A total of 1500 men drawn from the le Cap, Gatenois, Agenois, Cambresis, and Port-au-Prince Regiments together with 600 men from the Foix and Haynault Regiments. *Guadeloupe:* A total of 850 men from the La Guadeloupe, Armagnac, and La Martinique Regiments together with some artillerists."

Schermerhorn said that Davis, Balch, and "Les Combattants" list the following regiments: Bourbaonnais, Deux-Ponts, Saintonge, Soissonnais, Gatinois, Agenois, Touraire, Metz, Auxonne, Lauzun's Legion, Dillon, Champagne, Foix, Haynault, Auxerrois, Walsh, Armagnac, Grenoble, and Belzunce.

Verger's Journal (as quoted by Rice and Brown) lists the following units as being "selected to go to America" with Rochambeau and having embarked at Brest, April 4, 1780: Bourbonnais, Royal Deux-Ponts, Soissonnais, Saintonge, Auxonne, Legion of Lauzun.

Verger listed the following French units at Yorktown: Bourbonnais, Royal Deux-Ponts, Soissonais, Saintonge, Gatinais, Agenois, Touraine, Royal Artillerie (1 battalion of Auxonne Regt., 2 companies of Metz Regt.), Light Infantry and 400 hussars of the Lauzun Legion, 200 Voluntaires de Saint-Simon, and 800 garrison troops from the ships. Total: 8,000 men.

The Angoumois Regiment, Grenadiers de la Marine Royale, Regiment d'Infantrie de Monsieur, and La Sarre Infantrie Regiment were represented among the ships' garrisons of de Grasse's fleet at Yorktown, according to a listing of "journals" (Rice and Brown, Vol I, p 346) kept by French officers.

French navy and army forces also took part in the Spanish and French siege and capture of Pensacola, Florida, in April–May 1781 and in the expedition against Hudson Bay in the summer of 1782. Undoubtedly, the expeditions included French units which should be added to the list of those which took part in the American War. The author has not attempted to compile a list of the Pensacola and Hudson Bay forces.

"The American Campaigns of Rochambeau's Army, 1780–83" by Rice and Brown, 1972, also lists the Engineers, Corps Royal du Genie, as being with Rochambeau and St. Simon.

PAGE 142

French Navy regulations: Ordonnance . . . Marine, 25 Mar. 1765, quoted by M. Marcel Baldet in correspondence with Capt F. McMaster, USN Ret., letter dated 22 Aug. 1960.

Design & protocol: Letter, M. Baldet to Capt. F. McMaster, USN Ret.; Schermerhorn, pp 105–106; letter from Colonel Martel, Conservator, Army Museum, Invalides, Paris, to author, 26 Apr. 1977.

Standards—ancient: Preble, pp 103–117.

Rochambeau: It was not customary for generals to display personal standards, according to Colonel Martel's letter, above.

PAGE 143

Schermerhorn: Pp 141–144 state plainly that the French banner at the Metropolitan is not Rochambeau's but then proceed to call it "Rochambeau's Standard"!

Metropolitan Museum: Accession data on French-Kahlert banner.

Rochambeau's seal: Rice & Brown, p. xx, and illustration opposite p 126.

PAGE 144

British cartoon: D. H. Cresswell (comp), "The Amer. Revol. in Drawings and Prints," Lib. of Congress, 1975, fig 776.

Banner-Swiss Regt.: Marcel Baldet, "Enseignes, Drapeaux et Etendards," Histoire Militaire Section, French periodical review, dated before August 1960.

PAGE 145

Primary sources: G. Davis, F. E. Schermerhorn, and Van Blarenberghe's paintings of

the "Siege" and "Surrender of Yorktown" (Rice & Brown, "Campaigns of Rochambeau's Army . . . ," Princeton, 1972). Also used for reference are two letters (dated 1960) from Marcel Baldet to Capt. F. McMasters, USN Ret., and the flag replicas and miniature color guards presented by France in 1976 to the Yorktown Victory Center.

Photographs of Van Blarenberghe's paintings of the "Siege" and "Surrender of Yorktown" were kindly loaned by Dr. Howard C. Rice, Jr., co-author of "The American Campaigns of Rochambeau's Army."

Military history of regiments and personnel is based primarily on Schermerhorn, who goes into more detail on the units than their colors. There is some information on Lauzun's Legion in an article by E. Leliepre & R. Chartrand, "Voluntaires Etrangers de Lauzun," MC & H Vol 26, p 226. The story of Lauzun's last dinner is told by A. Whitridge, "Rochambeau," Collier, 1965, p 303.

Monsieur Baldet's comments to Captain McMaster were used for the proportions of the cross (same proportions in G. Davis) and of the overall dimensions (5½ by 5½ feet, whereas G. Davis has "about four feet square"). Baldet's comments have been used in describing and illustrating the following colors: Bourbonnais, Saintonge, Soisonnais, Gatenois, Metz, Dillon, Agenois, Touraine, Champagne, Fois, Haynault, Auxerre, Walsh, Armagnac.

PAGE 148

Colonels' colors at Yorktown: Kapp's biography of Steuben (1859) includes a translation of the Hessian sergeant's account (cited by Schermerhorn, p 110).

PAGE 154

Saintonge: There is disagreement among military flag historians on the exact sequence of color of the triangles forming the cantons of the Saintonge Regiment, but they do agree on the colors—blue, yellow, green, red.

G. Davis (1947) said the coloring sequence was different for the several authors he consulted. Therefore, he did not state a sequence, but did give the four colors listed above. Schermerhorn quoted Davis on this point and used what he said was Desjardins' sequence. Messrs. E. Leliepvre and R. Chartrand, in an article on the Saintonge Regiment's uniforms (MC & H, winter 1975), illustrate the flag with a different sequence (from Schermerhorn), as follows: 1st canton, top triangle, yellow, left-blue, right-green, lower-red; 2nd, R-B-G-Y; 3rd, B-R-Y-G; 4th, G-R-Y-B (and they list Desjardins as one of their references). Possibly different copies of Desjardins' book have different sequences of colored triangles.

Van Blarenberghe's painting of "The Surrender of Yorktown" pictures the Saintonge regimental standard with four colors for the triangles—red, yellow, blue, and white. The sequence of colors of the triangles is the same as Leliepvre and Chartrand, above, if white is equated to green. Also, the Saintonge flag replica at the Yorktown Victory Center is the same as that depicted by Leliepvre and Chartrand and by Van Blarenberghe (if white is green).

Monsieur Marcel Baldet, in a letter to Capt. F. McMaster, USN Ret., dated 14 Sept. 1960, said the sequence of color for the triangles was: 1st canton upper-yellow, left-blue, right-green, lower-red; 2nd, Y-G-B-R; 3rd, G-Y-R-B; 4th, G-Y-R-B. The author used Monsieur Baldet's sequence in the text and illustration but would now favor the sequence used by Van Blarenberghe, Leliepvre and Chartrand, and the replica at the Yorktown Victory Center.

PAGE 159

Belzunce Dragoons: Louis XI's sun device is illustrated in "Heraldry," Amer. Heritage, 1975. Colonel Martel, Conservator, Museum of the Army, Invalides, Paris, provided valuable comments on the Belzunce Dragoons guidon and other items in a letter to the author, dated 26 April 1977.

PAGE 161

General references: G. Davis. He cites S. M. Milne, "Standards and Colors of the Army," London, 1893, and a paper by a Major Carson in the "Bulletin of the Association of Graduates of the U.S. Military Academy," 1902. H. M. Chicester & G. Burges-Short, "The Records and Badges of Every Regiment and Corps in the British Army," London, 1895. C. M. Lefferts, "Uniforms of the . . . . Revolution," NYHS, 1926. Major N. P. Dawney, "The Standards, Guidons, and Colours of the Household Division, 1660–1973," Midas, Tunbridge Wells, England.

Description and illustrations of the British colors included herein are based on the above general references with specific additional references noted in the text and below.

PAGE 162

Loyalists—population: Franklin and Adams estimated one-third of the population was loyalist.

PAGE 163

Loyalist units: See C. M. Lefferts, pp 225–227, which lists 79 loyalist units.

PAGE 164

Dragoons: Stephen Jarvis, "An American's Experience in the British Army," Connecticut Magazine, XI, p 481 (as cited by J. T. Hayes, in "Connecticut's Revol. Cavalry: Sheldon's Horse," Pequot Press, 1975).

PAGE 165

1100 men: Uhlendorf, p 51.
Brigade of Guards: B. A. Uhlendorf, ed., "Revol. in Amer. . . . Ltrs. of Adj. Gen. Major Baurmeister," Rutgers, 1957, p 98.
Colors captured: Lossing, Vol II, pp 524–525, describes the Yorktown surrender. He says Washington was at the head of the American line on a white horse and that Rochambeau was at the head of the French line when the British troops marched out. Van Blarenberghe's painting of "The Surrender of Yorktown" shows a group of blue-coated mounted officers, one on a white horse on

the right side of the road at the head of the line. Lossing says the Americans lined the right side of the road and the French the left, which is opposite to Van Blarenberghe's painting when viewed from Yorktown.

Lossing (Vol II, pp 524–526) relates a family story heard from descendants of New York Ensign Robert Wilson "of Clinton's Brigade" that Ensign Wilson personally received the twenty-eight colors (10 English and 18 German) surrendered and that it was a special, separate ceremony conducted by Wilson, 28 British captains, and 28 American sergeants. The author cannot verify the above tradition. However, Van Blarenberghe's painting of the "Surrender" depicts pairs of cased regimenal colors being carried by regiments and being left standing upright and crossed in the surrender field among the rows of muskets which indicates no mass surrender of colors. (Tarleton's Memoirs lists 28 standards, 18 German regimentals, 6 British regimentals, and 4 British union flags, and in addition: 73 camp colors—32 German and 41 British).

PAGE 167

Colors left in Canada: F. G. Hudleston, "Gentleman Johnny Burgoyne," New York, 1927, p 265.

PAGE 169

General references: G. Davis, who corresponded in the early 1900's with various museums in Germany, namely, the Hist. Soc. of Bayreuth, Museum Friedericianum at Cassel, Hist. Soc. of Ober-Franken at Bayreuth, Hist. Soc. of Mittel-Franken at Ansbach, Vaterlandisches Museum at Brunswick, and Royal Staats Archiv at Marburg. He also cites William Ellery's description of a green Hessian flag captured at Trenton (Rhode Island Col. Rec., Vol VIII, p 170). Davis describes the two Hessian flags and the remnant of another (bequest of Mrs. Clymer) at the Hist. Soc. of Pennsylvania (these have disappeared since 1907), the German flags at West Point Military Academy (Ansbach-Bayreuth colors captured at

Yorktown), and the Hessian colors which are depicted in C. W. Peale's "Washington at Trenton," at the Metropolitan (see Ketchum's "World of G. Washington," Amer. Herit., 1974, p 179, for Yale Univ. copy).

C. M. Lefferts ("Uniforms of the . . . Revol.," NYHS, 1926) provides considerable information on German regiments. There are also recent articles on German military units (of the Revolution) in the publications of the Company of Military Historians, including O. K. Weinmaster, Jr., "The Hessian Grenadier Battalions in No. Amer." (winter 1975), and a book, "Military Uniforms in Amer.: The Era of the Amer. Revol.," J. R. Elting (ed.), Presidio Press, 1974.

Lossing (Vol II, p 412) describes and illustrates a "Hessian" (actually, Ansbach-Bayreuth) standard at the Alexandria-Washington Masonic Lodge in the 1840's, which had been presented to G. Washington by Congress. The flag is now one of the four in the West Point collection. One of the four is at the Smithsonian and another at Yorktown.

On the number of flags captured at Trenton, reports vary widely. As noted in the text, Hessian General Heister said fifteen (G. Davis, p 43), General Heath said four (Preble, p 328), and Ellery said four (R.I. Col. Rec., Vol VIII, p 170). Scharf & Westcott in "Hist. of Phila." (Vol I, p 535) say six colors and 900 Hessian prisoners were paraded through Philadelphia.

PAGE 172

Ansbach-Bayreuth: The following is quoted courtesy of the West Point Museum:

The Yorktown German Flags in the West Point Museum

The West Point Museum once had in its possession four regimental colors [once] carried by the Ansbach-Bayreuth Regiments of Voigt and von Seybothen (Accession Nos. 2431, 2432, 2433, 2434). All four of these flags were surrendered at Yorktown on 19 October 1781 and they appear to be the only flags surrendered on that occasion which have survived.

Physical Description

The four colors are all within an inch or so the same size: 50″ on the fly and 48″ on the staff. All are double flags made of two sheets of white damask silk. Each sheet is formed of three silk strips sewn together in vertical panels. The pattern of the damask is a small spray of flowers and leaves, now scarcely visible.

On the reverse of each flag is embroidered an eagle, originally red but now considerably faded, below the motto *Pro Principe et Patria*, in gold on a silver scroll. The obverse sides bear a wreath of green palm and laurel branches tied together with a pink ribbon, within which is a large monogram, a crown, and the letters "M.Z.B." for Markgraf zu Brandenburg (these letters have disappeared from 2432). Below the wreath is a date; on 2431 the date is "1770", on 2433 and 2434 it is "1775", while the date on 2432 has been obliterated. All devices on this side except the wreath are of gold bullion. The large monogram reads "S.E.T.C.A.", the first four letters meaning *Sincere et Constanter*, which was the motto of the Prussian Order of the Red Eagle and the Margraves of Brandenburg-Ansbach-Bayreuth. The fifth letter "a" stands for Alexander, the reigning prince, whose monogram also appears on the brass spearheads as "C.F.C.A." (Christian Friedrich Carl Alexander).

The flags are nailed to their staffs, a common German custom in the eighteenth century. Gherardi Davis in *Regimental Colors in the War of the Revolution* (p. 50) states that in a military museum in Munich there was a damaged spearhead, exactly like the ones at West Point, which was described as being the spearhead of the Ansbach-Bayreuth Regiment Voigt. Only two of the spearheads have survived (on 2433 and 2434). These bear monograms as described above. One of the colors (2433) still retains a streamer or ribbon of woven silver lace with a bullion tassel. The staffs are 7′9″ long (except 2433 which is 7″ shorter and slightly warped) and are painted white.

Restoration

All of the flags have been restored and, while fragile, can readily be moved and shipped. Apparently no restoration was attempted until 1914 when flag 2434 was selected for repair by the ladies of the Colonial Chapter of the Daughters of the American Revolution. Two years later another of the colors was restored through the generosity of the Priscilla Chapter of the DAR. The remaining two flags were subsequently restored in the routine flag restoration program. In 1914 and subsequently the West Point Museum conducted a considerable correspondence with foreign museums in order to determine the most suitable method of flag preservation. Unfortunately, a dark colored netting was used on all which has decreased the original brilliance of the white damask and given the colors a grayish yellow cast.

History

The 1st and 2nd Regiments of Brandenburg-Ansbach, under Colonel von Eybe and Voigt, arrived in North America in June 1777, each with a strength of 570 officers and men. In 1779 Voigt took command of the 1st Regiment while the 2nd went to Colonel von Seybothen. Both regiments surrendered at Yorktown in 1781, at which time the 1st had 471 officers and men, the 2nd, 461.

There is some difference of opinion on how many flags were carried by the two Ansbach regiments at Yorktown, and even if all of the flags now at West Point were actually being carried or were in the regimental baggage. But if the West Point flags were not surrendered at Yorktown there is no accounting for their present location. Most accounts agree that 18 German and 6 English regimental colors were surrendered. Since there were only four color-bearing German regiments at Yorktown there are thus more than the normal two or even three per regiment to account for.

General Washington, following the surrender, dispatched Colonel David Humphreys to Philadelphia with a list of the captured stores and the 24 colors to present to the Continental Congress. Word of Humphreys' mission preceded him and he was escorted into Philadelphia by the city's Troop of Light Horse. In the presence of Congressmen and the French ambassador the flags were "laid down" in the State House on 3 November. The ceremony is described in Westcott's *History of Philadelphia*.

Even before the flags had arrived, Congress, on 29 October, resolved "that two stands . . . be presented to his excellency, General Washington, in the name of the United States." By "stand" was meant a single flag; these two colors were sent to the Secretary at War, Benjamin Lincoln, who gave them to Washington on 28 December 1781. A letter of thanks from Washington to Lincoln at Philadelphia, dated the 30th, acknowledges the gift of the two stands. We do not know which flags these were, and it is highly possible that one was the color of the 7th English Regiment of Foot captured at Fort Chambley in 1775. Further, we have no idea if any other German colors found their way to Mt. Vernon in later years.

Two Ansbach colors are clearly shown in Charles Willson Peale's "Continental Type" portrait of Washington, now in the collection of the Metropolitan Museum of Art (Morgan and Fielding, *The Life Portraits of Washington*, p. 32, no. 18). There are believed to be some 27 portraits of this type, several of which are signed and dated Philadelphia 1779, which would be two years before the colors are believed to have been surrendered. This manifest anachronism must be resolved before the true story of the flags can be determined.

The two captured flags remained in Washington's possession until his death in 1799 when they were bequeathed to his adopted grandson, George W.P. Custis. Custis appears to have kept them in his home for a while and later placed them in the Masonic Museum at Alexandria, Virginia, where an Ansbach flag and the color of the 7th Foot (also now at the West Point Museum) were displayed with the label "Alpha and Omega", the first and last, captured in the Revolution. In the label the Ansbach flag was erroneously stated to have been captured at Trenton in 1776 and the British color surrendered at Yorktown. Both of these statements are palpably incorrect: the colors taken at Trenton were Hessian and of a very different design, while the 7th Foot was not at Yorktown.

Interest in Revolutionary War captured colors was rekindled during the War of 1812. In response to inquiries he had received, John Armstrong, Secretary of War, reported on 14 January 1814 that only six Revolutionary standards remained at the War Office in Washington, the balance being deposited at Philadelphia. No clue as to the nature of these flags was given. As a result of these inquiries a report on the preservation of trophy flags was made by Mr. Seybert, chairman of a Congressional committee appointed to review this subject. This resulted in the enactment of a bill by Congress, on 18 April 1814, directing the Secretaries of War and Navy to collect all trophy flags and to deliver them to the President of the United States. Possibly in acknowledgment of this law, Mr. Custis turned over to the War Department the "two stands of colors taken from the British Army under the capitulation of York" which had been bequeathed to him by Washington (Letter, Secretary of War to USMA, 9 September 1858).

The history of the captured flags during the next 44 years is not clear, but possibly could be discovered from the records of the War Department at the National Archives. On 11 September 1858 Mr. William B. Lee, Librarian of the War Department, presented the English color, mentioned above, and three Ansbach-Bayreuth colors to the United States Military Academy in a ceremony in which the battalion of cadets formed a guard of honor. The fourth Ansbach-Bayreuth color was received at the Military Academy from the War Department in 1900 marked "unknown". Its identity was not discovered until it was transferred some years later from Memorial Hall to the West Point Museum.

In 1958 the West Point Museum, with authority of the Secretary of War, transferred one flag (2434) permanently to the U.S. National Museum, Washington, D.C. Subsequently the Colonial National Historical Park, Yorktown, Virginia, requested that a flag be permanently transferred there. This was not allowed by the Department of the Army but the Museum did place one flag (2431) there on indefinite loan in 1959. Of the two remaining flags one (2433) is on public display in the West Point Museum and the other is in storage there.

Bibliography

Much has been published concerning these German colors but no critical examination of their provenance has been attempted. The principal works are:

Gherardi Davis, *Regimental Colors in the War of the Revolution,* New York, 1907, and Supplement, 1910.

Major J. M. Carson, "Trophies and Flags in the Chapel," in *Bulletin No. 2*, Association of Graduates of the U.S.M.A., January 1902.

PAGE 174

Riedesel colors: W. L. Stone, "Memoirs of . . . Maj. Gen. Riedesel . . . ," Albany, 1868, Vol II, p 126.

PAGE 175

R. Young: Account Book of T. Pickering, pp 281, 333, in Record Books of the Revolutionary War, WRD, National Archives.

PAGE 176

Standard carried: Statement, Ensign Morgan, 16 Sept. 1791, in American State Papers, Military Affairs, Vol I, p 23.

Painted poles: Letter, Knox to Butler, 9 June 1791, American State Papers, Indian Affairs, Vol I, pp 187–188. Estimate of Money in the Quartermaster's Dept., 18 July 1791, in the Estimate of Supplies Book, 1781–1793, Revolutionary War Book, 148, WRD, NA.

Wayne's Legion: Letters, Knox to Wayne, 21 Sept. 1792, and Wayne to Knox, 13 Sept. 1792, in Richard C. Knopf, ed., "Anthony Wayne," U. of Pittsburgh Press, 1960, pp 92–93, 104–105; Statement, Organization of the Army in 1793, 27 Dec. 1792, in ASP, Mil. Affairs, Vol I, pp 40–41.

4th S.L.U.S.: G.O. Pittsburgh, 23 Sept. 1792, in "Michigan Pioneer and Hist. Soc. Coll.," Vol 34, (1904), pp 364–373.

1793 budget: Letters, Wayne to Knox, 30 Mar. 1793, and Knox to Wayne, 6 April 1793; Knopf, "Wayne," pp 212, 216; Est. of Supplies . . . , 9 Apr. 1793, in Est. of Supplies Book 1781–93, Revol. War Book No. 148, p 134, WRD, NA.

Stillé: Stillé, ". . . Wayne," Phila., 1893, p 32.

And cases: G. O., Hobson's Choice, 25 July 1793, "Mich. Pion. & Hist. Soc. Colls." Vol 34, pp 364–733.

Toledo: Stillé, "Wayne," pp 331–334, quotes Wayne's report of the battle.

PAGE 177

The Powel Standard of the Troop of Philadelphia Light Horse: Through the courtesy of The First Troop, PCC, the following is quoted from J. Lapsley, "The Book of the First Troop, Philadelphia City Cavalry, 1774–1914," Phila., 1915.

THE SMALL STANDARD.

"As will be found in the fore part of the Annals of the Troop in its proper place, a standard was presented to the Troop in 1797 by Mrs. Powel. The identity of this flag has been somewhat obscured by the discovery of several bills, which were paid by Mrs. Powel in 1798–99, for material furnished and work done in the making of a 'colour' or 'standard,' and which work appears to have been under the direction of Captain Dunlap. It seems probable that the standard given in 1797 was in some way not a proper military flag and was replaced by Mrs. Powel by a standard made under directions of the captain of the Troop.

July 28, 1798
Mrs. Elizabeth Powel
1¾ yds. blue Sattin for a Colour for
Dunlap's Troop Horse—delivered
Mr. Blodget D 4.37
Philadelphia
Dec. 28, 1798
Received of Mrs. Elizath Powel
Fourthy Dollars in full for
Painting a Standard for
Capt Dunlap Troop
Chrs Gullergey

Pbs Feby 11 1799
Mrs. Powel

1 set of mountings for Colour staff and making Spear for 1st City Troop	Dol	35

The above work done by order of
Cap^n Dunlap
Recd the above in full
John Myers

Feby. 21 For the first troop of Philada
Cavalry viz

To 1 colour pole	11.3
" 8 Silver'd Tassels & lint	2.19 —
" Sattin Ribbon & Sewing Silk	2.6
" Silk to lap Round the pole	3.0
" Colour Case painted	7.06
" Sewing the Silk & fringe &c	14.3
	£4.17.6

Recd payment for
Thomas Jaquette
George Hicks
Philadelphia March 23 1799
The First City Troop

To Thomas Jacquette	Dr.
For 5 yards Silk fringe used for the Standard	$10.

Received Payment
Thos Jacquette
George Hicks

"The material of which this flag is made is a fine satin, originally probably of a bright blue color, but now pale from age and exposure. It is thirty inches in length and twenty-eight and one-half inches in width, formed of two pieces strongly sewed together at the edge, and surrounded on three sides by a heavy twisted and knotted silk fringe six inches in breadth; the fourth side is looped or folded into a pocket its entire length to receive the flag staff, which is of dark wood, one inch in diameter and nine and one-half feet in length, made in two parts hinged together, and made firm and unbroken when required, by a sliding ferrule. The staff is surmounted by a spear-head and socket of solid silver, the two taken together being ten inches in length; the spear-head is of carved open work of fifteen stars in which is seen an eagle holding a cavalry sabre. The device on this flag is shown on both sides, one of which is the exact reverse of the other, and consists of an eagle with out-spread wings painted in gold, shaded with purple and red; the head turned toward the left shoulder, is, with the neck, colored black, the mouth open as though screeching, the tongue red and beak white, a floating scroll depends from the lower beak, one-half below, and the other half floating above the head, on which are inscribed the words in gold, 'AD ASTRA.' The eagle is twenty-eight inches from tip to tip of wings, and ten inches from lower claw to top of head. The right half of the breast is concealed by a shield of two out-curving sides, meeting in a single point below, the top being formed of two re-entering curves; it is five inches in its greatest height and width, and bears upon it the arms of the State of Pennsylvania painted in proper colors with great beauty and finish, and is supported by the right claw of the eagle clasping it by the upper right half; the left claw projects forward and to the left, and grasps four arrow-pointed zigzag thunder bolts, extending to the right and left of the body. The head is surrounded by five golden radiating palmated halos, averaging three and one-half inches in length; above these and sprinkled through the field, are fifteen eight-pointed silver stars of seven-eighths of an inch diameter, extending from tip to tip of wings; the whole character of the work evidences the hand of an artist. The flag is in a very perfect state of preservation, notwithstanding its age. It was in service in the Northampton expedition and in the Mount Bull Campaign, and was carried on all important parades until Captain Hart's copy of the old standard was presented to the Troop in 1876, since which time it has been framed between two glass plates. In the armory of 1901 a special fire-proof safe was built for its safe keeping."

Glossary

General references: F. V. Greene, "The Revolutionary War . . . ," N.Y., 1911; H. L. Peterson, "The Book of the Continental Soldier," Stackpole Co., 1968; H. B. Carrington, "Battles of the Amer. Revol.,"

Bibliography

Berg, F. A. "Encyclopedia of Continental Army Units," Stackpole, 1972.

Carrington, H. B. "Battles of the American Revolution," 1877, 1881 (reprint Promontory Press, N.Y.).

Clark, W. B., ed., "Naval Documents of the American Revolution," for the U. S. Navy Department, GPO, Washington, D.C. (6 or more volumes), 1964 to present.

Cooper, G. R. "Thirteen-Star Flags," Smithsonian Press, 1973.

Davis, Gherardi, "Regimental Colors in the War of the Revolution," N.Y. 1907. Also, supplements, plus several books on German flags. Reprinted, in part, by The Flag Research Center, Winchester, Massachusetts. (The most incisive work on Revolutionary flags, very strict authentication requirements imposed by the author on flags included. Unfortunately, text is limited and only those extant flags known to Davis included. His notes, if found, should be informative.)

Dawnay, Major N. P., "The Standards, Guidons and Colours of the Household Division, 1660-1773," Midas Books, 1975 (12 Dene Way, Speldhurst, Tunbridge Wells, Kent TN3 ONX, England. (A very definitive, comprehensive, well illustrated reference on British Colors of the Colonial and Revolutionary era. The finest book on military colors known to the author.)

"The Flag Bulletin" (bimonthly periodical), The Flag Research Center, Winchester, Massachusetts.

Force, Peter, compiler, "American Archives," 4th Series, 6 vols., 1837-1846; 5th Series, 2 vols., 1848-1851, Washington, D.C.

Greene, F. V., "The Revolutionary War . . .", Scribner's, 1911. (Excellent accounts and maps of battles and campaigns).

Lossing, B. J. "Pictorial Field Book of the Revolution, 2 Volumes, N.Y., 1852 (The first comprehensive historical survey of sites and artifacts).

Mastai, Boleslaw and Marie-Louise O'Otrange, "The Stars and The Stripes," Knopf, N.Y., 1973. (A beautifully designed and illustrated book on the American Flag).

"Military Collector & Historian," Journal of the Company of Military Historians, Washington, D.C. (Quarterly), 24 Kay St., Newport, R.I. 02840. (Numerous, well researched articles on flags, uniforms, weapons, and units of the Revolution.)

The Standards, Flags and Banners of the Pennsylvania Society of Sons of the Revolution,'' privately published by the Society, Philadelphia, 1913 (originally published in 1903 without illustrations).

Papers of the Continental Congress, National Archives, Washington, D.C.

Patterson & Dougall, ''The Eagle and the Shield,'' Dept. of State, G.P.O., Washington, D.C., 1978.

Peckham, H. H., ''The Toll of Independence,'' Univ. of Chicago, 1974.

Preble, G. H. Admiral, ''History of the Flag of the United States of America . . .'' Boston, 1880 (The grandfather of American Flag books).

Quaife, M. M., Weig, M. J., and Appleman, R. E., ''The History of the United States Flag,'' Eastern National Park & Monument Association, Harper, 1961. (Excellent reference. Good analysis of the development of American flags).

Rice, H. C. Jr. and Brown, A. S. K. ''The American Campaigns of Rochambeau's Army, 1780-1783,'' Princeton and Brown Universities, 1972.

Schermerhorn, F. E., ''American and French Flags of the Revolution,'' Pennsylvania Society of Sons of the Revolution, 1948. (Comprehensive, basic reference. Primarily a compilation of previous books according to the author.)

Smith, W., ''Flags Through the Ages and Across the World,'' McGraw-Hill, 1975. (Scholarly, readable, comprehensive, well illustrated.)

Smith, W., ''The Flag Book of the United States . . .'' William Morrow & Co., N.Y., 1970 & 1975. (Thoroughly readable, well illustrated).

Smith, W., ''Flags of the American Revolution to Color,'' Bellerophon, 1975. (Accurate drawings and brief descriptions on about forty flags. Published as a coloring book for the Bicentennial.)

Washington, George, ''The Writings of George Washington,'' John C. Fitzpatrick, ed., 39 vols., Washington, 1931-1944.

The following Books and Periodicals appear as references.

Boatner, M. M., ''Landmarks of the American Revolution,'' Hawthorn Books, 1975.

Boyd, I., ''Light-horse Harry Lee,'' Scribner's, 1931.

Butler, Captain L., ''The Annals of the King's Royal Rifle Corps,'' London, 1913.

Chichester, H. M. and Burger-Short, G., ''The Records and Badges . . . of the British Army,'' London, 1895.

Coggins, ''Ships and Seamen of the American Revolution,'' Promontory Press, 1969.

Commager, H. S. & Morris, R. B., ''The Spirit of Seventy-Six,'' Harper & Row, 1958-1975.

59th Congress, ''John Paul Jones, Commemoration at Annapolis, April 24, 1906,'' GPO 1907, House Doc 804.

Cook, F., ''Journals of the Military Expedition of Major Gen. John Sullivan against the . . . Indians in 1779 . . . ,'' Auburn, N.Y., 1887.

Davis, B., ''The Campaign that Won America . . . Yorktown,'' Dial Press, N.Y., 1970.

DeKoven, R., ''The Life and Letters of John Paul Jones,'' 2 volumes, Scribner's, 1913.

Drayton, J., ''Memoirs of the American Revolution . . . ,'' 2 volumes, Charleston, 1821.

''Fanning's Narrative,'' by Himself, N.Y., 1806, 1808.

Ford, W. C., ''Correspondence and Journals of Samuel Blatchley Webb,'' 3 volumes, New York, 1903.

Fow, J. H., ''The True Story of the American Flag,'' Philadelphia, 1908.

Gottschalk, L., "Lafayette and the Close of the American Revolution," U. of Chicago, 1942.

Gottschalk, L., "The Letters of Lafayette to Washington, 1777-1779," Hubbard, N.Y., 1944.

Grose, Francis, "Military Antiquities of the English Army . . . ," 2 volumes, London, 1780.

Greene, F. V., "General Greene," N.Y., 1893.

Harrison, P. D., "The Stars and Stripes . . . ," Boston, 1906.

Hayes, J. T., "Connecticut's Revolutionary Cavalry. Sheldon's Horse," Pequot Press, 1975.

Hirsch, A. H., "The Huguenots of Colonial South Carolina," Duke University Press, 1928.

Historical Society of Pennsylvania Proceedings and Magazine.

Hollister, G. H. "The History of Connecticut," 2 volumes, Hartford, 1857.

Hough, F. B., "The Siege of Charleston . . . ," Albany, 1867 (reprinted by the Reprint Co., 1975).

Hudleston, F. J., "Gentleman Johnny Burgoyne . . . ," Bobbs-Merrill, Indianapolis, 1927.

Johnson, J., "Traditions . . . of the American Revolution in the South . . . ," Charleston, 1851.

Johnston, H. P., "The Yorktown Campaign . . . ," N.Y., 1881.

"Journal of the . . . Congress . . . 1774," Philadelphia, 1774.

"Journals of the Continental Congress, 1774-1789," Ford, Worthington C., ed., 23 vols., Washington, 1904-1909.

Ketchum, R. M., ed., American Heritage Book of the Revolution, 1958.

Ketchum, . . . "The World of George Washington," American Heritage, 1974.

Kidder, F., "History of the First New Hampshire Regiment . . ." 1868, and Baker, H. M., "New Hampshire at Bunker Hill," 1903, reprint, Peter E. Randall, 1973.

Lefferts, Charles M., "Uniforms of the American, British, French, and German Armies in the War of the American Revolution," 1775-1783, New York, 1926.

Library of Congress, Maps and Prints and Documents of the Revolutionary Era.

Library of Congress, "The American Revolution in Drawings and Prints" Catalog of the Bicentennial Exhibition, 1976.

Lee, Henry, "Memoirs of the War in the Southern Department of the United States," 2 volumes, Philadelphia, 1812.

Luzader, J., "Decision on the Hudson — The Saratoga Campaign of 1777," National Park Service, Washington, D.C. 1975.

McGrady, E., "The History of South Carolina in the Revolution, 1776-80, 1780-83," 2 volumes, Macmillan, N.Y., 1901-02.

Middlebrook, L. F., "History of Maritime Connecticut during the American Revolution, 1775-1783," 2 volumes, Essex Inst. Salem, Massachusetts, 1925.

Middleton, M. S., "David and Martha Laurence Ramsay," Carlton Press, N.Y., 1971.

Mongan, A., "Harvard Honors Lafayette," Fogg Art Museum Catalog of Bicentennial Exhibit, 1975.

Moore, F., "Diary of the American Revolution from Newspapers and Original Documents,' 2 volumes, N.Y., 1865.

Morison, Samuel E., "John Paul Jones, A Sailor's Biography," Little Brown & Co., Boston, 1959.

Morris, R., "The Truth About the American Flag," Wynnehaven, 1976.

Moultrie, W., "Memoirs of the American Revolution . . . ," 2 volumes, N.Y., 1802.

National Archives, Howe Collection of Maps.

Newman, E., "The Early Paper Money of America," Whitman Co., Racine, 1967.

Neubecker, O., "Heraldry, Sources,

Symbols, Meaning," McGraw-Hill, 1976.

Pennsylvania Archives, published by the Commonwealth of Pennsylvania, 17 vols., 1852-1892.

Peterson, H. L., "The Book of the Continental Soldier," Stackpole, 1968.

Ramsay, David, "The History of the Revolution of South Carolina . . . ," 2 volumes, Trenton, 1785.

Reed, John F., "Valley Forge, Crucible of Victory," Philip Frenau, 1969.

Rhode Island Historical Society, "Collections," Oct. 1925, Oct. 1934, Jan. 1940.

Scheer, G. F. & H. F. Rankin, "Rebels and Redcoats," New American Library Co., 1957.

Sherburne, J. H., "The Life and Character of John Paul Jones . . . ," N.Y., 1851.

Smith, S. S., "Fight for the Delaware 1777," Philip Frenau, 1970.

"The South Carolina Historical and Genealogical Magazine," S. C. Historical Society, Charleston.

Journals of the General Assembly and House of Representatives (of South Carolina), 1776-1780. Edited by W. E. Hamphill, W. A. Wates, R. N. Olsberg, University of S. C. Press, 1970.

Steuben, Baron Von, "Regulations for the Order and Discipline of the Troops of the United States," 1779.

Stillé, C. J., "Maj. General Anthony Wayne . . . Philadelphia, 1893.

Stone, W. L., "Memoirs and Letters and Journals of Major General Riedesel . . . ," 2 volumes, Albany, 1868.

Tarleton, Lt. Col., "A History of the Campaign of 1780-81 . . . ," London, 1787.

Thayer, T., "Yorktown: Campaign of Strategic Options," Lippincott, 1975.

Thompson, R., "The Story of Betsy Ross," Bicentennial Press, 1972-1975.

Tower, Charlemagne, "The Marquis de LaFayette . . . ," 2 volumes, Lippincott, 1895.

Uhlendorf, B. A. (trans.), "Revolution in America, Confidential Letters and Journals of 1776-1784 of Adjutant General Major Baurmeister of the Hessian Forces," Rutgers University Press, 1957.

War Department Records, National Archives.

Whitlock, B., "Lafayette," 2 volumes, Appleton, N.Y., 1929.

Wildes, H. E., "Valley Forge," Macmillan, N.Y., 1938.

Wirt, W. "Sketches of . . . Patrick Henry," Philadelphia, 1840.

Illustration Credits

The flags, paintings, prints, medals, and other artifacts listed below are included herein through the courtesy of the following institutions and collections:

Albany Institute of History and Art (AIHA)
Alexandria-Washington Masonic Lodge 22 (AWML)
Bedford Public Library, Bedford, Mass. (BL)
Bennington Museum (BM)
John Carter Brown Library (JCBL)
Chicago Historical Society (CHS)
Christie's, London (C)
Connecticut Historical Society (Conn. HS)
Connecticut State Library (CSL)
Craig Nannos Collection (CNC)
Delaware Art Museum (DAM)
Delaware Historical Society (DHS)
Detroit Institute of Art (DIA)
Easton Public Library (EPL)
First Troop, Philadelphia City Cavalry (FT)
Fogg Art Museum, Harvard University (FAM)
William Guthman, Westport, Conn. (WG)
Historical Society of Pennsylvania (HSP)
Independence National Historical Park (INHP)
The King's Royal Rifle Corps, Winchester, Hants, England (KRRC)
Library Company of Philadelphia (LCP)
Library of Congress (LC)
Maryland Commission on Artistic Property (MCAP)
Maryland Historical Society (Md.HS)
Masonic Library, Boston, Mass. (ML)
Massachusetts Historical Society (MHS)
Metropolitan Museum of Art (MMA)
Monmouth County Historical Association (MCHA)

National Archives (NA)
National Maritime Museum, England (NMM)
National Museum of History and Technology (NMHT)
New Brunswick Museum, Canada (NBM)
New Hampshire Historical Society (NHHS)
New York Historical Society (NYHS)
New York Public Library (NYPL)
New York Society of Sons of the Revolution (NYSSR)
North Carolina Historical Commission (NCHC)
The Old Print Shop, Kenneth M. Newman, New York (OPS)
Pennsylvania Academy of Fine Arts (PAFA)
Pennsylvania Society of Sons of the Revolution (PSSR)
Philadelphia Maritime Museum, Edgar Newbold Smith Collection (PMM)
Private Collection (PC)
Rhode Island Historical Society (RIHS)
Rhode Island State Capitol, Providence, R.I. (RISC)
Dr. Howard C. Rice, Jr., and Anne S. K. Brown (HCR)
Franklin D. Roosevelt Library (FDRL)
Royal Military College, Sandhurst (RMC)
St. Paul's Chapel, Trinity Parish, New York (SPC)
Schenectady County Historical Society (SCHS)
Society of the Cincinnati (SC)

U.S. Mint (Mint)
Valley Forge Historical Society (VFHS)
Virginia State Library (VSL)
West Point Museum (WPM)

William Penn Museum, Harrisburg, Pa. (WPM)
Colonial Williamsburg Foun. (CW)
Winterthur Museum (WM)
Yale University Art Gallery (YUAG)

ILLUSTRATIONS

COLOR PLATES

333

Index